*the*
# Pendulum...

*from Indian Removal
to buying Mille Lacs*

*the*

# Pendulum...

*from Indian Removal*
*to buying Mille Lacs*

**Clarence Ralph Fitz, BS, DVM**

with Lauralee O'Neil

VOLUME 2

ISBN:  978-1-60414-032-3 (hardcover)
       978-1-60414-551-9 (paperback)

FIRST EDITION

Published by
Fideli Publishing Inc.
119 W. Morgan St.
Martinsville, IN 46151

www.FideliPublishing.com

Dedicated to the memory of …

Joe Karpen

Donna Fitz

John Kiel

Carl & Freda Beaudry

Don Skogman

Bob Benner

Jerry Brandt

Sharon Peterson

Mayor Sandy Reichel

and Tom Henneck,

all Patriots,

in their own way,

in the struggle at Mille Lacs.

# Forward

Through countless hours of painstaking research this volume takes the reader on a journey that is factual, thought-provoking and disturbing.

You will learn much about those involved in establishing Federal Indian Policy, from Secretary of the Interior Harold LeClair Ickes through John Collier, Commissioner of the Bureau of Indian Affairs. Read about Colliers troubled early life through his years serving under President Franklin D. Roosevelt from 1933 through 1945. John Collier was primarily responsible for what is dubbed the 'Indian New Deal' as well as the Indian Reorganization Act of 1934.

It would appear that John Collier intended to reverse the previous long-standing effort of assimilation of the Indians by the United States. Much has been written as to the wisdom, or lack thereof, of his efforts. The Dawes Act of 1887 allotted tribal lands to individual Indians as a way to create individual homesteads in exchange for the Indians becoming U.S. citizens. The Indian Reorganization Act was also a part of the Americanization of Indians, giving them full citizenship. But John Collier, considered by many to have been an Indian enthusiast and a reformer, was opposed to forced assimilation, and did his best to reverse these policies. Collier has long been criticized for his progressive ideals.

E.A. Schwartz wrote that, *"A near consensus among historians of the Indian New Deal that Collier temporarily rescued Indian communities from federal abuses and helped Indian people survive the Depression but also damaged Indian communities by imposing his own social and political ideas on them."*[1]

Meticulously quoting from numerous historical documents, author Clare Fitz writes of the often seemingly schizophrenic thing called Federal Indian Policy.

---

1    E. A. Schwartz, "Red Atlantis Revisited: Community and Culture in the Writings of John Collier", *American Indian Quarterly* (1994) 18#45 p. 508.

You will journey through the days of the *Indian fighter* Andrew Jackson and the Indian Removal Act through the Indian Reorganization Act of 1934, its enactment and its consequences, particularly focusing on the tribes in the area of Mille Lacs, Minnesota.

Today we can hardly escape the often divisive and disturbing news concerning *Native Americans*, racism, *sacred lands*, *Indian Country*, etc. What is certainly apparent, however, is that our current system of Indian reservations is hardly enriching or enhancing the lives of tribal members.

In an article called *Native American Reservations: "Socialist Archipelago"* by Andrei Znamenski, Professor of History at the University of Memphis, the author writes,

> Imagine a country that has a corrupt authoritarian government. In that country no one knows about checks and balances or an independent court system. Private property is not recognized in that country either. Neither can one buy or sell land. And businesses are reluctant to bring investments into this country. Those who have jobs usually work for the public sector. Those who don't have jobs subsist on entitlements that provide basic food. At the same time, this country sports a free health care system and free access to education. Can you guess what country it is? It could be the former Soviet Union, Cuba, or any other socialist country of the past.

It is a little-known fact that Native Americans, as they prefer to be called in todays' politically correct English, receive more federal subsidies than any other ethnicity in the United States. Their housing, health care, education and food are all subsidized by taxpaying citizens in American. And yet, they are the poorest group in our country.

Again, quoting Znamenski:

> The poverty level on many reservations ranges between 38 and 63 percent (up to 82 percent on some reservations)[2], and half of all the jobs are usually in the public sector.[3] This is before

---

2  "Native American Aid, Living Conditions," available at http://www.nrcprograms.org/site/PageServer?pagename=naa_livingconditions

3  Rachel L. Mathers, "The Failure of State-Led Economic Development on American Indian Reservations," *The Independent Review 17,* no. 1 (2012): 176.

the crisis of 2008! You don't have to have a Ph.D. in economics
to figure out that one of the major sources of this situation is a
systemic failure of the federal Indian policies.

What is to be done about our malfunctioning and failing system of Federal
Indian Policy? In order to come up with solutions one must study and analyze
those policies that have brought us to this point in history. And you, dear reader,
will come away with just such an understanding as you journey through this comprehensive and well-researched chronicle — an expedition of the author's search
for the truth.

*—Lauralee O'Neil*

# Prologue

As I completed my first book, published in 2016, *...and the Mille Lacs who have no Reservation...*, it was very obvious that there was a lot more of the story to be told and so I added "Volume 1" to the front cover, not knowing if Volume 2 would ever happen. But after a full week in Washington, D.C., scouring the documents at the National Archives and each night riding the crowded metro with a briefcase full of copies of original documents to a motel in the suburbs that I could afford; and after a week in Kansas City, staying at a hotel that had a shuttle that would drop me off at the Kansas City National Archives each morning when the archives opened and pick me up when they closed, once again with a briefcase full of copies of original documents; and after a trip to Nashville, Tennessee to visit the Hermitage, the home of President Andrew Jackson; and after spending the winter of 2018-19 reading multiple books and trying to understand the life and times of Andrew Jackson, Harold Ickes and John Collier, I was ready during the winter of 2019-20 to start organizing, reading and studying the resources I had gathered. This book, *The Pendulum*, is the result.

In writing Volume 1 it became clear early on that the initial goal of the U.S. Federal Government was to concentrate the Chippewa Indians in one spot at White Earth. At an early date the attempt to convince the Red Lake Band of Chippewas to remove to White Earth failed but the plan continued in an effort to remove all the other Mississippi Chippewa bands to White Earth. It seemed though that at each treaty or agreement that the federal government made with the Chippewa Indians a clause would be included that would come back to haunt them and prevent the objective from being achieved. But why White Earth? And then it dawned on us; White Earth is west of the Mississippi River; just barely, but it is. With that realization I decided to include a chapter on Andrew Jackson and the Indian Removal Act, the Act that attempted to move all Indians west of the Mississippi River. An Act that I would contend was, once again, deemed necessary because of a clause in an agreement between the United States and the State of Georgia. The chapter on

Andrew Jackson begins before the United States of American existed and I think you will be amazed, as was I, at how slow life progressed at that time in contrast to our current life where everything seems to move at the speed of light.

In the chapters on the two men who were destined to become the future Secretary of the Interior and Commissioner of Indian Affairs under President Franklin D. Roosevelt, Harold LeClair Ickes and John Collier, I found both to have been deprived of parents at an early age which left them without an example of stable family life, both to have married influential women who played a major role in developing their husbands interest in Indian affairs and both having what I would consider dysfunctional families. In order to comprehend the actions of men and women in history that we cannot know personally, I find it necessary to do the best we can to know them through their own writings and the writings of others. Therefore, I include these chapters and I hope you, the readers, agree.

With that background I have attempted to understand both the Indian Removal Act and the Indian Reorganization Act, almost direct opposites we might argue. In this book we have delved into the events of the day, the events that prompted people like John Collier to promote the reforms he attempted, the effects of world events caused by the likes of Adolph Hitler, while weaving in some of the events of the day in order to establish the timeline. As the author I will also include some of the thoughts, fears and actions of a young boy on an Iowa farm who was born during the first year of the Indian Reorganization Act. And we will delve into how the Indian Reorganization Act was used by the federal government to buy land in Mille Lacs County, Minnesota in an effort to atone for the mistakes they had previously made; actions that still haunt the residents of Mille Lacs County.

In researching and writing this book I have gained an immense amount in understanding of that thing called Federal Indian Policy. I only hope I have been able to relate to you, the reader, a smidgen of that understanding. The story is far from over; there is a long road yet ahead in that effort to satisfy the goals of the Founders of the United States of American when they wrote in the preamble to the Constitution, "in Order to form a more perfect union."

— Clarence Fitz

# Table of Contents

# CHAPTER 1

# Andrew Jackson

In Volume I, ... *and the Mille Lacs who have no Reservation*, we traced the migration of the Chippewa Indians from the area around the mouth of the St. Lawrence River in what is now Canada, to their westward destination in Minnesota and Mille Lacs County. While we have no written records to confirm it, the Chippewa probably migrated of their own free will. But there was another migration in the southern part of what would become the United States which was not of their own free will and while not as direct, still had an impact on Minnesota and Mille Lacs County. That is the focus of this chapter.

## Andrew Jackson's Formative Years

In the eighteenth and nineteenth centuries there was a mass migration from Ireland to the English colonies in North America. Ireland was part of the British empire and King Charles I was striving to pressure the Presbyterians into the church of England. And so, in 1765, Andrew and Elizabeth Jackson, the parents of a future president, immigrated from Northern Ireland to America to escape the oppression of the British Crown so that they could freely practice their Presbyterian faith, and too, there was abundant land available in America. They built their home in the Appalachian valley, but before they could really get settled, the senior Andrew Jackson was dead.

Young Andrew Jackson would be born a short time after his father's death, on March 15, 1767 in Waxhaws, Province of Carolina (probably South Carolina). His mother, having been deprived of a livelihood due to her husband's death, moved in with her sister and served as a housekeeper. Young Andrew had two older brothers, Hugh and Robert. Andrew could already read by age 5 and his mother, apparently realizing that Andrew was a bright child, enrolled him in an academy operated by a Dr. Humphries. Because many older citizens of his community could not read, young Jackson took turns reading aloud to the gathered crowd the newspapers as they arrived. This included the Declaration of Independence, which appeared in their community when he was 9. Andrew's mother, Elizabeth, being a devout Presbyterian, was hopeful that young Andrew would become a minister, but Andrew was not much interested and never did develop an affinity for religion. He was a rambunctious boy who did not score terribly well in school. Being without a father, it was up to his mother to teach him right from wrong. She reportedly taught him that the way to settle an argument was with a duel, which, after all, was the way a gentleman handled a disagreement in those times. Whether or not she was the one who actually taught him to fight, we don't know, but as his life developed, he obviously learned it somewhere. The Scotch Irish did not hesitate to fight for their rights and Andrew had a bit of a temper when provoked.

When Andrew was about twelve years old his brother Hugh, having volunteered for the Patriot army in the Revolutionary War, died of heat exhaustion following a battle near Charleston.

When the war came to the Waxhaws area, Jackson's mother sent, or perhaps allowed, Andrew and Robert to drill with the militia that was being led by his uncle. They were made couriers in the victorious Battle of Hanging Rock in 1780. British forces discovered the Jackson boys at the house where they lived with their mother. In an act of defiance Andrew refused to clean a British officer's boots when ordered to do so, and as a result sustained a slash from the officer's saber on his forehead and one hand, the scars from which he would carry throughout his life. The two boys were later captured and imprisoned at Camden Jail. Prisoners there were not well cared for, and likely due to their starving condition, both boys contracted smallpox. Somehow their mother was able to negotiate their release from prison as part of a prisoner exchange.

Robert Remini, in his biography of Andrew Jackson, describes it this way:

> Elizabeth could not believe what she saw; her two sons wasted by malnutrition and disease. She procured two horses and placed the dying Robert on one and rode the other herself. Andrew walked the 45 miles to his home, barefoot and without a jacket. Two days later, Robert died and Andrew was delirious. Fortunately, the attention and care of his mother, the help of a local doctor, and his own strong constitution brought Andrew through the crisis. He remained weak for months but finally recovered.

After Andrew recovered, his mother volunteered to serve as a nurse for the American troops who had become infected with cholera. Sadly, she contracted the disease herself and died in 1781. Andrew described his mother as being "gentle as a dove and as brave as a lioness."

Apparently, his mother had taught Andrew to fear Indians, much like we teach our children in current times to fear strangers. So, at fourteen years of age, Andrew had lost his entire family to the British, and since many of the Indians had fought alongside the British, that likely helped mold Andrew's attitude toward both the British and the Indians. For a while after his mother's death, Andrew spent time in Charleston, drinking, gambling, cock fighting, and generally causing trouble. Somehow, however, he managed to avoid the law, returning home when his money was gone.

On September 3, 1783, the Revolutionary War was over and the Scotch Irish, along with many others, started moving westward. By 1784, the Treaty of Paris had been ratified by the United States government, a new and independent country.

Andrew, now seventeen, moved to Salisbury, North Carolina, and decided to study law. He was still a rowdy teenager, but not as unruly as he had been in Charleston. By 1786, he had learned enough law to be admitted to the bar. He and a classmate, John McNairy, became the public prosecutors in the western area that would become Tennessee. Andrew found lodging in Nashville at the home of widow Donelson, whose husband had been killed by the Indians. Nashville was a city of about five thousand and the Cherokee Indians would kill one of them about every ten days. About this same time, Jackson purchased his first slave, a woman named Nancy who was about eighteen to twenty years old.

Widow Donelson's youngest daughter, Rachel, was married to Lewis Robards of Kentucky, but apparently had filed for divorce. Rachel and Andrew immediately fell in love and lived together from 1790 to 1791 until her divorce was final in 1793. This, of course, set tongues to wagging in Nashville and after the divorce was final, the two legally married in 1794.

Jackson apparently became a rather successful lawyer and soon he and Rachel's brother Samuel formed a partnership, buying and selling land. They also ran a store close by the Cumberland River, near what would become the Hermitage.

It was also about this time that Jackson fought his first duel with a fellow attorney who reportedly had said something that hurt Andrew's feelings. Whether it was arranged ahead of time we don't know, but they both fired their pistols into the air and neither was hurt.

## Jackson, the Indian Fighter

Because of the untoward number of townspeople who were being killed by the Indians, the neighborhood organized a group of sixty or seventy men to counter the Indian attacks. And, although this was Andrew Jackson's first experience as an Indian fighter, he was emerging as a natural leader, and his six-foot one-inch physique looked the part. The Spanish in Florida were supplying the tribes with guns and ammunition and President Washington was of little help. At this time Jackson was spending more and more time in military endeavors in an effort to stop the killing of settlers. He had no mercy for Indians who slaughtered settlers, but as a lawyer he also condemned whites who murdered Indians, stole their land and/or acted without authority.

Governor Blount, governor of the Southwest Territory, and his friends decided that the way to deal with the Indian problem was to become a state instead of relying on the federal government. And so, a constitutional convention was called, and Andrew Jackson was named as a delegate. On June 1, 1796, Tennessee officially became a state and Andrew Jackson was elected to the new House of Representatives. His claim to fame was advocating that the federal government pay appeals of settlers who had been forced to attack Indians to protect their settlements.

Jackson did not seek re-election to the House of Representatives, but instead ran for the Senate and won. However, after a short time he resigned from the Senate. Perhaps he had his eye on an appointment as a state superior judge, because he was in fact appointed. As a judge, he insisted on respect for the law.

Throughout life, Jackson's eyes apparently gave him an advantage over anyone who dared to cross him. They were bright and blue and when he meant business, they seemed to have a fearless blaze. Remini tells an interesting story about Jackson as superior judge. A great hulk of a man named Russell Bean came before judge Jackson for cutting off the ears of a child while he was reportedly drunk. Bean marched into the courtroom, cursed the judge and jury and everyone present, and then marched out of the courtroom. Jackson ordered the sheriff to arrest Bean and lock him up. The sheriff obeyed but soon returned, saying that he could not apprehend him. Jackson then shouted orders to summon a posse and return the fugitive to court. Once more the sheriff returned, reporting that the posse could not subdue him. Jackson said to the sheriff, summon me then and I will do the job. Reluctantly the sheriff summoned Jackson and Jackson, with a pistol in each hand, walked briskly toward Bean, who was threatening to shoot anyone who got near him. Jackson and Bean glared at each other for an instant, then Bean dropped his guns and was taken off to jail. When asked later why he surrendered to Jackson, Bean replied that Jackson's eyes told me I was a dead man if I resisted.

In 1802, at the age of thirty-five, Jackson was elected Major General of the Tennessee Militia, receiving more votes than the current Major General Sevier. The election apparently caused enough of a reaction that the militia was divided into east and west with both Jackson and Sevier as Major Generals. In spite of that, this rivalry deteriorated into another duel — with neither man being injured. No wonder Jackson was feeling untouchable — two duels and no injuries. Jackson went on to excel at the job of Major General and, in 1814 was named a Major General in the United States army.

## Andrew Jackson's Military Career

On October 1, 1800, a secret treaty had been signed in which Spain would return Louisiana to France (the Treaty of San Ildefonse). By the time the treaty became known, Thomas Jefferson was the president and was fearful of the possible results, with Napoleon of France in control of New Orleans and with it, the Mississippi River. As luck would have it, however, the French under Napoleon were soundly defeated by the British in a naval battle at Santo Domingo and as a result, France decided to sell Louisiana to the United States in 1803 for fifteen million dollars.

The Louisiana Purchase enlarged the United States to the west, and President Jefferson knew that was significant, even though Lewis and Clark had not yet made their trek to the Pacific and the extent of the west was largely unknown.

As settlers were continuing to push westward, more and more skirmishes with hostile Indians were occurring. Andrew Jackson had been confronting this conflict between the settlers and the Indians all his life and was becoming more and more convinced that President Jefferson's Doctrine of Removal was the answer.

Back on his plantation Jackson was breeding fine horses and racing them. A dispute over the winner of one of these horse races resulted in Jackson's third duel between himself and Charles Dickinson. Dickinson had reportedly called Jackson a "worthless scoundrel" and a "coward." Jackson received a lead shot to the chest and two broken ribs. With blood dripping from his chest, Jackson fired a fatal shot to Dickinson. The lead ball remained there near Jackson's heart for the rest of his life, never properly healing.

THE DUEL.

In Washington, the federal government under President Madison was becoming increasingly disturbed by the continued meddling by the British in the affairs of the new republic. The British had put trade restrictions in effect which were hurting business, refusing to accept the fact that the colonists were no longer British subjects — and forcing American sailors into the Royal Navy. The British were also continuing to furnish arms and ammunition to the hostile Indian elements. It had been twenty-nine years since the colonist had defeated the British and declared their independence, but Britain still refused to honor United States' sovereignty as a nation.

On June 8, 1812, under President James Madison, war was declared by the United States against the British. The first two battles were disastrous for our fledgling country. The United States decided that striking Canada, then part of the British Empire, would be their method of attack. Andrew Jackson had offered to lead his troops in this effort but his offer was not accepted. Three attempts at victory against Canada were made, but all three failed.

Soon thereafter fifty British warships were spotted off the Chesapeake Bay shore, but what they were up to remained elusive. It soon became evident, however, as the British marched troops into Washington, overwhelming the American troops, burning the President's mansion, the United States Capitol and a newspaper office that had not been kind to the British in print. Only a violent rainstorm prevented further burning.

Meanwhile, back on the frontier, a party of Creek Indians were returning from the Great Lakes region and a conference with Tecumsah. Tecumsah was a Shawnee Indian who had plans to form a large confederacy of multiple tribes to rid the country of the white man's intrusive ways. His mother was a Creek Indian so his invitation to the Creeks to join his confederacy was a natural. David and Jeanne Heidler, in their book, *Indian Removal* quote Tecumsah as saying in a speech to Governor William Henry Harrison in 1810, "Once a happy race. Since made miserable by the white people, who are never contented, but always encroaching. The way, and the only way to check and stop this evil, is, for all the red men to unite in claiming a common and equal right in the land, as it was at first, and should be yet; for it never was divided, but belongs to all, for the use of each."

It was on their way home from their talk with Tecumsah that the Creek warriors massacred several white families at Duck River on May 12, 1812. The Duck River massacre aroused the passions of the people of Tennessee — and among them, Andrew Jackson.

In November of 1812, with concern for the safety of New Orleans and the territory of the Mississippi Valley, Jackson was ordered to assemble his troops and advance toward New Orleans. That he proceeded to do, but in March of 1813 he received a letter from Washington ordering him to dismiss his troops and go home. The new Secretary of War apparently wanted to concentrate on the east coast instead of the south. Jackson now had a dilemma: who would protect the country west of the Mississippi if he went home? And what about the effort on the part of the British to control the ports of Florida? Essentially, he was being asked to disband his army, send his arms to another commander, and leave his troops — without pay — to find their own way home. Jackson refused. He led his troops back to Nashville. Back in Nashville, a dispute between two members of his militia caused Jackson to promise to horsewhip Lt. Benton the next time they met. Jackson attempted to do just that and it escalated into gunfire in a hotel bar room, where Jackson was shot in the shoulder and upper arm. Having lost a lot of blood, a doctor recommended amputation but Jackson refused to allow it. The doctor then succeeded in stopping the bleeding and saved the arm. (The lead ball would remain in Jackson's body until much later, when it was removed by a white house physician — without anesthesia — during Jackson's presidency). Jackson was weak from blood loss and remained in bed for several weeks. He was still not fully recovered when the Creek Indians, under the leadership of half-breed William Weatherford, attacked Fort Mims on August 30, 1813, and massacred over three hundred American settlers.

This attack by the traditional Creeks (Red Sticks) on the innocent settlers at Fort Mims, led by half-breed William Weatherford, aroused Andrew Jackson from his sickbed. When word arrived that nearly all of the three hundred settlers at Fort Mims had been killed, Jackson was furious. He called for the Tennessee fighters to assemble. With his left arm in a sling and the bullet still lodged in the bones, he rode off on horseback to lead his troops. In addition to needing help to get on his horse or unfold a map, he had a case of dysentery, with severe stomach pains.

While still trying to recover and assemble an army, and with intelligence relayed from one of his spies, Jackson ordered John Coffee, his long-time friend who was leading a force of nine hundred troops, to attack the Red Stick Creeks at Tallushatchee. All of the nearly two hundred Creeks assembled there were killed except for one infant boy. When Jackson arrived and was asked what they should do with the child, he decided to send the boy home to his wife Rachel to be raised as his son.

Jackson had promised the friendly Creeks and Cherokees that he would defend them if needed. Both tribes were split into two factions; one friendly with the settlers and one hostile, who were being supplied with arms and ammunition by the British. Now that Jackson had joined his army, his chance arrived as word came that the hostile Red Stick Creeks were about to attack the friendly Creek faction. Jackson, in command of his some two thousand troops, and in excruciating pain, drafted a battle plan which worked exceedingly well. While William Weatherford and a considerable number of Red Sticks escaped the trap Jackson had set, some three hundred Red Sticks had been killed and the attack on the friendly Creeks was averted.

Commander Jackson now faced another challenge. The food supply for troops and horses was running dreadfully short and some of his troops were nearing desertion. Jackson, racked with pain and his arm still in a sling, propped his gun on his horse's neck and dared the deserters to leave. The glint in his eye that had caused Russell Bean to relent, also brought the deserters back to the mission at hand.

But with legitimate enlistments expiring, his troop numbers dipped to only 130 men. As word came that British troops had landed at Pensacola, Jackson appealed to the governor for more troops.

Finally, a few troops arrived, adding to his force, and with volunteers plus some U.S. Army regulars assigned to him, as well as John Ross and his band of Cherokees, Jackson's troop strength reached 3500.

Word then came from his scouts, one of which was Davy Crockett, that the Red Stick Creeks were organizing a village at Horseshoe Bend on the Tallapoosa River. After surveying the lay of the land and organizing the battle plan, on the morning of March 27, 1814, Jackson's army attacked the Creek stronghold. The fight was ferocious — with platoon leader Sam Houston continuing to fight even after being injured twice in the attack. A few Red Sticks were able to escape but in the morning after the battle 557 Creek Indian corpses were counted. With this attack, the Red Stick threat was eliminated and the few who escaped made their way to Florida for safety. But Jackson still wanted their leader, William Weatherford.

A few days later, a lone unarmed Indian rode into camp and asked for Andrew Jackson. He identified himself as William Weatherford. Jackson's first reaction was anger, but soon turned into admiration for the fearless courage and honor of the man. Jackson made a deal with Weatherford to stop the attacks on settlers by the remaining Creeks and, in return, Weatherford would be given his freedom and an ensuing peace. But there was a price to pay. With Weatherford's help, the Treaty of Fort Jackson was negotiated giving the United States 22 million acres of Creek land, even though it was only the friendly Creeks who remained there. The hostile Creeks were either dead or in Florida.

Jackson's many successes were beginning to impress the War Department. Perhaps they had misjudged him. He certainly was outperforming their other generals.

Brian Kilmeade and Don Yaeger, in their book, *Andrew Jackson and the Miracle of New Orleans* describe his effectiveness as a general this way. "His troops both loved and feared him. To everyone's surprise, he had made an effective fighting force out of volunteer militiamen. He knew when to be tough, and he knew when to temper that toughness with kindness. He was fearless in battle, but not reckless. In fact, he balanced his courage with great caution and surprising patience for gathering intelligence and listening to the advice of others. He knew when to stand firm on his convictions but wasn't blind to the possibilities of compromise. Finally, and most important, he possessed a natural instinct for military strategy that made up for his lack of formal training."

As a reward for his successes, Jackson was promoted to Major General of the United States Regular Army.

The British were still not ready to accept the fact that they had lost the Revolutionary War and that the United States was now an independent nation. They continued funneling arms and ammunition to the Indians in an effort to stir up trouble. With their wins in the Canadian attacks and with Washington burned, they moved on to a naval bombardment of Fort McHenry near Baltimore, Maryland. On September 13, 1814, British ships anchored in the Chesapeake Bay lobbed shells at the Fort. Francis Scott Kay had been sent to negotiate the release of a prisoner being held on one of the British ships. He watched shell after shell being fired at the Fort throughout the nighttime sky but couldn't see until the morning mist had lifted that the stars and stripes still flew over the Fort. The fort had not fallen. Key jotted down a poem that described his delight: "*'tis the star spangle banner, O! long may it wave, O'er the land of the free, and the home of the brave.*" Later his poem was set to music and became the national anthem of the United States of America.

The United States had held off the attack at Fort McHenry but Jackson still suspected, and his spies were telling him, that the British had their eye on New Orleans. He feared a British takeover of New Orleans would stop any further westward expansion of United States settlements. Lewis and Clark had returned from their excursion westward a few years earlier, so they knew there was a vast unexplored area to the west. Jackson pondered where he thought the British would land in order to attack New Orleans. Would it be Pensacola, then controlled by the Spanish, or would they attack Fort Bowyer which guarded the bay approach to Mobile, or would they attack New Orleans directly from the area where the Mississippi River emptied into the Gulf of Mexico?

After reinforcing Fort Bowyer, Jackson left the Fort in charge of Lt. Lawrence and headed with some four thousand troops toward Pensacola. Officially the United States government under President Madison objected to a move on Pensacola, but unofficially they would do nothing to stop him. The fort at Pensacola was under Spanish control, and while they were supposed to be neutral, the Spanish were allowing the British to man the fort. After failing to gain command of Pensacola diplomatically, Jackson and his troops rather easily took control. It was becoming evident to President Madison that Andrew Jackson was emerging as the best general he had in his army.

### The Battle that saved the United States of America and made Andrew Jackson the Most Popular Man in America

With Pensacola under his control and Lt. Lawrence in charge at Mobile, Jackson set off with his army for New Orleans. His fame as a victorious general preceded him, and he received an enthusiastic welcome from the townspeople of New Orleans when he arrived on the last day of November 1814. In an address to the assembled crowd he announced that he was there "to drive their enemies into the sea or perish in the effort." But the townspeople weren't so sure about this dirty backwoodsman-appearing man as he rode into town. However, Jackson appeared clean and erect in his best dress uniform at a reception later that evening, and the town was reassured that the right man had arrived to defend their town. Jackson set about getting the lay of the land and assessing the most likely route of attack the British would choose. On November 26, 1814, fifty large British ships had left Jamaica on a mission seeking revenge for the killing of their commander — the very one who had burned Washington as well as taking control of New Orleans and the Mississippi valley. The British came prepared to take control of the city and all the goods stored and ready for shipment from the port of New Orleans. In addition to all of the people on board who would be needed to administer the city, they were so confident that they also brought with them their wives and daughters.

While the British were sailing, Jackson was busy developing a strategy for defending the city, not knowing what approach the British might choose. At this same time, John Quincy Adams, Henry Clay and Albert Gallatin were in Europe trying to negotiate a peace treaty with the British.

Jackson correctly concluded that the British would likely use Lake Borgne as their route of attack. The British proceeded to ferry their troops from the anchored sailing ships across Lake Borgne where they would assemble for the march into the city. Some forty-five barges had to defeat the gunboats that Jackson had positioned in the lake, but because they were outnumbered, the gunboats were defeated. As the British were busy ferrying their troops from the ships across Lake Borgne, Jackson was organizing a parade in the city in an effort to generate enthusiasm and support for defense of the city. The parade was a brilliant idea, but even with his troops, and help from the friendly Indians, freed slaves, woodsmen, militiamen, French colonials and townspeople, he needed more troops and more supplies. He turned to the Bandit, Jean Lafitte, who had about one thousand troops and the much-needed muskets and ammunition. Jackson and Lafitte saw eye to eye and the much-needed agreement for support was cemented.

The first land battle of the attack commenced on Christmas eve. Jackson's forces did themselves proud with over five hundred British troops slain while only twenty-four American lives were lost. While the battle was raging, a peace treaty was being signed in Europe ending hostilities between the British and the Americans. The treaty would not arrive in Washington until February 14, 1815, and still had to be ratified by both countries.

Following the Christmas eve attack, and as the British were regrouping, American ships fired shells into the British camp while stealthy Choctaws used tomahawks to silence their sentries. The British found themselves with a river on one side, a swamp on the other, Americans waiting ahead of them and just a narrow path of retreat. They had no choice except to advance. The British had successfully destroyed one of the two American ships that were firing upon them but the other had been moved beyond their range, not by wind — because there was none — but by human muscle. The British troop line advanced toward the American stronghold but was soon forced to retreat. British forces were larger but Jackson's troops were better protected. By New Year's Day the British attacked once more, only to be forced to retreat yet again.

On January 8th, the British plan to attack with cannon fire from the west, creating a crossfire, failed because the cannon had not reached their position on time. But their assault from the front would continue only to discover that — for whatever reason — the unit that was charged with bringing ladders (and sugar cane bundles on which to position the ladders) had not brought the ladders and bundles. One of the British commanders suggested retreat, given all of the setbacks, but commander Pakenham refused. Pakenham's refusal to retreat cost the British army many men as well as the battle. And for Pakenham, it cost him his life.

At last the battle was over. Andrew Jackson's army had successfully defended New Orleans against the mighty British army. On January 17th, the British navy began to depart, and within a few days were all gone. Andrew Jackson emerged a hero. With some luck, some mistakes on the part of the British, but mostly on skilled preparation for and management of the defense of New Orleans, New Orleans and very likely dominion of the western half of North America was denied the British.

But as Jackson suspected, the British would not want to go home empty handed. The British ships headed for Fort Bowyer, which guarded Mobile. Since Colonel Lawrence realized that his few men would stand no chance against this massively larger force, he surrendered the Fort. However, at this same time, word of the signing of the Treaty of Ghent — ending hostilities between England and the United States — was spreading. When it reached Andrew Jackson, he

*The St. Louis Cathedral and Andrew Jackson Statue in New Orleans*

released his troops from service and, with Rachel at his side, made his way to the Hermitage.

Perhaps we could call this the real conclusion of the Revolutionary War, but it is known in history as the War of 1812.

After the war, the army was divided into two divisions; one in the north and one in the south, which was to include the northwest. The southern division was led by Andrew Jackson with headquarters at the Hermitage. Secretary of War Dallas's policy, and his orders to Jackson, were "civilize the Indians, by the establishment of competent posts on a lower route, from Chicago along the Illinois river, to St Louis … [and] is committed to your special care, as falling within the duties of your command."

Jackson's staff lived with him at the Hermitage and included Sam Houston and James Gadsden.

Jackson's primary concern was defending the southern border, which was complicated by the Creek Indians operating out of Spanish Florida.

The ninth article in the Treaty of Ghent that had been signed, ending the War of 1812, said all lands as they were in 1811 would be returned to the Indians. No way, said Jackson, and he prevailed.

The fact that the Seminoles, with their Red Stick Creek element, continued to torment the southern border, and the fact that some 300 runaway slaves were barricaded in a fort allowed by the Seminoles as well as the Spanish who governed east Florida, caused Jackson to ask permission of the Secretary of War to attack. The Secretary told Jackson to get permission from the Spanish governor, which was freely given, and the fort, housing the runaway slaves, was destroyed along with the arms and ammunition that had been provided the slaves by the British. This First Seminole War was Jackson's effort to gain control of Florida and eliminate the Seminole threat on the southern border. Although Jackson probably exceeded his orders, Secretary of State John Quincy Adams took advantage of the situation and made an offer to Spain: either take charge of Florida and prevent the attacks on the southern border or sell Florida to the United States. Spain chose to sell their interests in Florida to the United States — for five million dollars in 1819. Although Jackson was in trouble with Congress for the actions in Florida, in the end an effort to censure him was voted down in the House of Representatives. With Florida now in the control of the United States, President Monroe offered the Florida governorship to Andrew Jackson. After taking some time to deliberate, Jackson resigned from the military and entered the field of politics as the governor of Florida.

In today's age of almost instant communication, it is difficult to comprehend how anything got done in the 19th century. People were forced to rely on themselves, without benefit of the internet or instant chats, and make their own decisions. Jackson, with his Irish heritage and upbringing in a time when life and fortune were fragile, made the most of it. He formulated his own ideas and convictions, reached his own conclusions, acted upon them, and was not afraid to stand by them. That caused some conflict with those who disagreed with him but made him extremely popular with the people. He was a populist — and this is the wave that would fuel his political career.

## Andrew Jackson, the Politician

In June of 1821, Andrew Jackson's military career was over and his political career, with the exception of his brief time in the Tennessee House of Representatives, truly began. He had resigned from the United States Army and became the Military Governor of Florida Territory. He had survived the censure attempt led by Henry Clay — not the last time that he and Clay would clash — because of his actions in Florida, which Clay argued were beyond his official authorization. Clay was perhaps officially correct, but unofficially both President Monroe and Secretary of State Adams were happy to have the Spanish, and with them the British, out of Florida, which is what Jackson had accomplished, but also what drove Clay and Jackson to become solid enemies. That bitter relationship arose again when Andrew Jackson was on the ballot for President of the United States in 1824, along with Henry Clay, John Quincy Adams and William Crawford. When the votes were tallied, Jackson had the most popular votes *and* the most electoral votes, but not a majority. When the election was thrown to the House of Representatives, Clay, being unable to moderate his hatred of Jackson, gave enough of his electoral votes to second place John Quincy Adams in order to ensure Adams' win. The founders had feared that the power of the majority was dangerous unless checked, and therefore they had established the electoral college.

Jackson remained the most popular man in America and after being defeated in 1824, he set his eyes on four years hence.

In 1823 Jackson was elected to the United States Senate representing Tennessee, an office he held until 1825.

## The Cherokee Nation

By 1827, the Cherokee, who had taken seriously the opinion held by many that Indians — once civilized — could become U.S. citizens together with the whites, were becoming successful plantation owners and businessmen along with owning the slaves necessary to work the cotton fields. John Ross, whose father was a Scottish trader and mother who was one quarter Cherokee, was raised as a Cherokee, had emerged as the leader of the Cherokees. He had fought alongside Jackson in the beginning, until the removal movement changed his mind. The Cherokees, under John Ross, could see that if they were going to remain intact, they would have to become a territory or a state. They set about to do just that, holding a constitutional convention with John Ross as Chairman. They drew up and adopted a constitution very much like the one the colonies had formed some years earlier. John Ross became the leader of the government once the constitution was signed on July 4, 1827. Steve Inskeep in his book *Jacksonland* says white leaders were shocked to find that Cherokees were "acting as if federal Indian policy meant what it said, rather than what it actually meant." By about 1827 the only Indian land remaining in Georgia was the Cherokee land under John Ross's leadership.

While Andrew Jackson was busy with his presidential campaign, the Cherokees were preparing to print the first Indian newspaper in America — called the *Cherokee Phoenix.* The first issue was printed on February 21, 1828. The Cherokees had perfected the first written language for any Indian tribe so the newspaper was printed with both English and Cherokee words. John Ross knew that a newspaper would serve a powerful function for the Cherokee's new government, and so one of the first actions of that government was to commit a sum of $1500 toward the paper's establishment.

Samuel Worcester, a Congregational missionary, was in the Cherokee capital of New Echota as a result of efforts by the American Board of Commissioners for Foreign Missions. Jeremiah Evarts was the corresponding secretary for this Boston based board. Evarts was an ally of John Ross and was aiding Ross's efforts by publishing a series of essays favoring the Cherokees under the pen name of "William Penn." It was through the influence of Evarts and Worcester and the Missionary Board that got the printing press to New Echota.

Evarts was very religious, being against the war. He thought America's mission was to establish schools and religious missions throughout the world. He believed in abolition of slavery and in the Cherokee mission and believed that whites and Indians were and should be equal.

Lewis Cass, on the other hand, who would become Andrew Jackson's Secretary of War, believed that Indians were inferior and that they must be pushed away from civilization areas for their own good. The differing beliefs of Evarts and Cass were representative of the two schools of thought at play at the time. This is the same Lewis Cass that, while governor of Michigan Territory in 1813, led an expedition into what would become Minnesota, in search of the source of the Mississippi River. He identified Cass Lake as the source, but was proven wrong by Schoolcraft in 1830, whose expedition made it all the way to the actual source, Lake Itasca. This is the same Lewis Cass whom Hole-in-the-Day the Elder supported against the British, giving Hole-in-the-Day elevated status among the Chippewas.

Elias Boudinot, editor of the *Cherokee Phoenix*, was born Buck Watie. But when he met a man named Elias Boudinot, he liked that name better than his own, so he started using it for himself. Elias, whose wife was white, was a member of the Cherokee elite and lived in New Echota. Boudinot spent long hours working on the newspaper and helped it gain circulation by sending a copy of each issue to some one hundred other newspapers.

In response to the actions taken by the Cherokees, the State of Georgia passed a law adding the area occupied by the Cherokee Nation to the State of Georgia and extending the laws of Georgia over the area. They passed legislation annulling all laws made by the Cherokees, and which said that no Indian residing in Cherokee territory could be a witness in a Georgia court in which a white person was a party unless the white person resided in Cherokee territory, and that any white person living on the Cherokee Nation must get a license from the State of Georgia and swear to uphold the laws of the State of Georgia. That action on the part of Georgia was the impetus for the case of *Cherokee Nation v. Georgia*.

In the 1831 case of *Cherokee Nation v. Georgia*, the Cherokees asked the United States Supreme Court for an injunction to stop the State of Georgia from depriving the Cherokees of their rights. William Wirt, the attorney general in the James Monroe and John Quincy Adams administrations, argued the case for the Cherokee. Wirt argued that the Cherokee Nation was, by the United States Constitution (Article III) and by law, a foreign nation, and therefore not subject to laws passed by the State of Georgia. Chief Justice John Marshall wrote the opinion of the court, declining to rule on the merits of the Cherokee case on grounds that the Cherokee Nation was not a foreign nation and therefore the court had no original jurisdiction. He opined that the Cherokee Nation was not a foreign nation but rather a "domestic dependent nation." He continued to say that, "the relationship of the tribes to the United States resembles that of a 'ward to its guardian'." But the court indicated that it might rule for the Cherokees in a case that was properly brought before them.

## Andrew Jackson as President of the United States

In 1828, Andrew Jackson's popularity swept him to a landslide victory over John Quincy Adams in both popular votes and electoral votes. His wife Rachel was a homebody, content to be at home smoking her corncob pipe, and was not excited about being first lady. She reportedly said, "I had rather be a door-keeper in the house of God than live in that palace." If true, she got her wish because she died just prior to her husband's inauguration.

On March 4, 1829, Jackson was sworn in as President of the United States of America. The bitter John Quincy Adams did not attend the inauguration. Jackson

*Rachel Jackson*

would now lead the country that he had worked so hard to preserve. His inauguration was dampened, however, because of his beloved Rachel's death. In the book *The Graphic Story of the American Presidents* they write, "Looking older than his sixty-one years, Jackson was in poor shape to assume the burdens of the presidency in 1829. He was racked by tuberculosis, and the bullets he still carried in his body contributed to his poor health. Moreover, with Rachel dead he felt he had little to live for." His inauguration speech was so well attended that he had trouble getting back to the executive mansion as it was called at the time. The mansion was mobbed with exuberant supporters and Jackson slipped out and went to stay at a hotel up the street.

Andrew Jackson had said in his inauguration speech that it was his "desire to observe toward the Indian tribes a just and liberal policy, and to give that humane and considerate attention to their rights and their wants which is consistent with the habits of our Government and the feelings of our people." One must wonder what he meant. Secretary of State van Buren stated that Jackson's first objective was the removal of the Indians from the vicinity of white people and their settlement west of the Mississippi River.

During the 1820's colonization was becoming a popular method of dealing with the "non-white problem." In other words, solving social problems by the physical removal of "so-called" undesirables. The American Colonization Society was promoting the removal of black freedmen to a colony in West Africa — a colony that would eventually become the nation of Liberia. So, colonization of the Indians west of the Mississippi would appear to have been rather accepted as the norm.

In 1829, Catherine Beecher (operating anonymously as did Evarts) started a paper she mailed to women in the North and West opposing Indian removal. Interestingly, Catherine's little sister was Harriet Beecher Stowe, one day to be the author of *Uncle Tom's Cabin*.

With Evarts promoting his moral argument and Cass promoting his racist argument, Superintendent of Indian Affairs Thomas McKenney opined that Indians were being destroyed by contact with their aggressive neighbors — "we believe, if the Indians do not emigrate ... they must perish." Andrew Jackson's opinion fell somewhere between Evarts and Cass and rather agreed with McKenney. By moving the Indians west, Jackson thought, they would be "free from the mercenary influence of white men, and undisturbed by the local authority of the states." Was he truly being a friend to the Indians as he claimed, or rather was he submitting to the pressure for more plantation land for the settlers? Or was it both?

## The Indian Removal Act of 1830

This was the backdrop against which Tennessee Senator Hugh White, Chairman of the Senate Committee on Indian Affairs, on February 22, 1830, reported Senate Bill 102, A bill to provide for an exchange of lands with the Indians residing in any of the States or Territories, and for their removal West of the Mississippi. White pointed to the instruction of President Jackson in his recent State of the Union message in which the President had written, "Those States, claiming to be the only sovereigns within their territories, extended their laws over the Indians, which induced the latter to call upon the United States for protection. Georgia became a member of the Confederacy which eventuated in our Federal Union as a sovereign State, always asserting her claim to certain limits, which, having been originally defined in her colonial charter and subsequently recognized in the treaty of peace, she has ever since continued to enjoy, except as they have been circumscribed by her own voluntary transfer of a portion to the United States in the articles of cession of 1802. Would the people of Maine permit the Penobscot tribe to erect an independent government within their State? And unless they did would it be the duty of the General Government to support them in resisting such a measure? Would the people of New York permit each remnant of the six Nations within her borders to declare itself an independent people under the protection of the United States? Could the Indians establish a separate republic on each of their reservations in Ohio? And if they were so disposed would it be a duty of this Government to protect them on the attempt? If the principle involved in the obvious answer to these questions be abandoned, it will follow that the objects of this Government are reversed, and that it has become a part of its duty to aid in destroying the States which it was established to protect."

President Jackson went on to write, "Their present condition, contrasted with what they once were, makes a most powerful appeal to our sympathies. Our ancestors found them the uncontrolled possessors of these vast regions. By persuasion and force they have been made to retire from river to river and from mountain to mountain, until some of the tribes have become extinct and others have left only remnants to preserve for a while their once terrible names. Surrounded by the whites with their arts of civilization, which by destroying the resources of the savage doom him to weakness and decay, the fate of the Mohegan, the Narragansett, and the Delaware is fast over-taking the Choctaws, the Cherokees, and the Creek. That this fate surely awaits them if they remain within the limits of the States does not admit of a doubt.

"As a means of effecting this end I suggest for your consideration the propriety of setting apart an ample district west of the Mississippi, and without the limits of any State or territory now formed, to be guaranteed to the Indian tribes as long as they shall occupy it, each tribe having a distinct control over the portion designated for its use."

This was the basis and the objective of the bill that the Senate Committee on Indian Affairs was presenting to the Congress for consideration. Senator White explained how the actions of the Cherokees and the actions of the State of Georgia were testing the sovereignty of each, and the United States was being asked to take sides. He further explained that from one-third to one-half of the Cherokees had already removed from Georgia, but the remainder were being advised by white men or half-breeds [John Ross] to refuse to remove. He reported that, "The committee are well satisfied, that every humane and benevolent individual, who is anxious for the welfare of the great body of the Cherokees, *and is correctly informed of their true condition*, must feel desirous for their removal, provided it can be effected with their *consent*." Senator White enumerated the many and often overlapping treaties made with the Indians by various entities. He concluded by saying, "Should the Indians continue determined to reside where they now are, and become subject to the laws of the respective States in which they reside, no difficulty can occur, as your Committee see no reason to apprehend that either of the States have it in contemplation to force them to abandon the country in which they dwell; but, if they determine to remain, and continue to insist on a separate and independent government, and refuse obedience to the laws of the States, the consequences which must inevitably ensure, are such as the humane and benevolent cannot reflect upon without feelings of the deepest sorrow and distress."

The Senate Committee on Indian Affairs was clearly siding with President Jackson — that the only answer was removal of the Indians, arguably for their own benefit, a contention that would persist for many years and regarding many tribes.

*****

On April 9, 1830, debate on the Senate floor began with Senator Theodore Frelinghuysen of New Jersey, introducing two amendments to the bill as reported by the Senate Indian Affairs Committee. One amendment would guarantee that the Cherokee would not be interfered with either as to possession or enjoyment of their rights until they decide to remove and secondly that treaties would be negotiated with the Indians before any removal. Frelinghuysen went on to criticize

President Jackson for not following the procedure that George Washington had used, saying that Jackson was assuming powers rightfully possessed by Congress, and chastising him for backing the rights of the State of Georgia instead of the Cherokee.

Frelinghuysen objected to corrupting the country's honor by "buying over the consent of corrupted chiefs to a traitorous surrender of their country." He brought to light a directive from the Department of War dated May 30, 1829, which clearly advocates for bribing chiefs in private to secure treaties rather than attempting it in general council. Such treaties, he suggested, "will disgrace us in the estimation of the whole civilized world! It will degrade us in our own eyes, and blot the page of our history with indelible dishonor! ... It is not intended, sir, to describe this policy exclusively to the present administration. Far from it. The truth is, we have long been gradually, and almost unconsciously, declining into these devious ways, and we shall inflict injury upon our good name, unless we speedily abandon them."

Frelinghuysen then spoke about the rights of the Indians saying, "as the original tenants of the soil, they hold a title beyond and superior to the British Crown and her colonies, and to all adverse pretensions of our confederation and subsequent Union. ... no argument can shake the political maxim, that, where the Indian always has been, he enjoys an absolute right to still be, in free exercise of his own modes of thought, government, and conduct."

But then the Senator weakened in his argument, saying, "It is however, admitted, sir, that, when the increase of population and the wants of mankind demand the cultivation of the earth, a duty is thereby devolved upon the proprietors of large and uncultivated regions, of devoting them to such useful purpose. But such appropriations are to be obtained by fair contract, and for reasonable compensation." But then he goes on to say that, "Millions after millions [the Indian] has yielded to our importunity, until we have acquired more than can be cultivated in centuries — yet we crave more."

Senator Frelinghuysen argued that settlement of this country had been with the help of the Indians and now we are telling them, "away! we cannot endure you so near us! These forests, and rivers, these groves of your fathers, these firesides and hunting grounds, are ours by the right of power, and the force of numbers."

Continuing Frelinghuysen said, "Standing here, then, on this unshaken basis, how is it possible that even a shadow of claim to soil, or jurisdiction, can be derived, by forming a collateral issue between the State of Georgia and the General Government? Her complaint is made against the United States, for encroaching on her sovereignty. Sir, the Cherokees are no party to this issue; they have no part in this controversy. They hold by better title than either Georgia or the Union. They have nothing to do with State sovereignty, or United States sovereignty. They are above and beyond both."

He warns that "we [are] about to turn traitors to our principles and our fame — about to become the oppressors of the feeble, and to cast away our birthright!"

The Senator then asked, When, or where, did any assembly or convention meet which proclaimed, or even suggested to these tribes, that the right of discovery contained superior efficacy over all prior titles? He pointed to a 1763 proclamation of the King of Great Britain which stated that the Indians should not be disturbed in the possession of lands not ceded or purchased by them or their colonies. This alone, Senator Frelinghuysen intimated, should defeat this bill. But he continued with the history of the agreements made between the Indians and the United States government concluding saying, "We, after this, sir, can retain a single doubt as to the unquestioned political sovereignty of these tribes?"

"It is really a subject of wonder," the Senator said, "that after these repeated and solemn recognitions of right of soil, territory, and jurisdiction, in these aboriginal nations, it should be gravely asserted that they are mere occupants at our will; and what is absolutely marvelous, that they are part of the Georgia population — a district of her territory, and amenable to her laws, when ever she chooses to extend them.'

Frelinghuysen points to the Northwest Ordinance's treatment of Indians and its' statement that "these lands and property shall never be taken from them without their consent." Continuing he argues, "…how can we quietly permit her [Georgia], 'to invade and disturb the property, rights, and liberty of the Indians?' And this, not only not 'in just and lawful wars authorized by Congress,' but in the time of profound peace, while the Cherokee lives in tranquil prosperity by her side." He points to the trade and intercourse acts as supporting his opposition to passage of Senate Bill 102.

After arguing his case for about two hours, Senator Frelinghuysen concluded by quoting the language of an eloquent writer — one he obviously admired, "I had rather receive the blessing of one poor Cherokee, as he casts his last look back upon his country, for having, though in vain, attempted to prevent his banishment, than to sleep beneath the marble of all the Caesars."

*****

On April 15th, Georgia Senator John Forsyth, arguing for passage of the Removal Act, began his argument by explaining in detail that Senator Frelinghuysen obviously had no sympathy left for the white man because he had exhausted it all on the red man.

Forsyth leaned on the English legal theory of Blackstone saying that "legislation is the highest act of sovereignty." That the treaty of Hopewell clearly states that, "For the benefit and comfort of the Indians, and for the prevention of injuries or oppression on the part of the citizens or Indians, the United States in Congress assembled, should have the sole and exclusive right of regulating trade with the Indians, and managing all their affairs in such manner as they think proper." So, he argues, how can the Cherokee Nation be an independent nation? And by that same 1802 Treaty of Hopewell in the second article the United States "cede to the State of Georgia, whatever claim, right, or title, they may have to the jurisdiction and soil of any lands, lying within the United States, and out of the proper boundaries of any other State ... as the Eastern boundary of the territory ceded by Georgia to the United States." By this treaty he argues, "the United States obtained, by treaty, the power to legislate over the Cherokees, and transferred it to Georgia." Georgia, he argued, "stands justified in her course." Senator Forsyth intimates that their actions are benevolent, saying, "the condition of the remnants of the once formidable tribes of Indians is known to be deplorable: all admit that there is something due to the remaining individuals of the race; all desire to grant more than is justly due for their preservation and civilization."

Forsyth then addressed the efforts on behalf of the Cherokee by "the clergy, the laity, the lawyers, and the ladies," all designed to prevent the removal, "a project which has been steadily kept in view by three administrations." The Senator stated, "I feel and have ever felt the strongest anxiety to do justice to the Indian tribes. I have reflected much on the subject since the project of congregating them beyond the Mississippi, and establishing a great Indian government was first suggested during Mr. Monroe's administration." He continued, stating that he has become convinced that "the removal of the Indians beyond the States and Territories — was the only mode by which the power of the General Government could be properly and exclusively exercised for their benefit." "I shall vote for it," he said, "with a hope of relieving the States from a population useless and burthensome, and from a conviction of the Indians will be greatly improved by the change: a change not intended to be forced upon them."

Forsyth next described the current state of affairs, declaring, "without industry, and without incentives to improvement, with the mark of degradation fixed upon them by State laws; without the control of their own resources, depending upon a precarious, because ill-directed, agriculture, they are little better than the wandering gypsies of the old world, living by beggary or plunder." The Senator argued that, "In no part of the country have the Indians an admitted right to the soil upon which they live. They are looked upon as temporary occupants, who have not, and are not, intended to have a fee simple title to the land."

Perhaps Forsyth was describing the general attitude — at least of Georgia and probably widespread in that area — that, "this important object will be gained: a race not admitted to be equal to the rest of the community; not governed as completely dependent; treated somewhat like human beings, but not admitted to be freemen; not yet entitled, and probably never to be entitled, to equal civil and political rights, will be humanely provided for."

The President, he said, has "stated to the Indians what is their true position. They must remove, or remain and be subjected to the State laws ..."

Senator Forsyth pointed to the 1802 compact in which Georgia ceded considerable land to the United States; the compact which stated "that the United States should extinguish, (at their sole and proper expense,) the Indian claims to all the land not ceded by Georgia, within certain designated periods of time," and now twenty-eight years later, "a large territory still remains occupied by Indians." He continued, "We saw ourselves postponed, time after time, to suit the conveniences of other States, without murmur. Complaint would have been justified; it was not made; we relied upon the good faith of the Government for a performance of its obligations in reasonable time."

"In this hall" Forsyth said, "in the Representative Chamber, in every corner of the country, where a partisan newspaper is to be found, we are discussed without measure, and abused without mercy. This is not all; we are important enough to attract attention in transatlantic assemblies."

Nevertheless, Forsyth said, "I must not be withdrawn from my purpose, by the dishonorable artifices of editors of American newspapers, by the arts of Senatorial ingenuity, or by the uncalled for and grossly inconsistent censures of the British government."

The Senator related that when the Cherokees "sought to strengthen themselves in their position, by forming and publishing a constitution" and "transmitting a copy ... to the President of the United States ... the agent was directed to inform the Cherokees, that the formation of their constitution would produce no change in their relations with the United States."

After twenty-eight years, the Senator argued, "we found ourselves compelled to submit to the intrusive sovereignty of a petty tribe of Indians, or to put it down by our own authority, without the aid, and probably against the wishes of the Federal government."

Continuing, he argued, "the honorable Senator from New Jersey claims that the Cherokee Indians were, ever have been, and ever shall be, the owners of the soil, and independent of the Government of the State and of the Union; and he denies that the European discoverers, particularly the English, ever claimed or exercised the right to legislate directly over the Indians, as their dependents or subjects. The European doctrine [the Doctrine of Discovery] of the right conferred by the discovery of new countries, inhabited by barbarous tribes, was, I thought, well known."

The Senator went on to cite the Royal Proclamation of 1763, issued by King George III following the French and Indian War, which stated, "First, the sovereignty and dominion of Great Britain over Indians and Indian territory. Secondly, that the Indians were, as subjects, under the protection of the Crown. Thirdly, that the right to appropriate the land occupied by the Indians resided in the Crown. It contains grants to the whites, and reservations to the Indians as hunting grounds. Fourthly, that it was expedient to reserve the ground West of the sources of the rivers named in it," [a lime drawn along the Appalachian Mountains] "for the present, to the use of the Indians. Fifthly, that the lands East of the sources of those rivers, part of which was then actually occupied by the Indians, should be granted at the discretion of the proprietary or colonial authorities."

Continuing he argued, "On the Declaration of Independence, the States, respectively, took upon themselves all the authority Great Britain ever exercised, or claimed to exercise, within their limits. The Indians were at their discretion; and whether they were managed by direct enforced legislation, or by voluntary contract, no other Government could interfere between the State and the Indians residing within its territory."

During the Revolutionary War, the Senator claimed, "these savages became the allies of Britain, and were, with her, conquered in the struggle. We claimed them as our dependents, not only by the title surrendered by Great Britain, but of that obtained by victory in frequent and bloody battles."

In the Articles of Confederation, Forsyth asked, "Is there anything ... which deprives the individual States of any portion of their sovereignty over Indians or Indian lands?" He answered his own question with these words from the Declaration, "The Congress shall have the sole and exclusive right and power of regulating the trade and managing all affairs with the Indians, not members of any of the States; provided, that the legislative right of any State within its own limits be not infringed or violated."

Pointing to the United States Constitution, Senator Forsyth highlighted the provision which reads, "the powers not delegated to the United States, nor prohibited to the States, are reserved to the States respectively, or to the people. Has the power over Indians within the States been delegated by the constitution?" he asked.

He continued pointing out, that "the name of Indian is found no where else in the constitution but in that article and in this clause: 'Congress shall have power to regulate commerce with foreign nations, between the States, and with Indian tribes.' To the confederation was given power over all Indian affairs that could be exercised, without encroaching upon State sovereignty."

The Senator spent some time comparing treaties to contracts. "Now, sir, I assert explicitly, that the power to make a treaty with Indians within a States is not delegated to the United States, and I assert farther, that the power of making contracts with Indians is not prohibited to the States. The right of the United States to contract with, or legislate for, the Indians, beyond the States is not denied ... that the President has made, with the advice and consent of the Senate, various contracts with Indians, and called them treaties, is not to be denied ... What I assert is, that these instruments are not technically treaties, supreme laws of the land, superior in obligation to State constitutions and State laws ... the tenth section of the first article of the constitution proves that the Indian contracts were not in the contemplation of the convention, when the treaty-making power was discussed. By the seventh article, already quoted, it is shown that a distinction is made between foreign nations, States, and Indian tribes. Indian tribes are not, in the terms of the constitution, foreign nations or States ... A contract made between the United States and individuals or corporations, is not a treaty; a compact by State with State, or by the United States with a State, is not a treaty. How then, can a contract made with a petty dependent tribe of half-starved Indians be properly dignified with the name, and claim the imposing character of a treaty? No, sir, if a contract with an Indian tribe is not a treaty, alliance, or confederation, but is a compact or agreement, the State Government can make them at their pleasure, without consent of Congress ..." As proof the Senator turned to George Washington who, he claims, believed as he does, and to the Senate in a scenario he describes: "The Senate have decided that contracts made with Indians (on the treaty sent last year from New York) within a State, for their lands, were not such instruments as required the sanction of the Senate. The contract sent for ratification as a treaty, was returned to the President, neither ratified nor rejected. Within a few months the Governor of New York has, under a law of the State, called together the Oneidas, and made a treaty with them, in open day, and utterly disregarding the pretensions of the United States, under the treaty-making power, and the provisions of the laws regulating intercourse with Indians ... The State of

Georgia, after a fair investigation of her position, was confident that, never having surrendered to the United States her power over the Indians within her eminent domain, that the exercise of that power not being in any manner prohibited to her by the constitution of the United States, proceeded to follow the example of the other States, and the act of 1828 was passed, subjugating, after the 30ᵗʰ June, 1830, all the Indians in the State to the regular operation of the State laws. We were not permitted, unmolested, to follow in the footsteps of New York or Maine. What was not censured in either, was in us a crime."

As the debate for that day was drawing to a close, Senator Forsyth stated, "That we desire the Indians to remove, is certain. We believe their removal will be beneficial to us and to themselves. That we design to compel them by unjust legislation is not true — there is not a shadow of evidence of such intention."

But before the session ended Senator Forsyth took one more opportunity to chastise Senator Frelinghuysen for his position saying, in part, that "He believes everything stated by the persons favorable to the Cherokees, and distrusts all statements, by whom or whenever made, unfavorable to them."

*****

Senator Sprague of Rhode Island argued against the Removal Act and especially against the comments of Senator White and Forsyth. The question, he said, is, "The Cherokees now come to us, and say that their rights are in danger of invasion from the States of Georgia and Alabama; and they ask if we will extend to them the protection we have promised ..." Proponents of the Removal Act argue that the laws Georgia had passed were not prevented by the treaties.

Senator Sprague pointed to the Articles of Confederation that, in Article six says, "No state shall engage in any war without the consent of the United States, in Congress assembled, unless such State be actually invaded by enemies, or shall have received certain advice of a resolution formed by some nation of Indians to invade such State, and the danger is so imminent as not to admit of a delay till the United States in Congress assembled, can be consulted."

He continued arguing that the 1785 Treaty of Hopewell "secured to the Cherokees their previous right to exist as a community upon the territory in their previous possession." Such a treaty, he argued, "would have been obligatory upon any State, if the Articles of Confederation had never existed."

Followed by that treaty, Forsyth maintained, is the constitution which declares that "the United States cannot interfere in behalf of a State against a tribe of Indians, 'but on the principle that Congress shall have the sole direction of the war, and the settling of all terms of peace with such Indian tribes?" He then reminded the Senate that article six declares that "treaties made, or which shall be made, under the authority of the United States, shall be the supreme law of the land ..."

The proponents of this bill, according to Forsyth, say "that the existence of an Indian community, within the chartered limits of a State, is inconsistent with 'a republican form of government,' as guaranteed by the constitution of every State." If this was true, he answered, "a most unexpected result follows: it is, that Georgia has never yet had a republican form of Government: for there has never been a moment when such tribes did not exist within her borders."

The Senator pointed to the words of George Washington when addressing Indians: "That in future you cannot be defrauded of your lands. That you possess the right to sell, and the right of refusing to sell your lands ... The United States will be true and faithful to their engagements."

All of the treaties, he argued, "were ratified by the Senate ... But now that we, the United States, are called upon to 'be true and faithful to these engagements,' it is contended that they are not obligatory; and, in order to sustain that position, it is insisted that the constitution gives no power to make treaties with Indian nations, within the United States. Although every President of the United States and the members of his cabinet, every administration and all the great men by whom it was surrounded and sustained, have formed and established such Indian treaties."

"The second section of the bill under consideration," he avowed, "provides for the removal of 'any tribe or nation of Indians now residing within the limits of any of the States or Territories, and with which the United States have existing treaties,' and now we are told by the chairman that such treaties cannot exist — that there are not treaties." But, he argued, "if these contracts are not treaties, within the true meaning of the constitution, they could be made only by the authority of Congress. But the President and Senate alone — the treaty-making power — have always negotiated them, ratified them, and by proclamation announced them to the nation, as the supreme law of the land."

Senator Sprague pointed to the Northwest Ordinance and its article stating that "The utmost good faith shall always be observed towards the Indians: their lands and property shall never be taken from them without their consent: and in their property, rights, and liberty, they shall never be invaded or disturbed, unless in just and lawful wars authorized by Congress, but laws founded in justice and humanity shall from time to time, be made, for preventing wrongs being done to them, and for preserving peace and friendship with them."

The Senator from Rhode Island rather poked fun at Senator McKinley of Alabama when he said, "the gentleman insists that the true construction of the

[Northwest] ordinance gives all the right over the Indians for which his State contends, because the latter clause requires that 'laws shall from time to time, be made for preventing wrongs being done to them, and for preserving peace and friendship with them.' That is, laws restraining the whites, our own citizens, from encroaching upon the natives, and thereby endangering the public tranquility. If Maine or New York should pass laws for 'preventing wrongs being done to' the Canadians, 'and preserving peace and friendship with them,' would that give jurisdiction over the British province? But let us read the whole clause, the true construction of which confers this unlimited power: 'the utmost good faith shall always be observed towards the Indians,' which means that we may violate all our engagements at pleasure; 'their lands and property shall never be taken from them without their consent,' that is, both may be taken by violence, against their utmost resistance! 'In their property, rights, and liberty, they shall never be invaded or disturbed, unless in just and lawful wars, authorized by Congress.' 'there shall be laws for preventing wrongs being done to them, and for preserving peace and friendship with them,' the true construction of all which is, that a State may make war upon them at pleasure, deprive them of their lands, and annihilate their nation! To such arguments are gentlemen of great ability compelled to resort! The right of the natives, both natural and conventional, have been strenuously denied. What right, it is asked, have the Indians to the lands they occupy? I ask, in reply, what right have the English or the French, the Spaniards or the Russians, to the countries they inhabit?

"But it is insisted that the original claim of the natives has been divested by the superior right of discovery. I have already shown that this gives no ground of claim as against the discovered; that it is a mutual understanding or conventional arrangement, entered into by the nations of Europe, amongst themselves ..."

"The right of the aborigines," the Senator argued, "to the perpetual and exclusive occupancy of all their lands has been always recognized and affirmed by the United States. It was respected by Great Britain before the Revolution, as appears by the royal proclamation of 1763, in which all persons are commanded, 'forthwith to remove themselves' from lands, 'which not having been ceded to or purchased by us, are still reserved to the said Indians' ..."

Senator Sprague quoted extensively from a letter written by President George Washington's Secretary of State Thomas Jefferson to Secretary of War Henry Knox in 1791. "I am of the opinion that Government should firmly maintain this ground; that the Indians have a right to the occupation of their lands, independent of the States within whose chartered lines they happen to be; that until they cede them by treaty, or other transactions equivalent to a treaty, no act of a State can give a right to such lands; that neither under the present constitution, nor the ancient confederation, had any State, or persons, a right to treat with the Indians, without the consent of the General Government; that that consent has never been given to any treaty for cession of lands in question; that the Government is determined to exert all its energy for the patronage and protection of the rights of the Indians, and the preservation of peace between the United States and them; and that if any settlements are made on land not ceded by them, without the previous consent of the United States, the Government will think itself bound, not only to declare to the Indians that such settlements are without authority or protection of the United States, but to remove them also by the public force."

In wrapping up his argument the Senator from Rhode Island stated, "They now live by the cultivation of the soil, and the mechanic arts. It is proposed to send them from their cotton fields, their farms, and their gardens, to a distant and unsubdued wilderness — to make them tillers of the earth; to remove them from their looms, their workshops, their printing press, their schools, and churches, near the white settlements, to frowning forests, surrounded with naked savages — that they may become enlightened and civilized!"

"I am aware," he said, "that their white neighbors desire the absence of the Indians; and if they can find safety and subsistence beyond the Mississippi, I should rejoice exceedingly at their removal, because it would relieve the States of their presence. But let it be by their own free choice, unawed by fear, unseduced by bribes. Let us not compel them, by withdrawing the protection which we have pledged."

"It is said that their existence cannot be preserved; that it is the doom of Providence that they must perish. So indeed, must we all, but let it be in the course of nature, not by the hand of violence."

Senator Adams, the freshman Senator from Mississippi who would be dead before the $4^{th}$ of July the year that his term in the Senate began, argued in favor of the Removal Act. "I see nothing in the provisions of the bill before us unbecoming the character of a great, just, and magnanimous nation." He reminded the Senate of history, that by the 1802 compact with the State of Georgia, "the United States obtained from the State of Georgia a cession of territory sufficient, in extent, to form two large States" [Alabama and Mississippi] and in the compact the United States "agreed, on their part, in the most solemn manner, to extinguish, for the use of Georgia, the Indian title to all the lands situated within the limits of the State, 'as soon as the same could be done peaceably and upon reasonable terms!" He continued, "The bill under consideration proposes a mode by which this agreement may be performed ...," but "It is plain, ..., if the bill pass with this amendment, that the laws of the States and of the Federal Government must come into collision." Speaking of state sovereignty, Senator Adams stated, "The capacity to affect, by her legislative government, all persons and all property within her limits, is an essential attribute of the sovereignty which belongs to every State. I must conclude, therefore, that the Indians within the limits of the States did not form an exception, and that, subsequent to the declaration of independence, the States had the power to legislate over them. But it is insisted that, by the articles of confederation, the States surrendered up this power to Congress, and that any exercise of such power by the States after that was void."

Senator Adams argued that, "I have endeavored to show that the treaties in question, so far as they affect the legislative sovereignty of the States, are not consistent with the constitution; and as respects the States, they are not binding on them." "The argument" he declared, "is, that in the clause of the constitution conferring upon Congress the power to regulate commerce with foreign nations, among the several States, and with Indian tribes, contains no reservation in favor of the legislative rights of the States. Surely this was not the understanding of those who framed or those who adopted the constitution. On the contrary, did they not say, the States have now all the power and sovereignty, and that which they do not give up remains where it is, in the States respectively?"

Adams contended that "The grant of power in question to Congress is to regulate trade with the Indian tribes; and every power not necessary for the regulation of trade, so far as the Indians are concerned, remains with the States, not only upon the principles which I have mentioned, but by an express reservation, adopted from the most jealous caution, that all 'the powers not delegated by the constitution to the United States, nor prohibited by it to the States, are reserved to the States respectively, or to the people.'"

"Among the powers essential to State sovereignty" he argued, "is that of legislation over every rational being within the limits of the State, unrestrained except by the constitution of the United States and the constitution of the State itself."

"The constitution which the people of that State framed" he continued, "was submitted to Congress; and they admitted the State, with that constitution, into the Union. There is nothing in that instrument which takes away the power to legislate over the Indians, or modifies that power in any particular."

Senator Adams concluded his argument by declaring, "My principal object was to vindicate the right of the State, of which I am one of the Representatives, to legislate over all the population within her limits."

The next day the removal bill was removed from the table and a Senator Robbins made a thought-provoking argument on sovereignty.

"The President and Senate have the power to make treaties; but a treaty made with a party not competent to make it, is not a treaty; it is a compact, as distinguishable from a treaty; and the President and Senate are not competent to make a compact which is not a treaty; so that every such treaty is void, as a treaty, because the Indian nation was not competent to make it; and it is void as a compact, because the President and Senate are not competent to make it.

"I agree that an Indian nation, to be competent to make a treaty, must be a sovereignty; for that treaties, properly so called, can only be made by sovereigns with sovereigns ..."

He countered Alabama Senator McKinley saying, "A dependent sovereignty is still a sovereignty, and competent to make a treaty."

"Now what is sovereignty? It is to be *sui juris* [subject to his own law]– that is, to be subject, within itself, to no law but the law of its own making; externally, it may be subject to another jurisdiction, and then it is a dependent sovereignty — ... this is the condition of every Indian nation in our country, *sui juris*, and therefore sovereign, but subject externally to another jurisdiction, and therefore a dependent sovereign.

"Now the fact of being *sui juris*, and always of having been so, constitutes the right to be so. I would be glad to know if any nation has, or ever had, a better title to be *juri sui juris* than the fact of being so, and of always having been so? than a present position, fortified by a prescription that knows no beginning; that runs back as far as memory or tradition goes, and beyond, to where it is lost in that oblivion in which unknown times and their memorials are all buried and lost! And such is the title of every Indian nation now in fact *sui juris* to be, any better title to the right of being *sui juris*.

"Unquestionably, then, these nations are *sui juris*, of right *sui juris*; therefore, sovereign; therefore, competent to make treaties."

Changing gears, Senator Adams argued, "The population of the United States is taken periodically ...were the Indian nations within the United States ever included in any census as a part of the population of the United States? Never ... it is insisted ... that the constitution gives the Executive no authority to go within a State and make a treaty with a part of its population ..."

"As to the civilization of the Indians, that is his own concern in the pursuit of his own happiness; if the want of it is a misfortune, it is his misfortune; it neither takes from his rights, nor adds to our own. As to his being an inveterate savage, and incapable of civilization, I do not believe it; in that respect, I believe he is like the rest of mankind. The savage-state is the natural state of man ... Man at no time, ever rose from the savage state to the civilized man, but by the spur of an absolute necessity ... it was not until he could no longer live as a savage, or go where he could live as a savage, that he would submit himself to the incessant labor and severe restraint, which lies at the foundation of all civilization ..."

Talking about the Cherokee Senator Adams reasoned, "The new government, like the old, is made for their own internal regulation, and for that object merely ... If they now are a government within a government, at which such an outcry is made as justifying their destruction, so they always have been ..."

Wrapping up his argument against passage of the removal bill he said, "But if executed, and when executed, for one, I will say, that these Indians have been made the victims of power exerted against right — the victims of violated faith, the nation's faith ..."

On Saturday April 24, 1830 the amendments to the removal bill were voted down and disposed of and the Senate voted 28 to 19 to pass the Indian Removal Act (S. 102) and send it to its third reading.

*****

On Saturday May 15, 1830, the House of Representatives opened debate on the bill that the Senate had forwarded to them. Congressman Henry Storrs of New York argued long and hard against passage of the bill.

Storrs quoted from President Jackson's message on the State of the Union, "A portion, however, of the southern tribes, having mingled much with the whites, and made some progress in the arts of civilized life, have lately attempted to erect an independent government within the limits of Georgia and Alabama. These States, claiming to be the only sovereigns within their territories, extended their laws over the Indians, which induced the latter to call on the United States for protection. Under these circumstances, the question presented was, whether the General Government had a right to sustain these people in their pretensions."

Pointing to the Secretary of War's message to the Cherokee Storrs stated, "the President cannot and will not beguile you with such expectation. No remedy can be perceived, except that which frequently heretofore has been submitted for your consideration — a removal beyond the Mississippi, where alone can be assured to you protection and peace."

And so the Congressman said, "There is no reason to believe that the Executive Department is desirous to retrace its steps, and it is decisively avowed that these States have unalterably determined to proceed to the extremity of a strict execution of these laws in the face of the guaranties of our treaties."

To this state of affairs Congressman Storrs lamented, "While the Cherokee delegation have been at our door, anxiously waiting to know the fate of their nation, bands of profligate men have intruded themselves upon their people, and seated themselves down upon their lands. I know that this is not done under the authority of Georgia, or the countenance of the authorities of that State, but our agent has informed us that these intruders have taken courage in their aggressions, from the laxity of opinion prevailing in regard to Indian rights. A state of violence, disreputable to the country, exists there. Blood has already been shed. One of the Cherokees has been slain in open day. The forces of the Government have very lately been sent there to preserve the public peace, and there are some thousands of lawless adventurers prowling through their country, digging for Cherokee gold, and quarrelling among themselves for the division of the spoil.

"The protection which these unfortunate people have demanded of us, has failed to secure them against these evils. By surrendering the question of sovereignty, the Executive has, for all substantial purposes, virtually surrendered the treaties too. The intercourse laws of the United States are nullified with them."

The Congressman then chastised President Jackson by declaring, "If he has the power under the constitution to do what he has done, it is a mere mockery, and an insult to the Cherokees and to common sense, to talk about the treaty of Holston as a thing which has any existence."

He continued, "He maintains the right, in that department of the Government, to treat the obligations by which the United States are bound on the face of the treaties, as annulled from that time — that they shall be reduced to mean nothing any longer -..."

Storrs then said that the Executive's message was that "the treaty has now come into collision with the jurisdiction of the State, and must therefore be yielded." But, he argued, "the principle which lurks under this disguise, really goes to the total annihilation of the treaties from the beginning, and assumes that they were never binding on the United States at all. If they ever were so, no act of one of the States could discharge our obligations."

In regard to treaties the Congressman explained, "It is well known that the disposition of the treaty-making power was one of the most difficult points to be settled in the convention of 1787. In Europe, it was in the hands of the sovereign, and was liable to the greatest abuse. It was in the view of this evil, that under our constitution it was considered unsafe to trust it to the Executive. In Europe it was prerogative, but here it was to be limited by the constitution, and subjected to the control of the States in the Senate, where their sovereignty was equal ... it was even considered unsafe to entrust it to a majority of the States, and the concurrence of two-thirds of the Senators was therefore required. For this purpose the Senate is the council of the States, and the treaties are the acts of the States. The treaties, therefore, express the will of the States, and not the capricious inclinations or the pleasure of the Executive Department."

Continuing he stated, "I consider that the States have, in the strictest sense, retained to themselves, in the Senate, their own control of their reserved rights in the exercise of the treaty-making power. It is safely placed there under their own conservation, and they are bound in good faith to the Union to respect the treaties which are entered into."

Speaking of the President he charged, "His doctrines fall nothing short of an assumption of the power of Congress ..." Continuing to chastise the President Storrs declared, "He has given to the other party his own final determination of the question, and has acted upon it throughout. He asks us now for no opinion upon it; but, considering it settled, we are called upon to appropriate some millions to relieve the other party from the condition to which his decision has reduced them."

"The only power" he insisted, "which stands between the Executive and the States, is Congress."

The Congressman then turned to the Committee on Indian Affairs and charged the committee with "a spirit" ... "unfavorable to the claims of the native inhabitants of this continent." "If we consider what the state of society was," he said, "and how strongly the principle of self-preservation is implanted in the human heart, we should rather wonder that the Committee on Indian Affairs had not been able to find much more in our early history to sustain their positions."

Switching to the Doctrine of Discovery Storrs confessed, "I fully admit, that shortly after the discovery of America, the principle became established, by European nations, that they held their dominions here, as among themselves, by the right of discovery, and that this doctrine must be considered as settled at this day." He suggested that this doctrine was a defensive move in response to the "decision of the Pope, who claimed all undiscovered lands as his spiritual patrimony ..."

The Congressman suggested that, "We cannot deny that the European Governments originally held the rights of the Indian nations in very little regard." But, he continued, "I deny that our English ancestors, who first colonized these States, ever countenanced that disregard of Indian rights ..."

In regard to the treaties he opined, "But these treaties have been looked upon as something quite substantial, in the time of them. Things are firmly settled as these, are not to be easily moved."

"The Articles of Confederation" Storrs explained, "had narrowed the power of 'regulating trade and managing all affairs with the Indians,' by confining it to such as were not members of any of the States, and providing that the legislative right of any State within its own limits should not be infringed or violated. The Constitution" he stated, "omitted these restrictions."

Speaking of the Indians Congressman Storrs argued, "When they have just reached that point which is successfully calling forth their talent, and developing their capacity for moral improvement, we are about to break up their society, dissolve their institutions, and drive them into the wilderness."

Nearing the end of his argument, the Congressman concluded, "I have viewed this question in all the lights which have offered themselves to my mind, and I can see no way to dispose of it safely, but to stop where we are — to go no further ... I will take no share of the responsibility of carrying this measure through the House ... that part of the law of nations which commands the observance of treaties, is the law of the whole human family."

On the following Monday Georgia Congressman Wilson Lumpkin took to the podium to argue in favor of the Indian Removal bill. Congressman Lumpkin was a member of the House Indian Affairs Committee that was recommending passage of the bill and he attempted to make the case that it was for the welfare of the Indians that had prompted that recommendation. In regard to the Indians, he argued, "They have the capacity, to some extent at least, to take care of themselves. But to those remnant tribes of Indians whose good we seek, the subject before you is of vital importance. It is a measure of life and death. Pass the bill on your table, and you save them. Reject it, and [you] leave them to perish."

He continued, "I entertain no doubt that a remnant of these people may be entirely reclaimed from their native savage habits, and be brought to enter into the full enjoyment of all the blessings of civilized society."

"The means," he stated, "to improve the condition of the Indians, must, from the present state of things, very soon be withheld from these unfortunate people, if they remain in their present abodes ..."

Speaking from a personal viewpoint as well as that of the committee he argued, "The whole of my policy and views of legislation upon this subject has been founded in an ardent desire to better the condition of these remnant tribes. At the same time, I freely admit, their interest alone has not guided my action. From the time I became a member of this House, the great object of my solicitude and labor has been to relieve all the States (especially my own) from the perplexities, heart-burnings, conflicts, and strifes which are connected with this Indian subject."

In response to some of those who were arguing that Indian removal was initiated by President Jackson, Lumpkin referred to former President Monroe's message of January 27, 1825, in which he said, "Being deeply impressed with the opinion that the removal of the Indian tribes from the lands which they now occupy within the limits of the several States and territories to the country lying westward and northward thereof, within our acknowledged boundaries, is of very high importance to our Union, and may be accomplished on conditions and in a manner to promote the interest and happiness of the tribes, the attention of the Government has been long drawn, with great solicitude to the object. For the removal of the tribes within the limits of the State of Georgia, the motive has been peculiarly strong, arising from the compact with that State, whereby the United States are bound to extinguish the Indian title to the lands within it, whenever it may be done peaceably and on reasonable conditions." The Congressman went on to say that, "Mr. Adams, with great force of argument, while President of the United States, sustained these doctrines." And so Congressman Lumpkin argued, "there is no new measure, emanating from President Jackson and the Georgians, but that it is a measure tested by many years' experience ... Jefferson gave it the first official impulse ... Madison, Monroe, Adams, Jackson ... have, in their official capacities, repeatedly sustained the principles and policy of the bill on your table."

Just what, exactly, was this "compact" that President Monroe and others were talking about? When Georgia entered the Union as the thirteenth of the original thirteen states, it was considerably larger than today, containing — in addition to Georgia proper — the area that is today the states of Alabama and Mississippi. In 1795 the fledgling Georgia General Assembly, in order to spur its settlement, initiated a scheme to sell millions of acres of vacant land along the Yazoo River to speculators for just pennies, to speculators who were primarily Georgia legislators, state officials and other influential Georgians. Many of them then resold the land for huge profits, and the fraud was exposed. The State of Georgia, being swamped with claims, was able to negotiate the 1802 Articles of Agreement and Cession in which the United States Government agreed to (1) bear all expense of settling all the claims resulting from the Yazoo land fraud, (2) pay Georgia $1.25 million and (3) extinguish as quickly as possible the remaining Indian claims to land within the State of Georgia. In return the United States became the owners of the land which would become Alabama and Mississippi. It was this Yazoo land fraud deal and the agreement that the United States government had made with Georgia that President Monroe was referring to.

Congressman Lumpkin argued that much of the opposition to the Indian Removal bill was prompted by private interest. The traders, he pointed out, did not want their customers to be removed and the missionaries did not want the people they were trying to save to disappear. "Let it be remembered," he said, "that weak minorities make the most noise."

In regard to the opposition from religious groups the Congressman argued that while, "the religious opposition to this measure is not confined to any particular sect … these canting fanatics have placed themselves … behind the bulwarks of religion, and console themselves with the belief that the Georgians, whom they have denounced as atheists, deists, infidels, and sabbath-breakers, laboring under the curse of slavery, will never be able to dislodge them from their strong position."

Getting even more personal in his desire to have the Indians removed Lumpkin declared, "Yes, sir, amongst my earliest recollections are the walls of an old fort, which gave protection to the women and children from the tomahawk and scalping knife of the Indians."

Referring to the Yazoo land settlement compact of 1802 he argued, "This General Government; and every individual who administers any part of it, executive or legislative, must recollect that the faith of this Government has stood pledged for twenty-eight years past, to relieve Georgia from the embarrassment of Indian population. It is known to every member of this Congress, that this pledge was no gratuity to Georgia. No, sir, it was for and in consideration of the two entire States of Alabama and Mississippi." "This Government," he continued, "has, by its own acts and policy, forced the Indians to remain in Georgia, by the purchase of their lands in the adjoining States, and by holding out to the Indians strong inducements to remain where they are …" He argued, "but it should not have been done at the expense of Georgia. The Government, long after it was bound to extinguish the title of the Indians to all the lands in Georgia, has actually forced the Cherokees from their lands in other States, settled them upon Georgia lands, and aided in furnishing the means to create the Cherokee aristocracy."

"Sir," he argued, "my State stands charged before this House, before the nation, and before the whole world, with cruelty and oppression towards the Indians. I deny the charge, and demand proof from those who make it."

Congressman Lumpkin passionately claimed, "Georgia, it is true, has slaves: but she did not make them such; she found them upon her hands when she became a sovereign State. She never has, by her legislation, changed the state of freedom to slavery. If she has ever owned an Indian slave, it has never come to my knowledge; but more than one of the other States of this Union have not only reduced Indians to a state of slavery, but have treated them as brutes, destitute of any human rights — depriving them of their own modes of worshipping Deity — hunting them as wild beasts for slaughter — holding out rewards for their scalps, and even giving premiums for the raising of a certain breed of dogs, called bloodhounds, to hunt savages, that they might procure their scalps and obtain the reward offered by Government for them. Sir, compare this legislation with that of Georgia, and let the guilty be put to shame."

Speaking of the pamphlets that had been circulating he contended, "It is the statements found in these pamphlets and magazines, which are relied on as truth, that have induced so many worthy people at a distance to espouse the cause of Indian sovereignty, as assumed by the Cherokees."

"A large portion of the full-blooded Cherokees," he argued, "still remain a poor degraded race of human beings. I can readily conclude that but a very small portion of the real Indians are in a state of improvement, whilst their lords and rulers are white men, and the descendants of white men, enjoying the fat of the land, and enjoying exclusively the Government annuities ..."

On the wisdom of removing the Indians west he maintained that, "All the various emigrants to the West so far agree as to authorize the assurance that no inducement could be offered to them strong enough to bring them back again."

Speaking of the relationship of the federal government to the other original states Lumpkin reasoned, "Yes, sir, this Government was formed to protect, and not to destroy the State Governments. In all the States, we find, as soon as the Indians were reduced to a condition that no danger was to be apprehended from their power and hostility, the States have invariably taken their Indian affairs into their own hands, and no longer looked to the federal arm for aid."

He continued, "While the population of a State is small, and its territory extensive, large tracts of country are permitted to remain for the use and privilege of the Indians, to hunt and roam from place to place. They are also left to regulate their own affairs according to their own customs, without any interference on the part of the State. But when this state of things becomes changed, as it now has in Georgia, the State is, of necessity, compelled to assert and maintain her rights of sovereignty and jurisdiction."

In the event that the Removal bill is rejected, Lumpkin suggested, "Congress have sometimes failed to obey the will of their constituents, and they may do so upon the present occasion. If they do, I look to the unofficial sovereign people, to apply the proper remedy."

Wrapping up his argument he summarized, "In humanity, forbearance, and liberality towards the Indians, Georgia has no superior, if she does not stand pre-eminent. The prosperity and advancement of the Indians within her boundaries is the theme of Indian history, and the glory of missionary efforts. And yet sir, have you not, from day to day, throughout this long session, seen the provocations teeming upon President Jackson and the Georgians, and a spirit of asperity, rarely witnessed in this or any other country. If you want any evidence of the generous spirit and liberality of Georgia, turn your eye to the maps which adorn your walls; look upon the two flourishing States of Alabama and Mississippi, (for these States may, to a considerable extent, be considered a donation, on the part of Georgia, to this confederation of States.) It is true, Georgia did, at the time she ceded that territory to the Union, expect to relieve herself thereby of litigation and embarrassments, with which she was harassed, and which were of an unpleasant and perplexing nature, and her compact with this Government in 1802 secured the pledge and faith of the Federal Government to effect these desirable objects for Georgia. Yes, sir, from the signing of the compact in 1802, Georgia had a right to expect peace and quiet on the subject of the Yazoo speculation, as well as a speedy, reasonable, and peaceable relief from all Indian claims to lands within her borders. If you do not perform your duty, by withholding your opposition to long delayed justice, and fulfil the conditions of your contract of twenty-eight years standing, I would then advise you to let us alone, and leave us to manage our own affairs in our own way."

Congressman Ellsworth then argued against passage of the Indian Removal bill but had no new ideas to support his view.

Georgia Congressman Foster, contending for the passage of the bill, pointed to the words of Chief Justice John Marshall in the case of *Johnson v McIntosh*: "While the different nations of Europe respected the right of the natives, as occupants, they asserted the ultimate dominion to be in themselves, and claimed and exercised, as a consequence of this ultimate dominion, a power to grant the soil, while yet in possession of the natives. These grants have been understood by all to convey a title to grantees, subject only to the Indian right of occupancy. The history of America, from its discovery to the present day, proves, we think, the universal recognition of these principles ... France also founded her title to the vast territory she claimed in America, on discovery. However conciliatory her conduct may have been, she still asserted her right of dominion over a great extent of country not actually settled by Frenchmen and the exclusive right to acquire and dispose of the soil which remained in the occupation of Indians ... No one of the powers of Europe gave its full assent to this principle more unequivocally than England ... Thus has our country been granted by the Crown while in the occupation of the Indians."

On and on, hour after hour, day after day the Congressmen argued for and against the Indian Removal bill on the floor of the United States House of Representatives, repeating the same arguments over and over although using different words: Articles of Confederation, Constitution, sovereignty, treaties, laws, rights, obligations, promises, fairness and honor.

Finally, after some parliamentary maneuvering and passage of some amendments to the bill, the United States House of Representatives voted 102 to 97 to approve the Indian Removal bill as it had been amended on May 26, 1830, and the final approval of the bill was dated May 28, 1830. It was signed into law by President Jackson on that date.

*****

President Jackson, in his second annual message to Congress, said in part:

"It gives me great pleasure to announce to Congress that the benevolent policy of the Government, steadily pursued for nearly thirty years, in relation to the removal of the Indians beyond the white settlements, is approaching to a happy consummation. Two important tribes have accepted the provision made for their removal at the last session of Congress; and it is believed that their example will induce the remaining tribes, also, to seek the same obvious advantages.

"The consequence of a speedy removal will be important to the United States, to individual States, and to the Indians themselves. The pecuniary advantages which it promises to the Government are the least of its recommendations. It puts an end to all possible danger of collision between the authorities of the General and State Governments, on account of the Indians ... With Georgia, there is an express contract; with the new States, an implied one, of equal obligation ... With all convenient dispatch, the General Government should extinguish the Indian title, and remove every obstruction to the complete jurisdiction of the State ... It is, therefore, a duty which this Government owes to the new States, to extinguish, as soon as possible, the Indian title to all lands which Congress themselves have included within their limits ... No act of the General Government has ever been deemed necessary to give the States jurisdiction over the persons of the Indians."

*****

Following the case of *Cherokee Nation v Georgia*, missionary Worcester was being hassled in an effort to provoke a legal action. Quoting from Steve Inskeep's book *Jacksonland*, pages 250 — 251: "the silver-haired chief justice [John Marshall] remained formidable deep into his seventies, a political as well as a judicial figure. During the summer of 1831 he exchanged letters with William Wirt, telling the Cherokee lawyer exactly what to do: identify an individual with proper standing whose rights were denied before a Georgia state court. The decision by the state court could be appealed to Marshall's Supreme Court, which had the right to hear such appeals. This would create the basis for Marshall to draft a ruling that blocked Georgia from extending its laws over the Cherokees.

"In many modern-day courtrooms it would be considered unusual, if not unethical, for a judge to give private strategic advice to a plaintiff with whom he sympathized. But concepts of ethics were different in 1831 …"

The stage was set. The State of Georgia was endeavoring to get the Cherokees to remove and Worcester and the Cherokee newspaper he supported were making that task more difficult. The State of Georgia had passed a law requiring that any white man who lived on Indian land must have a license from the Governor of the State of Georgia or from anyone authorized to grant it, and to have taken an oath to support and defend the constitution and laws of the State of Georgia. The same law added the lands claimed by the Cherokee nation to various state of Georgia counties, extended the laws of Georgia over those lands, annulled all laws made by the Cherokee Nation and made it illegal for Creek or Cherokee Indians to testify in a Georgia court in which a white person was involved — unless the white person lived within the Cherokee Nation. The laws of the State of Georgia and the laws of the Cherokee Nation they served were in conflict. Georgia was clearly trying to make it uncomfortable enough that the remaining Cherokees would remove.

Eleven missionaries, all of whom refused to sign the document, were arrested, tried in state court and sentenced to four years of hard labor in the state penitentiary. Nine of the eleven accepted Governor Gilmer's offer of clemency and left the state. Samuel Worcester and Elizur Butler stood their ground and were put to work at the state prison.

This was the perfect case that John Marshall had asked for and John Ross knew it. The Cherokee attorney, William Wirt, appealed the case and *Worcester v. Georgia* was argued before the United States Supreme Court on February 20, 1832. Georgia, considering the case frivolous, sent no attorney to defend the State. Worcester argued that he was in the Cherokee Nation under authorization from the President of the United States and the State of Georgia had no jurisdiction over him. He argued that several treaties — that the United States had agreed to — acknowledged that the Cherokee Nation was a sovereign nation.

In the decision handed down on March 23, 1832, Chief Justice John Marshall wrote, "This duty, however unpleasant, cannot be avoided." Perhaps he had forgotten his earlier letters to attorney Wirt. He went to great length to explain how the common law of Great Britain that the United States had adopted did not authorize the taking of Indian land without purchasing it. He pointed to the treaties that had recognized the Cherokee Nation as a sovereign entity. He ruled that only the federal government was authorized to regulate Indian affairs, that the law passed by the State of Georgia was unconstitutional and that Samuel Worcester had been arrested under an unconstitutional law and his conviction and sentence was null and void.

John Marshall's opinion clearly states that it is the federal government that has jurisdiction over Indian tribes and is claimed as the justification for tribal sovereignty.

Following the Supreme Court ruling, President Jackson and his administration did nothing to enforce the ruling and Georgia didn't either. Federal Indian Policy was a function of the War Department and Secretary of War Lewis Cass, a strong proponent of Indian removal, was silent. Wilson Lumpkin, who had led the fight in Congress for passage of the Indian Removal Act was now the governor of Georgia. Governor Lumpkin signed a bill repealing the law under which Worcester was convicted and Worcester and Butler were freed on January 14, 1833.

It seems quite clear that had Chief Justice John Marshall's court been in a position to vote on the Indian Removal bill, they would have voted against it. In his opinion John Marshall makes the point that "several treaties had been entered into by the United States with the Cherokee Nation by which that Nation was acknowledged to be a sovereign nation, and by which the territory occupied by them was guaranteed to them by the United States." The court opined in regard to land that "according to the common law of European Sovereigns" the Doctrine of Discovery "gave the exclusive right to purchase," but only if the possessor was willing to sell. Marshall turned to the 18th century international lawyer, Emer de Vattel, to explain that being under the protection of a stronger power does not negate the sovereignty of the weaker power. Marshall referred to the 1763 proclamation issued by the King of Great Britain as "the settled state of things when the war of our revolution commenced." That proclamation "forbids the Governors of any of the colonies to grant warrants of survey, or pass patents upon any lands whatever which, not having been ceded to, or purchased by, us (the King) …are reserved to the said Indians."

"And we do further declare it to be our royal will and pleasure, for the present … to reserve, under our sovereignty, protection, and dominion, for the use of the said Indians, all the lands and territories lying to the westward of the sources of the rivers which fall into the sea [the line of the Appalachian Mountains] … we do hereby strictly forbid … our subjects from making any purchases or settlements whatever, or taking possession of any of the lands above reserved, without our leave and license …" and we "require all persons … who have …seated themselves upon any lands … above described … forthwith to remove themselves …" When our new government was formed Marshall explains, "Congress has passed acts to regulate trade and intercourse with the Indians; which treat them as nations…" He makes the statement that "The Indian nations had always been considered as distinct, independent political communities, retaining their original natural rights as the undisputed possessors of the soil from time immemorial." The Chief Justice opined on behalf of the court that the regulator of relations with the Indians, "according to the settled principles of our Constitution" is "committed exclusively to the government of the Union."

These are the opinions of the United States Supreme Court under Chief Justice John Marshall and indicate clearly why the Supreme Court very likely would have voted against the Indian Removal Act. But the people, through their representatives in Congress and with the support of President Jackson and Secretary of War Cass, had passed the act and it was now law.

## Back at the Executive Mansion

Included in Andrew Jackson's inaugural address, in addition to his comments on Indian affairs, was the calling for paying off the national debt, government reform (which meant removing incompetent and unfaithful government officials) and, to appease those who had feared having a general as president, his pledge that "military should be held subordinate to the civil power."

As we have learned, Andrew Jackson was fiercely loyal to his friends and not shy about his loyalty, an attribute that would surface early in his administration. Tennessee Senator John Eaton, who was Jackson's campaign manager and his first Secretary of War, had for some time been involved with the married but flirtatious daughter of the owner of the boardinghouse in which he resided. The young woman's husband was a naval officer away at sea. When the young woman's husband died while at sea, Jackson recommended that Eaton marry the girl to stop the rumors that were circulating. Eaton did just that, and when Jackson appointed him Secretary of War, the wives of the other cabinet members refused to associate with the new Mrs. Eaton. Taking the bull by the horns, the new President Jackson asked for the resignation of any cabinet member who continued to shun Mrs. Eaton. Their response was that they could not control the actions of their wives, which resulted in the President barely being on speaking terms with much of his cabinet. Secretary of State Martin van Buren sided with Jackson and Vice President John Calhoun sided with the dissenters, which probably resulted in Calhoun losing the support of Jackson for a future presidential bid.

The Doctrine of Nullification, which was backed by John Calhoun, was becoming worrisome to the President. In a nutshell it held that states have the right to declare null and void any federal law that they deem unconstitutional. Calhoun believed that "a state had a right to decide which federal laws it wished to observe and which it wished to reject." He also believed that states had a right to secede from the Union. In opposition, Jackson stated, "Our Federal Union, it must be preserved." Those differences of opinion were about to be tested. Shortly after the election, Vice President Calhoun's home state of South Carolina voted to nullify the federal tariff laws, which they believed, and probably rightfully so, gave northern businessmen an advantage over those in the south. South Carolina was prepared to secede from the Union if federal tariff's continued. In response, Jackson issued a Proclamation on Nullification: "Disunion by armed force is treason," and began preparing for civil war by mobilizing thousands of troops. John Calhoun resigned as Vice President and became a South Carolina Senator, thinking that the issue could be settled in Congress. President Jackson made it known that he intended to hang Calhoun if South Carolina went through with their plan. South Carolina backed down. Congress went on to pass the "Force Bill" which authorized the President to use troops to collect federal taxes, but it also passed legislation to gradually reduce tariffs. South Carolina rescinded its nullification legislation.

During these early days in our nation, the beliefs of the American people were very much influenced by the writers of the day. James Fenimore Cooper's novel in 1826, *The Last of the Mohicans* described Indians, who he thought originated from Asia, as being daring, boastful, cunning, ruthless, self-denying in war while in peace being just, generous, hospitable, revengeful, superstitious, modest and commonly chaste, a rather romanticized portrait of the Indians.

John Stone's stage play *Metamora or The Last of the Wampanogs* was a popular play first performed in 1829. The final lines of the play were, "White men, beware! The wrath of the wronged Indian shall fall upon you like a cataract that dashes the uprooted oak down the mighty chasms," an obvious play on the conscience for how the Indians were being treated.

Then in 1830 James Fenimore Cooper wrote the more thought-provoking *Notions on Americans*. In his book he stated that the most important tribes are the five civilized tribes and they are the only ones that can be called nations. He wrote that whites were superior to both Indians and blacks. That the Indians would gradually remove on their own. That they were the lowest level of humanity and were doomed because they were incompatible with white culture. All a rather sharp contrast to the picture he painted in *The Last of the Mohicans*.

With the writings of Jeremiah Evarts under the pen name of William Penn, and the writings of Harriet Beecher Stowe's older sister, Catharine, and even the articles in the *Cherokee Phoenix*, the young nations moral fiber and opinions were being molded. The nation was struggling with where the Indians and the blacks fit into what, at that point in time, was a predominantly white society.

Where would this moral struggling take the nation? The answer is yet unwritten.

As the campaign for Andrew Jackson' re-election for a second term got under way in 1832, the re-chartering of the Bank of the United States was an issue that was front and center. Jackson believed that control of the nation's monetary system should be left in the hands of a private corporation. In that same year, Congress passed a bill to re-charter the Bank of the United States, and President Jackson vetoed it saying as he did, "…when the laws undertake … to make the rich richer and the potent more powerful, the humble members of society, the farmers, mechanics, and laborers, who have neither the time nor the means for securing like favors to themselves, have a right to complain of the injustice of their government."

Henry Clay, Jackson's political enemy and a proponent of the central bank, ran against Jackson. A third party, the Anti-Masonic party, had nominated William Wirt as their candidate. The Democrats under Jackson handily won the election.

Andrew Jackson was inaugurated for his second term on March 4, 1833, the same year that the city of Chicago was founded. In his inauguration address he stated, "In the domestic policy of this Government there are two objects which especially deserve the attention of the people and their representatives, and which have been and will continue to be the subjects of my increasing solicitude. They are the preservation of the rights of the several States and the integrity of the Union."

During his second term, President Jackson was determined to

get rid of the Bank of the United States. His plan was to transfer the funds to state banks, even though he did not have the support of his cabinet. Secretary of the Treasury Duane refused to comply with the Presidents order; Jackson fired him and replaced him with Attorney General Roger Taney, who carried out Jackson's plan. *The Graphic Story of the American Presidents* describes the result quite well saying, "In retaliation, Nicholas Biddle, who headed the Bank of the United States, tightened up credit, recalled loans, and generally slowed down the American economy. When delegations came to Washington to ask the President to ease the economic hard times, Jackson replied: 'Go to Nicholas Biddle.' In this way, Jackson brought home to the people the immense financial power of Biddle and the Bank."

In 1835, when Chief Justice John Marshall died, President Jackson nominated Roger Taney, who would rule on the infamous Dredd Scott case, to take his place on the United States Supreme Court.

For the second time Henry Clay attempted to have Andrew Jackson censured by Congress, but the House of Representatives countered with a resolution supporting Jackson and calling for an investigation of the Bank. Nonetheless, the Senate under Henry Clay got the last word by refusing to approve Taney's appointment as Secretary of the Treasury.

## Indian Removal Begins

The first wave of the Indian removals was the Choctaws following the Treaty of Dancing Rabbit Creek. With very little by way of a plan they started, mostly on foot, toward the land across the Mississippi that had been promised to them. The first group left in the fall which meant that they continued their travel during the winter months, the very worst time for that kind of a journey. The War Department was supposed to be in charge of assisting the removal but had no organization in place for doing so, at least in the beginning, and some of the Choctaw groups simply wanted to travel on their own. After the summer of 1833, the Choctaw removal pretty much came to an end with some 9000 having reached their destination. Another some 7,000 just seemed to disappear into the woods and swamps.

The Chickasaw removal was delayed as a result of complications as to where they were to be relocated. And so, by 1837 when the details were finally worked out, the system for their removal was much improved. By the end of 1838 about 6,000 had reached their destination. The few hundred still remaining in Mississippi eventually removed.

The Creeks had originally refused to treat regarding their lands but as white settlers were essentially taking over their properties, the tribe eventually agreed to a treaty in 1832. This ceded all their lands to the United States — but with a provision giving a private reservation to a large number of individual Creeks. The massive intrusion of squatters, some 3,000 which grew to 10,000 within the few months of summer, 1833, prompted the federal government to attempt to evict the intruders but the effort proved useless. As the individual Creeks endeavored to sell their individual reserved plots they were met with unbelievable fraud. Eventually there was enough of an outcry from both Indians and whites that President Jackson ordered a commission to investigate the alleged fraud. However, before the investigation could even get started, a large group of hostile Indians attacked a stage carrying U.S. mail. The investigation was called off and General Thomas S. Jesup was ordered to organize a military campaign against the hostile faction, to subdue them and then remove the entire tribe beyond the Mississippi. The Second Creek War as it was called did not last long. Within a short time, the hostile group, some 800, had been chained and were marched along with women, children and old men — under military guard — to Montgomery where they were placed on boats for the journey west. Some 3,000 hostiles left the Creek homeland: some 2,300 reached their destination beyond the Mississippi. By the end of 1837 some 8,000 friendly Creeks had joined the hostiles in their new home beyond the Mississippi.

In 1830, before the Indian Removal Act, some 16,000 Cherokees still lived in the east and approximately 4,000 had already emigrated west. Those still in the east, under John Ross, were not about to leave. By the end of 1834 perhaps 1,000 of those remaining in the east had emigrated. But the Cherokees were starting to split into two factions; those under John Ross who were not going to emigrate, and the other under Major Ridge who were beginning to think that opposition was futile. Both Ridge and Ross had fought with Andrew Jackson against the Creeks back in 1814, and both were now successful plantation owners. Ross was the son of white traders and was married to a Cherokee woman while Ridge was of mixed race and also married to a Cherokee woman. When a meeting to be held in New Echota, the Cherokee capital, was announced for the purpose of negotiating a new treaty, it was declared at the same time that anyone who did not attend would be counted as being in favor of the treaty. Only Ridge supporters showed up for the meeting, a new treaty was negotiated and accepted on December 29, 1835, and, despite Ross's protests, the treaty was ratified by the U.S. Senate.

About 1,200 Cherokees left for the west in three groups following the treaty, but the deadline for removal was May 23, 1838, so most of the Cherokees were still in the east when Jacksons term ended on March 4, 1837. Eventually, although Jackson was no longer involved, the remainder of the Cherokees ended up in the west, but resentment for the split under Ross and Ridge, although never proven, most likely explains why Major Ridge, John Ridge and Elias Boudinot were all found murdered in their homes. Ross remained the leader of the Cherokees until the beginning of the Civil War and died in 1866.

In 1836 word came to Andrew Jackson that, under his old friend Sam Houston, who had been a platoon leader in his army, Texas had won its independence from Mexico and was asking to be annexed by the United States. There was opposition due to the slavery issue, but on the last day of his presidency President Jackson recognized the independence of Texas, which set the stage for annexation.

In his farewell address on March 4, 1837, President Andrew Jackson proclaimed, "The states which have so long been retarded in their improvement by the Indian tribes residing in the midst of them are at length relieved from the evil, and their unhappy race — the original dwellers on our land — are now placed in a situation where we may well hope that they will share in the blessings of civilization and be saved from that degradation and destruction to which they were rapidly hastening while they remained in the States; and while the safety and comfort of our own citizens have been greatly promoted by their removal, the philanthropist will rejoice that the remnant of that ill-fated race has been at length placed beyond the reach of injury or oppression, and that the paternal care of the General Government will hereafter watch over them and protect them."

## Back at the Hermitage

Andrew Jackson, back at the Hermitage, old, tired and ill, was under stress due to debts piled up by his adopted son, Andrew Jackson, Jr. Yet he remained active in the politics of the nation. The country had gone into depression in 1837 and Andrew Jackson patted himself on the back when the Bank of the United States failed and closed its doors. Jackson had assisted with the secret negotiations that achieved the annexation of Texas. President van Buren did not back annexation and Jackson, being always loyal to his friends, made sure van Buren

would not be the Democratic choice for president in the next election. Jackson instead, backed the successful James K. Polk.

Andrew Jackson died in his bed at his beloved Hermitage on June 8, 1845 at the age of 78. Reportedly his last words were, "I hope to see you all in Heaven, both white and black, both white and black."

In spite of his faults, Andrew Jackson drew praise from many directions. One such was on the occasion of the United States paying off the national debt under his resolve. At a banquet in Washington, Senator Thomas Hart Benton, who along with his brother Jesse was responsible for the bullet in Jacksons shoulder, rose to propose a toast: "This month of January, 1835, in the fifty-eighth year of the Republic," he said, "Andrew Jackson being President, the National Debt is Paid! And the apparition, so long unseen on earth, a great nation without a national debt! Stands revealed to the astonished vision of a wondering world!" Toasting the President, he said "President Jackson: May the evening of his days be

*Andrew Jackson's Gravesite*

as tranquil and as happy for himself as their meridian has been resplendent, glorious, and beneficent for his country."

William Cullen Bryant said of Jackson, "Faults he had, undoubtedly; such faults as often belong to an ardent, generous, sincere nature — the weeds that grow in rich soil. Notwithstanding, he was precisely the man for the period, in which he well and nobly discharged the duties demanded of him."

Chris Stirewalt, calling Jackson the father of the Democratic Party, in his book *Every Man a King* wrote, "…while Democrats may have taken his name off of the Jefferson-Jackson Day Dinner, they won't ever erase the way he made their party."

Remini, in the preface to the volume containing the three lectures he gave when asked to do so at the Walter Lynwood Fleming Lectures at

LSU in 1984, stated that Jackson believed that "Americans were citizens of an indissoluble Union, that they belonged to a Union of people, not a collection of States." This, he pointed out, was the basic rule that Lincoln used in 1861 to deny the southern states the right to secede. Remini went on to opine that Jackson had a major influence on the establishment of the two-party system. He took an active part in the organizational development of and shaping of the ideology of the Democrat party.

*****

Multiple books and sources were used in writing this chapter. See Notes.

# CHAPTER 2

# Harding to FDR

*Warren G. Harding*
PHOTO BY BY HARRIS & EWING

Almost 100 years had elapsed since the tumultuous times of the populist Andrew Jackson, with his daring yet brilliant defense of his fledgling country against the attempts of the British to reclaim what they had lost in the Revolutionary War. Jackson's presidency was likely highlighted by passage of the Indian Removal Act. Almost all of the events outlined in Volume I, ...*and the Mille Lacs, who have no reservation,* by this same author, were history.

It was 1921, the first world war was over, the 19th amendment to the U.S. Constitution had been passed giving women the right to vote and the economic boom called the Roaring Twenties was in full swing. Warren G. Harding, the Republican nominee for president, nominated by a deadlocked convention, had campaigned on getting back to normal after the First World War — which had ended in 1918. Calvin Coolidge had been chosen to be Harding's Vice President, and both were inaugurated on March 4th.

President Harding succeeded President Woodrow Wilson who had had the dubious honor of being Commander in Chief during the First World War. President Wilson was one of the signers of the Treaty of Versailles that ended the war as well as a major architect of the League of Nations. On a personal note, this author's father, Ralph G. Fitz, was a sailor on one of the destroyers that escorted President Wilson into the harbor at Brest, France, en route to the formation of the League of Nations.[1]

*President Wilson returning from the Versailles Peace Converence.*

In Mille Lacs County, Minnesota — and as discussed in detail in Volume I — the $40,000 that had been authorized by Congress on August 14, 1914 had all been used to purchase land for the Homeless Non-Removal Mille Lacs Indians. But by 1921 the lands had not yet been surveyed due to lack of funds. As a result, no allotments could yet be done. 1921, the same year that Franklin D. Roosevelt was attacked by the polio virus which resulted in the loss of the use of his legs for the rest of his life.

President Harding chose the infamous Albert B. Fall as his Secretary of the Interior. Fall was born in Kentucky but, for health reasons had moved to Las Cruces, New Mexico where he established his law practice. Secretary Fall chose Charles H. Burke, who had homesteaded in Dakota Territory, as the Commissioner of Indian Affairs. President Harding would be dead of a heart attack before it would be revealed that Secretary Fall had accepted bribes from two oilmen for leases to drill for oil in parts of the Naval Reserves located at Teapot Dome, Wyoming. Fall was found guilty of bribery in what became known as the Teapot Dome scandal and was sentenced to jail time and a fine. As a result, his tenure as Secretary of Interior was cut short and

*Albert B. Fall, c. 1923*

Hubert Work assumed the office of Secretary of the Interior where he remained

throughout the Coolidge administration. With President Harding's death, Vice President Calvin Coolidge was sworn in as the 30th president on August 3, 1923.

President Coolidge, or Silent Cal as he was called, was a rather shy man of few words who believed that less government was good government, the result of which was reduction of the national debt. In spite of the Roaring Twenties he was able to restore order to the White House by getting rid of the drinking (never mind that prohibition was in effect) and card parties of the Harding administration. Coolidge seemed to understand the plight of the Indian tribes and the contribution the Indians had made to the World War I effort. So he willingly signed the Indian Citizenship Act on June 2, 1924, which read, "BE IT ENACTED by the Senate and House of Representatives of the United States of America in Congress assembled, That all non citizen Indians born within the territorial limits of the United States be, and they are hereby, declared to be citizens of the United States."

In the 1920's the "Indian problem" as it had often been called, had those who were sympathetic to the woes of the Indian and those who had no problem exploiting them for their own personal gain. Albert Fall and Charles Burke were probably among the latter, not being above either obscuring their real intentions or outright exploitation. Hubert Work, who became Secretary of the Interior,

*Osage men with Coolidge after signing the Indian Citizenship Act — 1924*

had a reputation for being honest to a fault, and was extremely religious and of the opinion that the Indian's religious ceremonies were pagan and must be stopped. And then there was John Collier who had fallen in love with the Pueblos and in particular, their religion. Collier became involved with opposing the Bursum Bill. The Bursum Bill, proposed by Senator Holm Bursum of New Mexico, would have allowed non-Indians to retain any land they had squatted on before 1902, even though the Treaty of Guadalupe Hidalgo — the treaty that ended the Mexican-American War in 1848 — had guaranteed the Pueblos property rights and the right to citizenship. On several occasions Congress and the courts had infringed on the rights gained in the Treaty of Guadalupe Hidalgo which aroused a passion in John Collier.

In Mille Lacs County, Minnesota, in the spring of 1925, the government was finely ready to make allotments of from 5 to 15 acres each to the 282 Non-Removal Mille Lacs Indians, and by February 1926 the allotment process had been completed.

In 1925 Collier wrote for the "*The Christian Century, a Journal of Religion*"[2] saying, "There exists in America a national scandal which, being ancient and chronic, is not sensational. [In other words, it had been going on for so long that few paid any attention to it.] Involving at least through passive consent our whole electorate and much of our most revered institutional enterprise, and being not the vice or crime of one political party, the scandal is peculiarly enveloped with repressions. ... The victim directly is the American Indian." In large part, Collier quite correctly explained that "Indians are ruled by administrative decrees. Though citizens, they are government wards and are subject to the *plenary* power of congress, which in turn, through enactments and constructively, has remanded his plenary power to the secretary of the interior, that is, to the bureau of Indian affairs."

Perhaps troubled by the state of the Indian wards for whose welfare he was responsible, and likely goaded by the efforts of those who embraced John Colliers' view, Secretary of Interior Hubert Work, on June 2, 1926, requested the assistance of the Institute for Government Research which claimed to be an association of citizens who cooperate with public officials in the scientific study of government. Under the direction of one Lewis Meriam, the special staff visited ninety-five different jurisdictions; either reservations, agencies, hospitals, or schools, and also many communities to which Indians had migrated. In their words they considered their goal to be to determine what remains to be done to adjust the Indians to the prevailing civilization so that they may maintain themselves in the presence of that civilization according to at least a minimum standard of health and decency.

The study, commonly known as the Meriam Report, found an overwhelming majority of the Indians to be poor, even extremely poor, and not at all adjusted to the economic and social system of the dominant white civilization. They found the Indians living in a vicious circle of poverty and maladjustment. The study found the health of the Indians to be appalling as compared to that of the general population and the prevailing living conditions, poor diet and dreadful housing conditions of the majority conducive to the development and spread of disease.

They found excessive overcrowding in dwellings that were small shacks with few rooms and inadequate ventilation. They reported that "the furnishings of the primitive dwellings and of the shacks is limited. Although many of them still have very primitive arrangements for cooking and heating, the use of modern cook stoves and utensils is far more general than the use of beds, and the use of beds in turn is far more common than the use of any kind of easily washable bed covering…houses seldom have a private water supply or any toilet facilities whatever."

The study found the income of the typical Indian family low and the earned income extremely low. The study stated that "from the standpoint of the white man the typical Indian is not industrious, nor is he an effective worker when he does work."

So, what had caused this sad state of affairs they asked. The study determined that "The economic basis of the primitive culture of the Indian has been largely destroyed by the encroachment of white civilization. The Indians can no longer make a living as they did in the past by hunting, fishing, gathering wild products, and the extremely limited practice of primitive agriculture. The social system that evolved from their past economic life is ill suited to the conditions that now confront them, notably in the matter of the division of labor between the men and the women. They are by no means yet adjusted to the new economic and social conditions that confront them."

And what about the policies of the government? The study concluded that,

> Several past policies by the government in dealing with the Indians have been of a type which, if long continued would tend to pauperize any race. Most notable was the practice of issuing rations to able-bodied Indians. Having moved the Indians from their ancestral lands to restricted reservations as a war measure, the government overtook to feed them and to perform certain services for them which a normal people do for themselves. The Indians at the outset had to accept this aid as a matter of necessity but promptly they came to regard it as a matter of right, as indeed

it was at the time and under the conditions of the inauguration of the ration system. They felt, and many of them still feel, that the government owes them a living, having taken their lands from them, and that they are under no obligation to support themselves. They have thus inevitably developed a pauper point of view.

With the advent of the "governmental policy of individual ownership of the land on the reservations [the Dawes Act], the expectation was that the Indians would become farmers. Part of the plan was to instruct and aid them in agriculture, but this vital part was not pressed with vigor and intelligence. It almost seems as if the government assumed that some magic in individual ownership of property would in itself prove an educational civilizing factor, but unfortunately this policy has for the most part operated in the opposite direction. Individual ownership has, in many instances permitted Indians to sell their allotments and live for a time on the unearned income resulting from the sale... Many Indians were not ready to make effective use of their individual allotments."

With these and other problems, "the solution was to permit the Indians through the government to lease their lands to the whites. In some instances, government officers encouraged leasing, as the whites were anxious for the use of the land and it was far easier to administer property leased to whites than to educate and stimulate Indians to use their own property. The lease money, though generally small in amount, gave the Indians further unearned income to permit the continuance of a life of idleness."

The study also determined that,

> Surplus land remaining after allotments were made was often sold and the proceeds placed in a tribal fund [Dawes Act and Nelson Act]. Natural resources, such as timber and oil, were sold and the money paid either into tribal funds or to individual Indians if the land had been allotted. From time to time per capita payments were made to the individual Indians from tribal funds. These policies all added to the unearned income of the Indian and postponed the day when it would be necessary for him to go to work to support himself.

The sad truth revealed by this study was:

> Since the Indians were ignorant of money and its use, had little or no sense of values, and fell an easy victim to any white

man who wanted to take away their property, the government, through its Indian Service employees, often took the easiest course of managing all the Indians property for them. The government kept the Indians' money for them at the agency. When the Indians wanted something, they would go to the government agent, as a child would go to his parents, and ask for it. The government agent would make all the decisions, and in many instances would either buy the thing requested or give the Indians a store order for it. Although money was sometimes given to the Indians, the general belief was that the Indians could not be trusted to spend the money for the purpose agreed upon with the agent, and therefore they must not be given opportunity to misapply it. At some agencies this practice still exists, although it gives the Indians no education in the use of money, is irritating to them, and tends to decrease responsibility and increase the pauper attitude.

It is easy to conclude that this study revealed a relatively accurate description of the effectiveness — or lack thereof — of the government policy toward its Indian wards, but the study also probably correctly reported, "the typical Indian ... has not yet advanced to the point where he has the knowledge of money and values, and of business methods that will permit him to control his own property without aid, advice, and some restrictions; nor is he ready to work consistently and regularly at more or less routine labor."

In other endeavors the study found the government programs no more effective than those we have just described; improvement of health care, education of the Indians themselves, schooling provided for children both in boarding schools and day schools, employment opportunities, strengthening of family and community life, development of law enforcement, and others.

Under recommendations the Meriam Report stated,

The fundamental requirement is that the task of the Indian Service be recognized as primarily educational, in the broadest sense of that word, and that it be made an efficient educational agency, devoting its main energies to the social and economic advancement of the Indians, so that they may be absorbed into the prevailing civilization or be fitted to live in the presence of that civilization at least in accordance with a minimum standard of health and decency.

To achieve this end the Service must have a comprehensive, well-rounded educational program, adequately supported, which will place it at the forefront of organizations devoted to the advancement of a people. This program must provide for the promotion of health, the advancement of productive efficiency, the acquisition of reasonable ability in the utilization of income and property, guarding against exploitation, and the maintenance of reasonably high standards of family and community life. It must extend to adults as well as to children and must place special emphasis on the family and community.

Since the great majority of the Indians are ultimately to merge into the general population, it should cover the transitional period and should endeavor to instruct Indians in the utilization of the services provided by public and quasi public agencies for the people at large in exercising the privileges of citizenship and in making their contribution in service and in taxes for the maintenance of the government. It should also be directed toward preparing the white communities to receive the Indian.

By improving the health of the Indian, increasing his productive efficiency, raising his standard of living, and teaching him the necessity for paying taxes, it will remove the main objections now advanced against permitting Indians to receive the full benefit of services rendered by progressive states and local governments for their populations.

By actively seeking cooperation with state and local governments and by making a fair contribution in payment for services rendered by them to untaxed Indians, the national government can expedite the transition and hasten the day when there will no longer be a distinctive Indian problem and when the necessary government services are rendered alike to whites and Indians by the same organization without discrimination.

In the execution of this program scrupulous care must be exercised to respect the rights of the Indian. This phrase 'rights of the Indian' is often used solely to apply to his property rights. Here it is used in a much broader sense to cover his rights as a human being living in a free country. ... Recognition of the educational nature of the whole task of dealing with them will result in taking the time to discuss with them in detail their own affairs and to lead rather than force them to sound conclusions.

The effort to substitute educational leadership for the more dictatorial methods now used in some places will necessitate more understanding of and sympathy for the Indian point of view. Leadership will recognize the good in the economic and social life of the Indians in their religion and ethics, and will seek to develop it and build on it rather than to crush out all that is Indian.

The Indians have much to contribute to the dominant civilization, and the effort should be made to secure this contribution, in part because of the good it will do the Indians in stimulating a proper race pride and self-respect.

The Meriam Report was completed and submitted to Secretary Work on February 2, 1928. Secretary Work would resign less than six months later on July 24, 1928 and be replaced by Roy West who would serve in that capacity for the nine months remaining in President Coolidge's term as President.

Herbert Hoover would serve as Secretary of Commerce during both the Harding and the Coolidge administrations and when Coolidge announced after six years as president that he would not seek a second term, Hoover was nominated as the Republican candidate. Charles Curtis was nominated as his vice-president. Curtis was a successful politician having served in both houses of Congress. His mother was a Kansa Indian and he grew up in the Kaw tribe. Hoover, who was a liberal Republican, and Curtis won handily over the Democrat Al Smith who had promoted the repeal of prohibition.

Hoover was born on August 10, 1874 in the Quaker town of West Branch, Iowa, but when his father died at an early age Herbert was sent to live with his aunt whose husband was the U.S. Indian Agent at the Osage Agency in Pawhuska, Oklahoma. Sources vary as to how long he stayed in Oklahoma but sometime later he was sent to Oregon to live with an uncle and it is there that he was educated, such as it was. Despite his rather poor academic showing he was allowed to enter Stanford University the year that it opened its doors on the strength of his skills in mathematics. He developed an interest in engineering and geology that resulted in him becoming an extremely wealthy mining engineer, followed by humanitarian pursuits, government service and then politics. He reportedly was keenly interested in pursuing the recommendations of the Meriam Report. However, the Great Depression scuttled a lot of his endeavors.

President Hoover appointed Ray Lyman Wilbur as his Secretary of the Interior. Wilbur was born in Iowa but as a young child would move with his family to California. There he would become friends with Herbert Hoover while they were both students at Stanford University and ended up marrying a friend of Hoover's wife. It was Ray Wilbur who was responsible for renaming Boulder Dam to Hoover Dam. With Charles Rhoads, Hoover's Commissioner of Indian Affairs, they set about reorganizing the Bureau of Indian Affairs and promoting self-reliance among the Indians.

These actions were not to the liking of John Collier. In a 1932 issue of one of the weekly publications, *The Nation*[3] Collier wrote,

> When Secretary Wilbur and Commissioners Rhoads and Scattergood took office in 1929, we were led to feel a wonderful hope. They announced great programs and made wonderful promises. We assert that they have forsaken their programs. They have broken their promises. They have set up new evils of far-reaching kinds—evils which their predecessors did not sponsor .... We solemnly affirm that conditions among the Indians today. ... are more deplorable than they have been at any time since the United States became guardian over the Indians." This Collier wrote, was the message sent to Congress in the form of a petition from forty-nine Indian tribes and that had been read on the Senate floor on March 9th.

John Collier elaborated, first enumerating the improvements that Wilbur and Rhoads had made. He stated that the statistics that the Bureau kept had been erroneous in the past but now were truthful. He stated that the inspection system had been improved and the quality of government personnel improved, even though it was proceeding very slowly. He affirmed that the human relations programs were improved and that while not yet implemented, plans for improvement of schools looked promising, cooperation with states and counties regarding welfare programs was being advocated and that large amounts of Indian debt had been cancelled. But Collier went on to criticize the commissioners for not actively supporting the programs for education and social services being promoted, or at least talked about, by officials under the commissioners.

Collier criticized the Bureau's record saying that the harmful programs being promoted far outweigh the good ones, writing,

> The Wilbur administration inherited in 1929 a system of non-responsible absolution over Indian property and person. The 'system' had been elaborated across a century, steadfastly in the direction of an always more silent and more exhaustive spoliation of Indian property. Before 1929 the 'system' had become thoroughly understood.
>
> In 1914, the National Bureau of Municipal Research had lifted the veil. After 1922 many agencies had probed the 'system' and its effects, and the lines of remedy were clearly indicated. … Wilbur and Rhoads in 1929 stood, as it were, on a 'great divide.' They knew the facts and the truth, and proclaimed them. They marked out and publicly espoused a program of general direction and of detail—a program of reorientation, reconstruction, and, for Indians, salvation.
>
> Enthusiastic supporters eagerly rallied behind this program and behind Wilbur and his commissioners personally—among these supporters were Indians and Indian-welfare groups and the predominant elements in Congress. But opposed to the new program were the corporate and regional special interests which by means of the absolutist 'system' were battening on the Indians.
>
> These interests were, as they are today, powerfully represented within the Department of the Interior and the Indian Office; while their sway with and within the Department of Justice, whose role in Indian affairs is often decisive, has been greatly intensified since March, 1929.

While Wilbur and those under him promoted good plans for reform in the beginning, Collier continued, they have reversed course and "blocked efforts by Congress to rectify laws which they had initially denounced, and to pass laws which they had initially demanded as conditions precedent to good administration."

"The 'system' of 1929 is the 'system' of today," he wrote. "Among its starkest features… Indians are government wards and the wardship is peculiar in that the ward cannot seek accounting or redress in the courts. The guardian ultimately is Congress, and the guardian's authority is plenary and conclusive. The guardianship of person and the trusteeship of property have been delegated by Congress

to the Secretary of the Interior. Some protective and limiting statutes remain…
but to enforce these statutes through mandamus proceedings or otherwise, the
Indians must use money which the Department of Interior controls and lawyers
whom the department, the adverse party in the litigation, finds agreeable."

"These archaic statutes," Collier wrote, "constitute a sort of permanent mar-
tial law, suspended, used as a threat, or crushingly enforced, as administrative
opinion thinks most expedient." "It is this 'system,'" Collier continued, "as a total-
ity which the Wilbur administration since 1929 has successfully protected."

"Wilbur" Collier charged, "has issued a formula which amounts to terror-
ization of the Indians. It is, in substance, that if Indians are to be given rights,
including the right of responsible group self-help, it must be at the cost of assuming the tax burdens."

Collier makes no mention in his article for *The Nation* that 1929 had begun
as a country filled with optimism. Herbert Hoover had said during his campaign
that "We in America are nearer to the final triumph over poverty than ever before
in the history of any land." But by 1932 most of the country — as well as the rest
of the world — was suffering from the Great Depression. Most of the U.S. population was worse off than in 1929, not just the Indians. This was the John Collier
that was soon to become Commissioner of Indian Affairs.

Franklin Delano Roosevelt had been nominated in 1920 as vice president
with the unsuccessful presidential candidate James Cox. A period of twelve years
would elapse, during which Roosevelt would struggle with the aftermath of the
polio virus, before his name would once again appear on the ballot, this time for
president. President Hoover was being blamed for the Great Depression and so
the Roosevelt-Garner ticket was swept into office with a landslide victory. Roosevelt was about to take the reins of a country that was in desperate financial
shape when he was inaugurated on March 4, 1933. In his inauguration address he
uttered the famous line "…the only thing we have to fear is fear itself…"

Continuing he threatened, if he must, to use the war powers to attack the economic disaster that his country faced saying, "But in the event that Congress shall
fail to take one of these two courses, and in the event that the national emergency
is still critical, I shall ask the Congress for one remaining instrument to meet the
crisis—broad Executive power to wage a war against the emergency, as great as the
power that would be given to me if we were in fact invaded by a foreign foe…"

And so in his first 100 days FDR called a special session of Congress, closed
all of the banks in the United States until they could be inspected for soundness
with those found to be sound reopened one week later; called a conference of
state governors and threatened that the federal government would step in unless

*Outgoing President Herbert Hoover and Roosevelt on Inauguration Day 1933*

they figured out a way to deal with starvation in their respective states; got the Agricultural Adjustment Act (AAA) passed in order to limit the overproduction by farmers and give the farmers more purchasing power; got the National Industrial Recovery Act (NIRA) passed in an attempt to regulate business; created the Tennessee Valley Authority (TVA) to develop hydroelectric power for the Tennessee valley; created the Home Owners Loan Corporation (HOLC) to assist homeowners who were being threatened with foreclosure; issued an Executive Order taking the country off the gold standard in an effort to maintain U.S. gold reserves; set up the Federal Emergency Relief Administration to make grants to the states for relief to the unemployed; and organized the Civilian Conservation Corps (CCC) to provide work for unemployed youth. During his first term he developed the Federal Communications Commission, the Securities Exchange Commission, the Federal Housing Administration, the National Resources Board and the Rural Electrification Administration as well as restoring diplomatic relations with Russia.

By 1935 President Roosevelt was urging Congress to pass social security measures such as old age pensions, unemployment insurance, aid to dependent children and health services. The federal government was growing by leaps and bounds and Roosevelt's New Deal was well on its way, only to be dealt a blow by the United States Supreme Court when it declared the National Industrial Recovery Act (NIRA) and the Agricultural Adjustment Act (AAA) unconstitutional. That infuriated the President and he pushed Congress to set mandatory retirement ages for the Supreme Court and even to increase the number of members on the court, but Congress refused to make any changes.

Over the next several years naturally occurring vacancies allowed FDR to make new appointments that changed the makeup of the Supreme Court. The first FDR appointment was Hugo Black, a Ku Klux Klan member. Following the new appointments, the views of the court became more in line with the views of the president. And while President Franklin Roosevelt was making major changes in the federal government, over at the Department of the Interior Secretary Ickes and Commissioner Collier were making even bigger alterations to Federal Indian Policy, the Indian New Deal.

# CHAPTER 3

# Harold LeClair Ickes
# Secretary of the Interior

For those who could spare the two cents that it cost to buy a copy of the *New York Times* on October 29, 1929, the headline "Stock Prices Slump $14,000,000,000 in Nation-Wide Stampede to Unload…" must have been a shock. It all started on October 24 and culminated in what was called the Great Crash five days later. And while the stock market crash was the most visible cause of what would come to be known as the Great Depression, it was not the only cause. During the 1930's nearly half of America's banks had failed and since FDIC had not yet come into existence, depositors were the losers. This caused surviving banks to tighten their credit requirements triggering less capital for investing in businesses. As the dominos fell, purchasers were either extremely cautious or non-existent and jobs evaporated — until unemployment reached nearly thirty percent. In an effort to protect American businesses and farmers, tariffs were placed on imported goods which added to the strain on business internationally. And to top it off, the severe drought centered on the prairies of Oklahoma, Kansas and northern Texas hindered many farmers' ability to pay their taxes with the resulting loss of their farms.

President Hoover (1929-1933) must have been caught by surprise when the depression hit. He had said during the 1928 campaign for the presidency, "We in America are nearer to the final triumph over poverty than ever before in the history of any land. …" And while his administration initiated some programs to counteract the depression, it was too little too late and set the stage for the landslide victory of Franklin Delano Roosevelt (FDR) in 1932.

FDR was elected on November 8, 1932 and the filling of cabinet positions began. Roosevelt offered the position of Secretary of the Interior to two candidates, both of whom declined. Almost by default Roosevelt then decided on Harold LeClair Ickes, who incidentally wanted this job very badly.

So, who was this man, Harold LeClair Ickes? Perhaps the answer is that he was born into a dysfunctional family, tolerating and probably promoting a home life that by most standards would be considered dysfunctional. Ickes compensated by becoming a workaholic, a valuable trait for a Secretary of the Interior in those times.

Clair, as he was called as a child, was born in Altoona, Pennsylvania, an industrial railroad town, on March 15, 1874. His father, an alcoholic and a womanizer, was pretty much absent from his childhood and young Clair dropped out of school to work in an Altoona drugstore. His mother died when he was only sixteen and young Clair went to live with his Aunt Ada. That same year Clair, his sister Amelia and Aunt Ada moved to Englewood, a community in Chicago. Clair went to work in his Uncle Felix's drugstore in return for room and board, with time off to attend Englewood High School. He had no friends at Englewood but did develop a relationship with a teacher who became an advisor to him, something he had never had before. He also acquired a relationship with a classmate whose family became the only family he had ever had. T.H. Watkins, in his book *Righteous Pilgrim*, writes, "At the very least, the turmoil and uncertainty of his boyhood must have kept Clair off balance emotionally, and may have been the seedbed of the powerful contradictions that bloomed later in life."

Clair graduated from Englewood High School with good enough grades to gain entrance into Cornell, but he had no money for tuition, plus Cornell was too far to commute. In desperation, he made a trip to visit his alcoholic father in Altona, but the trip was unsuccessful in alleviating his financial problem. Clair had also qualified for Chicago University, but lack of tuition remained a problem. As luck would have it and most likely due to the influence of one of his Englewood teachers, he was able to impress the president of the University of Chicago enough that he was offered free tuition in return for work on campus. Clair found nearby room and board in return for housework and caregiving for an aged parent, and finally was able to move out of his uncle's house. His favorite subject in college was anthropology but he was only able to achieve a "C" average in college, a result of his having to spend so much of his time working in return for his tuition, room and board.

His first taste of politics occurred in college when he joined the campus Republican Club, later to become its president. While he did identify as a Republican, his position was still evolving. In his first election he voted for Republican McKinley for president and Democrat Altgeld for governor.

Clair's love life, or so he thought, also got its start at Chicago University. In his memoirs Ickes writes, as quoted in Watkins' *Righteous Pilgrim*, "She was said to be the richest girl in college and she probably was [her father had made his fortune in manufacturing light fixtures and in real estate] … I wished that I might be introduced to Miss Wilmarth, but I never suggested it to anyone … I realized that she travelled in an orbit so different and so far removed from mine that we might never meet. Then one day as I was mounting the first floor of Cobb Hall I looked up and saw Miss Wilmarth descending in the middle of the stairway … and just as I was about to pass her, of course without any sign of recognition, she bowed and spoke my name. …"

And so began the tumultuous courtship, home life and extra-marital affairs for Harold LeClair Ickes. Ickes and Anna Wilmarth ended up in a class together which provided the opportunity to begin their relationship. They managed several dates, always with a chaperone of course, as was the norm at that time in history. Ickes was on cloud nine. That is, until he was told that Anna would be going to Europe with her Mother for a year. Obtaining her permission to write to her, he did so faithfully, which helped his state of mind, but over time her return letters became fewer and fewer. His world was completely destroyed when an acquaintance, James Thompson, invited him to dinner (which he thought rather strange) and during dinner made it known that he and Anna were engaged and would be married soon.

Ickes graduated from the University of Chicago in 1897 without any plan for the future. True to form, none of his family attended graduation. He returned to Altoona but by the end of summer was back in Chicago.

The plot then thickened when Anna's new husband James Thompson invited him for a visit. Ickes accepted, and as a result of the visit became a reporter for a Chicago newspaper. As an employee of the newspaper, his love of politics blossomed and he became an assistant political editor. His newspaper career lasted about four years until the newspaper for which he worked was sold. After a short stint with a couple of jobs, Ickes became the campaign director for Independent Republican John Harlan in his run for mayor of Chicago. Harlan lost the election.

Now Ickes situation was about to become twisted in a way that is difficult to comprehend. Perhaps the only explanation is that both Ickes and Anna Wilmarth Thompson were the progeny of alcoholic fathers and both were searching for a healthy home life, something elusive as a result of never having had a wholesome example to emulate.

Anna and her husband had a son whom they named Wilmarth and Ickes would occasionally visit them, becoming quite fond of Wilmarth. Ickes was still living at the University and, during a bout of appendicitis, Anna's husband James visited him and invited Ickes to come stay with them until he had recuperated. Good judgment prevailed and Ickes declined the invitation.

A couple of years later, Anna's husband again visited, saying that Anna and Wilmarth were going to be away for an extended period of time and Anna wanted Ickes to stay with her husband until she returned. And so, Ickes packed his things and moved in with James. When Anna was about to return and Ickes was preparing to move out James convinced him that he and Anna wished Ickes to continue to live with them until he was ready to get married. When Anna returned home she, too, insisted that Ickes stay, adding that they would charge no rent. As strange as it seems, Ickes agreed.

It soon became obvious to Ickes that Anna's marriage was rocky, and Ickes and Anna grew closer. Interestingly, Ickes entered law school in 1903 with tuition money provided by Anna's mother. As their love blossomed, Ickes asked Anna to divorce her husband. However, what he got instead was Anna's husband being given the upstairs bedroom and Anna taking a bedroom on first floor near the one occupied by Ickes.

During all of this Ickes was able to graduate from law school in 1907. He opened a law office but had no real interest in traditional law practice. His real interest was in politics, being by now gravitating toward progressivism, and the social problems of the day, homeless children, battered wives, unemployment and on and on — interests that he fostered throughout his life.

About this time Anna brought home a thirteen-year-old girl, who was in foster care to protect her from her alcoholic and abusive father, with the intent of adopting her. She was given a bedroom on the second floor and shared a bathroom with Anna's husband. When the girl informed Anna that her husband James had twice molested her sexually, Anna went into a rage and insisted that her husband give her a divorce. Once the divorce was final, Ickes thought that now he and Anna could get married, but Anna, being intensely interested in protecting her public image, insisted that they not marry until her former husband was married to someone else. Yet they both held onto the idea of marriage even though they had frequent arguments. Finally, in 1911 Anna's ex-husband got married. Anna and Ickes were then married. Heading off on a two-month honeymoon in Europe, they began what would become an almost constant battle, both emotionally and physically, that would dominate their marriage — apparently set off by Anna discovering that she was pregnant.

Harold Ickes kept busy with his involvement in political movements, always ready to assume a leadership role, honing his skills as a political operative. He identified himself as a Republican, but always a progressive Republican. When the Chicago Progressive Republican League was organized, he became its president. He was a part of the progressive movement backing Teddy Roosevelt, and being rejected by the Republican convention, they organized their own convention. Woodrow Wilson, however, won the election and accomplished many of the programs the progressive Republicans believed in, and thereby weakening that movement. While it seemed like Harold Ickes was always choosing to be a part of a losing effort, his skills as a political operative continued to elevate his status in political circles, taking him to the national level. With his constant involvement and long hours he was working himself into exhaustion and, at times, depression, but at least that kept him away from the incessant fighting at home.

When President Wilson declared war against Germany many of the progressive Republicans opposed the war but Ickes supported it and offered his services to the President. Wilson accepted and Ickes was sent to the front lines in Europe distributing goods for the YMCA, even though he did not believe in the Christian values of the YMCA. In truth he was an agnostic. But his involvement in the war effort gave him a reprieve from the unceasing bickering at home. Upon his return, however, it immediately resumed — in spite of the love letters he had written from the front lines. At the end of the war, the Democrats supported the League of Nations, as did Harold Ickes, while most Republicans opposed it.

At the 1920 Republican convention, Warren Harding was nominated for President as a compromise candidate. Harold Ickes considered this move the end of his Progressive party. When the Democrats nominated James Cox for president with Franklin D. Roosevelt as vice-president, Harold Ickes switched from the Republican party to the Democrat party and joined the Cox-Roosevelt Progressive Republican League. Once again Ickes had chosen the losing side.

Along with President Harding and the end of the war came the Roaring Twenties with prohibition, speakeasies, moonshiners, the Model A and the Model T and movies. And while some in the United States were

*Warren Harding*

studying and becoming favorable to communism as a system of government, Ickes was not one of them. During this time both he and Anna kept themselves, busy with social work of one kind or another. Ickes accepted the position of president of the Chicago branch of the NAACP only to resign a short time later when he found out that the organization existed on paper but not in reality. But it demonstrated where his heart was.

A factor that would help to mold Harold Ickes's future career was the asthma attacks that Anna started having in the mid-1900s. To get relief she sought out the high dry air of New Mexico, fell in love with the area and ended up building a small house in the desert in the town of Coolidge (currently a ghost town) just east of Gallup, New Mexico. The New Mexico air relieved her asthma, the scenery was beautiful and she fell in love with the area and with the Navajo, Zuni and Pueblo Indians that called this area their home. It was here that she crossed paths with the future Commissioner of Indian Affairs, John Collier. This was how Harold, the future Secretary of the Interior, was introduced to Collier's work. In her book about the Indians of this area, *Mesa Land*, Anna mentions being at some of the same places as Collier.

When Albert Fall, Secretary of the Interior during the Harding administration, supported what they considered anti-Indian legislation in Congress, both Ickes and John Collier opposed it.

Ickes and his wife Anna continued to disagree about most everything and perhaps that is the reason for Ickes intense desire to belong — and hopefully to lead — as he became involved in political endeavors. And this also may have been the driving force behind his interest in stamp collecting and in developing flower gardens: these endeavors he could control. For once, he could be the boss and they didn't talk back.

Although Ickes had been investing some of Anna's money in the stock market, he appears to have survived it quite well, or at least he so claimed. In 1930, after considerable nagging, Ickes finally agreed to close his law office and accompany Anna and their two sons to what Anna called her "Dream House" in New Mexico. While still maintaining their residence in Chicago, Ickes apparently found some enjoyment in New Mexico as well as getting some first-hand knowledge of the plight of the Indians, especially the Navajo.

By 1932, with the depression in full swing, the Republicans nominated Herbert Hoover for a second term and the Democrats nominated Franklin Delano Roosevelt. Harold Ickes was asked by the Democratic National Committee to organize a Western Independent Republican Committee for Roosevelt, which would include ten Midwestern states. But he was already campaign manager for his wife, Anna, who was running for a third term in the Illinois General Assembly as a Republican, and she very much opposed his accepting a position with the Democratic National Committee, for obvious reasons. Not until he promised her that if Roosevelt was elected he would ask to be appointed Commissioner of Indian Affairs, did she relent. Apparently doing something to help "her Indians" was more important to her than her seat in the Illinois General Assembly.

Finally, after years of being on the losing side of so many political efforts he had chosen the winning team as both Roosevelt and Anna won their elections.

And so began an aggressive effort of letter writing, personal conversations and meetings, asking anyone whom he thought might be able to help to put in a good word for him in regard to being nominated for Commissioner of Indian Affairs. As it turned out, one of the first people he asked was aware that John Collier was campaigning for the same job and probably favored Collier over Ickes, and this person made Ickes request known to Collier. Apparently, Ickes was unaware of John Collier's efforts in that regard. Collier and his cronies organized a plan to recommend Ickes for first assistant Secretary of the Interior. That would clear the path for Collier to become Commissioner of Indian Affairs. Harold Ickes did not know that it was Colliers idea, but as he thought about the issue he decided that if he was qualified to be assistant Secretary of the Interior, then why not Secretary of the Interior. So, when Collier and his associates invited Ickes to Washington to talk about their plan, he accepted enthusiastically — but kept silent that he really wanted the job of Secretary of the Interior.

Harold Ickes was not on FDR's short list for Secretary of the Interior but when Hiram Johnson declined the offer and Bronson Cutting took too long to decide, Roosevelt rather unceremoniously chose Ickes. After all, Roosevelt did want someone from the west and he was also desirous of courting favor with the progressives, and Harold Ickes filled the bill.

Harold Ickes was thrilled with his appointment and given the workload — any excuse for avoiding staying at home.

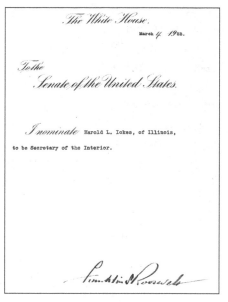

And so, Ickes set out to organize the Department of the Interior under his leadership. Nathan Margold was chosen as Interior Department solicitor on the strength of his work as legal advisor on Indian matters with the Institute of Government Affairs. Felix Cohen and Charles Fahy were given the position of assistant solicitor; both had been involved in the Pueblo Indian Rights issue in New Mexico. Harry Slattery was appointed personal assistant. Those were the easy positions to fill. Commissioner of Indian Affairs was not so easy.

Ickes and Collier had argued rather violently over policy in the past; Ickes really didn't much like Collier. And in addition, the job of Commissioner of Indian Affairs had traditionally been used as a reward for political favors. But Ickes had promised Anna, and in spite of their differences he knew that Collier exceled in his knowledge of Indian issues and would do what was best for the Indians without Ickes having to be involved to any great extent. And so, John Collier became Commissioner of Indian Affairs.

Ickes worked long hours at his job, normally twelve to sixteen hours each day. It seemed to be a benefit to both he and Anna as she was spending most of her time as an Illinois State legislator, her charity projects, and Indian issues in New Mexico, in addition to writing her book.

In spite of the workload, Ickes became sexually involved with an unnamed woman in D.C. and to complicate matters, the woman was engaged to a man who was able to make Anna aware of what was going on.

To add to his troubles, he was being pursued for an unpaid bill by a company in Chicago. It must have been beyond his ability to pay — or perhaps there were other issues — but it was serious enough that he offered his resignation to FDR. The President refused and somehow the matter got settled.

So, while that problem was resolved anonymous letters continued to arrive regarding his love affair, and Ickes suspected the fiancé. True to form, Ickes had given the fiancé a job at DOI in order to please his mistress, and while the fiancé was out of town his apartment was illegally searched and evidence was found that he was the writer of the letters. Ickes called him into his office and fired him.

In the fall of 1933 Ickes and Anna had leased a home in D.C. and there began a period of relative calm in the Ickes household. Anna was truly enjoying life in Washington, especially with her husband doing something for the Indians. In true form however, Harold Ickes could not leave well enough alone. He decided to confess to Anna that he was in love with another woman. Anna apparently went into a rage such as Ickes had not seen before and ended up in a nursing home for a period of time. Their son Wilmarth advised that they get a divorce but Anna refused.

A short time later, the mistress — that Ickes had given a job at the Department of Interior — marched into his office, gave him back his ring, resigned her job and shortly thereafter married her fiancé. However, just a few short months later the mistress left her husband and Ickes once again had a sexual paramour, although the romance had waned and they eventually drifted apart.

Harold Ickes was keeping himself very busy at work. The Interior Department was massive. Ickes found himself in charge of 500 million or so acres of federal land with the natural resources contained therein as well as water, irrigation, dams, national parks and monuments and reservations, the U.S. Geological survey, the Bureau of Mines, the Bureau of Reclamation, the territories of Alaska, Hawaii, Puerto Rico and the Virgin Islands, the office of education, The Freedman's Hospital and Mental Hospital and Land Grant Colleges, not to mention the programs initiated by Roosevelt to counteract the depression, the CCC, PWA and on and on. So much so that one of his first projects was to oversee the construction of a second Department of Interior building just south of the old one to house all the additional employees.

In spite of his personal antagonism toward John Collier, Ickes knew Collier would do the right thing for the Indians, so he gave Collier free reign and essentially rubber-stamped whatever Collier presented for approval.

Because of his involvement in many of Roosevelt's programs to counter the depression, Ickes had frequent personal meetings with the President. He thoroughly relished the personal satisfaction this gave him. But at times Ickes and FDR argued over funding of projects Ickes was in charge of, so much so that in his diary Ickes writes about considering resignation, and actually did so at one point — which FDR did not accept.

On August 31, 1935, Anna was killed in an automobile accident in New Mexico. Ickes oversaw a proper funeral in Chicago and then back to work.

Wilmarth, Anna's son from her first marriage, had married Betty Dahlman from Wisconsin. Sometime later Betty Dahlman's youngest sister Jane, contacted Harold Ickes and asked for help in relocating and finding a job, probably in an effort to get out of her mentally ill mother's house. Ickes was smitten with her from the moment she arrived in Washington, promptly gave her a job at the Department of Interior and started a relationship. Ickes and Jane Dahlman, nearly forty years his junior, were married on March 24, 1938, in spite of intense opposition from Jane's family, and in spite of Jane's attempt at one point to comply with her family's wishes.

On the work front the fear of communist infiltration of the government was growing. While Ickes appeared to have no leanings in that direction, his Commissioner of Indian Affairs, John Collier, was a suspected sympathizer and probably with good reason.

At the beginning of his second term, FDR was becoming frustrated that the U.S. Supreme Court was ruling against many of the programs that he was trying to implement. Roosevelt proposed a plan to counteract what he saw as obstruction by the Court. He would ask Congress to pass a law that would allow the President to appoint an additional justice anytime a sitting justice reached the age of 70 years. After considerable argument FDR's proposal went nowhere. But due to death and retirement, Roosevelt was able to appoint enough liberal judges to alleviate his problem.

Harold Ickes might be classified as a great humanitarian based on his efforts toward equality for blacks and in saving the Jews. While segregation was still in full swing he and Eleanor Roosevelt succeeded in organizing a Marian Anderson concert on the steps of the Lincoln Memorial. Ickes introduced Ms. Anderson with one of his most beautiful speeches and spectators — some seventy-five thousand and mostly black — stretched down both sides of the reflection pool.

September of 1939 was an eventful month, not only for the world but for Jane and Harold Ickes. On September 1st Germany attacked Poland by bombing a Polish fishing village. On September 3rd Great Britain and France declared war on Germany. And on September 4th Harold and Jane's son Harold was born.

As the next presidential campaign approached and war became more imminent, Ickes backed FDR for a third term, and Ickes was chosen by FDR to campaign for him. But after the election Ickes became worried because, what had previously been a close relationship with Roosevelt, now had changed such that Ickes would only see the President during cabinet meetings. Perhaps Roosevelt had other things on his mind? On Sunday, December 7, 1941 at 7:40 AM, Japan attacked Pearl Harbor.

While certainly supporting the war effort, Ickes was more concerned on a daily basis with what was happening to his department — a department he had spent the last eight years of his life creating. The National Park Service, the Bureau of Indian Affairs and the Fish and Wildlife Service were moved to Chicago to make room for the war effort personnel. All efforts were geared toward supporting the war. Fully one-third of the oil production went to the war effort and consequently gas rationing began on December 1, 1942.

*The last photo of President Roosevelt, taken at Warm Springs, GA by Nicholas Robbins for Elizabeth Shoumatoff. FDR died the following day, April 22, 1945.*

As FDR's government tried to manage the war effort and to acquire the cooperation of industries, Ickes and Roosevelt disagreed more and more often. At times Ickes thought Roosevelt was preventing him from having any significant say in waging the war, and that bothered Ickes greatly. Hawaii, which had been under Ickes control, was now under complete military control. Alaska was fortified with military personnel and the Alcon Highway was constructed as a route to Alaska. Ickes objected to the Japanese being put in concentration camps after Pearl Harbor and FDR put him in charge of relocating the Japanese back into California and other states when the concentration camps were dismantled. He also was given charge of 1000 Jewish refugees who were brought to New York for safety.

Franklin Delano Roosevelt died on April 12, 1945, just a few months into his fourth term as President of the United States. Harold LeClair Ickes had been his Secretary of the Interior for 13 years. Vice President Harry Truman became

President. Germany surrendered on May 7, 1945. President Truman and Harold Ickes did not get along well, but nevertheless Ickes lasted until February 12, 1946, when he resigned. The first atomic bomb had been dropped on Japan on August 6, 1945 and the war was over.

Much of this chapter reads like a romance novel but it is important that we know who this man Secretary Ickes was. He was a man of great influence and power and oversaw an important portion of United States history. Rather ironic given his early life and the torment of his personal life. Harold LeClair Ickes died February 3, 1952.

\* \* \*

Multiple books were used is writing this chapter. See Notes

# CHAPTER 4

# John Collier

# Commissioner of Indian Affairs

Fifty years had elapsed since the events in Georgia that we learned about in Chapter 1 of this book. The Civil War had been fought and lost by the Confederacy and the State of Georgia had been devastated with the great loss of life and destruction of property. The negro slaves, a major part of the Georgia economy, had been emancipated and Georgia's economy, which had been left in shambles by the war, had been rapidly rebuilt. Georgia, the last of the Confederate states to do so, had re-entered the Union on June 15, 1870 following Reconstruction. It had only been twenty years since the Battle of Atlanta when John Collier was born there on May 4, 1884, the fourth of a family of seven children.

John's father, Charles A. Collier, was first a distinguished lawyer and then a banker. Very active in civic affairs, Charles became a noted orator and served as

Mayor of Atlanta for four years. He was an avid proponent of public ownership of utilities. John's mother, Susie Rawson Collier, an attractive woman, was a lover of plants and animals and had a keen interest in literature.

The Colliers were a fairly typical wealthy Southern family of status who gathered for meals served by their negro cook, Lucy. As a young boy John's brother, Rawson, was his hero, and so he was disappointed when Rawson, apparently because of a penchant for brawling, was sent away to military school. In his memoirs John says that fighting was necessary for young boys in order to establish their status. And so, apparently because he couldn't fight due to his weakened arm from a previous break which had not been properly set, then re-broken and re-set, brother Rawson was his protector. His family, being good Methodists, cared much for the Jewish and Catholic minorities as well as for the negroes.

One passage from his memoirs describes John's entry into the world of the southern negro. "Lucy, our cook, a Negress, had her home in our yard, and Lucy's home was a second home to me. Her son was my companion in everything. Then the boy journeyed to stay with relatives in northern Alabama. There in northern Alabama, the boy's father was held in a chain-gang, rented out to work in a mine. After some months, Joe, my closest friend, came home. *He had learned that he was a Negro.* And he rejected me. He had learned to anticipate rejection, so he rejected even me."

John Collier's grandfather had been a part of the United States army that had moved the Cherokees westward and out of Georgia. John wrote that his grandfather had a safe full of Confederate money, perhaps saving it in case it again became valuable.

According to Collier, his father was busy attempting to heal the Southern wounds caused by the Civil War and the Reconstruction Period. He became involved in some kind of a financial scandal, bringing great dishonor on the Collier household. His mother became deeply distressed over the whole episode, started taking the relaxant, laudanum, becoming addicted. Although young John was not told its cause, he knew his mother was very sad about something. As a result, his mother died in 1897 when John was only 13.

After his mother's death John lived for a time in Sharon, Georgia, the home of a Roman Catholic convent school operated by the Sisters of the Sacred Heart. There, according to Kenneth Philp in his book, *John Collier's Crusade for Indian Reform*", "he became close friends with several nuns, turned away from the Methodism of his family, and temporarily embraced Roman Catholicism."

Three years later, apparently distraught with the family's tarnished honor as well as his wife's death, John's father Charles committed suicide. Now, with the loss of both of his parents, at but 16 years of age he went into a deep physical and spiritual depression that lasted for about six months; this would mold the life he was just beginning. He relates this profound incident in his memoirs, *From Every Zenith,*

> ...the crisis in which the determination of my life was set — in a rejection which was also an affirmation at the core of my being, at the unchanging fountain of my will ... The place was beside my mother's and father's tomb, and the time was the beginning of October in 1900. The details of what had killed my mother, three and a half years prior to that crisis of mine in the cemetery, and had killed my father three days before that crisis of mine, shall have no place in this writing. A doom ... had descended — had slowly crushed its weight down through years that were an eternity of pain.
>
> My identification with my mother and father was complete — deep as my brain and heart and soul. Where they had failed, through long torture ending in hopeless death, it was not I who could want to succeed. But the event within myself was not wholly negative, was not only the rejection of all desire for worldly or hedonistic success — of all that from within their own souls and from within social fate had been ultimately denied to each of these two. It was an affirmation of my own life's positive choice: to live in behalf of the world's hope.

This was to be the road map for John Collier's life. As we proceed through this chapter you will see that road map which John Collier devised in the cemetery unfold and be put into practice. He was true to the vision there uncovered. He had inherited from his mother a passion for the wild, an interest in astronomy, a dislike for any kind of cruelty and a love of literature. From his father he gained an identification with public affairs and the awareness of "community."

He was in his last year of high school when his father died. He finished his high school but he relates that he didn't learn much because his mind always wandered to nature, yet he graduated as valedictorian. Philp explains how, "... not because of scholastic merit. Along with most of his classmates he had cheated during the final examinations, and the principal responded by expelling two boys from poor families. Upset at this unfair punishment, Collier warned that he would expose the whole cheating system and the mediocre nature of the school unless the boys were reinstated. The principal agreed and nominated him for vale-dictorian." Good training for the activist he would become.

He spent the summer following high school out camping with his brother in the Appalachian Mountains — at least at first. After a while his brother had had enough camping, perhaps hastened by an experience when whiskey was offered by a mountain man, giving both boys a terrific hangover. This was followed by an uncomfortable flea-bitten nap — offered by a kindly mountain woman — during which their sleep was interrupted with constant terrible itching.

However, young John Collier continued his outdoors activity. In the prolonged isolation of the mountain wilderness, and at the conclusion of a severe thunderstorm, he claimed to have had a vision: a bird asked him to continue "onward, into the struggle not lost and not won," toward the "immortal effort toward creation in which I, the bird, need you." As he often did, he related the incident in a poem. From age eighteen on, Collier would spend time in the Appalachian Mountains, sometimes camping and sometimes staying with mountain folk. Most of these mountain folks were moonshiners who knew little of the outside world — except perhaps the penitentiary in Atlanta. Others were a remnant of the Cherokee Tribe that had escaped removal by hiding out in the mountains. Many of Collier's travels were in the area where the first Cherokee press had been located.

When he returned from his Appalachian wilderness adventures, John used money from his father's estate to enroll at Columbia University as a special student in literature. He really wasn't interested in the credits needed for graduation so he enrolled for graduate courses. It was after reading Peter Kropotkin's book, "*Mutual Aid*" that Collier became interested in larger social problems. Kropotkin was a Russian anarchist living in exile in London who believed in a classless society where everyone helps everyone in mutual aid. That was opposed to the Darwin theory of survival of the fittest. Does that not sound like the communal society that Collier would come to advocate for Indian tribes?

About a year after his father's death the family home was disposed of and Collier and his siblings lived here and there in Atlanta.

While at Columbia, Collier met Lucy Graham Crozier, a Knoxville woman who convinced him to change his major from literature to biology. Crozier was a follower of Friedrich Nietzsche whose belief was in the concept of the "beyond man" as the yet-unrealized potential within living man, present man, and of the entire task of life as the ordering of society and of thought so as to invoke the beyond man from present-man. Does this not also sound like the pledge that Collier made at his parent's grave?

Lucy Crozier had a plan to organize the railroads and chambers of commerce of the south in a system of distributing unemployed immigrants onto the land in Georgia, the Carolinas and Alabama. She involved Collier, but they had no success and abandoned the project in 1905.

Collier was then invited to be executive officer of the Associated Charities of Atlanta. In this position he advocated promoting work opportunities as the method of solving the problems of those in need of help. But after just four months with no success he was fired.

What did he do in the face of failure? He went camping. With several failures behind him, off he went into the wilderness where he spent the next six months. Upon his return from seclusion he took a job as a reporter for the *Macon Telegraph*, but soon became bored and secured passage on a ship bound for Europe. It was on board the ship that he met Lucy Wood, the lady who would become his wife in 1906.

True to his pledge in the cemetery, Collier transferred his share in the ancestral estate in Atlanta to his wife, Lucy. Following their wedding they again spent time in Europe where Collier studied the psychology of the cooperatives and labor movements of the European countries of France, Belgium, England and Ireland. Upon their return from Europe, he and Lucy spent three months camping in the Great Smoky Mountains. John Collier was a dreamer, a romantic searching for the perfect. Thus, was about to begin their New York years of 1907 to 1920.

Likely following their first son Charles's birth, and perhaps to give his daughter and grandson a stable home, Lucy's father had purchased a prerevolutionary Dutch farmhouse for them with a large apple orchard, barn, and an abandoned water powered mill beside a rushing stream. The couple added a large upstairs sleeping porch and a spacious downstairs playroom in addition to installing a big tank in the attic where water could be pumped with a hand pump to supply the house.

Collier was busy doing social work, moving from one societal problem to another and when his efforts failed would move on to the next one. He thought that money-making amusements such as saloons, dance halls and movie theatres needed to be regulated in order to protect the consumer, which led to a form of censorship.

While advocating on the one hand, Collier was also exploring the various movements of the time. That is how he met salon hostess Mabel Dodge, a woman who held weekly gatherings featuring a speaker — like Margaret Sanger, founder of Planned Parenthood — followed by lively discussion. Collier found this fascinating and stimulating. Quoting from Philps, Mabel Dodge described Collier as, "a small blond Southerner, intense, preoccupied, and always looking windblown on the quietest day. Because he could not seem to love his own kind of people, and as he was full of a reformer's enthusiasm for humanity, he turned to other races and worked for them." Mabel said Collier had attempted — at great odds — to stem the tide of Americanization by persuading immigrants to "keep their national dress, their customs, and their diets, their religion, and all their folk ways." But after seven years in this life in New York it was time for Collier to take a break. With Lucy and their three boys the Collier's headed for the North Carolina mountains for a year of camping.

Returning from camping Collier became the civic secretary of the Peoples Institute and Lucy helped found the Child Health Organization.

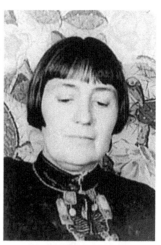

*Mabel Dodge*

From Lucy's organization they developed "The Home School" which they operated at their farmhouse while Lucy and Collier got an apartment in Manhattan during the week. The school itself housed twelve pupils — including the Collier's three boys. In his memoirs Collier describes the school this way:

> The Home School combined work, play and study. In summertime, the children went unclothed. They did carpentry work in the huge barn, they tended the garden, they paddled and swam in the mill pond. They were not disciplined, the school's method being permissiveness, but were perpetually absorbed in varied activities which were joyful. Rarely did the parents of the other pupils besides our own three sons meet the tuition fee. Lucy and I financed the school.

The school lasted for five years, but when the principal became incurably disabled, they closed the school and — true to form — the Collier family headed off on a three-month camping trip in the North Carolina mountains.

Collier's work with the Peoples Institute was guided by his previous studies. Philps explains it this way in his book: "He worried about the impact of industrialization and urbanization on the quality of human life, believing that organic society with its sense of community was being replaced by one in which the individual found itself isolated. He felt that the supremacy of machine over man led only to the uprooting of populations, the disintegration of neighborhoods, and the starvation of the soul."

This is the basis he used in his approach to the Peoples Institute, an educational organization devoted to giving the immigrant masses a sense of brotherhood in their local neighborhoods. The thought of the Peoples Institute was that "the poor and immigrants, could… sustain themselves through uncertainty, peril and pain, if offered the creative life of community within their urban environment." What controlled Collier's life these years he describes in his memoirs: "a belief that what I may call the Occidental ethos and genius were the hope of the world; that they might also become the world's doom; and my unwearying [sic] task was to make some difference in that Occidental ethos and genius."

Collier did make one important difference concerning the children of New York City in 1910. Children had no place to play except the streets, but the city ordinance prohibited playing in the street. The Peoples Institute studied the child street gangs which had developed and wrote about it. Through Colliers leadership the schools were then opened up for after school and weekend activities and community centers were created.

But due to his fascination with song, dance and the exotic, Collier would find himself being drawn to people like Isadora Duncan, whom he had met at one of Mabel Dodge's salons. Isadora was what I would describe as an erotic dancer who believed in free love and children without marriage. And while her dancing might be considered a form of free-spirited modern dancing of some value, she did not find much support in America and eventually moved to Europe.

By 1919, everything he and Lucy had been working for in New York seemed to be falling apart so he accepted an invitation from Los Angeles to lead adult education there under the sponsorship of the State Immigration and Housing Commission, the California State Board of Education and the Regents of the University of California. He left for California in September of 1919, and Lucy and the boys followed a few months later. This job lasted for three years except for the period December 1920 to the summer of 1921 when he discovered Taos and the Pueblo Indians.

In California Collier was welcomed by the movers and shakers in community education work. He led discussions on "the cooperative movement and the Russian Communist experience." In his second year in California, his salary started coming from the California State legislature. But his discourses were arousing concern and the Department of Justice began planting spies in his lectures. As a result, the Department of Justice — through their associations — was able to eliminate his salary. Collier resigned and, true to form, made plans to head for Mexico in search of remote wilderness.

Collier's view in 1920, according to his memoirs, reads, "the nature of man was believed to be found in traffic and acquisition of goods — and the human personality was therefore base, calculating, and shallow. Nothing beyond the individual was perceived; the human group was nothing more than a contract between self-seeking individuals." He was obviously bitter about his treatment in California. But Collier believed that man was social. Throughout time man lived the determining part of his life in face-to-face, primary, social groups; in village communities and federations of village communities.

Collier and the family headed for Mexico but enroute they decided to camp for a time on a southern California beach called Redondo Beach. While there, Collier received both a letter and a telegram from Mabel Dodge Luhan, asking them to visit Taos, New Mexico again. This is the same Mabel Dodge that had sponsored the New York City salons that Collier had frequented. She was now on her fourth husband, Antonio Luhan, a Taos Pueblo Indian, and they were living in Taos and attracting such people to the area as Georgia O'Keeffe and Ansel Adams among others. The Colliers were able to get train tickets to within 26 miles of Taos, and from there they took a stagecoach, arriving in Taos during a raging snowstorm.

Collier was mesmerized by the magic of Christmas at Taos with the Pueblo Indians, the Red Deer Dance, and the solemn demeanor of the Indians. But he was saddened because he was convinced that white culture would swallow up all this Indian magic. But then again, he thought, perhaps not.

Collier relates his experience in his memoirs:

> The discovery that came to me there, in that tiny group of a few hundred Indians, was of personality-forming institutions, even now unweakened, which had survived repeated and immense historical shocks, and which were going right on in the production of states of mind, attitudes of mind, earth-loyalties and human loyalties, amid a context of beauty which suffused all the life of the group. What I observed and experienced was a power of art — of life-making art — greater in kind than anything I had known in my own world before. Not tiny, not huge, this little group and its personalities seemed. There were solitary vigils which carried the individual out into the cosmos, and there were communal rituals whose grave, tranquil, yet earth-shaking intensity is not adequately suggested by anything outside the music of Bach.

John Collier was having a kind of "religious experience." His conclusion: "… it might be that only the Indians … were the possessors and users of the fundamental secret of human life — the secret of building great personality through the instrumentality of social institutions."

The Colliers stayed in Taos for eight or nine months, thus ending their plan to visit Mexico. Collier accepted a job as a teacher at San Francisco State Teachers College. They bought a house there intending to stay, but Collier couldn't get the Indians out of his mind. He was introduced to Stella Atwood who put him in touch with Kate Vosburg who was interested in Indian issues and had money. The result was that Collier quit his teaching job and became a research agent for the Indian Welfare Committee of Vosburg's General Federation of Women's Clubs.

Albert Fall of New Mexico was the Secretary of Interior under President Harding and Collier writes in his memoirs — probably correctly — that, "Fall intended the total destruction of Indian property rights, and the annihilation of the Indian as Indians, but he merely dramatized in his own person that which had been the unswerving government policy of one hundred years." As research agent for the Women's Clubs Collier visited all the Pueblos except Acoma and it was in doing this research that he learned of the Bursum bill.

The Bursum bill, introduced by New Mexico Senator Holm Bursum, was an attempt to settle the land dispute between the Pueblo Indians and the whites that had been created by the Treaty of Guadalupe Hidalgo which had ended the Mexican War in 1848, and the Enabling Act at the time of New Mexico's admittance into the union; the land dispute had been created by both the courts and the white expansion onto Pueblo lands. With Collier's and Antonio Luhan's help the Pueblo leaders organized in opposition to the bill. The Bursum bill was withdrawn, and with the resignation of Secretary of Interior Albert Fall as a result of both the Teapot Dome scandal and the Bursum bill, the crisis was at least temporarily delayed. Eventually, however, the Pueblo Lands Act was passed and signed by President Coolidge which set up a three-member Lands Board at Santa Fe to investigate, determine and report the status and boundaries of all Pueblo lands.

From now forward until he became the Commissioner of Indian Affairs, John Collier spent his time and energy advocating on behalf of the Indians. President Harding's administration under Commissioner of Indian Affairs Charles Burke was working toward assimilation and made certain tribal ceremonies crimes. On February 14, 1923, the Indian Bureau issued Circular 1665 which prohibited the gambling called "*ituranpi*", limited dances to one per month — and then only in daytime, in mid-week and performed in the center of the Indian district. There were to be no dances during planting and harvest (March through August) and nobody under 50 could do immoral dances. Secretary Work agreed, and also believed that the Bureau should attempt to modify Indian ceremonies into "harmony with the forms of Christian religion which civilization has approved, from which our rules of life are drafted and from which our government is founded." Collier, of course, objected. He wanted laws protecting native culture, which put him in direct opposition to most church missionaries. What this did was split the Pueblos into two groups; the progressives who followed the missionaries and the traditional who followed Collier. The Bureau was also wanting to prohibit the removal of boys from school for four days for religious training, which was their practice.

Collier also got involved in trying to save the sacred Blue Lake area for the exclusive use of the Taos Pueblo. This thirty-thousand-acre mountain area had been granted to the Pueblos by the Spanish Crown by the Treaty of Guadalupe Hidalgo.

In 1927, Collier and a group of western Senators succeeded in convincing the Senate Indian Committee to create and fund an Indian Investigating Committee. This committee held hearings where the Indians lived. During that same time at the urging of Interior Secretary Work, the Brookings Institute started another investigation into Indian affairs. Collier relates the result, writing, "At the end, Indian Commissioner Burke charged that Senator Pine, of Oklahoma, a member of the Senate's Indian Investigating Committee, and I were guilty of subverting the Indians, and of organizing them against the government. Called before the Senate Committee to substantiate his charges, Burke resigned from office."

On March 4th, 1929, Herbert Hoover was sworn in as President of the United States and the spirit of Indian affairs changed fundamentally, perhaps because Vice President Charles Curtis's mother was a Kaw Indian and Curtis maintained tribal ties. Ray Wilbur was chosen as Secretary of the Interior and Charles Rhoades as Commissioner of Indian Affairs with Henry Scattergood as his assistant. Perhaps the biggest changes initiated by the new administration occurred in regard to Indian schools.

The Indian boarding schools were in full swing at that time, and below are extensive quotes from John Collier's memoirs in

*President Herbert Hoover*

which he describes in detail events of which our federal government should not be proud.

> "Schooling included the enforced proselytizing of Indian children. Missionaries were a part of the schools, and parental consent did not enter the picture at all.
>
> Children were taken at six years of age and kept in boarding schools, indentured out, as serfs had been, to white families during vacation periods, until the end of adolescence. Child labor, in school time as in vacation time, was standard. The children's day would often begin at six in the morning and end at eight at night.
>
> Corporal punishment was usual — for children speaking their native tongues, for infraction of the rules, for running away to their homes. They would run away from school, be caught and taken back, sometimes by force from protesting, heartsick parents, and transferred to more distant schools."

A statement concerning this abuse, given by author Dane Coolidge to the Senate Investigating Committee, and publicized by the Indian Defense Association, was one of the many exposures which, by 1930, had doomed the whole medieval system in the Indian schools.

> "I am making a brief statement of my experience with what I consider the greatest shame of the Indian Service,' Mr. Coolidge's statement began, 'the rounding up of Indian children to be sent away to Government Boarding Schools. This business of kid-catching, as it is called, is rarely discussed by outsiders, either by the Indians or by Government officials, but during my numerous visits to the Navajo Reservation I have picked up a knowledge of its workings.
>
> In the fall the Government stockmen, farmers and other employees go out into the back country with trucks and bring in the children to school. Many apparently come willingly and gladly; but the wild Navajos, far back in the mountains, hide their children at the sound of a truck. So, the stockmen, Indian police and other mounted men are sent ahead to round them up. The children are caught, often roped like cattle, and taken

away from their parents, many times never to return. They are transferred from school to school, given white people's names, forbidden to speak their own tongue; and when sent to distant schools are not taken home for three years.'"

Mr. Coolidge went on to describe instances he had seen; the effect on children kept from their homes for years, and returned at last to a life they were no longer fitted to lead; the cases of children who repeatedly ran away; and the Government stockmen and agents who replied to pleadings to let children go: No Sir! That isn't the way the Government works ...' Mr. Coolidge ended his statement with the story of an old Navajo couple he had come to know:

"'The heart-break and misery of this compulsory taking of children was never more fully exemplified than on my resent visit to Lee's Ferry, Arizona, where old Jodie, or Joe, Paiute, lives. He is the last of his people in that part of the country and he and his wife had ten children. But as they came of school age, they were taken from him, and of the first eight all but one died in school. One daughter survived and was sent to Riverside [Indian School]. But like all of them she was given a white person's name; her Indian name was not adequately recorded; and though he had tried to find where she is, the school has lost track of her.

While working for me, Jodie informed me that the truck was soon coming over to take his little boy and girl, the last two children of ten. His wife, he said, sat and cried all the time, and he asked me what he should do. I told Jodie and I tell the world that a mother has a right to her children. They are hers, and since the others had all died or been lost, he should take these and his little band of sheep and hide far back in the mountains.

Poor old Jodie said nothing, and I suppose by this time his children are shut up in school. And every year in that school, as in most others, there are epidemics of influenza and other diseases. Very likely his last two will die. In special cases like this I think the Government should relent and allow them to grow up wild. And in all cases where the parents object or the children are afraid to go, I think the child-catchers should be called off.

I have heard too many stories of cowboys running down children and bringing them hogtied to town to think it is all accident, due to the unthinking brutality of a superior race. It is part of the regular system where the Indians are shy and wild — and no matter how crowded the buildings are, the children are caught just the same.

My reason for submitting these facts to your committee is that no Government employee, no matter how kind-hearted, would dare to mention the practice; while the traders and white residents on the reservation are even more compelled to silence. Yet it is a condition easily solved if day schools are installed and transfer to distant schools abolished. If they could see their children every day, as we see ours, the mothers would gladly send them to school. But if they are torn from their arms and transported far away, given strange names and taught an alien tongue, the mothers will sit like old Jodie's wife and weep and watch the road.'"

Had Mr. Coolidge embellished his testimony? Maybe! Maybe not!

With the change in tone from Washington, some improvements in the Indian schooling system occurred, but the system was unwieldy and difficult to alter. Indian services changed at a snail's pace from their former practices. And soon the primary focus of the Hoover administration was the Great Depression.

With the depression in full swing and blame being placed on President Hoover and the Republicans, the stage was set for the landslide victory of Franklin D. Roosevelt. Once FDR's election was assured, John Collier thought that the work with Indian affairs was in good hands. Colliers thoughts returned to his hoped-for trip to Mexico which had been long delayed, and to the book that he wanted to produce on the Indians of the Americas. But first he felt that he must make sure that Roosevelt chose the right person as Commissioner of Indian Affairs.

Collier made a list of those he thought would be acceptable, and while Harold Ickes was at the top of the list, he wondered if Ickes had the patience that would be required for the job.

Collier writes in his memoirs, "At this point I requested Ickes to come to Washington, where we talked over the situation, and where we met Nathan R. Margold. Then, through Raymond Moley, at the time a member of Roosevelt's inner circle, I arranged for an interview in New York between Ickes and Roosevelt, and accompanied Ickes to New York." While he favored Ickes, Collier thought that since he was not nationally known it was likely the best Ickes could hope for was either Commissioner of Indian Affairs or Assistant Secretary of the Interior.

Again, quoting from John Collier's memoirs: "The interview had been set for the first thing in the day, and at mid-morning, Ickes telephoned me with high excitement in his voice. I came on down at once, and we were joined by Professor Charles E. Meriam of the University of Chicago …Ickes told us, over generous drinks, that Roosevelt had asked him to become Secretary of the Interior, and that he had accepted. He had been part of a small group called together by Roosevelt to discuss land and conservation aspects of the New Deal program. As the meeting ended, Ickes was asked to stay on, and after the others had left, Roosevelt had pointed a finger at him, and said, 'You are my Secretary of Interior.'"

Joe Robinson of Arkansas, floor leader of the Senate, was pressing Ickes hard to choose Edgar B. Meritt, who had been Assistant Commissioner of Indian Affairs from 1923–1928, as his Commissioner of Indian Affairs. Ickes replied that he wanted Collier but Collier wanted time to think about it. Shortly, however, Collier told him to go ahead and submit his name. Ickes publicly announced that he would wait until he was confirmed before choosing anyone who needed confirmation but he went ahead and chose Nathan Margold as Solicitor and Charles Fahy as assistant Solicitor. In the end Roosevelt withdrew consideration of Meritt and John Collier was appointed Commissioner of Indian Affairs and confirmed unanimously.

It is interesting to ponder the differences in their stories — one told by Harold Ickes and the other by John Collier — of how the Interior Department's leadership came into being in the Roosevelt administration. But regardless of whichever is the true version, thus began the Indian New Deal.

The basic changes needed in Indian administration had been agreed upon by the time Roosevelt took office. They were, in essence, "the vesting, as bodies corporate, in the Indian tribes themselves, control over their own affairs — domestic, civil and fiscal."

A few months after his confirmation, Collier gave a speech to Navajo students at Fort Wingate, New Mexico, in which he elaborated on the purposes of his Indian New Deal. He told them that the government has a duty to bring education and scientific knowledge within reach of every Indian, and at the same time the government should reawaken pride in the soul of every Indian — not only pride in being an Indian, but hope for the future as an Indian.

Safely in office, Collier pushed Congress for passage of the Pueblo Relief Bill which became law on May 31, 1933. The bill appropriated $761,958 to the Pueblos in return for which they would drop their suits of ejection against non-Indians, and $232,086 to the settlers to make up for inadequate compensation ordered by the Pueblo Lands Board. It also gave the Indians veto power over the use of these funds which they had to spend for the purchase of needed land, water-rights, and other permanent economic advantages. In addition, the Taos Pueblo Indians got a fifty-year renewable lease of the sacred Blue Lake area.

Under the auspices of the Civilian Conservation Corps (CCC) the Indian Emergency Conservation Work was initiated. Seventy-two camps were established on thirty-three reservations, mostly in Arizona, Oklahoma, Montana, New Mexico, South Dakota and Washington. They built roads for fire control and dams to prevent erosion, constructed fences and wells, and on weekends attended workshops on operating machinery and principles of land management.

As we learned earlier, Secretary Ickes had appointed Felix Cohen as assistant Solicitor and with the approval of Commissioner Collier, Cohen was sent (loaned) to the Justice Department to develop — with the cooperation of Theodore Haas — the Handbook of Federal Indian Law. It presented legal and moral arguments demonstrating that Indians had certain sovereign rights, including political equality of races, the right to tribal self-government, federal jurisdiction in Indian affairs, and the government's duty to pass legislation protecting natives in their relations with non-Indians.

In cooperation with Secretary of Agriculture Henry Wallace, Indians were included in the Agricultural Adjustment Administration (AAA). Excess sheep and goats were purchased from the Navajos in the overgrazing reduction program and the meat was used for needy Indians in the northern plains states. The Bureau of Animal Husbandry organized a sheep breeding station at Fort Wingate, New Mexico to assist the Navajos in getting the right kind of wool for the weaving of rugs and blankets.

Secretary Ickes and Commissioner Collier were proud of their accomplishments in conservation and public relief, but many of the relief programs had little long-term effect.

Collier rejected the idea that the Dawes Act, which had been passed in 1887, had turned the Indians "into responsible self-supporting citizens" or enabled them "to enter urban industrial pursuits." Instead, he thought — and correctly so — that it had deprived them of vast quantities of property and created a class of landless paupers dependent on the federal government. On August 12, 1933, Collier wrote a letter to all his superintendents directing them to prohibit the sale of Indian trust land until further notice.

During that first year Collier continued to build on President Hoovers' beginning reformation of the Indian educational system. Eventually he would close twenty boarding schools and replace them with day schools even though some Indians objected to having the boarding schools closed. One of the objections was to the hogans built on the Navajo reservation being used as day schools, with their log and mud construction, low ceilings and dirt floors, which to some felt like a step backward from the wood frame school buildings. But Collier persisted.

Hogan

Building on his experience with the Peoples Institute in New York City, many of the Indian day schools doubled as community centers. Even with the obvious improvements in Indian education, the Navajos for which Collier had in earlier times had such great admiration, opposed the changes, stating that their children got fewer meals, the clothing allowance was eliminated, bad roads made attendance difficult, fresh water was often scarce, and because of the Navajos migratory habits.

Pursuing an answer to the allotment system, Collier called a conference to discuss solutions. At the conclusion the conference recommended (1) repealing the land allotment law (Dawes Act and Nelson Act), (2) consolidating Indian heirship and trust lands for agricultural purposes, (3) promoting tribal ownership of grazing and forest lands, (4) acquiring additional land for landless Indians, (5) providing a system of credit to further Indian economic development and (6) returning the five civilized tribes in Oklahoma to federal control and settling all claims arising from broken treaties. Collier was happy with these conclusions even though he was warned that the Comanches in Oklahoma were doing quite well and would not be happy with the plan.

In early 1934 Collier sent a circular to superintendents, tribal councils and individual Indians asking for their recommendation and was surprised by the amount of negative feedback he received. But he was convinced and ordered the solicitors to draft a bill. Solicitors Margold, Cohen and Fahy drafted the bill which would become the Wheeler-Howard Bill. In February 1934, Representative Edgar Howard of Nebraska and Senator Burton K. Wheeler of Montana introduced the forty-eight-page bill in Congress.

The contorted path of the Indian Reorganization Act will be examined in detail in other chapters as well as the Oklahoma Welfare Act and Alaska Reorganization Act.

As John Colliers' dream and his plans for bringing that dream to fruition progressed, he ran into many distressing road bumps along the way. His original fascination with the Indian way of life was through his experiences with the Pueblo and the Navajo and so it was heart-breaking that the stock reduction program, which admittedly was necessary (or at least something like it) to preserve the land for the future, had created such ill feeling toward him.

And perhaps even more distressing was the negativity exhibited against him by the Pueblos. After all, it was at the Taos Pueblo where the magic of their Christmas pageantry had deepened his love for the Indian way. But a controversy concerning peyote — a plant with both medicinal and psychoactive properties — had split the Pueblos into two groups and Collier and his government program was being blamed for the unrest over its use.

And then in 1935 he had reorganized the Pueblo administration, consolidating the northern, southern and Zuni jurisdictions into the United Pueblo Agency with headquarters in Albuquerque, New Mexico. And perhaps unwittingly he had appointed a woman, Sophie Aberle, as general superintendent, not exactly consistent with the native culture he so admired.

The unrest and antagonism against Collier surfaced in a most distressing way when Mabel Dodge Luhan and Antonio Luhan, the very people who had invited him to visit the Taos Pueblo in the first place, turned against him. Mabel thought Collier should have suppressed the use of peyote instead of supporting its use in native religion. She also objected to the appointment of Sophie Aberle. Her husband, Antonio, complained at a public meeting with Collier present, that the new Taos day school lacked furniture and teaching equipment, and that several girls had returned home pregnant from the Santa Fe boarding facility. And so, a war of words commenced between Mabel Dodge Luhan and John Collier.

The situation back in Washington wasn't much better. Senator Clark of Missouri had called for Collier's removal and Senator Wheeler agreed. Clark had come to dislike the Indian New Deal and on February 24, 1937, recommended that Congress repeal the Indian Reorganization Act (IRA) that he had sponsored three years earlier. He charged that the Indian Bureau had given tribal organizations powers not authorized in the IRA and that they discriminated against Indians who failed to support the act. Not one to take criticism without response, a second war of words commenced, now between Collier and Wheeler.

When World War II broke out it devastated Collier's programs and efforts. The draft removed many employees as well as many Indians, and much of the Indian Service was moved to Chicago to make room in Washington for the war effort. An attempt was made to completely eliminate the Indian Bureau but it failed: Congress was too preoccupied with the war. Jed Johnson, chairman of the House subcommittee on Interior Appropriations, wanted to slash funds for the Indian Bureau, considering Collier a radical who should be tried under the Hatch Act. The bottom line was that the Bureau's budget was drastically reduced.

With money reduced for Indian issues, Collier directed his attentions internationally, to the problems of dependent people throughout the world. His interest in the Far East began when he met Dr. Laura Thompson, a distinguished anthropologist who worked with Collier on his Indian Personality Study. While occupied with projects their relationship developed into a love affair. After divorcing his wife Lucy, John Collier and Laura Thompson were married in Reno, Nevada in August of 1943.

Collier's efforts for preserving the culture of minority groups would soon turn to the Japanese-Americans in detention camps. Vice President Wallace was in favor of Collier for handling the War Relocation Authority which was a United States agency charged with handling the forced relocation and detention of Japanese-Americans during World War II, but Roosevelt gave that job to Dillon S. Myer. Instead, Roosevelt gave Collier the job of supervising 20,000 Japanese at the Poston relocation facility on the Colorado river in Arizona. Collier involved the Indian Bureau in the activities at the Poston camp for several reasons, among which was using the Japanese agricultural experience to put 25,000 acres of land under cultivation by building check dams and opening range lands. And since the camp was on an Indian reservation this would help irrigate the reservation, and in the process would enable the Japanese to raise surplus food to feed the American troops.

In addition, true to form, Collier wanted to create a community atmosphere at Poston in order to restore Japanese morale and faith in democracy. But he failed in this mission because he and Myer did not agree. Director Myer wanted the Japanese dispersed throughout the country so they would assimilate more readily, preventing their return to Los Angeles and "little Tokyo." As a result, the Indian Bureau withdrew from the Poston project. But the projects Collier put in place set the stage for the gathering of smaller tribes into what would become the Colorado River Indian Tribes (CRIT).

With things rather falling apart for him, John Collier submitted his resignation as Commissioner of Indian Affairs on January 10, 1945, and President Roosevelt accepted it on the 22nd of that month. Kenneth Philp, in his book writes,

> "Roosevelt told Collier that the one achievement of his
> administration in which he took great pride was the new orienta-

tion in Indian affairs." Further quoting Philps, "Collier deserved Roosevelt's praise, but in retrospect the Indian New Deal had serious shortcomings. Collier's attempt to implement John Marshall's legal doctrine that Indian tribes were sovereign entities capable of exercising all powers of self-government not relinquished by treaties or acts of Congress proved difficult to implement after fifty years of assimilation. Many Indians rejected the notion of being treated as a separate class and Collier failed to convince Congress that the preservation of native heritage, with its cooperative institutions, would enhance the Indian's ability to cope with modern life."

Philps continues,

"The commissioner had limited success as an administrator because he overestimated his capacity to reconstruct Indian affairs and introduced too many ideas which often created confusion. ... Collier demonstrated inflexibility by firing Indians from the bureau who opposed his policies, and he created unnecessary problems when he appointed a woman superintendent to head the Pueblos."

But in 1945 Collier organized the Institute of Ethnic Affairs and became its president. The objective of the Institute: to develop the art of administering human affairs by joining the "scientific passion for developing truth" with the peoples' dream of an energetic, democratic society. He was also appointed by Secretary Ickes as an alternate advisor to the United States delegation on trusteeship matters at the first session of the United Nations General Assembly. Collier left for the meeting in London along with Abe Fortas and John Foster Dulles, the two who led the delegation.

Collier was unhappy with the outcome of the U.N. General Assembly meeting, plus his words and actions with the Institute were ruffling feathers with some in the government and military. As a result, the Internal Revenue Service revoked the tax-exempt status of his Institute and dried up its funding.

Two years later Collier became a visiting professor of sociology and anthropology at the City College of New York and continued his war of words with Commissioner of Indian Affairs Myer. But gradually Collier was losing his influence.

When Dwight Eisenhower became President, Collier tried to influence the choice for Commissioner of Indian Affairs but without success.

In the spring of 1955, Collier's wife Laura flew to Juarez, Mexico and obtained a divorce based on mental incompatibility. Collier was devastated and went into a nonproductive depression. An offer to become a visiting professor of anthropology at Knox College in Illinois helped to revive his spirit.

Two years later, back in Taos, he married a woman he had met at the Institute of Ethnic Affairs, Grace Volk.

In 1964, as he was nearing the end of his life, the Department of the Interior presented Collier with its Distinguished Service Award. And on May 8, 1968, John Collier died at his home in Taos, New Mexico.

John Collier was an anthropologist with a keen interest in preserving the culture of the American Indian and perhaps the Indians of the world, including their painting, pottery, weaving, music, dance, poetry and drama that were all a part of their cultures, and thus we can see his passions interwoven in his administration of Indian affairs.

As I finish this chapter, I have a sense of pity for this man, John Collier. Deeply wounded by the actions of his parents just when he was entering his teenage years, a loner of sorts, perhaps searching in the wilderness for the meaning of life that his parents had deprived him of, he spent his entire life in search of the perfect. He thought he could find that in the Indian culture and their communal way of life, but for whatever reason, that was not to be. He was an anthropologist, a romantic, a poet, a profuse author, an animal lover and a lover of nature and a dreamer. He failed to accomplish what he set out to do but, whether or not we support what his goal was, we must agree that it was not for lack of trying — with his unquenchable work ethic, his ability to move on to the next social problem in the face of failure, and his desire for the perfect.

\* \* \*

Three books were used is writing this chapter. See Notes.

# CHAPTER 5

# The Path to Passage

U pon his confirmation as Commissioner of Indian Affairs John Collier laid out his vision, first stating that Secretary Ickes had said that, "The Commissioner of Indian Affairs ought to be the representative of the Indians themselves in the Department of the Interior. He should be their advocate, fighting for their interests and pleading their case."

Collier seemed to understand that directive but continued to shoot himself in the foot by promoting the trust relationship of the federal government. While he conceived the job of the Bureau as being to bring about liberty and opportunity for the Indians, he made liberty and opportunity impossible by favoring "an undiminished responsibility by the United States for their welfare." He seemed to believe that there were many government services that could be afforded the Indians "while preserving intact the guardianship which the United States owes to the Indians." Saying it another way Collier stated, "I strongly believe that the responsibility of the United States, as guardian of the Indians, ought to be continued. Federal responsibility for the property-less or so-called non-ward Indians should be re-asserted. Within the continuing guardianship, it is possible to establish a framework of Indian rights and responsibilities, and of Indian self-help. Administrative reorganizations, and new legislation, will be required to this end. The constitutional guarantees, with all that they imply, can be made a reality for the Indians without any curtailment of the federal responsibility for Indian welfare." Good Luck! Had he forgotten the words he used when he scolded his predecessor Commissioner Wilbur?[1]

Using this roadmap, which he envisioned would enable Indians to become self-governing plus the conclusions of the conference he had called to discuss an answer to the allotment system, Collier directed the solicitors to draft a proposed bill to be presented to Congress. If one takes the time to read the notes of the attorneys assigned to this task one can't help but experience fear by the realization that citizens of the United States can be manipulated in this way. These notes state that "an acceptable system of self-government must include a system of property tenure which provides for the economic utilization of land and prevents the growth of large inequalities in land holdings. This can be established through the technique of a non-stock membership corporation from which members of the community will be entitled to receive a fair share of community income and the use of a fair share of community assets, and to which each member of the community will owe obedience in matters of government and business control."

Communal socialism? And then even more frightening, "To state these objectives in statutory terms is perhaps politically inadvisable and at all events legally unnecessary, since consent of the Indians to such a system will have to be secured by reasoning and bargaining, no matter what the statute provides…" The attorneys discovered a major problem with the system saying, "The most difficult problem is to formulate a system of allocating use and income which will at once preserve the necessary measure of equality and at the same time provide an incentive to use." That sounds like the same problem that faced the first English colony in America at Jamestown. History records that Captain John Smith solved the problem with his doctrine, "No Work — No Food."

Three bills were written by attorneys Stewart, Shepard, Siegel and Cohen for consideration. In reviewing the three proposed bills in preparation for a meeting to work on a final bill, a Mr. Robert Marshall, apparently not an attorney,

*American Wilderness Activist Robert (Bob) Marshall*

but probably was — or would become — Director of Forestry, made some interesting suggestions that from this vantage point in 2019-2020 seem to have been lost along the way. He wrote, "Some provision should be made to the effect that the liberties guaranteed in the bill of rights of the U.S. Constitution should be operative within the tribal jurisdiction, or do these apply without special mention because of the quasi-federal nature of the reservations? So far as I can see there is no provision in these restrictions which states who will enforce them when necessary." On another subject he wrote "…Siegel and Cohen propose that Indian communities should not be subject to taxation. If the Indian communities do not pay taxes then they certainly must pay some substitute by which states, counties and towns may receive their equivalent. Either the federal government should subsidize the local communities or the Indians should be forced to pay taxes any way."

Marshall then repeated a thought that he attributed to Mr. Roosevelt: "the rural tax problem will never be solved until the host of duplicating government agencies are tremendously reduced." He apparently was passionate when he stated, "for God's sake, I hope that no bill proposed by the present administration will continue the competent-incompetent mess which makes sound administration by either whites or Indians virtually impossible."[2]

In January 1934, Commissioner Collier solicited the help of superintendents, tribal councils and individual Indians in helping to develop the plan which would eventually become the Wheeler-Howard bill. He sent an outline to each and asked that they give the matter their early attention and return their opinions to him by mid-February 1934.[3]

In response the Consolidated Chippewa Agency, headquartered at Cass Lake, Minnesota, called a meeting for that purpose on January 30, 1934 to be held at the Lyric Theater in Cass Lake. Approximately 175 representatives from Onigum, Cass Lake, Winnibigoshish and Ball Club attended, representing the Leech Lake, Cass, Winnibigoshish and White Oak Point bands. Officers of the meeting were chosen with Ben Caswell as chairman.

There was a great deal of skepticism regarding the plan as outlined by Commissioner Collier. The attendees seemed to be a bit overwhelmed by the task when they were told at the beginning of the meeting that they should complete it that day, and rightfully so. Frank Broker commented saying, "This program probably took a year to plan, but they give us only half a day to consider and report on it."

Several others were concerned that this new program would interfere with the claims they had attorneys working on in the Court of Claims. Ed Wilson opined saying, "I enjoy listening to the speakers here. Now let's consider this. Remember the Rice Treaty, the act of 1889. This law states that when all the Indians were allotted in Minnesota, the 50-year period was to begin and this period does not expire for several years yet, but many things have been done by the Government before this period expired. We had per capita payments, we have tribal attorneys prosecuting our claims. Our claims are now in the Court of Claims lying there dormant. I wonder when these claims will materialize. In this program there are a lot of things that will conflict with our other claims. We should not accept this thing. There are lots of Indians that are not here that should have this information so they too will understand what is in this paper. We are at the point where we have no property. We would not be this way if the Government had given us all their treaty compromises, none of the laws have been carried out to benefit us. The Indians have never broken any agreements, but the Government has broken all their agreements with the Indians. That is the reason that we Indians are so poor today. The Government made us poor. We had lot of property years back, we had a reservation, we had everything, we used to make a living, today, we have nothing. It is a big responsibility on for us to accept this program in a few hours time."

Frank Broker spoke saying in part, "...I think for the Chippewas, there should be a separate program, and I think that this program will not work out for the Chippewas." William Fairbanks commented, "At this time the Commissioner should not try to take us back to the reservations and live again like our forefathers lived years ago. This does not look right to me...I hear some hearsay that those who sold their lands will accept this program and accept their share in the lands of the Community. I want to say this, that the Indian who still holds his land is very wise, but those that sold their lands were very foolish." Bill Morgan expressed the opinion that it would not be right or fair to the Indians who still had their allotments to put them into the community and let the ones who had sold their land share in what they still retained. Mrs. Rock stated that the land would never belong to the Indians, and at a man's death the land would return to the community. The only thing that a man could will to his family would be the home and all improvements on it. She did not believe it a practical idea to put the Indians in a community separate from the whites.

There soon developed a general consensus that this was a job that would take more than a few hours and they were in no rush to accept a new program and that winter in Minnesota is a hard time to have meetings. They decided they needed more time and could not finish the task in the short time given them, and so they adjourned. After another meeting on the 12th they still were not ready to reach a decision on the proposed plan.

On February 1, 1934, a meeting for the same purpose was held at the assembly hall on the White Earth Reservation. Approximately 170 were in attendance. Arthur Beaulieu was elected chairman. The letter outlining the proposed plan from Commissioner Collier was read and interpreted. Considerable discussion ensued on the proposal to create a wildlife refuge on lower Rice Lake which the Indians opposed because it was a wild rice field. Superintendent Burns reported to Commissioner Collier on Feb. 17th that after a follow up meeting on the 12th they voted, in substance, to support the proposal. However, that is not consistent with the minutes of the February 12th meeting which indicates that they voted against the proposal.

At a meeting of the Fond du Lac Chippewa held at the city hall in Cloquet on February 3rd the group in attendance voted unanimously to reject the program proposed by Collier. On the 5th of February 1934, the executive committee of the Fond Du Lac Band forwarded a resolution to Superintendent Burns who was Superintendent of the Consolidated Chippewa Agency, which read:

> Resolution — The Fond Du Lac Band of Chippewa Indians are satisfied that the destiny of the Chippewa Nation is linked with that of the American people or nation, and will bring its sterling qualities of the nation, to the melting pot in common with other foreign nationalitys [sic], forming citizenry of this great nation. In other words merge itself into the body politic of the nation. But looking forward to the Federal Government to fulfill its honor-bound treaty stipulations with the Chippewa Nation.

At a meeting on that same day held at Inger, Minnesota, the main objection by those who still held allotments seemed to be a resistance to turning them over to the community. The 63 in attendance voted unanimously to reject the proposal.

On February 4ᵗʰ at a meeting held at Nett Lake I.E.C.C. Camp, which was composed of members of different Minnesota reservations, a Mr. Selkirk opined that,

> "The allotment system in the beginning was intended to give the Indian a start in agricultural pursuits, but they found out that they could not make farmers out of Indians. It took hundreds of years to develop and educate the white man. They expect the Indian to become a farmer and work a year and become a success. The allotment system, while it was a failure, the intentions were right... ."

Among other things he continued saying,

> "I would hate to admit that I was not capable of getting along in this world, the same as the white man. I wish to go on record as opposing this problem of self-government." A Mr. Coffey objected, saying, "It is a very poor policy to reject something that we do not understand." And with that they selected the chairman of a committee to study the proposal and the meeting was adjourned. Supt. Burns reported in writing to Collier on the 17ᵗʰ saying, "I am informed that the committee members of this camp, held a session for the discussion of the program and were in favor of it, that the camp sentiment, as a whole, was in favor, but Mr. Selkirk, being a spokesman, made it appear that the delegation was opposed... ."

At a meeting held on the Nett Lake Reservation (Bois Forte) on February 5ᵗʰ, attended by some 60 people, there were some supportive comments, but Charles Day stated, "The Government has made treaties with the Indians and I think our present treaty should be fulfilled before we make another. We lost on most of our other treaties." Supt. Burns reported to Commissioner Collier that, "The 'Self-Government' program was somewhat bewildering to these Indians, as very few among them can be considered intelligent sufficiently to understand its underlying principles readily..." But after numerous questions they expressed their favorable view. At the close of the meeting they indicated that they would probably send delegates to the Cass Lake meeting to be held on the 12ᵗʰ, but apparently, they decided not to send anyone.

A meeting was held at Grand Portage on Feb. 7th, attended by about 50 people, at which it was agreed to further study the proposed program. During a follow-up meeting on the 9th the Grand Portage Band passed the following resolution: "RESOLVED, That the Grand Portage Band of Chippewas of Minnesota, wish to establish a Reservation along the lines, and in conformity with the suggestions of the Indian Department as contained in their recent letter to the Tribes of the United States, but with exceptions, and amendments to cover their existing conditions." They then enumerated their wish list for the reservation proposed.

On February 9th seventy-five Mille Lacs Indians met at the Trading Post where a Mr. Munnell read and explained the proposal. Chief Wah de nah commented, "Some of the Indians did not understand what you read a while ago and some of them did. I am in favor of this plan, but we must give it more study and thought. We would like to go in the other room and talk it over among ourselves."

The men then went into the other room for their conference. After hours of deep meditation, carefully weighing each point with the utmost thought, they returned to the main room. Chief Wah de nah said, "We understand this. Some of them like the idea." After Mr. Munnell explained that a joint Chippewa meeting was planned for the 12th, Chief Wah de nah announced, "We have to go home now. A lot of us came up from Isle and we have to go back on the school bus. We will hold our meetings and then we will send Mr. Burns a copy of our meeting and what we have done." And with that the meeting adjourned.

On the following day, Feb. 10th, the following letter was sent:

Isle, Minn
Feb 10, 1934

Mark L. Burns
Cass Lake
Minn.

Dear Mr. Collier,

We are having a meeting here. We elected our officers and our officers are as follows. President, Mike Sam, Vice-President, John Jekey, Speaking committee, Chief Wadena, Policeman, Pete Nay-quana.

We have come to [an] ending that we all have agree[d] to have our land to be bound into one.

We are asking you if you could let us have our game, as it has been before the white man came, we used to take it anytime.

We are asking you to give us a payment in near future.
We want you to present this matter for us.

Yours,

The Isle Village as whole
Mike Sam, President
John Jekey, Vice President
Pete Nay-qua-nay-be
Fred Sam, Secretary

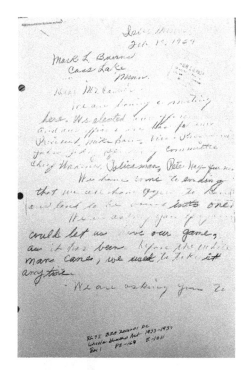

And 2 days later on Feb 12th the following letter was sent:

Onamia, Minn.<br>Feb. 12, 1934

Mark L. Burns
Cass Lake, Minn.

Dear Mr. Burns:

We are having a meeting here at Indian Trading Post and we have agreed to have our lands to be bound into one great reservation.

We are asking you if you could help us to have our game.

We are asking if they could speed up that Payment. We need it now.

We ask you to present this matter for us.

Yours,

The follows are officers of this meeting are —
President — Richard Gahbow
Vice President — Tom Skinway
Speaker of Committee — Chief Wadena
Secretary — Fred Sam
Policeman — Bill Bodskey

A public meeting was held at Cass Lake, Minnesota, February 12, 1934, with Superintendent M. L. Burns of the Consolidated Chippewa Agency by the delegates from Twin Lakes, Ponsford, Rice Lake, Pine Bend, White Earth village and Mahnomen, all from the White Earth Reservation, to discuss the Commissioner's proposed program for "Indian Self Government."

After opening the meeting Mr. Burns stated that the Fond du Lac Indians were against the program, Nett Lake undecided, Grand Portage in favor of it, and Mille Lacs not reported but believed to be in favor of it, Leech Lake undecided and requested an extension of time.

The delegate from White Earth village made a point that, "this self government program may sound very attractive and it has many good features about it but it operates like Socialism and Communism which we do not care to have and which the American Government does not recognize."

The Indian Emergency Conservation Camp (IECW) held that "The allotment system was a good thing but the management of the Department was wrong and they now tell you that the system was a failure in order to cover up the mismanagement of this entire matter." Their statement concluded, "…the time has now come when we must get out and take our places in the social, commercial and political life of the country and the Department then steps in and offers us this self government proposition. Why should we go back when we have an interest in the government of the country? It is class discrimination. It looks as though we are not good enough to share in the American government, and they want us to begin one of our own. We are citizens of the American nation –why can't we take our places with the American people? We honor the same flag and fought for it together."

At the end of the meeting the White Earth delegations voted as follows: Twin Lakes (Naytahwaush), Rice Lake, Ponsford and Pine Bend voting in favor of the program and White Earth and Mahnomen voting against it. These are the results that were to be handed to the Superintendent of the Chippewa Agency.

A letter to Commissioner Collier written February 14, 1934, from Red Lake Indian Agency Superintendent Raymond Bitney ended with the following words: "From what I have seen so far, it appears that the [Red Lake] Indians are not particularly interested at this time in this plan." At a council meeting held on February 17th the Red Lake council passed a resolution which read in part, "Whereas, all councilmen that got up to speak and discuss the object of the Circular came to the conclusion that the Red Lake Band of Chippewa Indians are not at this time, nor in the immediate future, qualified for the duties of self-government but rather they should occupy their reservation just as they have heretofore for the reason

that the Indians of the reservation have not advanced enough towards civilization and education and are not prepared enough to assume the responsibilities of
self-government...."

On February 17, 1934, Superintendent Burns sent off his report to Commissioner John Collier. He reported on each meeting held, the number of attendees and a short resume of each meeting. In regard to Mille Lacs he reported,
"The meeting with these Indians was held at the Ayers Trading Post, adjacent to
their community. These Indians are not as far advanced as other Indians are on
the other reservations, having practically no leaders of the intelligence sufficient
to comprehend the program, and took considerable time to read and interpret,
as well as explain the 'Self-Government' program. They have gone on record in
favor of it, however. These Indians, until within recent years, were without land,
roamed and camped about in the immediate territory of Mille Lac Lake. The
Government purchased land, in time, from which individual allotments of from 2
to 10 acres were made. They favor community ownership in lieu of allotments."[4]

A final version of a bill[5] to be presented to Congress — a forty-eight page
bill — was agreed upon, and while the Chippewa of Minnesota were still studying
and debating the proposed idea of self-government and attempting to get their
opinions to Commissioner Collier by the 15th as directed to do, Collier had
already sent the proposed bill to Representative Howard on February 6th and
asked the Congressman to please introduce it in the House of Representatives
promptly.[6] A copy of this original version can be found in the Appendix.

Already by March 2nd John Collier and his team were in Rapid City, South
Dakota, explaining the proposed bill to the Indians, and those sessions would
continue throughout March, ending with a final session at Hayward, Wisconsin
on April 23 and 24.

The Hayward session, which Collier did not attend due to conflicts with
congressional hearings, is the one that would have included the Mille Lacs band
had they chosen to participate. The Agency at Cass Lake lists two delegates from
Mille Lacs, Joe Eagle and Chief Wadena, but when it came time for the Mille Lacs
delegation to speak, Joe Eagle said, "My statement is very short. I just want to tell
why I am here. My people held a council last Saturday and delegated us to come
here — but we were not invested with the authority to accept or reject the bill —
but we were instructed to listen to what is being said here and get the opinions of
other Indians in regard to this bill."

Assistant Commissioner William Zimmerman, Jr. led the meeting and began
by reading a statement made by John Collier at the Rapid City, South Dakota
session saying,

"I shall first talk about the fundamental conditions of your life as I understand it. And what are these fundamental conditions which I shall suggest are wrong conditions and ought to be put right? What are they? They are, first, that the Indians of the United States, including your tribes, have for two lifetimes been steadily losing their property, becoming poorer and poorer on the whole. That is on the side of your property. If you take the United States as a whole, the wealth of the people has been increasing year by year steadily until the depression of three years ago. And, during those same years the wealth of the Indians, instead of increasing, has been melting away. I shall give you the exact facts after a few minutes. They are terrifying facts.

Now, the second condition is this: That the Indians of the United States are living under a condition which puts them at the mercy of the Indian Bureau.

The guardianship of the Federal Government over Indian life, which was intended to be a means of making the Indians both prosperous and free, has been having the opposite effect and has been making them poor while they are deprived of their freedom. Therefore, many people and some Indians have risen up and said that the only hope for the Indians is to put an end to the guardianship of the Government so that they may stand a chance in living. Some people have said the guardianship of the Government is injuring the Indian, is keeping them in a condition of slavery. Therefore, the responsibility must be brought to an end.

You have all heard that line of talk, and I do not hesitate to say I am speaking honestly my own feelings, that if the guardianship of the United States has to continue doing the things it has been doing; if it has to go on the old way, I think it had better be stopped, thrown aside, and the Indian better do without it. But, that is not the answer. The cure for the evils done by the Government is not to abolish but to reform it and make it do good things instead of evil things, and that is true of the guardianship over Indians.

The United States is not making a mess of its Indian guardianship because its employees are wicked or stupid. That is not the reason. They are not wicked and they are not stupid. But because the guardianship maintained by the United States is carried out under a body of laws which are wicked and stupid and which make slaves even of the Government employees hired to enforce the laws. There was a time when it was the policy of the United States Government to rob the Indians. There was a time when it was the policy of the United States Government to crush Indian life and even to crush the family life of Indians, and during that time laws were passed and those laws are still the laws, though it is no longer the policy of the Government to rob you or to crush you, but they are the laws [Dawes Act and Nelson Act], and by them we must work and you must live."

After more comments Commissioner Zimmerman read a letter from President Roosevelt:

"My Dear Mr. Howard,

My interest has been attracted to your bill, H.R. 7902, because of the virile American principles on which it is based. Opportunity for self-determination for the Indians in handling their property by providing modern corporate management, participation in local government, a more liberal educational system through day schools and advanced health measures are provided in the bill.

Adequate provision is made for his training in the management and protection of his property, and the conservation of his health during the period that must intervene before the Indian may be intrusted with the complete management of his own affairs. In offering the Indian these natural rights of man we will more nearly discharge the Federal responsibility for his welfare than through compulsory guardianship that has destroyed initiative and the liberty to develop his own culture.

Sincerely,
Franklin D. Roosevelt"

The bill, Zimmerman explained, is divided into four sections. "The first one sets up machinery by which Indians may organize for self-government; the second provides machinery by which Indians may be educated so that they may the better operate and manage business affairs; the third main title deals with the principal item of Indian property, namely land; the fourth deals with the proposed court of Indian affairs."

When Robert Marshall took the chair, he summarized what he was going to discuss in five sentences: "1. The Indians will keep the land they now own. 2. The Government will buy them more lands. 3. The lands will be owned in such a way that the Indians can really get the benefit of them. 4. They will be managed so as not to ruin them. 5. The tax-free period will be continued indefinitely."

Marshall continued, "…in regard to the matter of the Indians keeping the land they now own, The bill provides two phases of the same thing: 1. No more Indian lands can be sold to white men. 2. Those unsold ceded portions of the Indian reservations which by hook or crook have been thrown open by Congress and have become open for homesteading by White people — those lands which have not yet been sold or homesteaded will be returned to the Indian reservations and become part of the Indian land." Continuing, at one point Marshall said, "The bill proposes to buy land for landless Indians and I know a great many of you people, particularly Chippewas who through no fault of your own have lost their land — will in time be provided with land through the bill."

A question from a Bad River delegate to Field Representative Woehlke resulted in an interesting answer. **Question:** "An exception is made to one of your remarks. When were the Chippewa Indians at war with the U.S. Government? Where they became prisoners of war? Was it not through deceit that we became wards of government?" **Answer:** "I believe I made the general statement that the white race occupied the North American continent and that during this process of occupation it was at war with the Indian race. I believe in general that is true, but at the same time during this 300-year-war a great many of the tribes cooperated with the United States Government, as for instance the Crows and other tribes who were never at war with the United States. Several tribes in the Southwest always remained peaceful and helped the U.S. Government. But after all it was a condition of war in which the whites fought against the Red race, even though there were various alliances back and forth. Now as to the question of deceipt [sic] on the part of the Government, that is undoubtedly true."

I am including another question from the same Bad River delegate simply because it is, in my view, such a horrendous way for a representative of the U.S. Government to answer a question.

> **Question:** "If this so called self-government bill is accepted, how do we know that the Government will fulfill its promises? We have been deceived quite a few times."

**Answer:** "That is a very good question and it deserves an answer. Personally, none of us can guarantee that, but we can say that this administration has taken a new view, a new attitude toward the common man, whether White or Red. The first concern of our President is with the rights of man and not so much with the rights of property. I am quite certain that I can guarantee that whatever promises are made to you by this administration will be kept by this administration. As to the future, you must realize that up until very recent years the Indian race had land and properties that the white man wanted — especially land. The huge reservations of the '70s and '80s were right in the path of the white wave that swept across them. No matter what kind of promises the Government would make, the citizens would proceed to override them and take what they wanted; and frequently the Government had to break it's treaty promises and reduce your land holdings, because if it hadn't done so, the whites would have taken everything by force and the Government would be powerless to restrain them. The point is this: Of late years the white race has discovered that it took away too much land from the Indian race. It bit off and swallowed so much of the Indian land that now it has a national stomachache — it can't digest all the land. Because it took so much land and put it into cultivation and production, it now is faced with a condition under which it produces so much from the soil — so many things like cotton and wheat and corn — so many of these commodities — that there is no market for most of it and the prices have gone to the devil and the land values have also gone to the devil. Everything has gone to hell largely because too much land was taken from the Indians and put under cultivation. All of us are suffering from these past mistakes as you have noticed from the action of Congress in limiting cotton production, in trying to limit wheat production, etc. The Government realizes this, and in fact is now willing to buy back at low prices some of the land that was taken away and give it back to the Indians. That is why I believe that the promises made now will be kept. The theory now is not to take away from you, but to give it back to you."

Dr. Roe Cloud, Superintendent of the Haskell Institute, then took the chair and answered a question from a White Earth delegate this way:

> **Question:** "What does tutelage mean?"
>
> **Answer:** "It means instruction, guidance, education and nurture. It also has this added meaning — it means wardship and government control of Indians whenever we use that term."

And then came a second,

> **Question:** "What Minnesota Indians are included under Federal tutelage?"
>
> **Answer:** "Generally speaking I should say that all Indians in the United States — not only Minnesota — but all Indians are under Federal tutelage. In a more technical sense, the Supreme Court of the United States has said that wards and citizens are not incompatible terms — so that you and I as Indians can be wards and citizens at the same time and exercise under those terms the privileges that go with both names..."

Dr. Cloud gave a rather interesting answer to a fourth,

> **Question:** "After a community has been organized it develops that a considerable number of Indian members — say 75% refuses to work. What can be done with them? Will the other 25% have to feed and care for them?"
>
> **Answer:** "I believe someone is letting his imagination run away with him, but I would like to say that this new system — this new plan — provides in my judgment far more work opportunities to the Indian race than what you and I have experienced up to the present time. Generally speaking Indians are considered lazy, largely because of two things: There is widespread unemployment on reservations everywhere. A reservation is the hardest place in the world to find work for the Indian. Therefore, having no employment, he stands around the streets or mopes along the road in his lumber wagon. The second factor is because of wide-spread sickness resulting from not having enough to eat — malnutrition as it is called. Maybe tuberculosis has set in

and there is a dragging of the feet and a loss of ambition together with a generally weakened condition — he may not be strong enough to go to work.

Lately when these relief work opportunities have been given the Indian, he has demonstrated that he will work if he has the opportunity — as thousands proved this past winter. In the second place, this new system sets up a new form of self-interest that we have never before experienced. Here is the $10,000,000 loan fund that you and I can utilize to get started in something. To make industry we must have land, labor and capital, and hitherto we have not had anything but labor. Now for the first time in our experience the Government favors giving you the other two. In the third place, the bill says that beneficial use must be made of this land. The chartered communities must see to this.

Drones are a problem in any community and I trust in the best judgment of the Indians to solve the problem themselves. It is a thing that cannot very well be legislated against, but I believe that it can be controlled with a lot of good horse sense. Fourth, the chartered community brings to apply on the Indian the local public opinion.

Up to the present time when the Bureau asked us to go to work we said, 'Well, those birds are way off in Washington and we don't care very much about the white man's opinion.' But let the Indian public opinion be focused upon some one member of the community and watch the reaction. We naturally respond to what our fellows think of us and it is a most powerful force to make us do something useful in life. So I say that 75% of any community is not going to be lazy by any means."

**Question:** "Would ceded reservations in Minnesota under this bill be classified and considered as reservations?"

**Answer:** From Dr. Cloud, "Yes."

A White Earth delegate then **asked**, "Cite and interpret the so-called Curtis Act enacted in 1924, conferring citizenship upon the Indians of the United States, and state briefly how H.R. 7902 with its multitudes of provisions, can constitutionally be applied under grants provided for in the said act of 1924?"

The delegate was **answered** by Mr. Reeves saying, "That question has already been answered twice from this platform.... It was pointed out to you that citizenship and wardship are not incompatible. The Supreme Court has held and the Act of June 2, 1924 in conferring citizenship upon the Indians in no way deprived you of any property rights, privileges and opportunities granted to the Indians. There is no inconsistency between the two in any manner whatever, and enactment of the bill would only extend to you additional facilities and privileges without dispossessing you of present property rights or rights as citizens."

In response to the following **question** from a Lac du Lambeau delegate, "...Do we now own the water rights? ...", the **answer** from Mr. Reeves was, "...it provides that no lands, water rights or other assets owned by Indians shall be voluntarily or involuntarily alienated. Further, I might state that the water rights referred to, deal primarily in connection with arid southwest lands where it is necessary to resort to artificial application of water to raise crops. That is primarily the water rights dealt with in this bill. With reference to the water rights among you Chippewa people, your rights depend upon whether the waters are navigable or non-navigable. As to areas within the reservation, if they are navigable waters they belong to the State — if non-navigable they belong to the tribe or individual Indians in the event the reservation has been allotted."

Discussion as to who controls waters became rather heated. Mr. Reeves made the statement, "...as to hunting and fishing — if the streams are navigable the title is in the State and the State has the control, and if the waters are non-navigable the State has no jurisdiction." A **question** from a Bad River band delegate was, "If the State contends it has jurisdiction over navigable waters, would we be liable to State law and arrest if we pass over these waters with game out of season?" The **answer** was, "I think you would — I may be mistaken." And to that answer the delegate said, "I would like to know what good our treaty is then."

Mr. St. Germane then stated, "Someone has said — in fact the Supreme Court has said that the treaty is the supreme law of the land. I don't know what they mean by that — perhaps they should have said all but an Indian treaty. An Indian treaty, it seems, can be twisted any old way to suit someone else. A mere interpretation by a certain group of men should not change the law. My thought is this: That that interpretation of the law has never been argued by a member who really believes and knows that the Indians retain titles to these waters within reservation lands. Give us a chance — let an Indian go there and tell those grayhaired men what they should know."

Mr. Woehlke replied, "We are not only getting into navigable waters ... but we are getting into deep legal waters .... If you gentlemen from the Bad River or Lac du Flambeau reservations think that through the Wheeler-Howard Bill we are trying to take anything away from you, you are badly mistaken. It gives you greater security, adds to what you have, and takes nothing at all away from you...."

After the questions had all been answered the session then turned to a statement from each delegation. George Walters from White Earth made the following assertion:

> "I want to say a few words in regard to the subject under discussion here. At the time the councils were held in my locality I did not know that these papers were in existence [referring to papers explaining the bill] until the time when I was elected a delegate. These papers were not presented to me. These other delegates here know all about this, but all the time as for myself, only five days before I started for this conference did I know something about this. I am located very near where they are, but they never notified me. And I kind of in a way understand that I as an Indian am being approached to ask these questions. On my account as an Indian the government is holding this conference, and I want to say at this time that I don't have a show at all at this conference. It is at this place that I hear of the contents of this bill for the first time, and there are Indians of my tribe at home that should hear this news. It is not right that individuals must be here personally to hear of this deal.
>
> Why are we in such terrible and poor shape today? Am I responsible? The government is the cause of our privation. It is not the fault of the Commissioner of Indian Affairs we are in such privation. We are responsible for our own condition today. We did not follow the instructions of the Commissioner or the Government of the United States. I am the person that tried to hold back this person that wants to be a white man and there was not a single Indian that did not oppose me. The one that talked here previous he opposed me just the same. The White Indian is too susceptible to wrong doing. He always wants the money. That is the reason for such poverty. Our money in Washington is in very small amounts now and still we are writing the Government to give us some more. Isn't it a fact that future generations should be benefited by some of this money? What

is being left for our children — for the future generations? And what then will they live on? All these allottees have sold their 160 acres and I don't believe any of them possess even a twig of a tree and I don't believe they have as much as one shot of gunpowder or a parcel of land!"

Mr. Roe Cloud then spoke: "Mr. Interpreter, will you tell him that the new bill will protect his land so there need never be a loss, and also tell him it is safe for his children and grandchildren in future generations." And Mr. Walters replied, "That is all I want."

Jerome Arbuckle of the Bad River band presented a question — a very profound question — that did not get an answer, but his was a correct vision of the future.

> "When is the Indian going to be given the full rights of citizenship with the privilege of doing whatever a citizen does? No provision is made for this. We do not know how long we are going to be under Government supervision. We are classed as restricted citizens and it might be 100 years or more before this is changed."

Perhaps he answered his own question. As of 2020, 100 years has not yet elapsed.

Mr. Red Cloud of the Winnebago delegation opined saying,

> "There is a general impression among the public that the Indian will fail in the art of self-government. I believe the Indian can succeed because it is nothing new. They had experience in it long before the coming of the White race, and they governed themselves without the aid of jails, penitentiaries, insane asylums, etc. Most of us Indians, all tribes included, still retain the power and wisdom of the old chieftains. Most of us retain the wisdom of the old councils.
>
> Therefore, I cannot see why the Indians should fail in self-government.
>
> In some respects, this bill is too good to be true, but we know that it is the outcome of long consideration and deep thought, and that the Indians will receive the benefit of justice. Justice

may be blind, but Mr. Roosevelt and Mr. Collier are excellent eye doctors."

As the session was nearing its end Mr. Woehlke commented,

> "I have waited with this final word to you until I could find out just how your sentiment was drifting. … The Wheeler-How-ard Bill has not been passed, and while the Commissioner and his staff have been spreading this legislation before the Indian people all over the country so that he might inspect it — during that period powerful forces have been organized to defeat it in its entirety. … To many of the members of the House and Senate Committee there is arriving constantly a stream of letters from various individuals opposing this bill, and from those who will be benefited by it, those who favor it, there is hardly a word; until the committee has come to the conclusion that nobody wants this bill.
>
> On top of that you have the natural resistance of the Government itself against any increased appropriations for the Indians, and you must remember that this bill carries not only authorization for heavy appropriations immediately, but it also carries authorization for large appropriations to be made year after year — appropriations, the total of which will be a very large sum. …
>
> As a group and as individuals, let your representatives in the House and Senate know just how you feel about it, and write them and tell whether you are for or against the bill, and do it early and often!"

And following a few additional comments the session at Hayward, Wisconsin, ended. As I studied the transcript of the Hayward session, it seemed clear to me that in the beginning the government representatives thought the Indians were stupid, and even though they were asking intelligent questions they were being talked to like school children. As the session progressed however it seemed to become clear that the Indians had a pretty good grasp of the situation and the tone changed to one more of equals.[7]

While Indians across the country were debating the wisdom of this new proposal, many non-Indians were also weighing in on the subject.

Discussion in the formation of the education section of the proposed bill suggested some interesting thoughts in an unsigned archival document. For instance,

> "Education, in the biological as distinguished from the traditional meaning, is the process of fitting individuals and groups to act skillfully in a changing environment. 'Knowing' is only a preliminary to 'acting' either physically, intellectually, or emotionally. ... Since life and action are continuous, cumulative racial experience is a necessary part of the educational process; but learning this experience by rote from books can never take the place of learning from physical and intellectual action. Much of our white education, far out of touch with the real environment of modern life, has ceased more and more to have a vital influence on fitting the individual to deal intelligently with the modern environment. It has even less significance to a primitive people like the Navajos. ... The fact that false methods of education have had bad effects both on whites and the Indians is not an argument against education, but only against the education. Unless we escape from a difficult problem by taking refuge in intellectual nihilism we must assume that the educative process, soundly conceived and carried out, has a universal significance for all races and all times."

The document continues concentrating on the Navajos and I suspect that, although unsigned, this is John Collier in one of his anthropological thought sessions.[8]

Religious leaders were also making their opinions on the proposed bill known. A Presbyterian wrote,

> "It aims to correct the flagrant injustices of the land allotment policy." A Catholic director of Indian missions wrote, "It means training for and exercise of democratic self-government and the serious business of making a decent living..." and — quite profoundly I think — wrote, "Congress will count the costs. But it must recognize that here at least are concrete suggestions offered for the correction of past failures, both in fixed policies, like that of too general land allotment ... and in vacillating programs which have changed with almost every new commissioner, superintendent and farmer in the Indian service,

so that the Indian's head was kept in a constant whirl and his thumbs playing Tweedledum and Tweedledee." And an editorial in the "Churchman" stated, "The Commissioner is hated by those whose financial interests would be jeopardized by such legislation as that represented by the Wheeler-Howard Bill. ... They are fighting to kill the bill, using the same sort of pressure that is always used by selfish interests..."[9]

The Indian Rights Association, a white social activist lobbying group whose stated objective was to bring about the complete civilization of the Indians and their admission to citizenship, weighed in on the proposed bill, writing,

"Whether we wish it to be so or not, whether we encourage or discourage it, the amalgamation of the Indian with the white race in the United States is in process. In many sections it has already gone far. In others it has hardly begun and we look forward to certain sections being predominantly Indian for several generations. But these areas of Indian strength cannot indefinitely withstand the general forces that are working, even if they should desire to do so. ...

All friends of the Indians should look forward to and work for complete civil liberty, political responsibility, and economic independence of Indians. However, they will need for a considerable time, varying in different localities and situations, the protection and tutelage afforded by guardianship; but this does not mean permanent guardianship and wardship. We should not hold such a goal before Indian people. They and we must look toward the time when they will contribute to the support of government and maintain themselves economically without special aid or consideration (as a racial group) from any government. No other aim shows respect for Indians or will develop self-respect within themselves."

In commenting on the proposed Wheeler-Howard Bill the Association made some profound criticisms:

"It seems...entirely too inclusive in its scope. One of the primary difficulties of Indian legislation in the past has been its tendency to treat all Indians alike." and "Although the bill is urged in the name of self-government, many of its features are inimical to that end. The real governmental authority is handed over by Congress to the Secretary of the Interior and the Commissioner of Indian Affairs…No real responsibility is imposed on Indians. No civil liability can be enforced against any Indian community or its members." and "Holding before Indians an ideal of permanent guardianship for them by the Government is bad. It is destructive of human character. Also, the ideal of permanent freedom from taxation is a vicious one."

They also expressed concern that, although acceptance of the plan for chartered communities was optional, if a particular tribe did not accept the chartered community plan they would not benefit from proposed appropriations. "The importance of education" they wrote, "cannot be too greatly emphasized."[10]

We know that in the final days of the Congress in 1934, John Collier was doing his best to promote the Wheeler-Howard Act. It was important enough to him that he stayed behind in Washington instead of attending the session in Hayward, Wisconsin. The document, of which I now comment, is unsigned but it very well could have been Collier's testimony before Congress.

The document starts:

> "This Congress has an opportunity, even in these closing days of the session, to perform a great act of justice and restitution to the American Indians. … The bill in behalf of which I now appeal to you is intended to undo, so far as we can now undo them, a disastrous train of events which grew out of the act of 1887 and of the policy of Indian administration which grew out of and about this act. That policy and that act led well-nigh to the economic and spiritual destruction of the Indians. They have stripped the Indians of two-thirds of the lands they owned in 1887; have created a vast class of pauper Indians, landless and unemployed, and largely incapable of finding employment; have systematically destroyed Indian social and political institutions and the Indian arts and cultures; have deprived the Indians of all voice in the management of their own lives and affairs; and so far from solving the Indian problem, have left the problem infinitely more difficult and complicated. This system of law and

administration shackles the Indian Service as well as the Indians themselves.

It is an administrative measure which has the warm support of the President and of Secretary Ickes. ... It would give to the Indian at least a modest measure of economic security and economic opportunity. ... The general allotment act of 1887 sought to substitute individual private ownership of Indian land for tribal ownership. It provided for the parceling of the Indian reservations into small individual allotments and the issuance of trust deeds to all the enrolled members of the tribe. After a period of twenty-five years of trust ownership, or as soon as he might be declared 'competent', the allottee was to receive an unrestricted patent and could then do with the land what he pleased to do. In the debate that accompanied the passing of the allotment act, it is clear that the proponents of the measure were convinced that the private ownership of land was the one great step that was needed to civilize the Indians. The mere issuance of a fee patent would give to the Indians pride of ownership, thrift, industry, and the means of self-support; it would break down the tribal status of the Indians and convert them into typical American citizens; it would, at the same time, solve the Indian problem and in the course of a single generation relieve the Government of the immense and costly burden of caring for the Indian wards. ... The figures on the loss of Indian lands out of Indian ownership in the past forty-seven years are indeed staggering. ... Many reservations have in Indian ownership a mere fragment of the original land (and all the remaining allotted reservations are badly checkerboarded). ... Even if Indian allottees retained their land after receiving fee patents the heirship system inevitably leads to the ultimate loss of the land. Even the first generation of heirs is usually so numerous that physical partition of the land is impossible and it must be put on the auction block in order to divide the estate. ... For the administration of the remaining allotted lands there has been built up a fantastic and enormously costly real estate business which compels the Indian Service to expend an even greater share of its appropriations and energy in the sterile and fruitless administration of minutely parceled tracts. ... On allotted reservations, numerous cases exist where the share of each individual heir from lease money may be one cent a month. ... The cost of leasing, book-keeping, and distributing the proceeds in many cases far exceeds the total income. ... As the Indian estate has dwindled, Indian poverty and pauperism have increased alarmingly. ...This poverty contributes largely to the excessive death rate among the Indians ... It has long been held that the Indian policy of the past half century would lead to the rapid assimilation of the Indians into American civilized industrial life. The facts are precisely the opposite. ... Theoretically, the Indians are citizens of the United States, as declared by act of Congress of 1924; but this act was only an empty gesture ... In most of his actions, the Indian must today take his orders from a Federal Bureau, and against these orders he has no legal appeal. ... Land reform and home rule for the Indians are the essential and basic features of the Wheeler-Howard Bill. ... In carrying out this program, the Indian Service will become the advisor of the Indians rather than their ruler. The Federal Government will continue its guardian-ship of the Indians, but the guardianship envisaged by the new policy will constantly strengthen the Indians rather than weak-ening them. ... This program will pave the way for a real assimi-lation of the Indians into the American community on the level of economic independence and political self-respect. ... This Congress, by adopting this bill, can make a partial restitution to the Indians for a whole century of wrongs and of broken faith, and even more important ... can release the creative energies of the Indian in order that they may learn to take a normal and natural place in the American community."[11]

On February 19, 1934, Commissioner Collier sent a memorandum to the members of the House and Senate Committees on Indian Affairs explaining the bill that had been submitted. He started the memo by emphasizing that Indians in general were becoming more impoverished while the government was spend-ing increased amounts on the Indian Service, and he blamed it primarily on the allotment system.

Collier pointed out in detail that "through the allotment system, more than 80% of the land value belonging to all the Indians in 1887 has been taken away from them; more than 85% of the land value of all the <u>allotted</u> Indians has been taken away. And the allotment system, working down through the partitionment or sale of the land of deceased allottees, mathematically insures and practically requires that the remaining Indian allotted land shall pass to whites. The allotment act contemplates total landlessness for the Indians of the third generation of each allotted tribe." The bill that has been introduced, he wrote, "…is a Bill to correct the allotment system, saving the remaining lands, enabling the Indians to get their lands into usable shape, and providing the machinery and authority for restoring, to these Indians already rendered landless, usable lands, if they will demonstrate their wish to possess and use the restored lands." He made it clear that the bill "seeks to curb the administrative absolutism and it provided the machinery for a progressive establishment of home rule by tribes or groups of Indians." Collier clarified that the number of Indian employees in the Indian Service has been decreasing and states that the reason is that the educational opportunities available to Indians does not equip them to qualify for civil service jobs. He pointed out that the bill "authorizes appropriations of various sums for land acquisition, for the organization of Indian communities, and for education."

The Commissioner then provided the committees with a list of things that the bill, in his opinion, does not do. The bill does not disturb those allottees who have equity in their allotments; it would take nothing from any Indian. He assured the committees that, "the bill is not a scheme for taking lands from Indians who still possess land and dividing it among Indians who have no land." He assured the committee members that "The bill does not introduce any socialistic or communistic idea or device." He went on to say, "The bill does not bring to an end, or imply or contemplate, a cessation of Federal guardianship and special Federal service to Indians. On the contrary, it makes permanent the guardianship services. … The bill does not force upon the Indians anything, except that it stops the alienation of what lands they still possess…"

"It will properly be asked," Collier wrote, "what is the ultimate goal of this legislation? Does it contemplate for the Indians a permanent tribal status, isolation from the white man, collective as distinguished from individual enterprise, and non-assimilation into American civilization? The answer is a clear-cut one. No. The futures of the Indian tribes will be diverse, as their backgrounds and present situations are diverse. The Bill will not predetermine these futures. It is they who should determine their own futures."[12]

While the Wheeler-Howard Bill was making its way through Congress, rumors were flying among the Indians of Minnesota and those who were paying close attention to the proposed legislation.

A chief from the Nett Lake Reservation (Bois Forte) wrote to Commissioner Collier asking for more information, stating that "some say we will be required to move far away to some strange place. This is what the Indians don't want. If the reservation was to be created here somewhere I think it will be favorable to most ...."[13]

Dr. Hewitt, a dentist from Duluth, wrote to Commissioner Collier, declaring, "...it has seemed perfectly logical why the Indian has had, and has now, no faith in any proposal for their betterment emanating from Government sources. The recent attempt to explain your program for self-government through Supt. Burns, is a case in point, it being received either with indifference, or with hostility."[13]

A letter from Grand Portage to Collier read, "We the undersigned Chippewa Indians of Grand Portage did not vote to except [sic] the new deal" followed by four pages of signatures.[14]

In March of 1934, Joseph Latimer of Brooklyn, New York, wrote a rather profound article, parts of which I will cite. It is not clear whether it was a letter, an article to be published or just his thoughts. He writes,

> "It has been my experience that few Indians are interested in anything except to have Uncle Sam support and care for him. This is not the Indian's fault, but solely due to generations of paternalism under our Indian Bureau. The sweeping control granted in H.R. 7902 insures Indian Bureau paternalism for generations to come; forces the Indian to be a separated race; deprives him of his rights under the full citizenship Congress granted him in 1924, and revives, by dangerous experiment, the life of a condemned Bureau — an admitted failure after over fifty years of 'Indian care.' This Collier bill supports all those who think the Indian is only a helpless derelict in our civilization, and that he must be set off by himself to lead a community life as an Indian — an alien to all other Americans. ... But the Collier bill insures perpetuation of the Bureau; segregates both the Indian and his property from the laws, business and activities of life accepted by all other citizens of this country. Nullifies Indian citizenship, makes him a complete stranger to our National life, cuts him out, labels him 'Indian', and can more intensely than in the past establish him as a Bureau 'ward and incompetent.' Community property, community Government, community education and community life — all Bureau 'super-

vised' and 'helped' ('Supervising' and helping the Indian has been the Bureau's activity for fifty years). Certainly, there is no incentive in all of this to raise one's self from the same paternalized Indian as of the present. Paternalism kills individual initiative, and is the cause of the helplessness of the Indian of today. Indian 'community life' under this Collier bill will soon develop into a zoological curiosity for the entertainment of the American public, and of further experimentation by 'experts' on the Indian as a separated species of humanity. … To be sure, as the Commissioner recently said in Baltimore, 'many Indians are ignorant, cannot speak English and are unfit to govern themselves.' Then why rejuvenate, a Bureau which has not been able to correct such conditions, and now advocates intense segregation of the Indian? The millions of foreigners more 'ignorant' than the Indian, as equally unable to speak English, have landed on our shores and by mingling in all our life activities have become able American citizens. Could segregated racial Community life have accomplished this necessary change?"[15]

Denton Russell Bedford of the Columbia University Department of History wrote Commissioner Collier saying, "May I congratulate you on your monumental work in the rehabilitation of the American Indian as an individual and as a race."[16]

Wm. A. Brunette, in a letter to Commissioner Collier, wrote, "As a member of the Chippewa Indian Tribe, resident for about 30 years on the White Earth Reservation in Minnesota, I have been very much pleased with your plan for local self-government among the Indians." He added a P.S. that read, "There is much sentiment on the White Earth Reservation among a certain class of Indians, especially those of less than ¼ Indian blood, in favor of a division of the Tribal Funds. They do not desire to become members of any Chartered Indian Community, and seek to hinder others who would be eager for such an Indian Community from joining together for co-operative effort under the plan proposed in said Bill."[17]

C.F. Berry, a chiropractor from Manchester, New Hampshire, wrote Collier stating, "I wish that you could actually know how I feel in knowing that there is one pale face who is sincerely interested in his foster-ancestors. Greed and selfishness has since the beginning of time been the watchword of the fair-skinned ones of this land, whereas the reverse is true of our friend and helper the original American. … I have just written a forceful letter to my congressman asking for his whole-hearted support in the various bills before Congress in the interest of the Indian."[18]

Tom Skinaway, Onamia, Minnesota wrote Commissioner Collier. "I am told to ask you the following questions by my people. We have been told this idea of self government does not come from your office, is this true? Where is the money coming from to buy this land? Where will this land be? Will Mille Lacs and other reservations have their own self government or will it be in one big reservation? Please explain this to us…"[19]

It was April 1934, and there was obviously a push to convince Congress and the public that the Wheeler-Howard Bill was the right program for the United States to pass into law. John Collier was doing his utmost to convince Congress that this bill was in the best interest of the United States and that it should be passed before this session ended. The American Indian Defense Association, an organization that had been started by Collier back in 1923, through their California branch, published a comprehensive promotional pamphlet using their newsletter the American Indian Life in support of the bill. In part they wrote,

> "For the first time, we have legislation before Congress which confronts the *basic* problems of Indian administration constructively, courageously. The Wheeler-Howard Bill culminates a decade of study and investigation. It draws together the mature wisdom of many students and critics of the present system, Indian and white. Those who would reject it must offer in its place an equally constructive alternative, or keep their peace. … Without taking hasty action, there remains sufficient time to enact the Wheeler-Howard Bill in the present session. … *The Bill should be passed by Congress now!* … If the United States honestly wants to bring 'the new day' to the Indians, it is precisely at this point and at this time *that it must act!*"

The Association asked for wide distribution of the pamphlet, and through the pamphlet they asked the public for their personal approval and to make that approval known to their representatives in Congress.[20]

A newspaper article in the archival file that has no date or source contains an interesting paragraph, while writing about the opinions of Minnesota Chippewa in regard to the Wheeler-Howard Bill. "It is contended that individual land allotments carrying title are desirable and that former abuses were not due to the allotments themselves but to the government's failure to protect the recipients from exploitation. The Chippewas say the large Western Indian groups, remote from white settlement, may be benefited by the Collier plan but as to themselves they want it made more elastic to fit their peculiar needs."[21]

In an analysis of support by the tribes as of April 24th, the final day of the Hayward conference, it was reported that 47 tribes had voted and 38 tribes voted in favor while 9 tribes voted against the bill.[22]

Two days after the Hayward conference, a scathing article appeared in the *Cass Lake Times* voicing opposition to the idea behind the Wheeler-Howard Bill. Most of the article was consumed by a letter sent to President Roosevelt, written by Flora Warren Seymour, an attorney and author who was a former member of the Board of Indian Commissioners.[23]

As the bill was being debated in Congress, Congressman Will Rogers of Oklahoma wrote,

> "The administration heat has been applied to recalcitrant Congressmen the last few days in Washington in an effort to bring about the speedy enactment of the Wheeler-Howard Indian Rights Bill. ... Last week Secretary Harold L. Ickes took a hand in the matter and called several members of the House Indian Affairs Committee, one at a time, to his office to urge favorable discharge of the Wheeler-Howard measure from the Committee. Since several conservative amendments have been added to the bill, many of the original objectionable features have been eliminated. The Committee, however, is at the present time about equally divided on the matter. There are twenty-one members of the Committee and ten have expressed opposition to the bill."[24]

The *New York Times* on April 28th read, "President Roosevelt today advocated political liberty and local self-government for the American Indians and a move promptly was started to carry out his wishes. In a letter to Senator Wheeler and Representative Howard ... the President urged enactment of legislation introduced by them... ." A similar article appeared in the Sunday *Washington Star* the following day.[25]

Duane F. Porter, a Chippewa Indian and a Methodist missionary, wrote to Commissioner Collier on April 28th saying,

"I know the Indian. I was brought up among them. … Discussing the plan among the Chippewa Indians at White Earth Reservation I made a good success. … an Indian can do anything that you can do, do you know that he is human like yourself. It is true that the Indian Bureau has caused us to live separate from the rest of the world. That no one can be blamed for judging the Indian people in that awful wrong idea. The country is taxed fifteen million dollars every year to make the Indians useless and ruin them. The country ought to awaken and see that by freeing them from Indian Bureau control and conferring citizenship upon them that the country would save fifteen million dollars, and cause the Indian to be producers and wage earners, which would enrich the country many more times the fifteen million dollars. The Indian would fare better without the Indian Bureau and the country would gain much by the result of the Indians handiwork. While as wards they are an expense to the country. Keep in mind that the Indians are men and women and they can accomplish anything that others have done. If Indians have endured the bondage system of the Indian Bureau for fifty years, they can stand freedom forever."[26]

The screws were getting tighter and tighter on those who had any influence on the Bill. It even progressed to the point that Secretary Ickes sent a letter to all the employees of the Indian Service which in the last paragraph said,

"If any employee wishes to oppose the new policy, he should do so honestly and openly from outside of the service. This would mean his resignation. Any other course is unscrupulous and is detrimental to the Indian because it acts on the service like a canker. This condition has existed in the ranks for many years and has been partly responsible for the failures of the past. It retards and defeats the most conscientious effort toward good administration, and it will be summarily eliminated, wherever found, by dismissal."[27]

By April 30th it was reported that 62 tribes had voted on the proposed Bill with 51 voting in favor and 11 voting against.[28] On that same day the Duluth Herald ran an article of support.[29]

On May 17th Acting Solicitor Charles Fahy issued a memorandum regarding the power of the Federal Government to charter Indian corporations. He opined that "In the exercise of the congressional power to charter Federal corporations, there is no constitutional restriction upon the method of incorporation that Congress may select. A corporation may be created either by a special act, whereby a legislative body charters a corporation directly, or by a general incorporation law authorizing some administrative officer to issue a charter of incorporation to a body of 'incorporators' under prescribed conditions. Both methods of incorporation are equally valid and constitutional. ... The Wheeler-Howard Bill is, in effect, a general incorporation law for a defined class of Federal corporations, to wit, incorporated Indian tribes."[30]

On May 28th Principal Chief Joseph Bruner, representing the Indian National Confederacy in Sapulpa, Oklahoma, wrote a very caustic letter to Commissioner Collier saying,

> "As a full blood Indian (enrolled Creek No. 3142 of the Five Civilized Tribes,) I am deeply hurt. You have either deliberately insulted the Indians of Oklahoma, or you have exposed such colossal ignorance of the American Indians as to render you wholly unfit for the important office you hold. ... Approximately a third of the Indian population of the United States resides in Oklahoma. ... your articles deliberately deceive the reading public into the idea that all Indians are alike and that what you say of those Indians whom you know, is understood to apply to every Indian in the United States. I would be just as unfair to describe the very lowest class of residents in any American city and declare it to be representative of the citizenship of that city.
>
> In *Collier's Magazine,* we are insulted with the raw statement that the meanness cannot be educated out of us. That applies to such Indians as Former Vice President Curtis, Former Senator Robert L. Owen, Former Congressman Charles D. Carter, Present Congressman W.W. Hastings, the Humorist, Will Rogers, some of the most successful business and professional men in this State, some of the most prominent club women in the United States. You have stated publicly that you had never been in Oklahoma and that you do not understand conditions among Oklahoma Indians, but you write of us just the same...

In your *Washington Post* article, you emphasize the fact that Indians will be given government positions in the Indian service just as soon as they demonstrate their ability to function in such capacities. You say, 'for instance, we might turn over to them, the matter of law enforcement.' As a matter of fact, a Cherokee Indian was the first United States Marshall in this District after statehood; later he was called back into service after a white official had signally failed. ... Two Choctaws have served as Superintendents at the Five Tribes Agency. ... Here in Oklahoma, we participate in all government and civic affairs. ... In the forty counties of the Five Tribes territory, Indians are serving as judges of the courts, as treasurers, states attorneys, peace officers. They are not elected to these offices because they are Indians, but because they are believed to be capable and enjoy the respect of their fellow citizens....

You propose now to use public money to buy more land for these landless Indians. This would be a fine business for the Indian who has 'wasted his substance' but not so good for the American tax payer. Did any intelligent government thus <u>reward</u> it citizens or serfs? According to your plan, the Indian who isn't fit to own land will have two chances, while the Indian who has developed his allotment and made something of himself gets one chance. ...

So far, you have not furnished Congress with any definite information as to how many landless Indians there are, how much land you propose to buy for each, where you will buy it, or how you will manage to treat these beneficiaries alike. Indians will continue to be born landless for many years to come so it seems to many of us that if you ever start this 'endless chain' you will have the Indian out of step in the march of civilization before very long and he will be so hopelessly dependent that he will be useless to himself or society. All authorities on Indian matters have hoped to make the Indian self-supporting, self-respecting, independent. Now you come along with a 'New Deal' to reverse the general idea. Here in Oklahoma, ... we are not nearly so much interested in a 'new deal' as we are in just a plain, old-fashioned 'SQUARE DEAL.'"[31]

The Bois Forte (Nett Lake) band saw the Wheeler-Howard Act as a way to get the reservation back that they had ceded in the Nelson Act. They asked attorney Holmes of Duluth to attend a meeting and advise them on the issue. Holmes had not seen a copy of the amended bill and on May 29 wrote Collier asking for a copy.[32]

An unsigned archival document does a good job of explaining why the Dawes Act and the Nelson Act, which were most likely passed by Congress with good intentions, were a disaster for the Indians:

> "The Oto and Missouri Treaty of March 15, 1854, and the Omaha Treaty of March 16, 1854, cited herein, provided that after 'assignments' of 'permanent homes' had been made to all the Indian 'persons or families' the residue of the reservations might be sold 'for their benefit.' This was a pattern for subsequent treaties and acts of Congress; and the principle was incorporated in the General Allotment Act of 1887 [and the Nelson Act of 1889]. No provision was made for increasing needs of new 'families' founded in succeeding generations, nor for the needs of new-born children; and as more and more of the so-called 'surplus' lands have been sold the almost incredible short-sightedness of this policy has become apparent.
>
> Under this policy many millions of acres of Indian lands, now desperately needed by the increasing Indian populations because of economic pressure, have been sold; the most desirable and most desired of the Indian lands have passed from Indian ownership; and economical and profitable management and utilization of the remnants left has been rendered impossible by such selective alienation.
>
> The results of the system of allotting Indian lands in severalty did not become apparent for several years. But as the original allottees died and the lands passed to the ownership of their heirs, and this ownership became more involved by the death, in turn, of these heirs, the consequent subdivision of inherited estates into infinitesimal shares became intolerable. Indian and intermarried white owners of inherited lands could not make profitable use of their interests; and large areas of such lands were idle or leased for inadequate rentals. Demands for some relief developed both in and out of the Indian Service administration.

The act of May 27, 1902 (32 Stats. 275) authorized the sale of inherited Indian lands; and the alienation of Indian allotted land began. Indians and administration officials saw this as the easiest way to solve the problem; and no better way was offered. Indians received some immediate revenue from these sales and clamored for more. Demand was made on Congress for authority to sell allotments of living Indians, and Congress granted authority for the removal of restrictions on alienation and for the issuance of fee patents before the expiration of the trust period of twenty-five years; and the volume of alienation swelled. Today, of over 40,000,000 acres of land allotted in severalty to Indians, only approximately 17,000,000 acres remain in trust status; and of this amount, approximately 7,000,000 acres are in heirship status and potentially subject to sale."[33]

On June 6, 1934, Senator Wheeler spoke on the floor of the Senate saying, "The purposes of the bill are as follows: First, to stop the alienation, through action by the Government or the Indian, of such lands, belonging to ward Indians, as are needed for the present and future support of the Indians. The second purpose is to provide for the acquisition, through purchase, of land for Indians now landless who are anxious and fitted to make a living on such land. The third purpose of the bill is to stabilize the tribal organization of Indian tribes by vesting such tribal organizations with real, though limited, authority, and by prescribing conditions which must be met by such tribal organizations. ... As the bill now stands before the Senate the committee have given it long and careful consideration, and we feel that its enactment will be of great benefit to the Indians and in the long run will be much less costly than the present system to the Government of the United States. ... I, myself, think that this bill, as now presented, is the greatest step forward the Department has ever taken with reference to Indians."[34]

By June 6th, 1934, 92 tribes had voted on the proposed Wheeler-Howard Bill, with 74 voting in favor and 18 tribes voting against. The Minnesota tribes were listed as voting in favor at the Hayward conference; 376 from Grand Portage (Chippewa), 4,000 from White Earth, (Chippewa) and 562 from Pipestone (Sioux). Those that voted at tribal meetings; 250 from Winnibigoshish (Chippewa) and 889 from Leech Lake (Chippewa). A general council of Leech Lake, Cass Lake, Mississippi Chippewas and Winnibigoshish (Chippewa) had resulted in 259 Cass Lake votes in favor. The Red Lake Chippewa voted 1,938 votes in favor after an interview by the Superintendent with officers of the Council where they approved the bill but did not want the self-government part to apply to them. So, the total votes across the country as of June 6th was 158,279 for and 21,884 against.[35]

On June 15th Representative Howard gave a lengthy speech on the floor of the House in support of the Bill that bore his name. He concluded saying,

> "It may well be asked, What are the ultimate goals of the policy embodied in this bill? It seeks in the long run to build up Indian land holdings until there is sufficient land for all Indians who will beneficially use it. It will set up a gradual and voluntary revestment of allotted grazing and forest land, through purchase or assignment, into tribal ownership. Such ownership, combined with the consolidation of checker-boarded reservations, is an essential part of the proposed program of substituting Indian use of the land for the leasing system. It seeks to make the Indian as a group self-supporting through agriculture, livestock growing, forestry, and other rural pursuits.
>
> With a proper land system, credits, and systematic guidance, the majority of the Indians are amply capable of achieving the goal of self-support and thus save the expenditure of enormous Government appropriations and tribal capital. It seeks the functional and tribal organization of the Indians so as to make the Indians the principal agents in their own economic and racial salvation, and will progressively reduce and largely decentralize the powers of the Federal Indian Service.
>
> In carrying out this program, the Indian Service will become the adviser of the Indians rather than their ruler. The Federal Government will continue the guardianship of the Indians, but the guardianship envisioned by the new policy will constantly strengthen the Indians, rather than weakening them. This program will pave the way for a real assimilation of the Indians into the American community on the level of economic independence and political self-respect.
>
> The so-called 'assimilation' of the past has been largely the Federal abandonment of pauperized and landless Indians to make their own way, as best they might, in the white community. The Indians are now segregated far more through poverty and inferiority feeling than through any possible geographical

segregation. The program of self-support and of business and civic experience in the management of their own affairs, combined with the program of education, will permit increasing numbers of Indians to enter the white world on a footing of equal competition. There is an extraordinarily wide and sympathetic public interest in this proposed legislation. The President himself has strongly endorsed the principles of the bill and has asked for its passage in this session.

The Indians are overwhelmingly in favor of it. The responsible tribal councils representing about 155,000 Indians, after prolonged and full popular discussion of the bill, have voted in its favor; the tribal councils representing only about 17,000 Indians have voted against it.

This Congress, by adopting this bill, can make a partial restitution to the Indians for a whole century of wrongs and of broken faith, and even more important — for this bill looks not to the past but to the future — can release the creative energies of the Indians in order that they may learn to take a normal and natural place in the American community."[35]

Following the final lobbying and the conference to iron out the differences between the House and the Senate versions, the Wheeler-Howard Bill was approved on June 18, 1934 and became The Indian Reorganization Act.[36]

# CHAPTER 6

# John Collier Explains

The Indian Reorganization Act had been passed in a modified, shortened and amended version; now what does it mean? The only part that was not altered by Congress was the section that ended the allotment system of the Dawes and Nelson Acts. So, this was a very different act than the one discussed, debated and voted on by the Indian tribes across the country at the conferences held for that purpose, including the one at Hayward, Wisconsin. Unfortunately, much of the public assumed that the original version of the bill is the one that had been approved.

Commissioner Collier wrote an explanation of the newly passed bill entitled, "Facts About The New Indian Reorganization Act," and the following is his interpretation of the bill Congress had passed.

Section 1. Allotment of tribal land was ended.

Section 2. Indian lands will remain in trust unless changed by Congress, therefore no taxation of those lands. Oklahoma was exempted from this section.

Section 3. This section provides a method by which any surplus lands form the Dawes and Nelson Acts that have not been sold can be given back to the respective tribe.

Section 4. No Indian lands may be sold to anyone except an individual Indian or the Indian tribe. Oklahoma tribes and tribes on the Klamath reservation are exempt.

Section 5. Authority is given to Congress to purchase land for Indians and mandates that this land be held in trust. Congress was authorized to appropriate $2,000,000 annually for the purchase of land for landless Indians or for Indians whose holdings are too small or too poor to enable them to make a living thereon.

Section 6. This section gives the Secretary of the Interior authority to manage forests and grazing lands to sustain the forests and grazing lands for the future.

Collier wrote a lengthy explanation of the section dealing with a credit fund:

"The Act authorizes a revolving fund of $10,000,000 for financial credit to Indians.

At the present time and for many years past, only a comparatively small number of Indian land owners has actually farmed or used Indian-owned land. Most of it has been leased to white farmers and stockmen. This lease-money, with the installment payments on tribal or individual land sold to white people, has been the largest source of Indian revenue. When the installment payments ceased and the lease money, in many instances, dropped to almost nothing, poverty and distress came to thousands of Indian homes.

For fifty years a majority of the Indians have been living on per capita payments of money from the sale of their capital assets and on the small amount of rental they got from the shrinking capital that was left. They were in the position of a family of five that a long time ago received $2,000 for each member and deposited the entire $10,000 in a savings bank at 4% interest. The income from the amount of capital, $400 a year, was not enough to keep the family going, so every year the father would draw out some of the capital, $300 to $600 or more, and use it for family expenses. Now of the original $10,000 there is less than $3,000 left, and on this remaining capital the interest rate is only 1 instead of 4 percent.

To put it another way, fifty years ago an Indian family started out with fifty head of cows. In order to get by, the father sold every year not only the yearling steers but most of the young heifers as well. He did not leave enough heifers to replace the old cows as they became unproductive. Now only fifteen cows are left, and their product won't keep the family going.

That's what happened to thousands of Indian families. They leased their land and, through the years, sold some or all of it, and lived on the proceeds. And they did this, at the start, largely because they did not have the necessary capital to make a productive farm out of the raw land.

The land still owned by the Indians, and the land which will be bought for landless Indians, is of little use to them in its raw state. It must be fenced, plowed, seeded, stocked with cattle or sheep before it will support a family. This work requires plows, harrows, wire, seed, livestock, sheds, barns, homes. How are the landless Indians to obtain and pay to the Government for these things?

In order to give them a start, the Indian Reorganization Act authorizes a revolving credit fund of $10,000,000 — not appropriated as yet — from which to make loans to Indian tribal corporations which in turn will make loans to the individual members of the tribe. This fund is not large for the credit needs of a quarter million people. It will have to be administered very carefully, and the repayment of the loans must be safeguarded because, once all the money has been loaned out, the repayments will be the only source from which additional loans can be made. Within the limits of the available funds, loans can be made to individuals and groups to start and operate not only farms but all kinds of industrial enterprises, sawmills, fisheries, canneries, livestock associations, cooperative stores, etc. This credit fund is fully as important as the land-purchase fund; without the credit fund the present lease-and-lose system of land management would have to continue almost indefinitely.

When Congress authorized this credit fund, it directed that loans from the fund should be made only to Indian chartered corporations which in turn would make loans to individuals or groups. This was done so as to make the chartered corporation as well as the individual responsible for conserving the loan fund. As Congress did not extend to the Oklahoma tribe the right to organize chartered corporations, none of the Oklahoma Indians can have the benefit of this fund until the law is changed. Of course only tribes which vote for the acceptance of the Act and decide to incorporate will have the privilege of participating in the loan fund."

Collier then proceeded to explain how tribal incorporation (Section 17) would be accomplished.

"The section empowering the tribes to adopt a constitution gives them the right to run their own affairs about in the same way that a village or municipality operates. Section 17, on the other hand, gives the tribes additional authority to organize for business purposes to buy land, receive credit funds, sue and be sued, except that the Indian tribal corporation will have their property protected against taxation, seizure, attachment, etc., and cannot sell or mortgage any of the land within the reservation.

These tribal corporations also offer the key to the solution of the heirship problem on allotted reservations. They are expressly authorized to purchase restricted Indian lands, more especially the numerous parcels of heirship land which cannot be partitioned, and give the owners in return certificates of interest in tribal property. If, for instance, a young Indian owned small shares in five or six different pieces of land scattered all over the reservation, he and the other heirs could sell these lands to the tribal corporation, receive certificates of interest for them, and apply these certificates on single pieces of tribal land big enough to support a family, the tribal corporation loaning the young man enough money to build a modest house, buy stock, seed and implements and start in supporting his family on a place of his own. The title to this consolidated piece of heirship land would remain in the tribal corporation, but the young man would improve and use it wholly for himself and leave the use of the land and the improvements to his children just as though he had complete title to it. But after his death the land could not be split up into small unusable pieces.

The tribal corporation, not the individual members of the tribe, would do business with the Government, handle the part of the $10,000,000 revolving loan fund allocated to the tribe, loan it to the members and assume the responsibility for repayment of the revolving fund. If groups of members wanted to start livestock associations, operate their farm land in common, start a cooperative store or engage in other lines of business, they would apply to the tribal corporation for the necessary loans.

To prevent ill-considered action, the charter of incorporation cannot be granted until one third of the members of a tribe petition for it and it is ratified by a majority vote of all adult Indians living on the reservation. The Indians themselves will have to ask for it; after they have asked for it, they will have to determine through their properly elected officials what they want in the charter. When the charter has been drawn with the assistance of the Commissioner and his staff, then the tribe has to vote on its ratification. Once the charter has been issued and accepted, it cannot be cancelled or altered by the Secretary or any other Administrative official, nor can it be surrendered by the tribe. Only Congress can revoke it.

To provide aid and assistance to the various tribes which want to organize, Congress authorized an appropriation up to $250,000 a year. When Congress makes such an appropriation, the money can be used to pay the costs of the elections that must be held, to pay the expenses of tribal delegates and officials engaged in drafting the constitution, the by-laws and the charters, to pay the salary and expenses of experts hired to assist the tribes in the organization work, to cover the cost of holding meetings, to pay printing bills and similar items.

This organizing appropriation will, of course, be available to only those tribes which decide to accept the benefits of the Act and assume the duties and responsibilities that go with the benefits."

In regard to Section 11 which deals with education for Indians Collier wrote, "One of the very important provisions of the Act is Section 11 which authorizes an annual appropriation of $250,000 for reimbursable loans to enable young Indians of both sexes to obtain a higher vocational or technical education. Under this section it will be possible to send larger numbers of promising young Indians to schools of forestry, agriculture, business administration, medicine, nursing, engineering etc., so as to fit them to do either the technical work of the Indian Service or to establish themselves professionally in the white world."

And in regard to involving more Indians in Indian Service of the Government he wrote:

"Another important provision of the Act authorizes the Secretary to establish a special Indian civil service through which positions in the Indian Service as they become vacant through death, resignation, retirement etc., would be gradually thrown open to qualified Indians who have the character and experience necessary to do the work, but who have not gone to high school and college and who, therefore, cannot now qualify for such positions under the general civil service laws. The Secretary is directed to set up special standards for Indians who want to enter the Service; he is directed to state the age limits for any of the positions, to state that only healthy, able-bodied Indians can be hired for the various jobs, that they must be of good moral character not given to drinking, loafing, cheating and lieing [sic], that they must have certain experience, education and proven ability to be appointed to the higher positions.

This section does not mean that any Indian can get a Government job just because he is an Indian, or that he can loaf on the job he already has. Such a result would be disastrous to the Indian Service and unfair to the Indians as a whole. Like any white person, an Indian is hired to do certain work for which the Government pays him. To hold his job he must work faithfully, and in fact he should work harder and more tirelessly than white employees because he is rendering service to his own people. The Indian employee will be a failure if his work is merely a job to him or her. Congress let down the civil service bars to <u>improve</u> the service rendered the Indians through the employment of more Indians; unless the old and new Indian employees thoroughly understand this intention and give to their own people the best that is in them, the Indian civil service provision of the Act will be a failure."

Section 13 highlights the exemptions from the Act as it relates to the tribes in Oklahoma, on the Klamath reservation and in Alaska.

Collier explained that,

"All of the tribes, except those in Oklahoma and Alaska, must first state through their ballots whether they want to accept or reject the application of the Act to their reservation.

Section 18 directs the Secretary of the interior to call an election on every reservation to have the residents decide acceptance or rejection. The election must be by secret ballot. Every member of a recognized tribe, 21 years old or older, is entitled to vote at this election. But the descendants, the children and grandchildren, if non-members can vote at this election only if they were actually living on the reservation on June 1, 1934. If a majority of all these entitled to vote cast their ballot against acceptance of the Act, it will not apply to that reservation.

This means, of course, that those who reject the Act must reject all of it. If they do this, they remain exactly as before the passage and approval of the Act. The tribe that rejects the Act does not have the trust period automatically extended; the tribe does not share in the land-purchase fund; its members cannot receive the new educational loans; they cannot receive exemption from the general civil service law; they cannot participate in the ten-million-dollar credit fund; they cannot incorporate under the terms of the Act; the Government can continue to do as it pleases with their tribal assets; they cannot share in the tribal-organization fund."

Rejection of the Act, however, will not mean abandonment of the tribe by the Government. Its members will continue to be Federal wards and the tribe will continue to receive its share of the appropriations and services open to the Indian race as a whole. There cannot be and will not be any discrimination against a tribe which in the exercise of its best judgment declines to accept the Act. It will merely drift to the rear of the great advance open to the Indian race. It will stand still and will probably continue to lose its lands while those who accept the Act, its benefits and responsibilities can preserve and increase their lands and will move forward. [1]

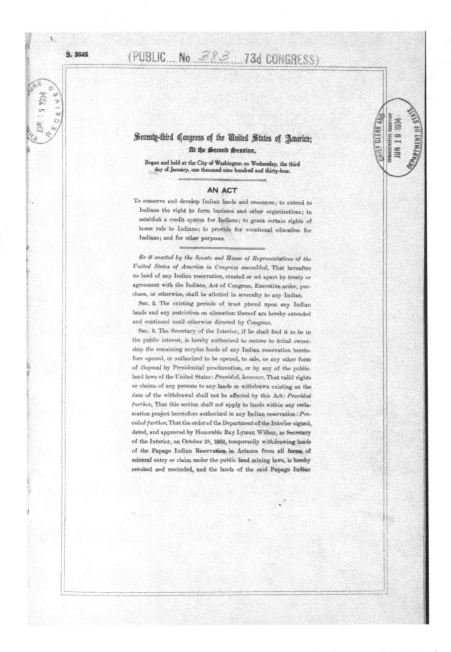

In another document authored by Commissioner Collier entitled, "Analysis and Explanation of The Wheeler-Howard Act," he explains further:

**"Section 1 — Prohibition against future allotment.**

This section provides that no Indian land which is now unallotted shall hereafter be allotted. The section does not disturb or affect in any way existing Indian allotments. Neither does it deprive Indians of the right to secure 'fourth section allotments' upon the public domain. The purpose of this section is simply to preserve tribal lands for the use of the Indian tribes and to prevent these lands from being broken up and turned over to individual Indians who may sell the land, or lose it in other ways, to non-Indians.

**Section 2 — Continuance of restrictions on alienation.**

This section provides that land which is now held by Indians under trust patents or under any restriction on alienation shall continue to be held in that manner, unless Congress enacts legislation to the contrary. This section changes all existing laws which provide that the trust period on Indian lands or other restrictions on alienation shall, regardless of the consent of the Indians, expire upon a definite date, usually 25 years after the original allotment. This section does not change existing laws or regulations regarding Indian applications for fee patents. The policy of issuing such fee patents in exceptional cases, laid down in Order 402, will continue in force." Indians of Oklahoma are exempt from this section.

**Section 3 — Restoration of surplus lands.**

This section gives the Secretary the right to turn back to an Indian tribe any surplus lands of the reservation that have not yet been sold or otherwise disposed of under existing laws. [Dawes and Nelson Acts]

The surplus lands affected by this section are lands not allotted to Indians, which have been opened for sale or entry as public domain lands. This section does not disturb the rights of those Indians or whites who have already acquired or entered upon such lands. Furthermore, this section does not apply to any 'Reclamation Project' heretofore authorized. A Reclamation Project, under this section, is an area of land which has been selected from a reservation, improved by irrigation, and then opened for settlement to the general public, subject to assessments upon each irrigable acre for the cost of developing the land." Lands of the Papago Indians were to be handled differently.

### Section 4 — Transfer of restricted land.

This section sets forth the three permissible ways in which restricted Indian lands may be transferred and prohibits any transfer of such lands except as so authorized.

First, restricted land may be transferred by an Indian owner, with the approval of the Secretary, to an Indian tribe or corporation, by sale or by will or in any other way.

Second, restricted Indian land may be inherited by members of an Indian tribe or corporation or any other heirs, Indian or non-Indian, of the deceased. Any will disposing of restricted allotted lands must be approved by the Secretary of the Interior, as is the case at present. The Secretary may approve such will only if the beneficiaries are either members of the same tribe or corporation as the deceased or heirs of such deceased. In the absence of a will, restricted allotted lands will descend, as is now the case, in accordance with the State laws in force at the time. On those unallotted reservations where rights of occupancy to tribal land are now inherited by tribal custom or department regulation, this section does not change the existing situation.

Third, restricted Indian lands may, with the approval of the Secretary of the Interior, be exchanged for other lands of equal value, whether such lands are owned by Indians or by non-Indians. Title to the lands thus acquired through exchange is to be taken in the name of the United States in trust for an Indian tribe or for individual Indians, and such land will be exempt from State and local taxation. ... Such exchanges may be authorized only when they do not interfere with the policy of consolidating suitable areas of land under Indian ownership. Thus an Indian whose land is surrounded by other Indian's lands will not be allowed to exchange lands with a non-Indian.

The foregoing statement of the methods by which restricted Indian land may be transferred has no application to unrestricted land owned by individual Indians in fee.

This section applies to heirship lands, as well as to lands owned by living allottees. Under the provision of this section, heirship lands which are not partitioned among the heirs of the deceased can be sold only to the local Indian tribe or corporation.

Under this section, the same restrictions that apply to the transfer of restricted Indian lands are applied to the transfer of shares in the assets of any Indian tribe or corporation, whenever such shares shall be issued by any organized tribe or corporation.

This section does not apply to the Indians of Oklahoma or to the Klamath Indians."

### Section 5. Land acquisition.

This section authorizes the Secretary of the Interior to acquire lands for Indians in need. Under this section, the Secretary may acquire lands, water rights, or simply surface rights to lands. He may acquire lands within or without existing reservations. He may acquire white owned or Indian owned lands, fee patented or restricted lands, lands of living Indians or lands in heirship status.

It is the primary purpose of the Interior Department, under the authority granted by this section, to purchase white-owned lands interspersed in Indian reservations or adjacent to such reservations, so as to block out suitable grazing, timber, or farm areas for Indian use. Such lands will be acquired through outright purchase, whenever Federal appropriations shall be made available, and also by exchange, wherever a non-Indian, who owns land within an area that is predominately Indian-owned, is willing to exchange such land for land of equal value that is now occupied by an Indian, who would prefer to move into the area that is being consolidated under Indian ownership.

A second purpose of the Department under this bill will be to acquire lands outside of existing Indian reservations, upon which Indians who are now landless, and are not affiliated with any tribe that still has land, may settle.

A proviso to the second paragraph of this section excludes the Navajo Indians of Arizona and New Mexico from the benefits of any money that may be appropriated in the future under this section, if the two Navajo boundary bills become law. The Arizona bill has already been enacted. The New Mexico bill has not yet been enacted. Until the latter bill is enacted, the proviso against land purchases for Navajo Indians is without force.

This section authorizes the appropriation of not to exceed two million dollars each year for the purchase of lands. This Act, however, does not actually appropriate any money. Appropriation of Federal funds are customarily made by a 'general appropriations bill,' which covers all the various Government services. Such a bill will be passed at the next session of Congress, which begins in January, 1935.

Title to lands acquired under this Act will be taken in the name of the United States, and held in trust either for an Indian tribe or for individual Indians. It will be the policy of the Interior Department to hold such title in trust for Indian tribes, and to assign individuals possessory rights in such lands as long as the lands are actually occupied and improved. Where an Indian surrenders land which he now owns, in exchange for white owned land, such white owned land may be taken by the United States in trust for the individual Indian who has made the exchange.

### Section 7. Proclamation of Reservations.

"Under this section, land acquired by the Secretary of the Interior for the use of Indians may be added to an existing reservation or else set apart as a new Indian reservation. If added to an existing reservation, the land is to be used for the benefit of Indians entitled to reside on that reservation. If set aside as a new reservation, such land will be open to settlement by landless Indians." This section does not apply to Oklahoma Indians.

### Section 8. Exemption of public domain lands.

This section provides that Indian holdings of allotments or homesteads upon the public domain shall not be affected by this Act, unless they fall within the boundaries of some Indian reservation, now existing or established hereafter.

### Section 12. Indian preference in employment.

This section requires that qualified Indians are to have preference in appointments to vacancies in existing positions in the Indian Service as vacancies occur. It directs the Secretary of the Interior, without regard to Civil Service regulations, to establish standards of eligibility for Indians for all positions maintained now and hereafter by the Indian Office. This calls for a review and revision of the requirements for present positions, and also for advance planning for positions which may hereafter develop in connection with local self-government by Indian tribal organizations.

### Section 15. Claims, suits and judgments.

This section provides that no claims or suits of Indian tribes against the United States shall be in any way impaired or prejudiced by anything in this Act. It also provides that Federal expenditures made under this Act shall not be deducted from any future judgment which any Indian tribe may secure against the United States on any claim.

### Section 16. Tribal organization.

Under this section, any Indian tribe that so desires may organize and establish a constitution and by-laws for the management of its own local affairs.

Such constitution and by-laws become effective when ratified by a majority of all the adult members of the tribe, or the adult Indians residing on the reservation, at a special election. It will be the duty of the Secretary of the Interior to call such a special election when any responsible group of Indians has prepared and submitted to him a proposed constitution and by-laws which do not violate any Federal Law, and are fair to all the Indians concerned. When such a special election has been called, all Indians who are members of the tribe, or residents on the reservation if the constitution is proposed for the entire reservation, will be entitled to vote upon the acceptance of the constitution. Such constitution can be adopted only by a majority of all such Indians (not merely a majority of those voting). If a tribe or reservation adopts the constitution and by-laws in this manner, such constitution and by-laws may thereafter be amended or entirely revoked only by the same process.

The powers which may be exercised by an Indian tribe or tribal council include all powers which may be exercised by such tribe or tribal council at the present time, and also include the right to employ legal counsel, (subject to the approval of the

Secretary of the Interior with respect to the choice of counsel and the fixing of fees), the right to exercise a veto power over any disposition of tribal funds or other assets, the right to negotiate with Federal, State and local governments, and the right to be advised of all appropriation estimates affecting the tribe, before such estimates are submitted to the Bureau of Budget and Congress.

The following Indian groups are entitled to take advantage of this section: Any Indian tribe, band, or pueblo in the United States (outside of Oklahoma) or Alaska, and also any group of Indians who reside on the same reservation, whether they are members of the same tribe or not.

### Section 17. Tribal Incorporation.

This section authorizes any Indian tribe (outside of Oklahoma) to obtain a charter of incorporation, issued by the Secretary of the Interior. A petition for such a charter should be signed by one-third of the adult Indians of the tribe or reservation for which a charter is sought. Such a charter of incorporation becomes effective when ratified by a majority vote of the adult Indians living on the reservation. When once ratified, such a charter may not be revoked by the Secretary of the Interior. Only future legislation of Congress can revoke such a charter.

A charter of incorporation may convey to any tribe the right to engage in business, to obtain loans from the Indian Loan Fund authorized by Section 10 of this Act, to acquire property, to issue certificates of corporate interest to the members of the corporation who transfer land to the corporation, and to do all other incidental things necessary to the conduct of corporate business. Among these incidental powers may be mentioned the power to elect or appoint officers and employees of the corporation, to promulgate and amend by-laws, to pay out dividends, etc. No Indian corporation, however, may sell or mortgage any land at all within the reservation nor may it lease such land for a period exceeding ten years.

Any tribe which desires a corporate charter may request the assistance of officials of the Interior Department in preparing such a charter, or may, if it so chooses, consult private attorneys or advisers in the preparation of such a charter.

### Section 18. Referendum on application of Act.

This section provides that the Indians of any reservation may, by a vote of a majority of the adult Indians on the reservation, exclude themselves from the operation of the entire Act. It is the duty of the Secretary of the Interior to call a referendum election for this purpose upon each reservation, at some time before June 18, 1935. Such an election must be held by secret ballot, and 30 days' notice of the election must be given to the Indians of the reservation.

### Section 19. Definitions.

This section defines certain terms, namely, 'Indian', 'tribe', and 'adult', as these terms are used in various provisions of the Act.

The term 'Indian' is to be construed as including three classes of persons:

(a) All persons of Indian descent who are members of a recognized tribe, whether or not residing on an Indian reservation and regardless of the degree of blood.

(b) All persons who are descendants of any such members of recognized Indian tribes and were residing within an Indian reservation on June 1, 1934, regardless of degree of blood.

(c) Persons of one-half or more Indian blood, whether or not affiliated with any recognized tribe, and whether or not they have ever resided on an Indian reservation.

This section further provides that Eskimos and other aboriginal people of Alaska may be considered Indians, under those provisions of the Act which apply to Alaska.

The term 'tribe' is defined to include any Indian tribe, organized band, or pueblo, and also to include any group of Indians residing on a single reservation, whether or not they have been previously organized as a single tribe. Wherever practicable, the Interior Department will treat the Indians of a single reservation as a single tribe.

This section finally specifies that the term 'adult' is used to refer to persons who have reached the age of 21 years."[2]

# CHAPTER 7

# Implementation and Sidetracks

The Indian Reorganization Act had been passed, but that did not mean that all of the Indians were happy. On August 27th and 28th, 1934, a group of Indians from California, Oklahoma, Arizona and New Mexico met in Gallup, New Mexico. At that meeting the American Indian Federation was organized with Joseph Bruner of Oklahoma as its president and J.C. Morgan, a member of the Navajo Tribal Council as vice-president. Adam Castillo, who was head of the Mission Indians of California, was chosen as the first district representative, and it was the publication of the Mission Indians of California that became the official publication of the new organization.[1]

The formation of the American Indian Federation set off a war of words objecting to what the Federation was espousing. J.C. Morgan apparently wrote an article in "The Christian Century" to which Mrs. D. B. Chillers, an Oklahoma Indian, wrote a lengthy letter of rebuttal.[2] Commissioner Collier also joined in supporting his views on the Navajo religious practices.[3]

Joseph Bruner and the American Indian Federation were not to be silenced. On December 21st, 1934 they sent off a letter to President Roosevelt and Congress writing in part,

> "Having been granted un-qualified American citizenship in 1924, we beg to emphasize that we should be considered and treated in accordance with that part of the immortal Declaration of Independence reading: 'We hold these truths to be self-evident, that all men are created equal; that they are endowed by their Creator with certain inalienable rights; that among these are life, liberty and the pursuit of happiness.' ... From 1871 until our grant of citizenship in 1924, the American Indian was held as a political prisoner, or, as the United States Supreme Court has defined the status, as 'political wards' — his person under the immediate jurisdiction of the Bureau of Indian Affairs, and subject in all personal relations to the arbitrary rules and regulations of said Bureau. ... Until the present administration, no official of said Bureau has ever publicly questioned our rights as American citizens: but, now, Commissioner Collier has publicly repudiated the Act of Congress in granting us citizenship."

Their letter quotes Collier from a May 6, 1934, issue of the *New York Times*; "The Indians are citizens of the United States, made so by a special act of Congress passed in 1924, as a gesture for their services to the Nation in the World's War. Notwithstanding, Indians having the status of Government wards today, that is, two-thirds of the total population — cannot make contracts, cannot borrow money, etc. without the permission from a Special government bureau, the office of Indian Affairs." They continue by quoting Ward Shepard, a Bureau of Indian Affairs official from the *New York Herald-Tribune* issue of November 3, 1934; "The Government has given up trying to make the Red Man into a 'White Man' and has decided that his best future lies in being allowed to 'be himself.' ... to allow him to live his own life in his own way — at the same time giving him modern sanitation and other beneficial features of White Civilization."

Quoting from the same article:

> "The efforts to civilize the Indian according to White stan-
> dards was doomed to failure from the start because it was an
> attempt to transplant a people still in the Stone Age into the
> high powered democracy of Modern America." To this they
> responded in writing: "To the foregoing we state as fact: that
> under Commissioner Collier, the Indians have been denied free-
> dom of speech and free assembly, Indians opposing the policy of
> the Bureau have been subject to vindictive treatment; the per-
> sonal rights of the Indian as guaranteed to American citizens
> under our Constitution have been completely ignored, and, in
> fact, by Commissioner Collier denied to exist; ... and to fully
> establish the intent of the present Commissioner to segregate
> the Indian, keep him an Indian, not an American citizen; to
> cut him off from the greatest education for citizenry, namely,
> personal contact with American life — we cite the Bill which
> the Bureau forced through at the very close of the last session of
> Congress. ...
>
> "Approved," [they write] "means <u>consent</u>, for the first time
> in history, by the Indian Tribes to Bureau jurisdiction and rule;
> this means the limitation of personal rights under citizenship. ..."

Continuing, they call for the removal of Commissioner John Collier. They offer for consideration by Congress the following three guidelines aimed at restoring the "personal rights now due the American Indian as an American Citizen."

"1.  Free the Indian at once from Bureau wardship of his person.

2.  Each State through its already established channels under which and in the same manner they now treat their other citizens, but the Indians — to educate, to guard health, to police and to open all its established

Courts to the Indian. Congressional appropriations from Indian funds where treaties provide, or from taxes now voted annually to the Bureau (and more if needed) to go to the State to cover all cost of foregoing. In cases of emergency the Red Cross should be given all power, free from Bureau Control, to immediately take charge of the Indian health and life situation.

3. Begin at once with competent heads to untangle the Indian property-mess existing in the Bureau with the view of creating, legally, active trustee-ships, subject to court review, of this property, including tribal funds; preferably creating a separate trust for each reservation and tribal fund. These trusts should be created on same fundamental legal basis as other innumerable trusts which now hold property all over the United States. At no time, of course during the above program, is the Indian to be inequitably disturbed in the rights, occupancy and use of any Indian property now by him possessed."[4]

President Roosevelt referred the letter from the Federation to Secretary Ickes for an answer. Ickes responded in part writing,

"In this Memorial you make a series of statements which have no foundation in fact. ... you aver that 'under Commissioner Collier the Indians have been denied freedom of speech and free assembly, ... the personal rights of the Indians as guaranteed to American citizens under the Constitution have been completely ignored, and, in fact, by Commissioner Collier denied to exist.' The basis of your complaint seems to be the continued wardship of the Indians. In this administration continued efforts have been made to relax and liberalize the guardianship and to diminish the control which, under the law, the Office of Indian Affairs exercises over the person and property of Indians having the status of wards.

Apparently you believe that these efforts are insincere and ineffective. ... I am wondering if it has ever occurred to you that the power to accept or reject an act of Congress as bestowed on the Indian by Section 18 of the Indian Reorganization Act was one of the most extraordinary privileges ever granted any part of the American people. ... In other words, the Indians themselves were given by Congress the privilege to decide their own legislative status, a privilege never accorded to any other fraction of the population."[(5)]

*Rep. John R. Murdock from Arizona*

It seems obvious from today's point in history that the Federation's understanding of the Act was fairly good, and perhaps they did have some foundation in fact. The fact that they could reject the Act was not completely sincere because of the perks that were included for those who accepted it.

The American Indian Federation had friends on the Navajo reservation as evidenced by a letter written to Representative Murdock on April 10, 1935 with the Federation being copied. This letter was reportedly signed by many Navajos and included statements like,

"… Under Commissioner Collier's rule and order we sold more than half of our sheep. We cannot afford to sell any more. If we do, our children will die of hunger. We raise no corn and other stuff because our land is without water. … We do not believe Commissioner Collier is our friend, otherwise he wouldn't make us go hungry … We ask our friends in Congress to remember that we do not believe Mr. Collier knows much about Indians therefore he should be removed from office. … We hold conference here today to write this letter to you."[(6)]

At the sparsely attended 1936 convention of the American Indian Federation, held in Salt Lake City on July 24, 1936, at least in the opinion of one of the attendees, the organization focused hardly at all on Indian affairs, but was almost entirely focused on the dangers of Communism. Joseph Bruner, Chairman of the organization, set the tone with his opening address during which he said, "Communism is destructive. It would mean the destruction of all that Americans hold sacred — sanctity of the home, private property, free speech, free press and the Christian form of government. The aim of the Communist party, directed by Stalin from Moscow, is to establish communism by means of a world-wide class revolution. The New Deal for the Indian," he said, "is in line with that program.

To allow anyone who is even remotely identified with that program to continue in public office is a very real danger to all Americans."[7] They were using the Communist label to try to get rid of John Collier as Commissioner of Indian Affairs.

At their 1938 convention held in Tulsa, Oklahoma, they passed a resolution to be presented to all of Congress, asking Congress in part, to "stop introducing any Bills into Congress pertaining to Indian Affairs except such Bills as shall be specifically requested by the Indians themselves."[8]

At its founding the American Indian Federation espoused some well-founded principles. And while it was a thorn in the side of the Interior Department, John Collier and even President Roosevelt, it was of little lasting importance because of their focus at times on Communism. While the concepts of communalism, communism and socialism have things in common, they are not the same. John Collier was influenced by his childhood to explore these concepts, and they continued to creep into his adulthood, and so it is easy to see how his adversaries could focus on the fringe of the new Indian program he was designing.

On October 25, 1934, Solicitor Nathan Margold issued an opinion that had been requested of him as to "what powers may be secured to an Indian tribe and incorporated in its constitution and bylaws by virtue of the following phrase, contained in the Wheeler-Howard Act (Public No. 383, 73d Congress): 'In addition to all powers vested in any Indian tribe or tribal council by existing law, the constitution adopted by said tribe shall also vest ....'" The lengthy opinion written by Solicitor Margold can be found in the Appendix.[9]

In February 1935, Solicitor Margold was asked to issue an opinion on the vote to accept or reject the Indian Reorganization Act by a Tribe. Following a lengthy discussion, he wrote,

> "I am, therefore, of the opinion that the Wheeler Howard Act continues to apply to those reservations wherein less than a majority of the adult Indians have voted to reject the act. Nothing in this opinion, however, is intended to modify the previous ruling of this Department ... that under certain circumstances such a reservation may have a new opportunity to vote upon the rejection of the act."[10]

Attorney General Homer Cummings agreed with the opinion of Solicitor Margold but suggested another issue that needed resolution. "The sentence also presents another probable ambiguity. Your Solicitor apparently assumes that the statute applied to particular reservations until and unless rejected by a majority

**Homer Cummings**
*HARRIS & EWIING PHOTO PORTRAIT (1920)*

of the adult Indians thereon. On the other hand, it has been suggested that the statute was not intended to be applied to any Indian reservation until approved by a majority of the Indians concerned. ..."[11]

On March 6, 1935, Commissioner Collier sent a circular to those Indian tribes that had expressed an interest in drawing up plans for tribal organization under the new Indian Reorganization Act, even though no funds had yet been appropriated by Congress for that purpose. But Collier suggested that tribes might want to begin working on a plan for organization. "It is important," he wrote, "that every Indian on the reservation who wants to help plan the future of the tribe should have the opportunity to work with some committee." He wrote that it was not necessary to put their proposed constitution and bylaws in legal form but just to note what they wanted to live under. He made a rather revealing comment when he wrote, "On most reservations some of the older Indians will be able to give valuable help in explaining how the tribe dealt with basic social problems before the tribal government was broken or curtailed by the white man."

Collier continued, "When the final recommendations of the tribe are submitted to the Secretary of the Interior, a constitution and by-laws will be drafted in proper legal language on the basis of these recommendations, so far as they are consistent with justice and do not conflict with existing laws."

When the final documents are approved, he wrote, "...the Secretary of the Interior will call an election for the purpose of voting upon the constitution and by-laws ...." If it is approved by the voters, he wrote, "...it will be submitted for the approval of the Secretary of the Interior. If he approves it, it will have the force of law and will supersede all conflicting regulations of the Indian Office."

Thereafter, he wrote, it "will not be subject to change except by the Indians and the Secretary, concurring together, or by Congress. At the time of the first election, if one-third of the adult members of the tribe have petitioned for a charter of incorporation, the Secretary may submit for the acceptance or rejection of the tribe such a charter. This charter will not upset any of the provisions of the constitution. Rather it will strengthen these provisions by recognizing the tribe as a person in the eyes of the law, with all the ordinary rights of a private person to manage his own property, to engage in business," etc. The charter, he explained, would be effective only after ratification by a majority of the adult Indians of the tribe or reservation.[12]

In Chapter 4, I wrote about the mystic side of John Collier and his tendency to wander into the abstract. I quote from an article in the April 20, 1935, issue of the "Harlows Weekly" written by John Collier following a trip into the Everglades to visit a Seminole camp. "Not many words were exchanged, for the medicine-men and clan-leaders were going to meet us formally the ensuing day. What communicated far more was the handclasp of those long delicate dark hands — electrical hands, vibrant with a heatless fire, hands of women and men deeply evolved as living spirits and yet faithfully animal — animal, and possessed of the long-lost unrecoverable wilderness heritage we grown up white men cannot have for our own. We adult whites can watch as on another planet's shore the earthfire flush and wane, build and fade through sky, through prairie and marsh and jungle-trees and through the wild creatures (whose sensitiveness so far exceeds our own) and these wild men (whose gentleness exceeds our own)." This was John Collier, an anthropologist with a mystical side.[13]

While much of the rest of the country's tribes were starting to take advantage of the Indian Reorganization Act, Oklahoma, which had been exempted because of opposition from some residents, and Alaska, which had a different set of circumstances, were working on legislation. Alaska was brought under the Indian Reorganization Act by the amendment passed May 1, 1936, a copy of which may be found in the appendix of this book. Legislation called the Thomas-Rogers Act became law on June 26, 1936, known as the Oklahoma Indian Welfare Act. That act brought the Indian tribes in Oklahoma, except for exempted Osage County, in large part under the Indian Reorganization Act. The Oklahoma Indian Welfare Act can also be found in the appendix of this book.

During the promotional phase of the Wheeler Howard Act you will recall that the tribes were assured that if they were not convinced that the Act would be good for them, they were free to reject it, and the impression given them was that there would be no pressure placed on them to accept it. Well, the Navajo Tribe did just that — reject it. In a letter from Commissioner Collier to the Superintendent of the Central Navajo Agency in Gallup, New Mexico, he wrote, "The tribe, although by a narrow majority, has voted not to accept the Indian Reorganization Act. ... The tribe's decision is, for the present, a final one. To change the result, the tribe must go to Congress for an Act permitting a new election to be held."

And then in opposition to the assurance that the tribe was free to reject the Act, he put the pressure on:

> "… by rejecting the Indian Reorganization Act it has left itself exposed to the danger and actual, though not immediate, possibility of losing its land and its other resources.
>
> On a per capita basis, the Navajo Tribe, had it adopted the Act, would have been entitled to $993,950 in grants and loans during the fiscal year beginning July 1. That fund has now been rejected by the tribe.
>
> The Tribe's share, on a per capita basis, in the organization fund of the Indian Reorganization Act would have been $37,700 in the year ahead, but that money has been rejected by the tribe.
>
> The Tribe's share in the land-purchase fund for the year ahead would have been $259,200, on a per capita basis. That money has been rejected by the Tribe.
>
> The Tribe's share in the student-loan fund for the year ahead would have been $49,050. That money has been rejected by the tribe ….
>
> It will be a great achievement if the tribe proves able, under all the physical handicaps that exist, to work out its destiny in a happy way during the next years. Through rejecting the Reorganization Act, the tribe has made its task indefinitely harder. …"[14]

In a letter from Superintendent Faris to Commissioner Collier it would appear that even in 1935 there was fraud at the polling place. Farris discovered that at least three census numbers had voted twice. In another case there was one vote each cast by Hohtolee Jim, Jim Hohtolee and Jim Hartole. Coincidence? Commissioner Collier replied in part, "It does not appear that there was any fraud at the polls and it probably would require some argument to convince the Indian Committees that an election in the absence of fraud should be held over again instantly."

And then Collier made a very disappointing statement for a government official, writing, "True, there was gross misrepresentation in the Navajo language to non-English-speaking Navajos. True, they voted under the misleading of these falsehoods. But in white elections falsehoods are told and some voters believe them."[15]

In a letter to Representative Duffy Commissioner Collier wrote, "The Navajos voted themselves out of the Indian Reorganization Act ... The result was governed by statements, totally false, which had been spread by word of mouth among non-English speaking Indians by men connected with or inspired by Bruner and Morgan. [American Indian Federation] The particular falsehoods were to the effect that if the tribe adopted the Act, its goats and sheep would be confiscated, whereas if they rejected the Act, no further stock reduction in the interests of soil conservation would be necessary.

> "It hardly can be called a 'triumph of Christianity over paganism' that these falsehoods were told to the Indians by certain missionaries, a minority of the missionary body on the Reservation. On the contrary, these missionaries have given to the Christian cause a serious setback among the Navajos."[(16)]

Before two years had elapsed, some in Congress were having second thoughts about what they had done by passing the Indian Reorganization Act. One of those was Senator Wheeler — the same Senator Wheeler whose name as a sponsor was on the Wheeler-Howard Bill that became the Indian Reorganization Act upon passage. Senate Bill 1736, known as the Wheeler-Frazier Bill, was introduced in the Senate on March 1, 1937, by Burton K. Wheeler and Lynn J. Frazier in an effort to repeal the Indian Reorganization Act. The primary reason for Senator Wheeler changing his mind was probably that he thought the Indians were being given powers, by approval of the constitutions that tribes submitted, that had been stricken from the Wheeler-Howard bill before it was passed.

Remember that the original bill had been 48 pages long (in one communication Collier says it was 52 pages long ??) and the final version was but 10 pages long. If one reads the opinion on the powers of Indian tribes written by Solicitor Margold (included in the appendix of this book) one can understand why Senator Wheeler had changed his mind. Nearly the only power remaining to the United States was that of paying the bills. Yes, the Department of the Interior had the final say, but that was pretty much a rubber stamp process. Secondarily, Indians who were under the Act were treated as a separate class of people on reemphasized reservations instead of being merged into the general population, as had been the previous intent. Thirdly, Indians want the educational advantages afforded to white people. And lastly, that some of the Blackfeet Indians of Montana were unhappy with the Act and there were charges that Indians who had not adopted the Act were being discriminated against. Bills had also been introduced in Congress by James E. Murray of Montana, Dennis Chavez of New Mexico, Pat McCarren of Nevada, Usher L. Burdick of North Dakota, John Steven McGroarty of California and Thomas O'Malley of Wisconsin with the intent of exempting certain Indians or changing certain provisions in the Act. The American Indian Federation was quick to endorse the bill which would repeal the Indian Reorganization Act and Commissioner Collier was ready to lobby against its passage.[17] Obviously the repeal bill died in the Senate.

On August 17, 1940, a circular was sent to Indian tribes apprising them of a law Congress had passed on July 8, 1940, which abolished the old Indian custom adoption. The law provided that no adoption will be recognized for the purpose of inheritance, unless it shall have been:

1.  By a judgment or decree of a State Court.

2.  By judgment or decree of an Indian court.

3.  By a written adoption approved by the superintendent of the agency having jurisdiction over the tribe of which either the adopted child or the adoptive parent is a member, duly recorded in a book kept by the superintendent for that purpose.

4.  By adoption in accordance with the procedure established by the tribal authority, recognized by the Department of the Interior, of the tribe either of the adopted child or the adoptive parent, and duly recorded in a book kept by the tribe for that purpose.

5.  If the adoption has been recognized by the Department of the Interior prior to January 8, 1941, or in the distribution of the estate of an Indian who died prior to that date; provided, that an adoption by Indian custom made prior to January 8, 1941, may be made valid by recordation with the superintendent if both the adopted child and the adoptive parent are still living, if the adoptive parent requests that the adoption be recorded, and if the adopted child is an adult and makes a request or the superintendent on behalf of a minor child approves the recordation.

This Act did not apply to Indians of the Five Civilized Tribes or the Osage Tribe of Oklahoma or to the distribution of estates of Indians who had died prior to January 8, 1941.[18]

A memorandum was sent to the Indian tribes by Superintendent Scott on October 4, 1940, informing them that on October 16, 1940, the War Department would start registering males between the ages of 21 and 36 for the draft under the Conscription Act, and although non-citizen Indians had been exempt in the past, all Indians were made citizens on June 2, 1924, and so all Indians of the designated age group are by law required to register for the draft.[19]

Since the Hatch Act had been passed by Congress in 1939, another memorandum was circulated by the Consolidated Chippewa Agency giving guidelines for Government employees under that Act. Government employees were warned that it is unlawful for them to 1) take an active part in a political campaign, 2) to solicit or receive campaign funds from another Federal employee or official or for anyone to solicit politically in any Federal building and 3) for anyone to solicit or receive campaign funds from a Federal employee who receives his salary from an appropriation provided for in the Emergency Relief Act. The memo listed as things that are lawful; 1) to make a voluntary contribution to any political party but cannot be forced to make a contribution and must not be discriminated against for not doing so, 2) to put a political picture in the window of his home, 3) to wear a political badge or button, and 3) to put a political sticker on his private automobile.[20]

By November of 1941, John Collier and the Office of Indian Affairs were embarking on an anthropologic study of the Indian tribes with the objective of determining the extent to which Indian autonomy in the United States had been affected by the many years of Federal rule. The study was being organized in cooperation with the University of Chicago. Collier compiled an impressive group of academic researchers to lead the study.[21]

On December 7, 1941, Japan bombed Pearl Harbor starting at just before 8:00 am and lasting much of the day. As a young boy of five years old, your author has that day indelibly etched in his brain. Television had not yet arrived on the Fitz farm in central Iowa so I am sure the news arrived by radio. Grandma and Grandpa Hill had come for Sunday dinner, probably fried chicken as was often the case on a Sunday. But what I, your author, remember most is my mother and grandmother talking about something very serious in the kitchen of our farm home. I remember looking up at the faces of my mother and Grandma, not really comprehending what was bothering them, but knowing that something had them very concerned. The air was filled with apprehension.

The next day the United States entered World War II. John Collier wrote, "We are in the World War. The stake is everything — literally everything — that we as Americans (white and Indian) hold dear. ... It is going to be a long war. It can have no indecisive ending. What we love will go down for a long age, or its enemy will go down for a long age."[22]

Winston Churchill took this opportunity to invite himself to spend Christmas at the White House. Like it or not, the United States was now in the war, and Churchill was hopeful that he could convince President Roosevelt to join England and the allies to work together in defense of both.

The people of the United States were furious with Japan, but Churchill wanted a cooperative effort in Europe against Hitler.

On Christmas Eve, Roosevelt and Churchill spoke jointly to the nation in a radio address. Churchill is quoted as saying that on this "strange Christmas eve" Americans should endeavor to "make the children happy in a world of storm."[23]

My parents, Ralph and Edith Fitz, were doing just that. Ralph knew how serious this was; after all, he had enlisted in the Navy in World War I and experienced the atrocities of war. But the small plastic Rudolph the Red-Nosed Reindeer was in its place on the buffet leading the miniature sleigh with its 8 tiny reindeer, and all was ready for the arrival of Santa. Rudolph had become part of the Christmas magic only two years previous when the department store — Montgomery Ward — gave away thousands of comic books telling the story of Rudolph to thousands of children there with their Christmas shopping parents.

Christmas came to our home that morning and sure enough, I found that farm set that I had wished for under the tree, complete with a barn, cows and pigs, all made of cardboard but perfect for a budding farmer. Little brother Melvin, now 2 years old, was more interested in the colorful wrapping paper which was quickly snatched away, smoothed and folded for use again next year.

But in the adult world, and even for children like me, life was about to get very different.

Overnight, much of the focus of the government, including the Department of the Interior and the Office of Indian Affairs, was turned to the war effort. There were approximately 127,000 Japanese in the United States, 47,000 of whom were foreign born and almost 94,000 of whom lived in California. On February 19, 1942, President Roosevelt issued Executive Order 9066 and the evacuation of Japanese Americans from what was considered sensitive areas, mostly on the west coast, began. "The Interior Department," Acting Chief Caskill of the Planning and Development Branch wrote, "is better equipped than any other Agency of Government to handle this problem."

Commissioner Collier made it known that,

> "If it is to be a program merely of keeping them under guard
> in concentration camps, we are not interested other than per-
> haps to make available some limited areas of public lands where

such camps could be located. On the other hand, if there is a willingness on the part of the Army, and other Governmental authorities concerned, to do a constructive job of supplying these people with useful work, providing education — particularly of a civic nature — health, and other services, and rehabilitating them subsequently to the war, we are disposed to have a part in the program."

One of the sites under consideration for interment was Owens Valley, California, which is one of the sources of water for Los Angeles. The Los Angeles Department of Water and Power objected and made a strong case for locating a camp on the Colorado River near Parker.

Chief Engineer & General Manager Van Norman wrote,

"I have been advised that there is approximately 8,000 acres of cleared land, under the jurisdiction of the United States Indian Service, that has been farmed and is supplied with pumped water from the Colorado River and I also understand that approximately 6,000 acres of this area is not being used at present and is available. ... Further you might point out that it would be desirable to extend the area under water to a very great extent, possibly to a total of 40,000 to 50,000 acres. The Japanese could be employed to clear, level and put into production the additional acreage needed which would result in a permanent improvement that could be settled by return soldiers at the expiration of the war. A dam has been built by the United States Reclamation Service just above the town of Parker on the Colorado River which will raise the water to an elevation which will command all of these lands by gravity flow, making it possible to abandon the pumping plant that supplies the 8,000 acres above referred to."[24]

A Memorandum of Understanding was drawn up between Secretary of War Stimson, Secretary of the Interior Ickes and the coordinator for civilian interment for building and operating an internment camp on the Colorado River Indian Reservation. [25] By March 13, 1942, Secretary of War Stimson made it known to Secretary Ickes that an agreement had been reached with the City of Los Angeles and that construction had started on the Owens Valley facility and that as soon as Secretary Ickes gave permission work would start at the Colorado River Reservation. Four days later Superintendent Gensler of the Colorado River Indian Agency in Parker, Arizona made it known to Commissioner Collier that there was a push to find areas to grow the guayule plant as a source of rubber for the war effort and the Colorado River Reservation was being considered as a location that the guayule could be grown. He continued writing,

> "The reservation cannot be made to take care of ten to forty thousand Japanese, and then produce its maximum of guayule. … There is no question but that the Japanese must be removed from the coast, and the Colorado River Reservation perhaps lends itself to this movement as favorably as any place in the country. On the other hand, the Colorado River Reservation is also one of not too many areas where the guayule may be grown and it is reasonable to expect that a place could be found for the Japanese where the guayule would not grow."

Even children like me became part of the endeavor to supply the war effort. I remember well the slogan that appeared in store windows and newspapers, "Slap the Japs with Rubber Scraps." I took apart an old abandoned pedal sewing machine because any child that brought 50 pounds of iron to the collection point got a ride around the city square in an army jeep. I got my ride! Through our school we were asked to scour the road ditches and pick milkweed pods. The contents were to be used in life preservers. I picked a bag of pods. These are just some examples of the total commitment of the United States to winning this war.

Apparently, the Pima Indian Reservation was chosen to grow guayule on some 5,000 to 8,000 acres.

Many Indian reservations were being looked at as possible sites for Japanese interment including the Red Lake Reservation in northern Minnesota.

By March 18, 1942, President Roosevelt had, by Executive Order, established the War Relocation Authority in the Office for Emergency Management of the Executive Office of the President. Milton Eisenhower was named by the President as the Director of the Authority and put in charge of supervising the relocation of the Japanese in cooperation with the Secretary of War. By early April a memorandum to be approved by Director Eisenhower and Secretary Ickes had been developed in respect to the relocation on the Colorado River Indian Reservation in Arizona of approximately 20,000 Japanese, and on April 14th it was signed by both.

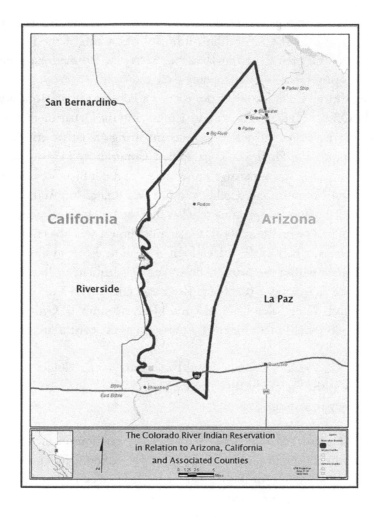

The Colorado River Indian Reservation
in Relation to Arizona, California
and Associated Counties

In a letter to one of the administrators of the War Relocation project, John Collier wrote, "In essence, the Japanese project is to be administered in much the same manner as an Indian jurisdiction would be. You are directly responsible to the Commissioner of Indian Affairs…"

Office space in Washington was becoming an issue with the demands of the war effort. Collier wanted the Indian office to remain in Washington and Eisenhower was hoping the War Relocation Authority could be housed at the Department of Interior. John Collier was busy brainstorming how his interest in community organizing could be useful in molding the thoughts and opinions of the Japanese confined at the internment camp. Since most of the Japanese expecting to be housed at Parker would come from the city of Los Angeles, Collier asked the city for assistance in procuring the electrical equipment needed at Parker. By the beginning of May the Relocation Authority was asking if the Parker camp could accept another ten thousand Japanese. Secretary Zimmerman stated that approved sites thus far accommodate only sixty thousand.

Apparently, the Colorado River project at Parker was the only one administered by the Office of Indian Affairs under Collier, but the Department of Interior was involved with other war effort projects involving Indian reservations such as leasing land on the Pima Maricopa Indian Community in Arizona for the growing of cotton. It was a massive undertaking and conflicts were starting to surface between Commissioner Collier and the War Relocation Authority under Eisenhower. Collier was complaining to Ickes that the Indian Service should be in charge of the Pima project but W.P.A. under Eisenhower was objecting, wanting to manage Pima themselves. In the end ten relocation centers were established with five of them within the jurisdiction of the Department of Interior, two of them on Indian Reservations (Colorado River and Gila River) and three on Reclamation projects (Tule Lake, Minidoka and Heart Mountain). Only the colony on the Colorado River Indian Reservation was under the control of the Office of Indian Affairs.[26]

On June 27, 1942, in a speech given by Commissioner Collier to the Japanese evacuees at the Colorado River Indian Reservation, he reveals his ideas on what democracy is, stating,

> "Democracy means this — that all the functions of society, not only the political functions but also the economic functions, and the social relationships, are so organized and carried on that every human being, as he comes up through the years of his childhood, may participate with increasing activity in the dominant functions of society. Democracy means that everybody takes an active responsibility and that the community nourishes the life of each one. Life in a democracy, where one merely enjoys certain privileges such as the ballot and the guarantees of the Bill of Rights, is not a very inspiring thing as compared to the quality of life and of challenging experiences in a through and through democracy where the entire local community unites in mutual aid and in aid to the great society."

He obviously intended to operate the Japanese camp as a commune patterned after what he had set up in the Indian Reorganization Act and thought that his system would be a demonstration project that would become that of the United States and of the world. He said to the Japanese, "I am satisfied in my own mind, and we of the Indian Service are satisfied, that this colony, as the months go on, as the years go on, is going to provide a demonstration of the efficiency and the splendor of cooperative living. It is going to provide that for the advantage of our whole country."[27]

With Japanese colonies at Parker and at Poston it seemed that the Office of Indian Affairs was spending a large percentage of its time dealing with the Japanese internment camps. Just the constant communication with the social scientists that had been placed at Parker and Poston seemed to keep Commissioner Collier busy. Tension was high at the Poston location for ten days in November 1942, as criminal activity surfaced among a group of evacuees resulting in a strike and demonstrations before it came under control.

In June of 1942, Dillon S. Myer succeeded Milton Eisenhower as director of the War Relocation Authority. On January 20th & 29th, 1944, a new Memorandum of Understanding was signed by Abe Fortas, Acting Secretary of the Interior and John H. Provinse, Acting Director of the War Relocation Authority transferring responsibility for the administration of the Colorado River Relocation Center from the Department of the Interior to the War Relocation Authority. By May 28, 1944, some 22,000 of the Japanese evacuees had been relocated into the interior of the country, with some 5,000 of them in the Chicago area. Any who were deemed to be loyal American citizens were free to go anywhere except the West coast states. It is obvious that John Collier had wanted to be in charge of relocating the Japanese when they were allowed to leave the internment camp but that was not to be.

By January of 1945 things were falling apart for John Collier and on January 22, 1945, President Roosevelt accepted his resignation.

William A. Brophy was appointed to the position of Commissioner of Indian Affairs.[28]

By later in 1945, May 7th to be exact, Germany surrendered after wreaking havoc in Europe for six years. As a 3rd grade pupil in the one room country school in rural Iowa I remember that Monday. Most country schools had a bell tower whose bell was primarily used to call students in from recess. But on that very special day we students, kindergarten to eighth grade, with Miss Nelson's permission (or maybe direction) kept the bell ringing the entire day. From the first student to arrive until the last one to leave, we pupils took turns pulling the rope to ring the bell. There was still much war to be fought, but victory was in sight.

# CHAPTER 8

# The U.S. Government
# Buys Mille Lacs

I n 1914 the United States had started buying land at Mille Lacs in an effort
to allot land to the homeless non-removal Mille Lacs Indians who had not
removed as they had agreed to do several times. Since there was no available
land in Mille Lacs County that was not already claimed by settlers, and since the
Government had agreed to allot all the Chippewa Indians, and since the Indians
continued to live on land that was owned by someone else, Congress chose the
following method of solving the problem. 1,994 acres were purchased by the U.S.
Government and allotted to the non-removal Mille Lacs Indians in small parcels
of ten acres or less. These allotments were put in 25-year trust status for each
allottee, and because of the timing these allotments were still intact at that time
the trust agreements were extended indefinitely. By 1955 only 26 of the original

282 Mille Lacs allotments were still in the name of an individual Indian; the rest had been deeded to the United States Government. But the Government was just getting started.

It was 1935 and the Wheeler-Howard Bill had been passed by Congress and signed by President Roosevelt and was now law known as the Indian Reorganization Act. The first allotments of land to the Mille Lacs Chippewas, on land purchased for them by congressional act, had taken place only ten years before the passage of the act which would end the allotment system, and so most of the issues faced by Indians in other areas had not yet occurred at Mille Lacs. Most of the Mille Lacs Indians did not live on their allotments of from four to ten acres, but instead continued to live in the three villages in the area near the trading post, in Isle and at Danbury.

The 365 Mille Lacs Indians, classified as the non-removal Mille Lacs, were registered on the annuity rolls of the White Earth reservation. The homeless non-removal Mille Lacs agreed in council to the Act of January 14, 1889 — the Nelson Act — in which they agreed to remove to the White Earth Reservation. But they then refused to remove, even though they had agreed to do so and even though there were allotments of from 80 to 160 aces waiting for them at White Earth. Consequently, in 1914 Congress authorized appropriations to purchase lands that could be allotted to these homeless Indians. 1,960 acres were purchased in the three areas — the Trading Post, Isle and Danbury — and put in trust for their use.

We can debate who was at fault, but the fact remains that these Indians were in dire straits. Their primary problem was one of subsistence, as may be recognized in the following quote from a 1935 Indian Service report:

> "The years of squalor, ... have produced in this group, more than in other Chippewa bands, negative attitudes and backwardness in every aspect of life. Like a sedentary gypsy colony, they have become squatters along the United States highway and in the desolate wastes of the back country. It is an ugly, pathetic situation for any Indian band to be in ... a sordid picture of poverty. ...
>
> Single-room tar-paper shanties of small dimension house large families; to have an adequate supply of pure water is beyond their hopes, and firewood is gleaned surreptitiously from the countryside. Gardens are unknown to the community, as are livestock, poultry and machinery, and this is no criticism of the

Indians, for the possibilities for having or using such things in their present condition and location are out of the question.

If health conditions are not alarming, it could only be because the Indians have become inured to exposure, malnutrition and insanitation. The children show the effect more of a lack of proper food and warm clothing, and of a miserable home life. That they go to school at all, or benefit by school work, is surprising.

The Indian population, particularly at Isle, are looked down upon as wretched paupers by the white inhabitants. This white prejudice, added to the miasma of degradation created by other circumstances, makes life for the Indians intolerable and disgraceful by any civilized standard. In Mr. Ayers, trader at the Mille Lacs post, however, the Indians have a real friend, as shown by his constant effort to give the Indians employment, store credit and help otherwise.

From a cultural point of view, this group is conspicuously Indian as compare to bands like the White Earth Chippewa. Very few are conversant with the English language. There is a large full-blood element. Some ceremonial still persists. Native crafts, (basketry), ricing, sugar gathering and other subsistence pursuits are still practiced. Those, together with work relief and casual wage work allows the Indian colony to survive on this lowest rung of modern human existence.

School facilities are fair. The Mille Lacs Indian school (8 grades) has 68 in attendance, more than half of whom are in the first to third grades with only three in the eighth grade. The Isle public school has five Indian pupils, the Bill Horn day school of Aitkin County eleven Indian pupils. The presence of Indian pupils in the public schools is said to be resented by the whites, although they are admitted.

Of all the Chippewa reservation groups in Minnesota the need for social and economic rehabilitation in this Indian area is preeminent."

This Indian Service government representative recommended purchase of lands for the Mille Lacs Indians with the following goals:

"a. To furnish fuel for Indian use.

    b.   To control valuable lake shore property.

    c.   To fulfill our obligation to the Indians under the terms of the Indian Reorganization Act.

    d.   To increase both Band and individual incomes.

    e.   To facilitate the building and encourage the maintenance of better homes, better health and community enterprises.

    f.   To give this group their first opportunity for economic development."[1]

If this government employee's description of conditions among the Mille Lacs band at this time is even half accurate, and I suspect that it is, then no wonder the band leaders responded to Commissioner Collier's request for their opinions on self-government in such a child-like fashion. You will recall that in an earlier chapter we quoted from Superintendent Burns' report to Commissioner Collier saying in regard to Mille Lacs,

> "The meeting with these Indians was held at the Ayers Trading Post, adjacent to their community. These Indians are not as far advanced as other Indians are on other reservations, having practically no leaders of the intelligence sufficient to comprehend the program ... These Indians, until within recent years, were without land, roamed and camped about in the immediate territory of Mille Lac Lake."

In respect to procuring land for the Mille Lacs Indians, J.S. Monks, the acting superintendent of the Consolidated Chippewa Agency, wrote to Commissioner Collier on July 1, 1936, asking that special attention be paid to an Isle property (SW/4 NE/4, Sec. 1, Twp. 42N, R 25W, 4P.M.) which had been purchased by John Jekey in 1913 and was in danger of being forfeited to the State because of unpaid taxes. The forty-acre parcel was assessed to John Jekey but owned in parcels ranging from two acres to five acres by John Jekey, Jim Skinaway, Mrs. Old Sam, Andrew Quiack, Charles Moose, William Henry, Fred Day, Mike Sam, Sam Davis, Tom Benjamin and Pete Anderson — some of whom were deceased. This parcel bordered land that had been allotted to Isle Indians and was home to some ten Mille Lacs band families. While white Isle residents were reportedly not happy having Indians living within their midst, the Mayor of the Village of Isle, O.A.

Haggberg, reportedly was in favor of the government helping these families, as was the superintendent.

A few days later an encouraging response arrived from J.M. Stewart, Director of Lands, but it was short lived. On July 30th Land Field Agent A.L. Hook wrote to the Director of lands in Washington, saying that the ownership of this property is so complicated that there is no way that they can get it all in order by the time the State would assume ownership and suggesting that perhaps another way to get the taxes paid could be found so that the property may be saved for these Indians. A response was received saying that they had no money with which to pay the taxes and suggested negotiation with the State.

Acting Superintendent Monk then appealed to Mille Lacs County Auditor Florence Munier with that suggestion. Mille Lacs County Auditor Munier replied that the property will revert to the State on September 5th unless the taxes are paid but suggested a method by which the property could be purchased from the State after it had been forfeited. On August 31st Land Field Agent Hook wrote Director of Lands Stewart with information on the current situation, stating,

> "It has been ascertained that notices of sale for delinquent taxes have been served on the Indian owners and forfeiture to the State will be effective September 5, 1936. However, the Minnesota law provides that the present owners have one year from that date in which to redeem their property by payment of all taxes and a discount rate of approximately 50%. The law also provides that occupants of the property may not be dispossessed for a period of two years prior to date of expiration of notice, which in this case is September 5, 1936. At the end of the redemption period, September 5, 1937, this property will be forfeited to the State. When the title to the property passes to the State it will be necessary to deal directly with the State authorities and the property will have to be purchased on a per acre basis, which in all probability will be in excess of the amount required to redeem at this time. We have just discussed this matter with Mr. Mark L. Burns, Coordinator, and he advised us that immediate steps should be taken for acquisition of this property from present Indian owners."[2]

On November 28, 1938, Superintendent Burns, superintendent of the Consolidated Chippewa Agency, wrote to Land Agent Hook urging further consideration of purchasing the Jekey property in Isle. Albert Sundberg, who was now auditor of Mille Lacs County, had furnished the following:

> "In regard to the tax status of the SW1/4 of NE1/4 of section one (1), Township 42, Range 25, Village of Isle, I hereby wish to state that according to our records, this description has forfeited to the State for non-payment of taxes, has been classified and appraised at $200, for which amount it can be purchased, under terms of 50% cash, balance payable 25% on or before one year and 25% on or before two years, unpaid amounts bearing interest @ 4% payable annually: Provided, however, that no standing timber, timber products or buildings, shall be removed until an amount equal to the appraised value of the timber, timber products or buildings has been paid."

Agent Hook replied to the Superintendent writing, "In consideration of the circumstances involved, it is rather difficult to support this recommendation. … the price of $5.00 an acre may be considered excessive in consideration of the type of land involved unless a reasonable valuation could be given to the buildings on the property, which, I understand, belong to individual Indians.

> "The matter of title will also involve considerable difficulty. It will not be possible for us to accept the State's title to the property and we would have to clear through the title by the original Indian owner and since he is now dead, it would involve going through probate proceedings.
>
> The most serious objection I find to this proposed purchase is that it would tend to perpetuate a living condition which, I am sure everyone connected with the Indian Service will agree, is very unfavorable. I think the real solution of the problem is the removal of these people to a more desirable location, preferably on the shores of Mille Lacs Lake."

His immediate suggestion was to move the families now living on the State-owned property to the adjoining property that is owned by the Indians.

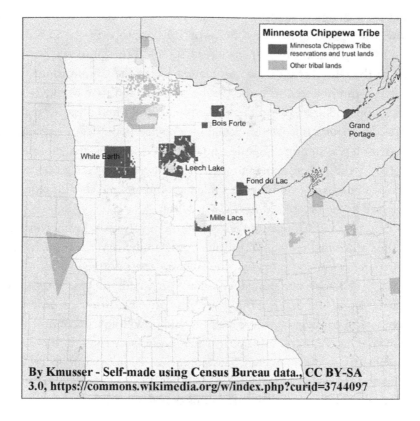

By July of 1936, the Minnesota Chippewa Tribe had a constitution and bylaws ready for a vote of ratification by the Minnesota Chippewa Tribe. The Mille Lacs Indians were apparently not concerned that they were not listed as a reservation in Article II, Section 1 of the Minnesota Chippewa Tribe's proposed constitution. That section reads: "This constitution for representation shall apply to the White Earth, Leech Lake, Fond du Lac, Bois Fort (Nett Lake) and Grand Portage Reservations, and the nonremoval Mille Lacs Band of Chippewa Indians."

On June 21, 1936, the Mille Lacs Indians voted overwhelmingly in favor of ratification.[3] The constitution and bylaws can be found in the appendix of this book.

In August of 1936, Mille Lacs County Commissioner Emmons from Onamia appealed to Senator Elmer Benson with a special request. He related that John Shincobe (Shin goob), a disabled Indian ex-serviceman, his wife Mary Davis, and his family, had been squatting on 56 acres of land adjoining the village of Onamia (Lot 4, Sec. 31, T. 42 N, R. 26W. or in another letter listed as R. 27). His father had lived there before him, there were many graves on the property, and they were now being asked to move by the owner of the property, the D.S.B. Johnston Land Company, so the property could be sold. This property was located just west of the village of Onamia on Onamia Lake. The Commissioner related that he had communicated with the Land Company and they would be willing to sell the property for $2,000 if the Government could find a way to make that happen, and then allot it to Mr. Shincobe — who had never before been allotted. Senator Benson was informed by the Bureau in Washington that allotment had been ended by the Indian Reorganization Act but that the Government was in the process of purchasing land for the Mille Lacs Indians and that his request was being referred to the Land Field Agent, Mr. Hook.

The Consolidated Chippewa Agency became involved and were considering two possible outcomes; ejection of the Shincobe family from the property by the owner or purchase of the property. The Agency was informed by Land Agent Hook that, "The tract is not located within the proposed purchase area but could be justified for purchase as a rice camp site. The price which the company is asking for the land is considerably more than I would be willing to recommend, however, I am confident that a considerable reduction in price could be obtained."

On February 2, 1937, Agency Superintendent Monks wrote to the D.S.B. Johnston Land Company and attempted, whether on purpose or not, to put some doubt into the soundness of their title to this parcel of land. He wrote,

> "If the price asked was more reasonable it might be the Indians at Mille Lacs would desire the tract for camping grounds during wild rice season. Our investigation also discloses that this land has been occupied by Indians from time immemorial, that many Indian graves are situated thereon, and there is a possibility of certain technical questions coming up such as that portion being used for a burial ground becoming a public ground after so many years of that kind of use according to State Statutes, as well as the question of adverse possession."[4]

On August 24, 1936, Assistant Commissioner of Indian Affairs William Zimmerman, Jr., announced by letter to Land Field Agent Hook that the preliminary plan for the 1937 Land Acquisition Program for the benefit of the Mille Lacs band had been approved and that $25,000 had been allocated for the plan. The plan listed 138 families currently with a total population of 503 and with 1960 acres currently held in trust and 40 acres in fee. The ultimate goal, they stated, was 4500 acres of agricultural land and 10,000 acres of timber land. The plan explained that, "Dairy farming is the most promising industry for this community. It is estimated that at least 100 of the Mille Lac Indian families should establish small dairy farms ...." These dairy farms, they suggested, could get funds from the Indian Reorganization Act Revolving Fund to get started.

By the end of 1936 the Federal Government had sent many letters to Mille Lacs area property owners which said,

> "The Federal Government is planning to purchase a few tracts of land in the vicinity of Mille Lacs Lake in Mille Lacs County, Minnesota. The land so purchased will be owned by the Federal Government and held in trust for the use of the Mille Lacs Band of Chippewa Indians. It appears that you are the owner of ... Will you kindly advise whether you would consider selling ... and advise us the price. ..."

It is important to remember that the country was in the midst of the Great Depression and so many people had great incentive to sell. The Mille Lacs Timber Company of Isle responded to the government's request saying, "...we have land for sale at nearly all localities around Mille Lacs Lake and would like to know how much and what type of land you would be interested in, and also the preferred location." Howard O. Haggberg of Isle offered his 40 acres for $65 an acre but his offer was rejected because of the price he was asking.[5]

By the time the final project plan for the Mille Lacs 1937 IRA Expendable Project was finished it included multiple parcels of real estate in Mille Lacs, Pine and Aitkin Counties.

Under the heading of the "PRESENT SITUATION AND NEED FOR ADJUSTMENT" it states,

> "The Mille Lacs Band originally occupied a reservation in Mille Lacs County on the shores of Mille Lacs Lake. The original reservation was comprised of approximately 61,000 acres. The reservation was opened to public settlement under the general land laws of the United States. The Indians were moved to the White Earth Reservation. A few of them stayed on the White Earth Reservation, but many of them came back to their original home, due to the fact that they were not contented or satisfied at White Earth.

By the Act of Congress of August 1, 1914 (38 Stat. 591) the purchase of land for the Non-Removal Mille Lacs Indians was authorized." Under that act 1,994.1 acres of land was purchased. "In the year 1926 the lands purchased under the Act of August 1, 1914 were allotted to the individual Indians, the allotments varying in size from 5 to 10 acres.

The Indians in the Mille Lacs District [Vineland] do a considerable amount of craft work, a market for the articles manufactured being provided by an Indian Trading Post which is operated by a white man in the community. Highway U.S. 169 runs through the reservation and for this reason the demand for souvenirs and Indian Art Work is considerable and a good market is provided.

The Indians in the Isle District are not as fortunate in regard to the sale of Indian Art Work. However, they do sell some articles which they have made. This group has been dependent in a large measure upon work relief projects under WPA and similar projects.

... there are 280 acres of trust allotments in the Isle District. This acreage is divided into 37 allotments ... The land in the allotments is of rather poor quality and does not lend itself to agriculture. There are 20 families in this district. A majority of the families are residing on a tract of fee owned land which adjoins the allotments. This 40-acre tract was purchased several years ago by a group of the Indians but has become tax delinquent ... but is subject [to] purchase by the owners until September 5, 1937 ... As a great many Indian graves are on the tract it will be desirable to purchase next year.

There are 25 families residing in the Danbury District which is located in Pine County, Minnesota. The 901.45 acres of trust allotments are scattered over a large area ... A few of the Indians purchased tracts of land which were not under the jurisdiction of the Department. Most of these tracts have become tax delinquent .... An IECW road was constructed in this area, giving employment to a majority of the Indians residing in this district. .... On March 16, 1937 at a meeting of the Pine County Board, R.H. Barnes, Assistant Land Field Agent explained the land purchase project to enlarge the Indian holdings in Ogema Township and the Board approved the project.

There are about 10 families residing at Sandy Lake in Aitkin County. Lots 2 and 3, Sec. 32, T. 50N., R. 23W, containing 35.35 acres was reserved for the Indians by Executive Order dated March 4, 1915. ...

About 15 families reside in the vicinity of East Lake. There is no trust or tribal property in this vicinity. East Lake is in Aitkin County. A few tracts of land have been purchased by the Indians but now are tax delinquent .... There was some discussion as to whether this area should be part of the Mille Lacs project or the White Earth project but Land Agent Hook favored Mille Lacs.

A majority of the Indians of the Mille Lacs Band gather wild rice during the harvest season. They have been handicapped in recent years by not being allowed access to some of the good wild rice lakes in the regions. It is thought advisable to purchase tracts of land on the shores of some of the good wild rice lakes in order to provide camp sites for the Indians during the wild rice harvest season. ..."

Under the heading of "DETAILED DATA RELATING TO THE PURCHASE AREA," the following statement was made,

"Two rice camp sites have been definitely selected and proposed for purchase. Both camps are located in Township 42 N., Range 27 W., in Sections 5 and 25. The camp site in Section 5 is on the shore of Ogeche Lake and the other, in section 25, is on the shore of Onamia Lake."

Details of each of the proposed land purchases and the names of the sellers can be found in this file in the National Archives at Kansas City.

Each of these many real estate deals had its own set of circumstances and legal details to be worked out before the transaction could be finalized. One of those parcels was described as Tract No. 3 (Lots 3 & 4, Sec. 27, Twp. 43 N., R. 27W) owned by Joseph Eagle containing 79.90 acres of timber land and 5000 feet of lakeshore on Lake Mille Lacs valued at $2000 and an adjoining parcel described as Tract No. 4 (Lot 4, Sec. 27, Twp. 43 N., R. 27 W.) owned by his sister Alice P. Martin containing 2 acres of timber land and valued at $50. The property was located between the Indian Trading Post and a small island on Sha-bosh-Kung Point. Joe Eagle had a house where he lived on the property, so a small parcel was carved out for that purpose as a life estate. His sister Alice did not live on her parcel. These parcels were the public domain allotment, allotted to their father Me-gee-zee (or Eagle) on October 1, 1907, as a 25-year trust patent that was extended another 25 years by Executive order on December 20, 1920, and inherited according to his will dated April 10, 1922, by his children; Joe Eagle, who lived on the property, and Alice Martin, who lived in Ponsford, Minnesota, and an adopted daughter, Way we nah be quay who inherited one acre.

On January 23, 1937, Joe Eagle's attorney, Hilding Swanson of Brainerd, Minnesota, wrote to the Consolidated Chippewa Agency in Cass Lake stating, "This, as you know, is a very valuable piece of land, suitable for the Indians, and we believe that all the Indians at Mille Lacs Lake could be quartered on this piece of land, ...." He continued suggesting that the island located east of the parcel, "technically should belong to Joe Eagle." He stated that Joe Eagle had an interest in selling the property.

On June 15, 1937, Director of Lands Stewart directed a letter to Consolidated Chippewa Agency Superintendent Burns, informing him that the Executive Order of December 7, 1920, had extended the trust period on the Me-gee-zee allotment for an additional 25 years, so no patent in fee was ever issued and the land is exempt from taxation. "It is not believed necessary" he wrote, "to purchase an abstract of title before making application for cancellation of the taxes. Since there is no question but what the land has at all times been exempt from taxation, you are requested to make application to the County Commissioners for cancellation of all tax assessments, tax sale certificates or tax deeds and request that the land be removed from the tax assessment rolls."

But by July 8, 1937, the issue of who owned the property was still not resolved. Quoting from a letter of that date sent from Land Agent Hook to J.M. Stewart, Director of Lands in Washington: "Mr. Rex H. Barnes, who handled the case, discovered from an examination of the County court records in the early part of his negotiations that there was a cloud in Mr. Eagle's title to this property resulting from a homestead entry ten years prior to the date of the allotment. This question was referred verbally to the Cass Lake Office and we were informed that Mr. Eagle's title to the property was valid and the cloud in title referred to above had, or could be, set aside by proper Judicial action.

In a recent interview with Mr. M.L. Burns, Area Coordinator, prior to his departure to the Washington Office, the matter of the Eagle purchase was brought up and he informed us that he had obtained a pencil copy of an abstract covering title to the above property prepared by the Cass Lake office which indicated that Mr. Eagle had no claim whatsoever to the property and that title had reverted to the State of Minnesota through tax delinquency and would be offered for public sale."

Director of Lands Stewart replied on July 26th,

> "… The land is the allotment of Me-gee-zee, deceased, and remains in trust status.
>
> There is enclosed herewith a copy of Office letter of June 15 to the Superintendent of the Consolidated Chippewa Agency relative to this land, which it is believed will fully explain the situation. It is expected that the Superintendent will have the lands removed from the tax assessment rolls, and all tax assessments, tax sale certificates, tax deeds, etc., canceled at an early date.
>
> It may be stated for your information that Olof Johnson made homestead entry covering the land in question September 30, 1891, but by Departmental decision of July 5, 1900, in the case of *Ma-gee-see v. Johnson* (30 L.D. 125, 294), the entry was ordered to be cancelled and the allotment to Ma-gee-see thereafter approved."

On June 17, 1937, an "OFFER TO SELL LANDS TO THE UNITED STATES" was executed by Joseph Eagle and Katherine L. Eagle for a price of $5000 and with 5 acres carved out as a life lease.

A few days later a letter was written to Joe Eagle by Land Agent Hook rejecting his offer and writing, "the option as submitted cannot be recommended for purchase because there has been included in the option a reservation of five acres covering land on the extreme point of Government Lot 3. Our purpose in recommending the purchase of your restricted property was to provide the use of same for the Mille Lacs Indians as a tribe. When the matter of the purchase of your property was brought to our attention we made an effort to determine the true value of same and it was our intention to approve an offer from you at approximately the present market price of your property less such reduction as would be justified by the continued occupancy of your home which is located on the property and the benefits you would receive from same as a member of the Mille Lacs Indian Group.

We wish to inform you that if you desire to have your property recommended for purchase by the United States Government, it will be necessary to offer same at a price of $5,000 without any reservation whatsoever, with the understanding that you transfer title to the United States in trust for the Indians and obtain an assignment as a home site from the Tribal Council, or accept $4,000 for the property and a life assignment of five acres to comprise an area surrounding the present location of your home and including the adjoining lake frontage."

Toward the end of the month Agent Morrison stopped to visit with Joe Eagle and was told by Joe that he did not receive the letter of rejection. Morrison verbally gave him the gist of the letter and he said he would talk it over with his attorney and decide.

On April 12, 1937, H.D. Ayer, manager of the Mille Lacs Indian Trading Post, wrote to Land Agent Hook suggesting an exchange of a 35-acre tract owned by him (SW1/4 — NE1/4 –S 28 — 43 — 27 — Less Cemetery) for the allotment owned by the heirs of the now deceased Chief Wadena. "The allotment," he says, "I now occupy on a five-year lease. The above 35-acre tract has the CCC Camp on it and about 12 acres is under intensive cultivation." A couple of weeks later Mr. Ayer received a letter which said that it is doubtful that that could be worked out because of the way the two parcels are held.

"The object in setting up this project" they write, "is to provide land for landless Indians of the Mille Lacs Band of Chippewa Indians of Minnesota and to provide additional lands for those already holding small allotments." While they are proposing to purchase lake front property it will simply allow, they say, the Indians to fish for their own use. The report states that, "Fishing on a commercial scale is not permitted in Mille Lacs Lake."[5]

As is often the case, rumors were flying. Indian Field Agent Hook received a letter from the American Legion Auxiliary, Isle Unit 405 in Isle saying, "One rumor is that there is to be 150 Indian families to be moved here from Leech Lake. Another that they are from Danbury Wis., and that it is to be used to move the Indians we have here on to farm." Agent Hook replied saying, "The purpose of our Acquisition program is to provide a small amount of land whereon the Indians may make their homes."

Agent Hook also received a letter from Walter Stevens, who apparently was a part of the Cleveland Realty Company in St. Paul and owned a summer home in the area of Sunset Bay on the east shore of Mille Lacs Lake. Mr. Stevens wrote, "We have just been advised that the Federal Government is considering the purchase of considerable areas of land in this vicinity for the use of Indians. While agreeing that this movement by the government is an admirable one, surely some locations could be selected that would not bring a tribe of Indians near to homes that have been built up by a community of home owners, who have made considerable investment for the benefit of their families, to give their children the benefit of a lake home during the summer months away from the dangers of city life during school vacation periods. I am strongly protesting a movement that would locate a tribe of Indians anywhere near the shores of Mille Lac Lake, between the Town of Isle and Opstead."

Agent Hook replied saying in part,

> "… we wish to inform you that it is not the intention of the Office of Indian Affairs to carry out any program of land purchase which would be detrimental to the general welfare of the community. …we have no plans for re-locating other groups of Indians in this vicinity. Whatever is done at Isle will be for the benefit of the Indians who now live there. …"

Senator Henrik Shipstead also weighed in on behalf of his constituents and was assured — like the others. Apparently, the citizens of Isle had had a meeting on January 7th to talk about the government's project for purchasing land and Henry Paulsen of the Mille Lac Timber Company attended. Following the meeting he wrote to the Bureau of Indian Affairs protesting the project as they understood it and suggesting that the Indians of Isle be moved to the east side of the lake. The Land Agent replied suggesting that in the future if they have a meeting he would like to be invited to explain the project.

On February 17th the Isle Civic and Commerce Association wrote to Land Agent Hook and invited him to their next meeting to be held on March 4th at 6:00 PM with supper at The Isle Café. Agent Hook accepted the invitation and spoke to the group at length saying, in part,

"One of the common objectives to this legislation [Wheeler-Howard Act] is the charge that the Indian is being considered as a special class and the Act itself is one of special class legislation. We accept that challenge and admit that the Indians are being considered as a special group and are fully deserving of such consideration. We maintain that the Indian has lost his birthright, his way of living, and that he has never been repaid. You may point out that all of the land which the Indian once claimed was sold in a legal manner and that the former Indian owners received compensation in cash. However, I wish to point out that in return for his former holdings where he lived a primitive life, obtaining his living from the natural resources, the Indian received the white man's goods at a time when his state of civilization prevented his making any adequate use of these gifts. In addition to the loss of his land, the Indian lost his old tribal organization and was thrown into white communities where it was impossible for him to function in his then state of development. ... Undoubtedly what you are most naturally interested in are our plans for the Indians living in the Isle Community. From the rumors we have heard it might be well to state first the things we do not intend to do. It has never been our intention to remove Indians now living in other parts of Minnesota and concentrate them at Isle. Whatever we do here will be done for the benefit of the Isle Indians and the scope of our work will be limited by the needs of the present group of Indians now living in the community. ... it might be well to state also that we will not consider the removal of this Indian group from their present homes to some distant reservations ...We know that very few of our Indian people will ever become successful farmers on the same basis as their white neighbors. We do know, however, that every Indian family under proper guidance can be urged to put in a garden which will supply a large portion of the food required for family use. ... we realize that the gathering of rice is one of the most valuable economic assets now remaining to the Minnesota Indian. We propose to aid him ... by acquiring wild rice fields or suitable locations along wild rice lakes which will serve him as camp sites during the ricing season. ... We dislike the present situation wherein the Indian must obtain this fuel supply [for heat in winter] by trespass on his white neighbor and it is our purpose to include in our acquisition program such lands as will provide the basis for a sustained fuel supply."

By May 1937, rumors were again flying in regard to the government buying lakeshore land for the Indians of Isle and Congressmen, Senators Ernest Lundeen and Henrik Shipstead and Representative Harold Knutson were getting involved in the letter writing, as well as the Isle Civic and Commerce Association. One rumor was that the government intended to purchase all of Section 22, township 43N., range 25W. in Mille Lacs County. The truth — Assistant Commissioner Zimmerman wrote, "at present there is no definite plan for acquisition of land along the lakeshore."

The presence of the Indian Service in Isle once again caused concern among Isle residents and that activity was explained by Land Agent Hook.

> "The activity of the Indian Service in the Isle District was for the purpose of inspecting the lands on which the Indians are now living and in making a general survey relative to any possible betterment of their present living conditions. At the present time it is felt that little can be done at Isle other than restoration of the lands on which the Indians are now living and on which title will revert to the State of Minnesota through tax delinquency. However, if it should seem advisable, after further study, to recommend additional land purchases at Isle, the program will be discussed with the committee appointed by the Commercial Club in accordance with the understanding arrived at when the writer attended a meeting of this group on March 18."

On November 23, 1937, Louis Balsam, Superintendent of the Consolidated Chippewa Agency at Cass Lake, wrote Land Agent Hook saying that he had received a letter from Fred Sam, a tribal executive committeeman from Mille Lacs stating that it was urgent that additional land be purchased for the Indians in Isle especially as a wood source for fuel. Agent Hook replied,

> "Our proposed program of land acquisition at Isle was blocked because of political pressure exerted by the white citizens of Isle, Minnesota. The matter was taken up with members of the Minnesota Congressional delegation and protests were

forwarded to the Office of Indian Affairs. The opposition was so strenuous as to intimidate prospective land owners with whom we attempted to negotiate; in fact, it completely blocked our program for the time. Since we were unable to accomplish any results, it was deemed advisable to drop the matter rather than carry on a controversy from which we could not hope to profit under existing conditions. Mr. M.L. Burns, Superintendent of the Consolidated Chippewa Jurisdiction, and Acting Area Coordinator, concurred in this decision. I would suggest that sometime at your convenience a conference be arranged which I might attend in order that we may discuss fully land matters relating to Isle, Danbury and East Lake."[5]

On June 21, 1937, Assistant BIA Commissioner Zimmerman and Assistant DOI Secretary Chapman accepted options to purchase four properties: 99.75 acres (N1/2NE1/4, Sec. 28, and Lot 5 Sec. 21, T.43N. R. 27W.) from E.A. Cooper for $1540, 80 acres (S1/2 NW1/4, Sec. 28, T. 43N. R. 27W) from Miss Stella K. Manning for $800, 90 acres (N1/2 of NE1/4, Sec. 20 and east 20 rods of SE1/4 of SE1/4, Sec. 17, all in T.43N, R.27W) from the Vermont Savings Bank for $1600 and 156.45 acres (Lots 1 and 2 and N1/2 NE1/4, Sec.25, T. 42N, R. 27W) from Henry W. Haverstock et al for $2600. A week later Land Agent Hook rejected the offer from Mrs. M.S. Weide of Santa Monica, California to sell her property for $8,500.

On August 3, 1937, Land Agent Hook reported to Consolidated Chippewa Agency Acting Superintendent Monks that Agent Barnes, William Nickboine and Fred Sam had made a tour of the wild rice camp sites that the Mille Lacs Tribal Council was requesting be purchased. These sites were located on Swamp Lake which was east of Glen, White Elk Lake located north of Aitkin, Mud Lake located east of Bennetville, all three in Aitkin County and Dean Lake located northwest of Crosby in Crow Wing County, in addition to Ogeeche Lake in Mille Lacs County. In regard to the Lake Ogeche site he reported,

"We find it will be necessary to purchase approximately 300 acres on the lake as the tracts are held by two owners who are unwilling to sell a part of their holdings without selling all. The D.S.B Johnston Land Company owns 237.60 acres on Ogeeche Lake which they have agreed to option and also will convey approximately 15 acres on the tract on which John Shingboob lives at Onamia. The portion of this tract which they intend to convey will include the present home of John Shingboob and also the Indian graves."

Coordinator Burns, Ag. Extension agent Stinson, and land clerk Munnell all signed a letter to Director of Lands Stewart in Washington on August 21st, in regard to purchasing land on Ogeche Lake for a wild rice camp.

> "The Indians of the nonremovable Mille Lac Band [notice the terminology used] … recommends the purchase of lots 7 and 8, Sec. 5, Twp. 42N., Rge. 27W. Mille Lacs County as a permanent rice camp … This camp site has been used for generations for the White Earth Indians and the nonremovable Mille Lacs band and other Indians who like to come back to the old historic rice fields for early ricing. Approximately one hundred families gather annually on this rice bed to gather the season's supply of wild rice. The Government owns no land on the rice bed and the Indians have been trespassing in gathering rice for the last 15 or 20 years. … The rice bed is one of the most productive in the Mille Lacs area. It is approximately one half mile wide by three miles long, and in normal years it is completely filled with wild rice. In normal years the Indians would take twenty five to fifty tons of rice from this lake."

The same group of three on the same day recommended a wild rice site be purchased on Lake Minnewawa in Aitkin County, one on Laura Lake in Cass County and one on Bowstring Lake in Itasca County in addition to the five sites recommended by the Mille Lacs Tribal Council.

As 1937 was nearing an end, the $25,000 that had been appropriated by Congress for the plan called the Mille Lacs 1937 I.R.A. Expendable Project were exhausted and Land Agent Hook explained that while properties could be negotiated and contracts written, no money would be available until Congress appropriated it in 1938.

But planning continued and a preliminary project plan was accomplished entitled the MILLE LACS 1938 PROPOSED ENLARGEMENT. The scope of this project, they explained, was to acquire land within the present areas to further block out said areas with the lands purchased in 1937 and to establish other purchase areas for other groups of Indians living in this territory who are in urgent need of land. This was planned for the Mille Lacs, Isle, Danbury, East Lake and Sandy Lake districts.

In early 1938 it was obvious that the government service was very desirous of acquiring the Joe Eagle Property and the Weide property when funds were available.

By February 11, 1938, The United States had accepted options on eleven wild rice camp sites and among them was the 250.6 acres on Ogeche Lake owned by the D.S.B. Johnston Land Company. By May 28, 1938 the Ogeche Lake site documents were in their final stage and it was approved by Assistant Secretary Chapman on July 23rd, and the company was paid on September 15th.

The Andrew P. Jorgensen property (Lot 4 and SW1/4 of SW1/4, Sec.28 and NE1/4 of NE1/4, Sec. 32 and NW1/4 of NW1/4, Sec. 33 all in T. 43N, R. 27W.) had been on the want list for the United States back in 1914 when the government was buying land on which to allot the Mille Lacs Indians but the asking price was too high at that time. Now in 1938 they were once again interested. The property contained a quarter mile of frontage on Lake Mille Lacs.

On March 22, 1938, options were accepted on two additional wild rice camp sites making a total of 13 sites to be owned by the United States in trust for the Minnesota Chippewa Tribe.

On April 7 and 8, 1938, the Executive Committee of the Minnesota Chippewa Tribe passed the following resolution:

### Resolution No. VII

WHEREAS, The communities of Isle, Fon du lac, Inger and Ball Club are without reservation lands, and

WHEREAS, W.P.A. requirements are that projects can only be constructed upon lands public in character, and

WHEREAS, W.P.A. is co-operating with the Indian Service in the rehabilitation project being planned to construct a limited number of homes in Indian communities of the State,

NOW, THEREFORE, be it resolved that the Tribal Executive Committee does hereby respectfully petition the Department of the Interior, the Cass Lake Agency and the Land Acquisition Department, that requisite reservation lands be acquired in the communities of Isle, Fon du lac, Inger and Ball Club as early as possible and that the same be acquired from funds available to the Land Acquisition Department for such purposes.

In April 1938 Representative Knutson was asking for additional land for the Pine County Indians and was told by Commissioner Zimmerman that there were no funds currently available from Congress for that group of Indians.

In 1939 Coordinator M.L.Burns commenced a study on the land and economic conditions on the Mille Lacs Lake Reservation. His report, in part, said, "The Indian-owned land consists of small tracts on or near the shore of Mille Lacs Lake in Sections 17, 20, 27, 28 and 29, in Township 43 North, Range 27 West, and a 120-acre tract in the Northeast Quarter of Section 1, Township 42 North, Range 25 West, in Mille Lacs County. Lands in Aitkin County consist of the Southwest Quarter of Section 31, Township 4 North, Range 24 West.

Mille Lacs Lake area is a popular summer resort and the lake is noted for its excellent fishing. Summer recreation multiplies the population many times during the three or four summer months. Also, a large portion of the tourists traveling to resorts farther north pass through this region and often stop over night to enjoy the fishing and natural scenic beauty. A paved highway, No. 169, passes directly across the reservation and connects with east and west roads at various points. The lake shore is dotted with individual summer homes, cabin resorts, small hotels and taverns and other small settlements which cater largely to fishing parties and summer tourists.

The Mille Lacs Indian Village is located on the southwest shore of the lake and is ideally situated from the standpoint of scenic beauty and might be developed along commercial lines.

The Mille Lacs Lake Indians are very adept at making birch-bark handicraft work and sell large quantities of these materials, along the highway, to tourists in the summer time. This business can be greatly expanded if these Indians had a cooperative store, located at some strategic point along the main highway. All of the products could be sold from this central point. These people are industrious, reliable and greatly in need of assistance.

The Isle group are situated some fifteen miles east, away from the lake and on land unsuitable for any economic development. They live in an isolated community, inaccessible to schools, churches or community activities and in homes entirely unsuitable for human habitation. The general condition of the group is very poor and they are an extremely impoverished group from any angle. They have no incomes other than direct relief or relief work and are in need of suitable land for the location of suitable homes."

As 1939 began the Minnesota Chippewa Tribe was busy lobbying the Bureau of Indian Affairs in an effort to get more land. On January 11th the Executive Committee of the Minnesota Chippewa Tribe passed Resolution XVIII which read:

> "Whereas, the Executive Committee of the Minnesota Chippewa Tribe is assembled in special meeting duly called pursuant to notice, at the City of Duluth, Minnesota … and
>
> Whereas, it is learned that there are approximately 10,000 acres of tax delinquent land which has reverted to the State of Minnesota, and subject to disposal under the State Tax Laws, said land situated in Township 41N., Range 16W., and Section 1, 12, 13 and fraction of 24, Twp. 41N., Range 17W., 4th P.M., Pine County, in Ogema Township, and
>
> Whereas, the said township borders St. Croix River and within it are some ten individual allotments of the members of the non-removal Mille Lac Band of Chippewa Indians, and
>
> Whereas, the said township 41N., Range 16W., is bordered to the west by the township 41N., Range 17W., within which township, in Sections 2, 3, 6, 8, 18 and 30 thereof, are situated ninety or more individual allotments of the said non-removal Mille Lacs Band, none of said allotments exceeding ten acres, and
>
> Whereas, the acreage allotted to this band is generally known to be inadequate for their proper economic needs and even for fuel supply, and
>
> Whereas, the Township 41N., Range 16W., hereof mentioned, is now and has been from time immemorial frequented by a large number of the Mille Lacs Band of Chippewas, including the River of St. Croix, and is the logical ground for permanent home-sites and a reserve for the Danbury group of the Mille Lacs Band, and
>
> Whereas, it is understood the officials of Pine County indicated it is possible for the Indian Department to acquire the

lands for a nominal consideration not exceeding fifty cents or one dollar per acre, Therefore

Be it Resolved that the acquisition of these lands be, and is hereby, urged sanctioned and approved, and the Commissioner of Indian Affairs is urged to use his power to initiate negotiations with the State of Minnesota, with the view of acquiring the tax delinquent lands for the benefit of the Minnesota Chippewa Tribe, and

Be it Further Resolved that if said land or any portion thereof is to be acquired by condemnation, that the same be handled by the Tribal Attorney."

On the same day the Executive Committee of the Minnesota Chippewa Tribe passed Resolution No. XV which read:

"Whereas, the home conditions of the Indians at Isle, Minnesota, they being a part of the Mille Lacs Band of Chippewa Indians, are generally known to be exceedingly bad, and

Whereas, a Rehabilitation project has been set up and approved to improve the home conditions of these people, and

Further, in connection with this project, there is pending a road project to construct suitable roads or trails to the lands allotted to this band to enable them to have excess [access] to them for the purpose of wood supply and erection of homes, and

Whereas, there are ten families residing with poor homes on taxed delinquent land, being the SW/4 NE/4, Sec. 1, Twp. 42N., R. 25E, 4PM, which was purchased by a group of this band, and that the said land is needed to tie-in with the allotted lands, and by reason of the fact that it is not permissible to expend Rehabilitation funds for the repair of homes on taxable land, therefore

Be it resolved by this Committee that the Secretary of the Interior be and is hereby authorized and urged to acquire the said land for the Minnesota Chippewa Tribe, to be used as a permanent home for the said Indians."

And not to be out done, on January 17, 1939 the Mille Lacs Band passed the following resolution:

WHEREAS, the Mille Lacs Band of the Minnesota Chippewa Tribe is duly assembled in special meeting on this 17th day of January, 1939, at the Mille Lacs Indian Village for the purpose of determining the land needs of the Band, and,

WHEREAS, the present land holdings of the Band are grossly inadequate for the economic rehabilitation of the Band and,

WHEREAS, it is understood to be a purpose of the Indian Reorganization Act to provide suitable lands for Indian homesites, subsistence gardens, self-help projects, etc. now,

BE IT THEREFORE RESOLVED, that the Bureau of Indian Affairs is hereby urged and requested to purchase tracts of land specified below for the benefit of the Mille Lacs Band:

1. All that portion of land lying east of the center line of Sec. 28, T 43N, R 27W,

2. The east half of the SW1/4, Sec. 21, T 43N, R 27W

3. All that portion of land located within Sec. 16, T 43N, R. 27W.

The foregoing resolution was duly adopted by the Council of the Mille Lacs Band on Jan 17, 1939 by a vote of 22 for and 0 against.

(s) TOM HILL
Acting Chairman, Mille Lacs Council

(s) MRS. JIM HILL
Acting Secretary, Mille Lacs Council

On March 8, 1939, Acting Superintendent Burns wrote the Commissioner of Indian Affairs urging a new look at acquiring land for the Isle Indians; either the former Jekey property or a 100-acre lakeshore property that they had identified and that the Isle Indians could be moved to.

In a March 28th issue of the *Minneapolis Star* an article ran with the headline "WHERE ONCE LORDLY TRIBE LIVES IN SQUALOR." The article describes one of the households they visited, that of Fred Day: "There are 13 in the household, Day's wife and seven children, also his son-in-law, John Wayas, with his wife and two small children. Their one-room tarpaper house is 18 by 24 feet. The flooring is of rough lumber showing holes and cracks. This home contains among other things one iron bed, two home-made wooden beds. Day is in poor health. He received for November a $12 grocery order from county relief.

HE STATED HIS ALLOWANCE HAS BEEN CUT AND THAT $12 WAS INSUFFICIENT TO FEED HIS FAMILY. Due to Day's health, it is necessary at times for his wife and daughters to supply wood for the home by hauling it on their backs or shoulders some distance. His son-in-law was put on WPA a short time ago."

On April 12, 1939, Land Agent Hook wrote to the Isle Civic and Commerce Association, which he had promised to do prior to any purchase for the Isle Indians. He stated that "We recommend that Lots 1, 2, 3 and 4 and the E1/2 of Section 22 and Lots 1, 2 and 3 of Section 27, T. 43 N., R. 25 W., be purchased for the Isle group of the Mille Lacs Band." Of this lakeshore land just north of Isle he wrote, "…[It] will furnish this group with excellent home sites, school facilities, a sugar bush for revenue, and an outlet to the lake for fishing, guiding, recreation and, later, a possible resort development." He asked the Isle Civic and Commerce group for their reaction to this proposal. Of the area currently occupied by the Isle Indians he wrote, "So far as I have been able to determine, not more than one of the 37 original allotments is being used by the Isle Indians although some of them adjoin the 40 acres they now occupy which is fee patent land and has now reverted to the State of Minnesota for non-payment of taxes." Superintendent Burns had recommended that the tax forfeited property be purchased for the Indians but Land Agent Hook recommended that that purchase not be approved.

Within about a week Agent Hook received an answer from the Isle Civic and Commerce Association: "About the year 1937 this issue was brought to the attention of this Association and was strongly opposed. And on January of the same year we went on record by a unanimous vote by all our members and was supported by two petitions of several hundred signers from the property owners and taxpayers on the territory concerned to oppose the move in all ways. However, we will have a meeting again on May 4th to reconsider the issue once more. But from all indications the attitude among the people has not changed."

Shortly after the May 4th meeting the Association sent off a strongly worded response letter to the Department of the Interior, writing in part,

> "This move was under way which you may recall some time
> ago, and was at that time very bitterly opposed by the white
> community adjacent to this tract at that time. And this associa-
> tion had a meeting to take this matter up again at this new pro-
> posal, and our meeting was well attended by interested parties
> from this vicinity, the Village of Isle, Township of East Side, and
> property owners residing in other large cities who have summer

homes near this tract of land. Everyone at our meeting voiced a very strong opposition to this move, and it was unanimously voted by our members to take all steps we could to have this move set aside for all time." They suggested that the best solution is to move the Isle Indians to the Vineland area where they already have lake access. They concluded their response by writing, "We hope that it will not be necessary for us, at this time to take such drastic steps to prevent this move to go through as most of our members suggest."

By the first of June it appeared that there was a strong push on the part of the government Indian Service as well as the Chippewa tribe to pursue the purchase of the land on the east side and move the Isle Indians there. But the white population rather violently opposed the move and the Isle Indians themselves opposed the move.

It is interesting to note that by mid-1939 the term "Non-removable Mille Lac Indians" is becoming common in Indian Service letters.

In an attempt to purchase 65 acres of land on Ogeche Lake (Lots 7 & 8, Sec. 5, T. 42N., R. 27W.) owned by the Onamia Land and Development Company a letter from the First State Bank of Onamia President W.A. Benzie indicated that the depression was taking its toll: "Replying to your letter relative to the above [land] will say that we lost this land through the taxes as the state took it, I have been laid up for the past two years and last fall I went down to Milaca to see about the taxes and found that they had been sold to the State, if you had taken it over at that time we could of handled it but we have lost all our land as we had to let it go as we was unable to hold it." By August 10, 1940, the Indian Service had decided to reject the option to purchase this land as a wild rice camp site since the land could not be obtained from the party that had offered the option — and the Indians already have access to the lake.

Mille Lacs County Sheriff Oscar Dahl, in a conference with Alcohol tax investigators, had indicated that the sheriff's office would appreciate cooperation from the Federal authorities in the matter of liquor control as the Indians are being fleeced of what little money they have by the violators of the liquor laws. Examples, he stated, were "bootleggers and 3:2 operators in his county who were selling intoxicating liquor and 3:2 beer to the Indians living in the vicinity of Mille Lacs Lake." They had picked up two Indians, he said, "at Milaca ... and that they had 8 pints of 3:2 beer and 1/3-pint Old Quaker Tax Paid Whiskey in their possession." Dahl said that "the 3:2 beer had been purchased by the Indians at Buds Place Long Siding, Minnesota and that the Tax Paid Whiskey had been sold to the above-mentioned Indians by one, Tommy Joseph, who works in the Marudos Bros. Chevrolet Garage at Milaca, Minnesota, that Joseph charged the said Indians $2.75 for the pint of Old Quaker Tax Paid Whiskey."

On September 1, 1939, Land Agent Hook wrote to Acting Superintendent Burns informing him that options had been signed on the Weide and Haverstock properties that the Indian Service had desired previously but had rejected because of the price being asked. Mrs. Weide lived in California but was visiting Minnesota for the summer. These properties that formed the point above the Mille Lacs Indian settlement are described as the Mille S. Weide property (Govt. Lots 1, 2, 3 Sec. 16, T. 43 N., R. 27 W.), comprising 90.50 acres and the H. W. Haverstock property (Govt. Lot 4 and NW1/4 SW1/4 Sec. 16, T. 43 W., R. 27 W.), comprising 68.75 acres. The option was for $14,000.

Agent Hook said that the options would not be submitted to Washington unless they were approved by both the Office of the Consolidated Chippewa Agency and the Tribal Council. In response Superintendent Burns sent off a letter to Assistant Commissioner of Indian Affairs Zimmerman writing, in part,

> "During the past year we have had considerable difficulty in making proper adjustment of the Isle group of Indians ... Seventy taxpayers and homeowners ... residing in Eastside Township, have protested against the purchase of land for these Indians ... there has been some talk ... of asking the Indian Department to move the Indians to some other location. ... this past summer I contacted the Indians of this area to see if I could induce them to move on the west side of the lake with other Indians at Vineland where there are good school accomodations [sic] for the children, good roads, and other desirable facilities which are not available at Isle. Within the past week seven or eight families of the Isle group have consented to move ... if proper housing facilities are available. ... For some time there has been under consideration the purchase of property owned by Mille S. Weide and Mr. H.W. Haverstock. ... Those families at Isle who have examined this property during the past week were very enthusiastic about it and are willing to move there. ... For your information there are five houses on the property, three of which are sufficiently large to care for two families each. The five houses should take care of at least seven families .... The houses

on the property I would estimate to represent a value of from
$6,500 to $7,000. ... To summarize, it appears that the one and
only solution for the economic and social problem of the Isle
group is to purchase the above described land."

Attached to the letter were descriptive remarks including,

"The west shore line of Mille Lacs Lake has been extensively
developed for commercial summer resorts and private summer
homes. The land under consideration, ... consists of a projecting
peninsula. It is one of the few remaining points ... that has not
been commercially developed. The property has something over
6000 ft. of lake frontage .... The two cottages built of stone ...
are exceptional ... the frame houses ... are all in good condition.
There are two wells on the property ..."[2]

On December 6, 1939, Land Agent Hook received a letter from the Assistant Commissioner of Indian Affairs in Washington which read, "It has been
concluded that the lands described in your letter should be acquired, providing
the option price is satisfactory. For this purpose an allocation of $14,000 is being
made from the 1940 contractual authority." On January 24, 1940, the Secretary
of the Interior accepted the options.

On May 20, 1940, Director of Lands Steward in Washington received an air
mail letter from land agent Hook asking for a hasty conclusion of the purchase
in light of the fact that one of the houses had been broken into and the Indians of the area were suspected. The purchase of both properties was granted by
Acting Commissioner Armstrong on June 24, 1940. On July 13, 1940 a check
for $7,000 was mailed to Mille M. Weide in full payment for her property and
Land Agent Hook complied with her request to have certain personal items from
the house delivered to the Miller Tea Room since she was back in California,
and while it wasn't really official business, he complied. On July 18th a check for
$7,000 was received by Catherine B. and Henry W. Haverstock in full payment
for their property.[2]

By November of 1939 Consolidated Chippewa Agency Superintendent Burns
was again asking Land Agent Hook to take another look at the Joe Eagle property
following a visit by Joe Eagle to the Superintendent's office. Hook responded
saying that Eagle's price had been out of their range in the past but that the Superintendent should find out what price Joe Eagle would now accept, but that the
"Weide's Point" property is first in line for any appropriations in 1941.[4]

John Jekey was not giving up on the property he had purchased in conjunction with others back in 1913, some twenty-five plus years ago. The property had been claimed by the State due to tax delinquency and was now for sale from the State for $200, which John Jekey apparently paid and again became the owner on July 28, 1939. So, by November 25, 1939, Jekey and his wife were attempting to donate the land to the United States in trust for the Minnesota Chippewa Tribe but were faced with title issues. The Land Title Examiner informed them that "… tax lands will not be acceptable until the State or its grantees quiet title through court action or, until quit claim deeds can be obtained from all persons who might have an interest in the land."[2]

On February 26, 1940, Tribal Executive Committee Chairman Frank Broker called a special meeting of the Tribal Executive Committee to be held on March 16th to discuss "proposed legislation relative to the segregation of Tribal lands between the Red Lake Band and the Minnesota Chippewa Tribe. …"

Governor Stassen directed all males of draft age to register at their regular polling places including Mille Lacs County on Wednesday October 16, 1940. On March 25, 1941, Assistant Superintendent Walz reported that 41 Indians had been registered for the draft by the Mille Lacs County Local Board.[6]

On May 16, 1941, Stella K. Manning acknowledged receiving a check for $800 for her 80 acres of land under the 1937 Mille Lacs Expendable Land Acquisition Program.[7]

In early 1941 the Consolidated Chippewa Agency had asked each county to report the law violations by Indians in their respective counties. Mille Lacs County Attorney Nyquist replied admirably as follows:

> "It is impossible for me to give much of a detailed report such as you request. We keep a record of our criminal cases as I get them from the various Justices of the Peace over the County, but no record is kept as to whether the defendants are Indians or not."[8]

By March of 1942, the Consolidated Chippewa Agency was referring to 6 reservations being under their jurisdiction with the sixth one being listed as the "Non Removal Mille Lacs (Purchased Lands)." By 1942 there were 408 Mille Lacs Indians enrolled with 354 residing where they are enrolled.[9]

On March 26, 1942, Consolidated Chippewa Agency Superintendent Scott asked Land Agent Barnes for help with a request from the Mille Lacs Land Board and Council for purchase of two tracts of land, one being at Sandy Lake and the other Lot 1, Sec. 21, Twp. 43N., Rge. 27W designated as the NW/4 NW/4 in Mille Lacs County containing 32.35 acres. Scott wrote that he didn't know if any money could be found for this purpose.[10]

By 1943 reports show that the income of the non-removal Mille Lacs was $2500 for wild rice, $750 for fish, $600 for furs, $500 for game, and $500 other products such as berries, $3280 for leather and beadwork, $1500 for basketry, $2721 from agriculture, $1177 for employment with the Indian Service and $5000 from non-Indian employers. In addition, payment to service men's dependents was $17,000, Social Security Assistance was $9941, relief by the Indian Service was $1050 and direct relief was $883.[11]

On March 21, 1943, the Minnesota Chippewa Tribe Executive Committee passed a resolution approving the wishes of the Mille Lacs Band to purchase the 75 acres owned by Mrs. Jerry Besser (Lots 1 & 2, W3/4 SE1/4, Sec 17, T 43, R 27), but on May 13th that resolution was rescinded because of the price asked for the parcel, and instead they authorized purchase of a wild rice camp site on Mallard Lake in Aitkin County.[12]

On October 20, 1944, final payment was made on the wild rice camp site on Mallard Lake in Aitkin County.[13]

In 1943 the emphasis on land purchases shifted from the Lake Mille Lacs area to the Sandy Lake and Danbury areas.

On August 18, 1947, C.V. Roland from Onamia, Minnesota, who was opening a resort on Mille Lacs Lake called Roll-In Lodge, wrote a second letter to The Department of the Interior, Office of Indian Affairs asking for their assistance. He and two other G.I.s, he stated, were opening a resort business on Lake Mille Lacs. R.E.A. in Aitkin had agreed to extend electric lines to their area, he wrote, but "due to the fact that the Boyd family (Indians) who own the property across which the R.E.A. must place their poles (3 or 4 poles) still refuse to give consent until they have received permission from your department in Washington," the project is stalled. He continued listing reasons why it was vitally important to have electricity for the proper operation of his resort and hopefully before winter. On August 29, 1947, he received approval from Washington but now was asking the District Director of the Office of Indian Affairs in Minneapolis for assistance in getting the proper legal easements in place. Mr. Roland emphasized the urgency writing,

> "We are only 1-1/10 miles from the power line at the present time and in the case of myself, I have installed an oil burner furnace, modern rest rooms, shower rooms, minnow tanks with

running water, etc., and it is vitally necessary that I have electricity to operate my place of business. Furthermore, I have taken out a G.I. loan and also invested much of my own money and cannot do business properly without the service of electricity."[14]

On September 6, 1949, Land Officer Barnes made it known by letter to the Commissioner of Indian Affairs that they were desirous of acquiring a 574.1-acre site in Pine County for the Danbury Indians. The parcel was owned by the State of Minnesota as tax-forfeited land. The Town of Ogema and the Board of County Commissioners had indicated in 1943 that they were agreeable to a price of $1.025 plus costs.

Louis T. Gottwalt, who apparently owned the Louis T. Gottwalt Lumber Co. in Pierz, Minnesota, owned a tract of land at Mille Lacs (Block A of Walser's Subdivision, Sec. 16, Twp 43N, R, 27W, 4ᵗʰ P.M.) containing 8.1 acres. In September of 1948 he had offered to trade his tract for that of the deceased Non-Removal Mille Lacs allottee No. 104, She kaug, which the probate court, about a year later, found was inherited by a single heir, her daughter, Mrs. George Boyd or Jennie N. Boyd, formerly Mrs. Jim Noonday or Ah be no je. Mrs. Boyd's property (N1/2 NE1/4 NE1/4 SW1/4, Sec. 28, T. 43N., R. 27W, 4ᵗʰ P.M.) contained 5 acres. The Minnesota State Highway Department was in the midst of choosing the exact route for U.S. Highway 169 which was being rerouted and reconstructed. Both properties however would be affected by the project.

Sister Laura, a part of the Order of St. Benedict, being a friend of the Indians of the area as well as being aunt to Louis Gottwalt, was in the middle of the transaction, as evidenced by a letter from Sister Laura to Land Agent Barnes on January 9, 1950, in which she writes, "… I called on Mrs. Boyd last Friday and found both she and her daughter, Mabel, home. We talked for a while and in the course of the conversation Mable said: 'Ma is going to build a house for me and Charlie on the new land we are going to get.' I asked her if the deal is all settled now and Mabel said: 'Yes, but we have to let them know in Cass Lake if we want to trade and mother said I should write to them she agrees to everything and wants to trade.'" Sister Laura concluded the letter with some small talk writing, "What a diligent wife you have, Rex! Mending stockings while she rides with you. If only my Indian women would have a little of her ambition. I very seldom find them busy when I visit their homes. Naturally, the homes look accordingly. — Well, I am doing my utmost to help them to raise their standards of living but, it's a slow process.—"

A month later Sister Laura again wrote to Land Agent Barnes reporting that Mrs. Boyd had still not heard anything from Cass Lake and that she had to buy wood for heat while other Indians were helping themselves to the wood on her future 8 acres. And Sister Laura being Sister Laura continued saying, "If February continues to behave as he does now wood wont [sic] be in such great demand. Was it ever cold in January! Once we had 38 below. In spite of the cold weather I drove our regularly to my 'Injuns.' Once I drove out at 21 below to meet the group of women whom you saw there, and to my surprise 34 reported on that very cold day."

By February 18, 1950 Mr. Gottwalt was notified that his offer had been accepted by the Area Director.

The real reason, it appears, that the Gottwalts were willing to make the deal is that Mr. Gottwalt's aunt, Sister Laura, being a missionary to the Mille Lacs Indians, was using a small cottage that her nephew had built for her on land that he was leasing for that purpose, and that is what she would use as a meeting place for her work among the Indians of Mille Lacs. That leased land was adjacent to Mrs. Boyd's land and by making this trade Gottwalt could move the cottage used by his aunt a very short distance to land that he would soon own.

By June 18, 1950, they were still trying to find the south lot line, but the southeast corner was buried in the old highway. Sister Laura was under the impression that buildings must be removed by July 7th. But the plot was thickening. Mr. Gottwalt was notified on July 14, 1950, that the Highway Department had set a new date of September 1, 1950, for all buildings to be off the right of way for the new highway. He was advised that since the exchange was not yet final, he could move the building to a temporary foundation on either the Mrs. Boyd property or to a temporary foundation on his leased property. It just had to be off the highway right of way by September 1st.

On November 29, 1950, Sister Laura again wrote to Land Agent Barnes. "Long time no see and no hear from you. — How are you? I suppose not home half of the time. Right? What are the chances for getting the deed to that parcel of land? The last I heard about it, I was told that it is up to you to put the 'final touch' to it. We moved our Little Flower Inn on the new land. — We also have a basement dug for the addition to it, which will be built soon. How is your good wife? Greetings to you both and God bless you."

On December 14, 1950, attorney Phillips wrote to the Office of Indian Affairs in Minneapolis informing them that the deed from Mr. Gottwalt to the United States in trust for Jennie N. Boyd has been duly recorded and the abstract continued to date as requested. And the next day the Area Land Officer provided the deed of Jennie N. Boyd to Louis T. Gottwalt and wife, Marie M. Gottwalt. So, the documents were making their way through channels and the trade was completed by early 1951.[15]

On January 26, 1957, the Superintendent of the Minnesota Chippewa Tribe, along with the Chairman and Secretary, attended a general meeting of the Mille Lacs Reservation members. One of the items discussed was the applicability of State law and order to Mille Lacs Indians. Quoting a February 21, 1957 report, "Some Indians did not seem to know that they were privileged to use local courts and also that they were liable through county courts for offenses committed against each other."

The 1957 report also stated that a takeover agreement on the Mille Lacs Community road was received from Mille Lacs County in which, "they agree to assume maintenance responsibility for the Arrowhead Point Road."

An interesting paragraph indicates that even with the massive government involvement in their affairs, all was not well with the Chippewa Indians of Minnesota. "Two railway carloads of Green Giant peas and corn, consisting of 4,083 cases, were donated to the Minnesota Chippewa Tribe by the Green Giant Canning Company of Le Sueur, Minnesota. They were off color and not marketable through regular mercantile channels."

In a January 1957 report the statement is made that, "The proposed termination legislation affecting certain tribal groups within the Minneapolis area have again been discussed with the Central Office. It is generally agreed Federal responsibilities to certain Indian groups could be terminated in an orderly manner in the near future without adverse effects on the people concerned."

In 1957 Government officials reported,

"On a trip into Minnesota with Area Relocation Specialist Lay, we visited a small, but promising, manufacturing enterprise conducted by Mr. Francis LaQuier and three or four other Indians at the tiny community of Wealthwood near the Mille Lacs Reservation. They have established market outlets for their products, but need machinery, storage space and assembly line organization to produce in the volume required by their market outlets. They are not interested in financial assistance. They want to expand gradually, say they can obtain the necessary machinery without assistance, and will incorporate in a month or so. As they expand and hire new employees, they have indicated an interest in looking further into a possible training agreement. They will manufacture souvenir or toy items and the wholesalers who are prepared to take their entire output are all located in Minneapolis, only about 157 miles distant."[16]

# CHAPTER 9

# Wild Rice Camp Sites

W ild rice is actually not a rice at all, but rather the seed of a grass that
grows in the marshy or shallow edges of lakes in northern sections
of the United States and in Canada. It has traditionally been a staple
of the diet of the Chippewa Indians and probably still is, but once non-Indians
discovered it, a stable market for the harvested supply developed and still exists.
Wild rice was traditionally harvested in canoes with one person moving the canoe
through the grass with a pole and the other bending the grass tops over the boat
and knocking the rice grains loose with a stick so that it falls in the boat, allowing
plenty of seed to fall back in the water to reseed next year's crop. Most natural wild
rice is still harvested this way. The rice then would be parched to loosen the hull.

The government service estimated that 85,000 pounds of wild rice had been
harvested during the 1933 season and that not consumed by the Indians themselves was selling for 18 to 20 cents per pound. The 1934 crop though, had been
reduced by irregular water levels and an early frost.

*Wild rice harvesting, 9th century.*

The Department of Agriculture was assisting the State of Minnesota in 1934 with plans for setting up a cooperative marketing association for the marketing of wild rice, berries and handicrafts. Congress had appropriated $5000 for "Establishment of a system of cooperative marketing for Indian crops, including wild rice, berries, fish and furs." The goals the Government Service had set were:

1. To raise the quality of the product marketed.

2. To stimulate the harvesting of Wild Rice in all the lakes when the production was sufficient to warrant.

3. To increase the amount of Wild Rice held over winter by each Indian family to 125 pounds or more.

4. To establish an organization for handling and marketing native crops, as Wild Rice and blue berries.[1]

With the work force organized under President Roosevelt's Civil Works Administration (CWA) and Federal Emergency Relief Administration (FERA), five modern wild rice camp sites of about ten acres each were built at least one of which was on the White Earth Reservation.

Once the Indian Reorganization Act was passed, the search for wild rice camp sites shifted into high gear.

The Final Project Plan for the Mille Lacs 1937 I.R.A. Expendable Project identified two definite sites for wild rice camps that were being proposed for purchase. Both sites were located in Township 42N., Range 27W., in Sections 5 and 25. The site in Section 5 was on the shore of Lake Ogeche and the one in Section 25 was on the shore of Lake Onamia.

The site on Lake Onamia (Lots 1 and 2 and N1/2 NE1/4, Sec. 25, Town 42N., Range 27W) was owned by Robert G. and H.W. Haverstock. The site had about a half mile of shoreline, 75 acres of hardwood timber and two small cabins used for hunting camps. In total the site included 3 acres of crop land, 45 acres of hay land and 107 acres of woodland and swamp. An option to purchase this site was accepted by the Government for $2,600 on July 7, 1937. [2] [7]

The site on Lake Ogeche (Lots 7 and 8, Sec. 5, Town. 42N., Range 27W.) contained 65.35 acres and was owned by the Onamia Land and Development Company. It too had sufficient timber for firewood for parching. [3] [7]

On August 3, 1937, Land Agent Hook identified five wild rice camp sites that the Mille Lacs Tribal Council was asking the government to purchase:

1. Swamp Lake site (Lots 10 & 11, Sec. 26, T. 46N., R. 25W.) containing 77.15 acres and located 3 miles east of Glen in Aitkin County. It was common for 35 to 40 families to use this site for camping during wild rice harvest by either trespassing on white-owned property or by paying a fee for camping. This lake contained a rice bed of about 150 acres, one half the area of the lake. The Superintendent of the Consolidated Chippewa Agency was also urging the purchase of this site. [4] [2]

2. White Elk Lake site (Lot 4, Sec. 19, T. 50N., R. 27W) located 21 miles north of Aitkin in Aitkin County and containing 26 acres and Lot 3 containing 39.5 acres.

3. Mud Lake site (Lot 2 and the SE1/4 SW1/4, Sec. 11, Lot 5, Sec. 2, T. 45N., R. 27W) located one mile east of Bennetville in Aitkin County and containing 124.3 acres.

4. Dean Lake site (Lots 1 & 2, except the south 10 acres of Lot 2, Sec. 18, T. 36N., R. 25W.) located 13 miles northwest of Crosby and 12 miles northwest of Aitkin in Crow Wing County and containing 96.11 acres. Practically this entire 500- acre lake was a wild rice bed and hardly ever failed to produce a crop, usually producing 35 to 40 tons of rice in a season. There was a 24 x 26 ft house on the site

as well as a good well, 30 acres of crop land and 70 acres of hardwood timber.[5] [2]

5.  A second Lake Ogeche site just west of Onamia owned by the D.S. B Johston Land Company containing about 300 acres.[6]

In addition to the requests of the Mille Lacs Tribal Council, several other sites were being recommended by the Chippewas of Minnesota for purchase as wild rice camp sites. Among them were:

1.  Lake Minnewawa site (MR/4 SW/4 and lot 5, Sec.32, Twp. 49, Rge. 23) in Aitkin County. This site was 40 miles from Fond du Lac and 45 miles from Mille Lacs and had been used in the past by about 75 families either by trespassing on private land or paying a camping fee. This site contained about 400 acres of rice bed and normally produced 40 to 50 tons of rice annually. Ample firewood was available on the heavily wooded site.[7]

2.  Another Mud Lake site (Lots 2 & 3, Sec. 28, Twp. 144, Rg. 26) located 5 miles from Ball Club and 35 miles from Cass Lake and 20 miles from Sugar Point. 75 to 100 families used this lake for ricing which contains an estimated 5000 acres of rice beds and 100 tons of rice could easily be harvested annually. The site contained 40 acres of hardwood timber and 40 acres of meadow land.[8]

3. Laura Lake site (Lots 1 & 2, Sec. 36, Twp. 141, Rge. 29) in Cass County was 35 miles north of Mille Lacs, 50 miles from Fond du Lac and 35 miles from Onigum. 75 to 80 families normally riced Laura Lake annually which produced about 25 tons of rice from about 250 acres of rice bed. This site contained 89.61 acres with plenty of firewood.[9] [2]

4.  Bowstring Lake site (no description) which was adjacent to Inger and close to White Oak Point, Ball Club, Sugar Point and Cass Lake. 50 to 60 families normally riced this site annually by trespassing on Indian allotments. This rice

bed normally produced 25 to 30 tons of wild rice and had ample wood supply for parching.[10]

The government Indian Service had successfully purchased 13 wild rice camp sites by 1939 and they were still looking for additional properties. In searching for these properties, the primary objectives were finding lakeshore on wild rice beds that would accommodate the camping of the Indians for the several week periods during harvest as well as access to timber from which to secure the wood needed for parching the rice.[7]

The Minnesota Chippewa Tribe, with the aid of the federal agents, were forming a corporation, the purpose of which was to purchase, transport, grade, finish and market the wild rice. This would give the individual Indians a ready market for the rice they harvested as well as establish a price point for sale of the rice to the public.

By 1939 the corporation had secured a $20,000 loan from the Revolving Credit Fund that had been established under the Indian Reorganization Act.

But all was not well in the fall of 1939. The Government had purchased a wild rice camp site on Dean Lake in Crow Wing County, but Mr. Laughlin, from whom the property was purchased, would not vacate the property until he received his check and the Land Agent would not give him his check until he vacated. The check had been issued by the United States Treasury on July 20th in the amount of $1450. $906.64 had been paid to the holder of a contract for deed on the property, $493.36 was being held in escrow to be released by the Land Agent when all title matters had been resolved and Mr. Laughlin had supposedly received a check for $50.

Several Indian families were camped on this site and some of the rice was ready for harvesting. Game Warden Christensen told them they could start harvesting on Tuesday — which they did — but on Wednesday they were told by the game warden that all lakes in Crow Wing County were closed. When questioned, game warden Christensen said he had received a phone call from his superior notifying him that all lakes were closed. Frank Broker, President of the Indian Tribal Council, who was at Dean Lake on a visit, gave the Indians permission to start ricing and notified the game warden to that effect. While there Mr. Broker had learned that Mr. Laughlin was charging the Indians 25 pounds of rice per family for camping there.[11]

By September 9, 1939, the Credit Agent for the Wild Rice Corporation Enterprise was struggling with the proposed budget for the business. If her estimates were correct that the wild rice would be purchased from the Indians who gathered it for 11 cents per pound and sold for 35 cents per pound, and if her estimates of the cost of operations were correct, the corporation would be losing money. Superintendent Burns replied saying that some sales of the finished product had been made at 35 cents per pound for second grade rice and 40 cents per pound for first grade rice. Corporation manager Paul LaRoque had sent letters to several companies in an effort to secure sales of rice, including Sears Roebuck, Applebaum's Market and Montgomery Ward, in which he was asking a price of 40 cents per pound for Grade 1, small and 45 cents per pound for Grade 1, large.[12]

Apparently, the venture, for whatever reason, did not survive due to Public Law 108 in the 104th Congress, passed in 1996. The act was entitled "An Act to make certain technical corrections in laws relating to Native Americans, and for other purposes." Section 13 of that act was entitled "Revocation of charter of incorporation of the Minnesota Chippewa Tribe under the Indian Reorganization Act" and read "The request of the Minnesota Chippewa Tribe to surrender the charter of incorporation issued to that tribe on September 17, 1937, pursuant to section 17 of the Act of June 18, 1934, commonly known as the 'Indian Reorganization Act' (48 Stat. 988, chapter 576; 25 U.S.C. 477) is hereby accepted and that charter of incorporation is hereby revoked."

Currently Minnesota Stat. § 84.10 provides: "It shall be unlawful for any person to take wild rice grain from any of the waters within the original boundaries of the White Earth, Leech Lake, Nett Lake, Vermillion, Grand Portage, Fond due Lac and Mille Lacs Reservations except said persons be of Indian blood, or residents of the reservation upon which said wild rice grain is taken."

Minnesota Department of Natural Resources Wild Rice Regulations state, under the heading of "Indian Reservation Restrictions (General),"

> All native wild rice within the existing boundaries of the White Earth, Leech Lake, Bois Forte, Grand Portage, Fond du Lac, and Mille Lacs Indian Reservations is managed by the respective reservation wild rice committees. These committees establish the opening date, days, and hours of harvest no less than 24 hours prior to the opening. These regulations may be altered by the wild rice committees after the season has been announced by posting the major entrances to affected waters no less than 12 hours prior to the changes taking effect. It is unlawful for any person to take wild rice grain from any of the waters within the original boundaries at the White Earth, Leech Lake, Nett Lake, Vermillion Lake, Grand Portage, Fond du Lac and

Mille Lacs reservations except for Native Americans or residents of the reservation upon which said wild rice is taken.

The Mille Lacs Band Statutes Annotated (amended through May 14, 2004) read as follows:

§2301 Band license — "Every enrollee of the Mille Lacs Band of Chippewa Indians who harvest wild rice within the Mille Lacs Reservation shall have in his or her possession a proper Band ricing license..."

§2302 Non-Band license — "If the Commissioner of Natural Resources determines that it is in the best interests of the Mille Lacs Band of Chippewa Indians, he may issue a non-Band ricing license to any enrolled member of a federally recognized tribe..."

§2303 Non-Indian license — "If the Commissioner of Natural Resources determines that it is in the best interests of the Mille Lacs Band of Chippewa Indians, he may issue non-Indian ricing licenses in numbers determined by him to be suitable..."

## CHAPTER 10

# The Minnesota Chippewa Tribe

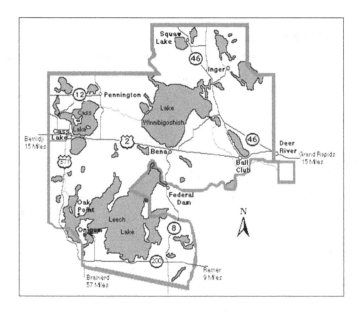

U
p to 1922 the Federal Government had manned Chippewa agencies at White Earth, Leech Lake, Fond du Lac, Nett Lake and Grand Portage, all reservations that had been allotted as well as an agency at Red Lake which had not been allotted. On July 1, 1922, the agencies for the allotted reservations were merged into the Consolidated Minnesota Chippewa Indian Agency and located at Cass Lake, Minnesota.

In September of 1934, a request from a Rev. W.K. Boyle from Bemidji, MN, as to the financial status in Washington of the Minnesota Chippewas, resulted in the following answer.

"The tribal funds belonging to the Chippewa Indians amount to $836,000. Practically each year there has been a per capita payment from this fund of from $25 to $50 for each man, woman and child, and without any means of increasing or adding to this fund, it is rapidly diminishing in size." The answer to his inquiry continued saying, "It is not intended when these funds are entirely exhausted that these Indians shall be made the responsibility of the State. The Federal Government through gratuity appropriations will continue to look after those Indians who are our responsibility. ... We realize that many of the Indians in the Chippewa country have disposed of or lost their lands and are in need of assistance. ... Furthermore, as you probably know, these Indians have pending in the Court of Claims suits against the Government seeking to recover large sums of money. We have no way of knowing when action will be taken, what amount will be awarded the Indians, or when Congress will make the appropriation to cover the sum. This money and the purposes to which it may be put will have an important bearing on the future of the Chippewas as well as any program that may be worked out for them."[1]

On April 4, 1938, Acting Secretary of the Interior Oscar L. Chapman notified Superintendent Lewis Balsam that he was authorized to remove the furniture and records of the Consolidated Chippewa Agency as he had been instructed to do by the Commissioner of Indian Affairs, and move everything in the office to Duluth. A few days before this message from the office of the Secretary of the Interior, an incident had occurred at Cass Lake, apparently in response to the instructions from the Commissioner to move the office. A former White Earth Chippewa, who apparently now lived in Oklahoma, sent a clipping from the *Oklahoma News* of March 29th which described the incident:

"A dozen enraged Indian women beat Supt. Lewis Balson of the Consolidated Chippewa Agency today in protest against an order from Washington transferring the office from Cass Lake to Duluth, Minn. The attack occurred while Indian braves in full war paint and regalia picketed the agency office. Balson was not injured seriously but retreated to the office. The women closed in on Balson as he stood in front of the office reading aloud a formal order from Washington for removal of the headquarters to Duluth. The braves, meanwhile, continued their march around the agency office, preventing removal of agency files. Balson feared further violence."

Louis Balsam, the Superintendent of the Consolidated Chippewa Agency, wrote a lengthy explanation, at least in his opinion, to Commissioner Collier on April 7th from Duluth, stating that when he arrived at Cass Lake last September he found "corruption, skullduggery, intimidation, graft and even murder" to be the state of affairs at Cass Lake Agency headquarters. He accused his predecessor, Superintendent Burns, a Chippewa whose own allotment was at Cass Lake, as well as the regional office in Minneapolis, of knowing about it but doing nothing. Balsam made it known to Collier that when he had taken over the office in Cass Lake he tried to make some order of the office but,

> letters simply could not be found, much of the filing being a year behind, unpaid bills were as much as five years old and it was common talk that some houses could not sell to the Agency because they never got paid, no office hours or days for transaction of regular and special business had been fixed, etc., etc.: after months of the foregoing, the Co-operative which had been found in a mess, ripened into an acute situation. The new superintendent tackled that. Four hundred pages of hearings are in D.C. now and tell their own story. At once, all the old gang rallied. Board members of the Co-op., on their manager's payroll, rallied others equally battening upon tribal funds. A hue and cry were raised about the white superintendent mistreating poor Indians, etc., etc. — always the white against the Indians: the usual smoke screen.

He related that the president of the local boosters' club had told him that "Power in high places brought this agency here. Nothing you or the present Commissioner can do will ever move it." The merchants of Cass Lake, he charged, were a loud voice in opposition to moving the agency, not wanting to lose the business the agency's presence generated. He ended his letter to the Commissioner writing, "It is not an unusual picture: A new man in entirely new environment, standing alone; changes where change is feared and hated; and now this yowling and demand for the old order. It must not triumph, else, as I see it, all we are struggling for may just as well be forgotten."

Minnesota Governor Elmer Benson sided with those that wanted the agency to stay at Cass Lake and the Duluth Chamber of Commerce favored the move to Duluth. The Executive Committee of the Minnesota Chippewa Tribe passed a resolution asking for the removal of Louis Balsam from any connection with the Consolidated Chippewa Agency.

Minnesota Governor
Elmer Austin Benson

Apparently, the Cass County Sheriff and a group of local Indians had occupied the Cass Lake office and were preventing the Indian Service access to the records remaining there. Secretary Ickes contacted the Attorney General and asked that he direct the United States Attorney at St. Paul, Minnesota, to use the appropriate means to prosecute the offenders who were obstructing the work of the Indian Service.

Secretary Ickes, in an effort to settle the dispute, called for an election of the Minnesota Chippewa to determine where they want the Consolidated Chippewa Agency to be located. The choices on the ballot were Bemidji, Cass Lake, Duluth, Grand Rapids, Minneapolis, White Earth Reservation, and also with an opportunity for write-ins. The votes were tabulated and Cass Lake was the clear winner. As a result, and after conferring with Superintendent Balsam, Commissioner Collier recommended that the Agency be moved back to Cass Lake, that Superintendent Burns be reappointed to that post and that Superintendent Balsam be moved to a new area. Secretary Ickes complied with Commissioner Collier's recommendation but with certain conditions.

These conditions he enumerated to Frank Broker, the president of the Tribal Executive Committee of the Minnesota Chippewa Tribe writing that reestablishing the Agency headquarters at Cass Lake was contingent on Cass Lake to "clean house and keep it clean." Decent living conditions at fair rental prices must be provided the Indian Service employees, and, he added, drunkenness and prostitution must be eliminated from the streets of Cass Lake. Cass Lake must be made a desirable place to live.

It would appear that this description of conditions at Cass Lake was not an exaggeration as evidenced from a letter from Special Officer H.P. Davis to Assistant Commissioner of Indian Affairs Zimmerman written August 17, 1938. In this letter Agent Davis writes,

"The following is my report of conditions as I found them in Cass Lake during the four days I was there ... The lack of proper law enforcement is very noticeable. Drunkenness on the streets by both men and women, Indians and whites, is open and common. It is not uncommon for groups of drunks to congregate on the sidewalk near the drinking places and argue and quarrel loud enough to be heard a block or so away. Profane and vulgar remarks are heard often on the streets.

Indians can obtain liquor easily. I saw them drinking over the Bar and in booths in four different places in the town. In two of them, Indians were about their only customers. Open gambling is permitted and a poker game is run in the Fuller Recreation Parlor each evening and is patronized mostly by Indians. Drinking establishments stay open until late hours in the morning or as long as there are customers sufficient to make it worthwhile. I was informed that the City Ordinance provides that they close at 11 P.M. only on Saturday, then at 12 o'clock midnight.

In addition to the ten drinking places in town, there are three night clubs — The Red Rooster ... the Green Grove Inn ... and the Silver Star .... The Red Rooster does not solicit Indian trade, but sells to Indian girls when they are accompanied there by white men. The other two places solicit Indian trade, especially the Silver Star where they can buy hard liquor and beer by the drink or bottle. The night clubs in the country stay open all night. The only house of prostitution reported to me was in the south part of town and is being run by Mrs. Sythers and her daughter Birdie where they have four other girls. It seems to be a well known place.

A Mr. Johnson and I went out at about daylight one morning and was met outside by Birdie who informed us they were all busy and wouldn't let us come in the house, but told us to go down town and get a quart of "10 High" whiskey and return in an hour or so. As I didn't care to partake of their hospitality, I didn't return. There are dozens of girls on the streets in the evenings, some of which are looking for a partner who is willing to buy them liquor and food, and if you would care to lease a cabin on some lake, they would go and stay with you all night. This was suggested to me a couple of times.

Such were the conditions in Cass Lake at the time."[2]

The Emergency Relief Appropriations Act of 1937 had been passed by Congress and with this authority the Office of Indian Affairs had allocated $50,000 for the benefit of the Minnesota Consolidated Tribe. Of this amount $4,500 was earmarked for houses, house repairs and a well at Mille Lacs.[3]

On December 31, 1954, the Minneapolis Area Director reported to the Commissioner of Indian Affairs that, "The consolidation of the Red Lake and Consolidated Chippewa Agencies, now the Minnesota Agency located at Bemidji, Minnesota, was effective on December 1."

Reports from the Minneapolis Area Office of the BIA to the Commissioner in 1955 stated that the Red Lake Fisheries had a 100,000-pound increase in the catch from last year and that the Minnesota Chippewa Tribe wild rice business was thriving. They worried, however, that, "As conservation measures are not applied to this ancient activity, it appears that the whites and Indians are going to ruin the possibilities of future crops." They reported that the 1955 Minnesota State Legislature had made available $12,500 to Indians with one-fourth or more degree of Indian blood, to be used for scholarship grants for higher education. The report stated that "Two Mille Lacs allotments were purchased in the name of the Minnesota Chippewa Tribe, which leaves only 26 allotments of the original 282 in individual trust ownership ...." In the health field they related that weekly clinics were conducted by part-time doctors at Grand Portage and Mille Lacs Reservations. They reported that among others an application for funds in the amount of $42,000 was completed for new school construction at Onamia, Minnesota, under Public Law 815, Title 4.

It is interesting that the Minneapolis Area Office of the BIA had under its supervision Indian groups and reservations in Minnesota, Wisconsin, Iowa and Michigan. Their supervision of timber and lumbering was extensive and in 1955 they reported that "over 2,200,000 board feet of timber with a value of about $6,200 was scaled during the month" of December.

Illegitimate births and cohabitation were concerns of the Bureau of Indian Affairs. Their report states, "This illegitimate birth rate [24% in 1954] is very high in comparison to non-Indian communities." Commenting on cohabitation they related that,

At the present time there are approximately 50 cases of illicit cohabitation. Many of these cases are quite involved due to one party being married and the presence of children. Others are short term arrangements where the individual lives with a succession of mates. It is necessary to have many individual interviews with the court and clients involved with this type of problem.

Apparently, the social work that the BIA was involved in — that they felt was not getting adequate attention — included unmarried mothers, juvenile delinquency and cohabitation.[4]

# CHAPTER 11

# Ten, Fifteen, Seventy-Five, Eighty-Five Years into the Future

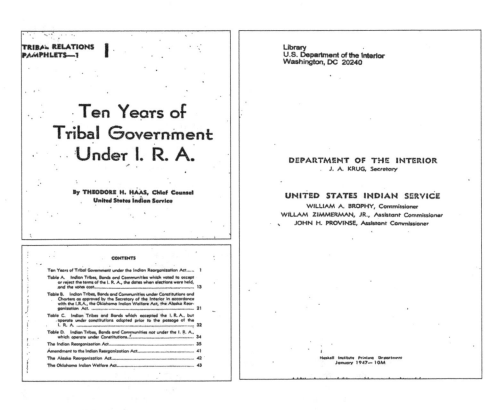

In 1947 William A. Brophy was Commissioner of Indian Affairs and Julius A. Krug was Secretary of the Interior all under President Harry S. Truman. Theodore H. Haas, Chief Counsel for the U.S. Indian Service wrote an analysis of the effect of the Indian Reorganization Act (IRA) on tribal government.

He opined that under the IRA Indian tribes were "authorized" to "take over control of their own resources and to conduct tribal enterprises as membership corporations which would be subject to diminishing federal supervision as the tribal leadership showed a desire for more control and an ability to direct their affairs." He stated that at the present time there are 195 tribes under the IRA. He classifies the Minnesota Chippewa as a confederacy or several groups combined. Haas seems to indicate that the intent is for the federal government to get out of the business of directing federal Indian policy saying, "Most of the I.R.A. charters provide that after the charters have been in effect for a specified period of years certain supervisory powers of the Secretary of the Interior may be terminated by action of the tribal council, the Secretary and the tribe."

Haas correctly explained that "Since the Indians were denied their natural way of life, the government had to establish the odious ration system which sapped initiative and resourcefulness. Many of the Indians became dependent upon government aid as a consequence. A tradition of need for assistance therefore has been developed…"

He blames some of the difficulty in implementing the I.R.A. on Indian Service officials who were skeptical that the IRA was sound policy. In fact, he says, "there were some who did not believe in Indian self-government. The attitude of the local administration in such cases may be likened to that of a colonial administrator who feels a keen sense of duty as a supervisor over an inferior people whose lives he controls."

> **3. Lack of familiarity among the Indians with white culture.** With the exception of a comparatively few tribes and individual Indians, American Indians are among the most economically depressed groups in the country. Educated Indians and those experienced in white methods often leave the reservation. While there has been a great improvement in the amount of education which most Indians receive, it is still several years less than that of most whites in neighboring communities. This leaves a dearth of educated leadership to carry on at home. Also the inability of many of the older Indians to understand English and many of the younger Indians to understand their native Indian tongue adds additional barriers. Lack of understanding and cooperation between the new and the old generation, an inevitable consequence in a rapidly changing culture, is often used to keep Indians in a divided status. Indians in some states are disenfranchised, and even in states where they vote, nowhere, save possibly in the State of Oklahoma, are many Indians elected or appointed to important offices. All these factors indirectly reflect on local Indians. For example most Indian councilmen had little experience in local government or in political matters generally prior to the institution of self-government on the reservation. Deeply frustrated groups are often plagued by internal rivalry and factionalism. Scapegoats are often sought. The Indians' plight is blamed on a person, a Bureau or a statute. The Commissioner of Indian Affairs, the Indian Office, the Superintendent, the Council or the I. R. A. may be attacked as the cause of all woes.

Haas states that "American Indians are among the most economically depressed groups in the country. Educated Indians and those experienced in white methods often leave the reservation. … Also the inability of many of the older Indians to understand English and many of the younger Indians to understand their native Indian tongue adds additional barriers."

The report then in general terms exemplifies the accomplishments of tribes since enactment of the IRA.[1]

## Minnesota Chippewa Tribal Council — April 7, 1949

While Legal Counsel Haas seemed to be convinced that the Indian Reorganization Act was alive and well, Sam Zimmerman of Grand Marais, President of the Minnesota Chippewa Tribal Council, seemed to think otherwise. In a letter to Congress but especially the Minnesota Senators and Representatives Zimmerman writes,

> "Pursuant to your request we are herewith giving you an analysis of our problem to date.
>
> As you well know the Indians of Minnesota are directly under the so-called Indian Department, and incidentally under the Department of Interior. During some 150 years there have accumulated a large number of regulations issued out of that department and the war department ordering us what to do. These number into the thousand. These are not laws but are regulations which are used by the department agents to control us. When the subject is raised in court, invariably the courts hold that they do not supply [apply?], but when the Indians then follows the ruling he is stepped on. Some of these problems are as follows:
>
> An Indian cannot hold land unless approved by the President of the United States. This land is held in trust and disposed of as the Government sees fit. Many times the Indian does not know he has any land or money coming to him unless he asks. If he fails to do so he may never get his money.
>
> The Indian is discriminated against and cannot live like a white man, which is in violation of former treaties. He is unable to apply the write [writ] of habeas corpus; to drink beer which by law has been declared to be non-intoxicating. He cannot be

sold soft drinks because it may be used for mixing with strong drink. (There have been and still are indictments for the selling of coke to Indians.) See Federal Judge Nordbye. The courts have held he was a human being, but so far that ruling apparently has been disregarded.

He cannot cut his timber or grow crops without the consent of the Indian Bureau, and he must rely on state aid for relief although he may have a fortune in timber he wishes to cut. (See Nett Lake Reservation — Lawrence Connors.) Much of this timber has reached its maturity and is now rotting, but it must rot since he cannot get the consent of the Bureau to cut it.

He cannot contract his timber for the best price; he must rely on the government agents to contract it. As a result, in Minnesota he is being deprived of a living because the Weyerhauser interests have, through the Indian bureau, tied up his timber; he was never consulted. For 150 years the government has thrown hundreds, even thousands of lawsuits in his lap, but very little money or justice.

In every single instance of exploitation of the Indian, the government through the Indian Bureau has been a party. Every contract of logging, sale, or other business was conducted soley [sic] by the Indian department and the record included in the many lawsuits pending shows deliberate dishonesty, and the history of government scalers is something to shudder over. Examples of every kind and description can be found in the saling [sic] records which have not been destroyed. For records see the log scales of 1913 in the Grand Portage case. Where as much as three thousand dollars per eighty acres were extracted from the Indian this way. The enemy of the Indians is not the business man — the Indian is now wise to him and in many cases wiser.

The above should make you ponder our problem — Now can we of Minnesota get:

1. The absolute right of citizenship.

2. Since in Minnesota, he has set up his own corporation, and has demonstrated he is superior to the Department in his ability to administer, he should be released from the Indian Department in Minnesota. For proof of this

statement, see Mr. Savage, business manager for the Minnesota tribe.

3. The elimination of intoxicating liquor discrimination. Since many of the young men have come back from the army, they have criticized the department for this regulation.

4. The right to cut their own timber so they can make a living. Since the corporation has set up a sales agency, the [that] can deal directly with the buyers of timber and their men can do their own logging. As it now stands he gets little for his timber and no work. The way it is now handled he is constantly cheated and winds up with a lawsuit instead of a living and since the government controls his funds he must of necessity have the lawyers finance these lawsuits.

5. There is ample proof of their diversion of funds to violate the directive of Congress in the order for cancellation of reginal offices. For your information see your own directive. For testimony see the Minnesota Tribal Council. The Minneapolis office must be closed; so far it is just a bottleneck and the cost to the government has been some $100,000 per year.

6. The United States has ample proof of their ability to transfer title since the title of the United States Government is in the form of treaty deeds from these Indians — now they cannot deal with his own property.

7. We want the Minnesota Tribal Council to take over the duties of the department in Minnesota. They will give you much more efficiency and less cost that the department. Where they need help on roads they can make deals with the local agencies and not go to the government.

He has nothing to say about his budget, nor who will govern him, a direct violation of democratic rule, which was foisted upon him through a series of regulations which are not law, but are more fearsome — a dictatorial policy. Under the policy of the Government he can still be hunted like an animal and a bounty paid for his scalp. These laws are still on the books and were vividly called to the public's attention when a man was being tried for running down and killing three Indians. The case was not only dismissed, but the perpetrator tried to collect the bounty. (See Minnesota case — for reference see Minnesota Chippewa Council.)

His funds have been taken in violation of laws for over a hundred years, and when the Congress of these United States created the Indian Claims Commission to give him justice, because other courts had narrowed down the law, the authorities seem to consider it still a court of law and not one of equity. In this the intent of Congress will be abrogated. Congress should issue a directive clarifying this subject or the rotten root of Indian injustice will still remain. He wants his just chance in court.

He cannot go to a state school unless he pays the state. For many years the Chippewa was paying a fee for this purpose until their funds ran out. Now he is there by sufferance. A grand heritage for the people who deeded around three million square miles of territory which makes up this country. There has been no parallel under any other government comparable to this treatment — even taking into consideration Stalin, Hitler, Tojo, and others — for similar treatment we are hanging our enemies.

He has only restrictive citizenry — only that given him [by] the Department. Many of their regulations have been set aside by courts, but they pay no attention to those decisions. (See decision regarding guardianship.)

He has no right to seek an accounting without the consent of Congress. When he goes to seek some right or information he is thrown out. The Grand Portage Indian Reservation is in the process [of] destruction by reason of the arbitrary wilderness area, which will starve him upon his own reservation — he was never consulted. He has supported the State of Minnesota in pushing through the Indian Department and Congress in obtaining a right of way through their reservation which was to bring tourists to him and thus give him a solution to his economic problems. Now it seems the State in conspiracy with other departments and the Isaak Walton League intend to destroy the remnants of his home. The matter was promised by Congress — by the State of Minnesota, and much time, money and energy was spent on this project. The Indians intend to fight this matter. Oberholtser. Zimmerman, Chapman, Hoffman and others should be set right in this matter.

In may [many] instances where the department has made a bosh of things they have gladly transferred that problem to the Indian council and in every instance the Indians have worked it out without much trouble. See Nett Lake Cooperate, the Indian Farm and others.

Where the council with its board of directors have shown much more efficiency and diligence that the department, what reason have you to delay turning over to the Indians their inherent right, unless you, yourselves, adopt the creed of the department.

We believe the Minnesota delegation to a man, and with other interested members of Congress if need be, should confer without delay with the new Commissioner of Indian Affairs [probably referring to John Nichols], and without fanfare, remove this bug a boo from our State.

We believe that the new Secretary of the Interior, whoever he may be, should not be confirmed until he has released these slaves. You have the power, and should exercise it.

If you do not, we have but one alternative — to test these laws and regulations through the courts and reach back to our treaties for the inherent right of a political body, to do these things without the consent of the Indian Bureau.

For your further information we have served notice on the State of Minnesota through the Governor, that we will close highway 61 where it runs over our tribal property, and where the State of Minnesota has no easement or right of way. We intend to do this during August or [of?] this year. Much harm will be done — much poor advertising for the State will result, and the tourist business will receive a serious setback — all can be corrected by the State doing what they promised Congress — build eight miles of road as they promised to the village of Grand Portage, Minnesota.

> You have all met us and we believe we have offered proof of our ability. Please help us.
>
> Minnesota Chippewa Tribal Council
> By Sam Zimmerman, Its President"[2]

• • • • • • • • • • • • • • • • • • • • • •

## THE INDIAN REORGANIZATION ACT — 75 YEARS LATER
### *Renewing Our Commitment to Restore Tribal Homelands and Promote Self-Determination*

HEARING

Before the
COMMITTEE ON INDIAN AFFAIRS
UNITED STATES SENATE
ONE HUNDRED TWELFTH CONGRESS
FIRST SESSION
June 23, 2011

Daniel K Akaka, Hawaii, *Chairman*
John Barrasso, Wyoming, *Vice Chairman*
Committee members:
Daniel K Inouye, Hawaii
Kent Conrad, North Dakota
Tim Johnson, South Dakota
Maria Cantwell, Washington
Jon Tester, Montana
Tom Udall, New Mexico
Al Franken, Minnesota
John McCain, Arizona
Lisa Murkowski, Alaska
John Hoeven, North Dakota
Mike Crapo, Idaho
Mike Johanns, Nebraska

Opening Statement by Daniel Akaka:

> *"... When Congress enacted the Indian Reorganization Act in 1934, its intent was very clear. Congress intended to end Federal*

*policies of termination and allotment and begin an era of empowering tribes by restoring their homelands and encouraging self-determination. Those fundamental goals still guide Federal Indian policy today.*

*When Congress amended the Indian Reorganization Act in 1994, it reaffirmed the original intent of the IRA and ensured that all tribes would be treated equally, no matter when their relationship with the Federal Government was recognized.*

*In addition, the Congress explicitly rejected the Department of Interior Solicitor's opinions implementing policies which divided tribes into separate classes. Since 1934, the IRA has stood as the bedrock of Federal Indian policy.*

*However, a Supreme Court decision in 2009 narrowly construed the text of the IRA and completely up-ended the status quo, which had existed for 75 years, contrary to Congressional intent, legislative history, and affirmative actions by the Administration.*

*I have a great deal of respect for the Supreme Court and the hard work that they do. However, when the court gets it wrong, it is the responsibility of Congress to fix it. ... "*

Frederick E. Hoxie, History Professor, University of Illinois:

*"... When Congress approved the Indian Reorganization Act in June, 1934 it articulated and advanced three broad goals.*

*First, the IRA was intended to end allotment ... by the Dawes Severalty Act ...*

*Second, the IRA made possible the organization of tribal governments and tribal corporations ...*

*Third, by ending the allotment policy and providing for the future development and even expansion of reservation communities, Congress endorsed the idea that individuals could be both U.S. and tribal citizens. For the first time in history, the Federal Government codified in a general statute the idea that tribal citizenship was compatible with national citizenship and that Indian-ness would have a continuing place in American life."*

William Rice, Professor, University of Tulsa College of Law:

*"Mr. Chairman, ... I ... would like to note with appreciation your work on ... all the hearings you have conducted on the*

*Declaration on the Rights of Indigenous People.... [adopted by the United Nations General Assembly on September 13, 2007 by a vote of 143 for, 4 against and 11 abstaining. Australia, New Zealand, Canada and the United States voted against the adoption.] They are intertwined with this idea of the IRA. The IRA was something of a precursor to this. ... "*

Question by Chairman Akaka for Professor Rice:

*"Professor Rice, in your testimony, you mentioned the recent hearing the Committee held on the United Nations Declaration on the Rights of Indigenous People. Do you think the policies in the Indian Reorganization Act and the U.N. Declaration are compatible when it comes to treatment of Indian lands and self-governance of indigenous peoples?"*

Answer:

*"... I believe they can be made so. They are very, very close as we sit here and look at the text of the Declaration. The statutory authority in the IRA calls for self-determination by tribes, self-governance by tribes, and recovery of tribal homelands that have otherwise been lost. The Declaration calls for those same things. ... "*

Carole E. Goldberg, Professor, UCLA School of Law

*"...And what this policy did was abandon the goal of assimilation in favor of the belief that Native American societies had a right to exist on the basis of a culture different from the dominant one in the United States, and this could only be achieved through establishment and reestablishment of the territorial basis for tribal self-determination. That was a key component of the purpose of the Indian Reorganization Act. ... There was no comprehensive list of federally recognized tribes at the time of enactment of the IRA* [Author's note: see list in appendix of "and the Mille Lacs who have no Reservation"] *... ."*

Question by Chairman Akaka for Professor Rice:

*"Professor Rice, in your research of the Indian Reorganization Act, did you ever come across documentation that indicated that*

*Congress intended the Indian Reorganization Act to exist only for a limited number of tribes or for a limited amount of time?"*

Answer:

*"The short answer to that, Senator, is no. As has already been said, at the time there was no list of federally recognized tribes. ... "*

Ms. Goldberg:

*"... one of the things that seems to be evident in some recent opinions of the United States Supreme Court is a departure from some very fundamental, what we call canons of construction, rules for interpreting statutes that have been part of the U.S. Supreme Court doctrine since the early 1899s and Chief Justice John Marshall.*

*And what those doctrines dictate is that when a statute is presented to the court that is ambiguous, the terms are not clear, that all of the uncertainties or ambiguities are supposed to be resolved in favor of supporting outcomes that favor tribal self-determination and land rights. ... "*[3]

• • • • • • • • • • • • • • • • • • • • • • • •

## A LEGAL REVIEW

### Tribal Jurisdiction over Nonmembers
#### *November 26, 2013*

"As a general rule, Indian tribes lack criminal and civil jurisdiction over non- enrolled members. However, there are exceptions. First, Congress re-vested Indian tribes with inherent authority to exercise criminal jurisdiction over non-enrolled member Indians, as well as non-Indians who commit dating and domestic violence against Indians within the tribes' jurisdictions, provided the non-Indian has certain enumerated ties to the tribes. Second, under the first *Montana* exception, tribes may exercise civil jurisdiction over non-members when the non-members have entered private consensual relationships with the tribe or its members, provided the conduct at issue relates to the consensual relationship. Third, under the second *Montana* exception, Indian tribes may exercise civil jurisdiction over non-members when the non-members' conduct threatens the integrity of the tribe. Fourth, tribes may exercise jurisdiction over non-members when Congress authorizes them to do so.

Although the Supreme Court has recognized the tribal right to exclude non-members from tribal land as a basis for regulatory authority, it is not clear whether the right to exclude is independent of the *Montana* exceptions. While the Supreme Court has drawn tribal jurisdiction over non-members narrowly, it has also held that defendants in tribal court who challenge the tribal court's jurisdiction must exhaust their tribal court remedies before seeking relief in federal court."

This entire legal review can be found in Appendix 6 of this book.

• • • • • • • • • • • • • • • • • • • • • •

## 2020 — Mille Lacs Band owns these Businesses

Grand Casino Mille Lacs with adjoining hotel and convention center and several restaurants

Grand Casino Hinckley with three hotels, RV resort, restaurants, spa, golf course and convention center

Woodlands National Bank Onamia with branches in Hinckley, Sturgeon Lake, Zimmerman, Minneapolis, Cloquet and Grand Market

East Lake Convenience Store, McGregor

Grand Market, Onamia

Grindstone Laundry, Hinckley

Grand National Golf Course. Hinckley

Grand Makwa Cinema, Onamia

Hinckley Medical Office, Hinckley

Doubletree by Hilton & Rival House Sporting Parlour Restaurant, St. Paul

Doubletree by Hilton Minneapolis Park Place Hotel, Saint Louis Park

Embassy Suites by Hilton Oklahoma City Will Rogers Airport, Oklahoma City

Intercontinental Saint Paul Riverfront Hotel & Citizen Restaurant, St. Paul

Big Sandy Lodge & Resort, McGregor

Mille Lacs Super Stop, Onamia

Sweetgrass Media, Onamia

Subway Restaurant, Onamia

2020 Brand Solutions, South St. Paul

Taco Johns, Onamia

Crossroads Convenience Store, Hinckley

Eddy's Resort, Onamia[4]

# Epilogue

*"to everything there is a season, and*
*a time to every purpose under the heaven"*

~ Ecclesiastes 3:1

*We the People of the United States,*
*in Order to form a more perfect Union…*

As we conclude Volume 2, let's look back over what we have learned:
The 1452 order of Pope Nicholas V authorizing Christian nations to take ownership of any lands they discovered and the desire of the monarchs of Europe for more power, which translated into more land and people (subjects) and the desire on the part of these people (subjects) for religious and economic freedom. This resulted in these courageous pioneers embarking on unknown journeys across an often unrelenting and merciless ocean in search of a better life for themselves and their families. What they found upon arrival was a land already populated. Sparsely, yes, but populated. And even though sparsely populated, the natives far outnumbered the pioneers, putting the pioneers in a perilous position in the event of conflict. How were these pioneers to know how many natives were out there? They had no idea how far the land extended to the west until Lewis and Clark made their expedition to the Pacific Ocean.

The European nations had decided that, from their respective, any land claimed by the explorer nations would then belong to that nation. England and France established most of the colonies in North America, but the original thirteen colonies were British. England crafted a policy of making treaties with the natives in which the British acquired land, and, following the Revolutionary War and the establishment of the United States of America, the treaty-making process was inherited by the new nation.

There is little or no doubt that the societies of Europe were more advanced in what we term 'civilization' than the societies then inhabiting what would become the United States of America. Was one better than the other? Debatable. But what is clear is that the system that England — and eventually the colonies followed by the United States government — were using to acquire land was not well understood by the natives. That, combined with the language barrier, made it easy for the natives to be misled, especially in the beginning. And natives were no different than other populations in their desire to have new possessions in order to make life easier or to give them an advantage. And so, they willingly bartered with the colonial traders for things in exchange for the beaver hides that were in high demand in Europe.

As settlements pushed further and further west, the wilderness that had provided livelihood for the natives became more and more scarce. Many such factors played a part in putting the natives at a disadvantage in the negotiations for land. While I am not saying that all treaties were fraudulent, some clearly were. There were honest negotiators on both sides and there were fraudulent negotiators on both sides.

In Volume 1 *"…and the Mille Lacs who have no reservation…"* we learned how the Chippewa tribe migrated westward, eventually reaching what would become the State of Minnesota. When they reached Sioux territory, they encountered resistance to their westward occupation of the land. But by the mid 1700's they were able to defeat the Sioux who were in occupation of the area around the southern shore of Lake Mille Lacs and drive them further south. As the white settlers moved westward, at first primarily interested in the timber for the lumber industry, the settlers encountered the resistance of the Chippewa. Much of Volume 1 deals with those encounters.

And thus, over many years, the entire nation would come under the control of the United States of American with the Indians being relegated to reservations.

What are these things called reservations? We won't deal here with the reasons for, or wisdom of relegating the natives to specific areas. However, we do need to be mindful that these were very different times than the times we experience today. While television pundits we listen to talk today about the prevalence of racism, erroneously — I would contend — there was indeed real racism during the settlement of our country. Some is easy to understand because the settlers were, so to speak, invading and acquiring the land that the natives considered to be theirs. Casualties on both sides were common; death breeds fear, and fear breeds racism. Yet simple decency prevailed, prevented the now dominant society from completely exterminating the natives, at least in most cases. And so, natives were placed on reservations where they would be out of the way of settlement.

Suffice it to say that by the luck of location, some reservations have become economic goldmines and some have become centers of economic despair. But regardless of how economically successful the tribal industry is, the Indian people are suffering. Why? Even as far back as Plato and Aristotle, opinions varied in regard to the virtues of ownership of property, and this argument continues to today. The writings of the founders of our country and the Constitution, the framework for our country's government, were based on private ownership of property. The conception that one's private property is the result of one's manual and intellectual labor, and that private property creates freedom, and with it comes the promise of the opportunity of realizing the 'American Dream'. Private property is the very basis for achieving the 'American Dream', which can be defined as providing for one's family in such a way that it will leave the next generation with the opportunity to realize a better life.

Ownership of property and, consequently, a chance at realizing the 'American Dream' is denied the residents of Indian reservations. How did that happen? As we said previously, Indians were placed on reservations in order to get them out of the way of settlement. But confined to a reservation, Indians had little chance of providing for the needs of themselves and their families. They were made wards of the federal government; the government would provide for all their needs for food, housing, schools, medical care and necessities.

In 1887 and 1889 the federal government tried to correct that situation with the Dawes Act, and in the case of Minnesota, the Nelson Act, which, if it had been successful, would have made all reservation land private property. But as so often happens, those bills were not well thought out and resulted in Indians losing control of a large amount of their land.

Then came John Collier, a complicated man who would cause great harm while at the same time doing great good. Collier, as we have learned, did not believe in free enterprise or private ownership of property, as a result of the tragic events that had destroyed his family in his early life. As he matured, he studied the socialist and communist philosophy's and became an advocate of socialism. His early career involved him in community organizing, causing him to clash with the dominant capitalist class. It is interesting that in his early life he would disappear into the wilderness and live off the land for months at a time, reminiscent, I would contend, of the life of the natives in earlier times.

Collier, I believe, was, above other things, an anthropologist. He was in his glory when he could study societies, especially native societies. He became enamored of the Pueblos during his visit to the Taos Pueblo. During his early days as Commissioner of Indian Affairs he had set in motion a study of Indian cultures and had scientists involved in the study when it was then brought to an end by the bombing of Pearl Harbor and that resulting in the United States entering World War II. And then when Collier was put in charge of the Japanese internment camp in Arizona, he had scientists studying the effects of internment on the Japanese and had hoped to be in charge of the resettlement so he could bring the study to its conclusion, but he was denied that opportunity.

John Collier was the primary author of the Indian Reorganization Act that Congress passed in 1934. The beneficial element of that act was the ending of the federal government's role in deciding who was competent to take ownership in fee of their allotment land, which usually meant an immediate sale of that land to a non-Indian. That system had resulted in massive amounts of Indian land being sold to non-Indians. Perhaps just as important was the system for ending the inheritance plan that was administered by the federal government and had resulted in tiny plots of land that were too small to be beneficial, and all administered by the federal government, at great cost to the taxpayers.

But making Indians wards of the federal government *in perpetuity* and causing all reservation land to be owned by the federal government in trust for the use of the Indians were two horrendous inclusions in the Indian Reorganization Act. Why? Because by so doing, all Indians to this day are wards of the federal government, deemed too incompetent to take charge of their own affairs; a very demeaning condition. And further, by making Indian land inalienable it deprives the Indian of the opportunity to mortgage that property in order to raise the funds necessary to start a business. All these conditions solidify the Indian wardship status and limit opportunity, leaving reservation Indians living mainly on government dole. No man or woman will work if their livelihood is simply handed to them. The result, I am firmly convinced, is idleness and loss of incentive, resulting in the alcoholism, drug addiction and crime that runs rampant on Indian reservations.

It is now 2020 as I complete this volume, and more than 85 years since John Collier convinced Congress that his plan, called the Indian Reorganization Act, would create a utopia for the Indians — a utopia that would soon be copied by non-Indians as well. This was the progressivism of Theodore Roosevelt and Woodrow Wilson, brought to fruition by the influence of the Progressive Republican John Collier and accepted with minimal opposition under the FDR administration's New Deal — moving further and further away from the separation of powers envisioned by the Founders when they drafted the United States Constitution. The United States was originally founded on the principles of capitalism, and that remains the dominant system in the United States today, except on Indian reservations which remain pockets of communalism.

Supreme Court Justice Clarence Thomas has written that Federal Indian Policy is schizophrenic. He is absolutely right! On the one hand, Indians are citizens of the United States by the Act of 1924, with all the rights and responsibilities of citizenship, yet they are still wards of the federal government, not covered by the United States Constitution, and exempt from taxation because the federal government owns their land. Does this not seem incompatible?

In Chapter 11 we listed the many businesses owned and operated by the Mille Lacs Band of Chippewa. At least in this example it seems incomprehensible that this degree of success can be accomplished by a group of people who are deemed too incompetent to manage their own affairs and therefore must be wards of the federal government. Many of these businesses are located on land owned by the federal government, thereby making the land non-taxable and giving that business an unfair advantage over privately owned businesses. Schizophrenic?

The bottom line, in my opinion, is that people are people. Indians are people. Non-Indians are people. Neither is superior or inferior to the other. So why does our federal government insist on separating the two? Why do we have the Bureau of Indian Affairs? Why do we not have a Bureau of German Affairs? Or English Affairs? Or Italian Affairs? And on and on? We can all study history, and some can rewrite history, but history is history — it is fact. It is what it is.

Can we not look to the future? Can we not come up with a plan to correct this travesty?

Let us first look to what I would call the mission statement of the United States of America: *"... We hold these truths to be self-evident, that all men are created equal, that they are endowed by their Creator with certain unalienable Rights, that among these are Life, Liberty and the pursuit of happiness. --- That to secure these rights, Governments are instituted among Men, deriving their just powers from the consent of the governed. ..."*

I started this epilogue with words from the preamble to the Constitution, *"We the People of the United States, in Order to form a more perfect Union ..."*

These profound words by our Founders have, in large part, been lost along the way, with *"We the People"* being squeezed out of the picture by a Congress that is shirking its duty. A Congress that is adopting — not officially but in practice — a 'living constitution', instead of honoring the Constitution created in

1787. By delegating powers that, if they were following the Constitution, should be performed by the Congress, and therefore accountable to the people through elections, Congress has abdicated their duties to unelected bureaucracies made up of career bureaucrats that are accountable to no one. The result is that the separation of powers has been lost, and with that the protection against tyranny.

The Bureau of Indian Affairs, for example, has been given the power to make laws (regulations) which is constitutionally only legislative function. The Bureau enforces those laws (regulations) — an executive function, and issues binding opinions on those laws (regulations) — a judicial function. This is exactly what James Madison feared and wrote about in Federalist No. 48 on February 1, 1788: "No political truth is certainly of greater intrinsic value, or is stamped with the authority of more enlightened patrons of liberty than that on which the objection is founded. The accumulation of all powers, legislative, executive, and judiciary, in the same hands, whether of one, or many, and whether hereditary, self-appointed, or elective, may justly be pronounced the very definition of tyranny."

We don't have to reinvent the wheel to correct this travesty. President Abraham Lincoln has given us a road map. I certainly hope that we, as a country, have matured since the days of the writing of the Constitution and the necessity of compromising to allow slavery to continue in order to get all the original thirteen states to agree to the Constitution and forming of the Union. If those states which opposed slavery had not compromised, our union may not have resulted, and who knows what would have ensued. And I hope that we have moved on from Judge Roger Taney's ruling that Indians were not yet civilized enough to be full citizens, although he envisioned that occurring sometime in the future. As I commented earlier, pundits like to talk about racism, but while racism does exist, it is miniscule compared to that of the time of the founding of our country, or even still in the times of John Collier.

The first step in correcting these injustices, in my opinion (and since Congress seems to be impotent) is for the President to issue an Executive Order freeing the Indian people from the wardship of the federal government and bringing them into the full status of citizens, as President Lincoln did for the negroes.

And following that, we must have an organized effort to reorganize or eliminate that portion of the government involved with federal Indian policy since it would no longer have a needed function.

The Indian wars are over. There is no longer any reason to have *Indian Country*, the original definition of which was those areas where conflicts with Indians (Indian wars) were still occurring. It is absurd that an entire class of people is deemed incompetent to manage their own affairs, given current conditions. And yes, provisions should be made to help those who cannot help themselves (true wards) for all citizens, without giving preference simply because of a particular racial classification.

If Indians were no longer wards of the federal government, then there would be no reason (except that it has been done that way for 85 years!) for the federal government to own the lands that comprise Indian reservations and other trust land areas. And just imagine how much money could be saved by eliminating duplication of services; money that could be redirected to areas of real need. Once Indian wardship is terminated, the Indians would become full citizens of the United States with all the privileges and obligations of the United States Constitution. That would bring them under the influence of the fourteenth amendment of that Constitution.

With the fourteenth amendment in full force there would be no need for a Bureau of Indian Affairs. That would require amending the Indian Reorganization Act or, even better, replacing the Indian Reorganization Act with a new act that does not pit race against race. Perhaps by so doing we could get closer to the utopia that John Collier envisioned, not as the communal society that he sought but instead as a capitalist society, the blueprint of which can be found in the Constitution of the United States of America.

There is more to our nation's history that has occurred, and will occur, and more books to be written. As I conclude this epilogue, and with it complete Volume II, this thought is in my head. Will I write Volume III? I don't know. The Indian Reorganization Act and I are essentially the same age. It is inevitable that I will depart this world at some point; will the Indian Reorganization Act as well?

Can we please, sometime in the near future, become the "*one nation, indivisible*" that we profess to be? It is time for the Federal Government to get out of the Indian business! I pray that will happen.

# Notes

## Chapter 1: Andrew Jackson

*Jacksonland* by Steve Inskeep

*Andrew Jackson* A Biography by Robert V. Remini

*Indian Removal* by David S. and Jeanne T. Heidler

*The Long, Bitter Trail* by Anthony F.C.Wallace

*The Graphic Story of the American Presidents* by Danbury Mint

*Every Man a King* by Chris Stirewalt

*The Legacy of Andrew Jackson* by Robert V. Remini

*Andrew Jackson and the Miracle of New Orleans* by Brian Kilmeade

American History magazine — February 2011

Congressional Record

## Chapter 2: Harding to FDR

1. On a personal note, the author's father, Ralph G. Fitz, was a sailor on one of the destroyers, the USS Allen, that escorted President Wilson into the harbor at Brest, France enroute to the formation of the League of Nations.

2. RG75, BIA Records, DC, Records of Indian Affairs Commissioner, John Collier file 1919-1945, File of letters sent, Box 1, PI-163, Entry 180

3. Ibid

## Chapter 3: Harold LeClair Ickes, Secretary of the Interior

*The Secret Diary of Harold L. Ickes — The First Thousand Days (1933-1936)* by Harold LeClair Ickes

*The Secret Diary of Harold L. Ickes — The Inside Struggle (1935-1939)* by Harold LeClair Ickes

*The Secret Diary of Harold L. Ickes — The Lowering Clouds (1939-1941)* by Harold LeClair Ickes

*Righteous Pilgrim — The Life and Times of Harold L. Ickes 1874-1952* by T.H. Watkins

*The New Democracy* by Harold L. Ickes

*Mesa Land* by Anna Wilmarth Ickes

## Chapter 4: John Collier — Commissioner of Indian Affairs

*On the Gleaming Way* by John Collier

*From Every Zenith — a Memoir* by John Collier

*John Collier's Crusade for Indian Reform 1920-1954* by Kenneth R. Philp

## Chapter 5: The Path to Passage

1.  RG75, BIA Records, DC, Records of Office of Indian Affairs Commissioner, John Collier file 1919-1945, File of letters sent, Box 1, PI-163, Entry 180

2.  RG75, BIA Records, DC, Wheeler Howard Act 1933-1937, Box 10, PI-163, E-1011

3.  RG75, BIA Records, DC, Wheeler-Howard Act 1933-1937, Box 8, PI-163, E-1011

4.  RG75, BIA Records, DC, Wheeler Howard Act 1933-1937, Box 1, PI-163, E-1011

5.  RG75, BIA Records, DC, Wheeler Howard Act 1933-1937, Box 8, PI-163, E-1011

6.  RG75, BIA Records, DC, Wheeler Howard Act 1933-1937, Box 10, PI-163, E-1011

7.  RG75, BIA Records, KC, Consolidated Chippewa Tribe-Cass Lake, MN Council of MN Chippewa, Testimony-Howard Wheeler Bill, Box 5, Hm:1989, Row 3, Comp:19, Shelf 2, and RG75, BIA Records, DC, Wheeler Howard Act 1933-1937, Box 2, Pi-163, E-1011, Stack 11E-2, Row 10, Comp 13, Shelf 2-4

8. RG75, BIA Records, DC, Wheeler Howard Act 1933-1937, Box 8, PI-163, E-1011

9. Ibid

10. Ibid

11. Ibid

12. Ibid

13. Ibid

14. RG75, BIA Records, DC, Wheeler Howard Act, Box 6, PI-163, E-1011

15. RG75, BIA Records, DC, Wheeler Howard Act 1933-1937, Box 7, PI-163, E-1011

16. RG75, BIA Records, DC, Wheeler Howard Act, Box 6, PI-163, E-1011

17. RG75, BIA Records, DC, Wheeler Howard Act 1933-1937, Box 3, PI-163, E-1011

18. RG75, BIA Records, DC, Wheeler Howard Act 1933-1937, Box 6, PI-163, E-1011

19. RG75, BIA Records, DC, Wheeler Howard Act 1933-1937, Box 1, PI-163, E-1011

20. RG75, BIA Records, DC, Wheeler Howard Act 1933-1937, Box 9, PL-163, E-1011

21. RG75, BIA Records, DC, Wheeler Howard Act 1933-1937, Box 7, PI-163, E-1011

22. RG75, BIA Records, DC, Wheeler Howard Act 1933-1937, Box 10, PI-163, E-1011

23. RG75, BIA Records, DC, Wheeler Howard Act 1933-1937, Box 9, PI-163, E-1011

24. RG75, BIA Records, DC, Wheeler Howard Act 1933-1937, Box 8, PI-163, E-1011

25. RG75, BIA Records, DC, Wheeler Howard Act 1933-1937, Box 9, PI-163, E-1011

26. RG75, BIA Records, DC, Wheeler Howard Act 1933-1937, Box 10, PI-163, E-1011

27. RG75, BIA Records, DC, Wheeler Howard Act, Box 6, PI-163, E-1011

28. RG75, BIA Records, DC, Wheeler Howard Act 1933-1937, Box 8, PI-163, E-1011

29. RG75, BIA Records, DC, Wheeler Howard Act 1933-1937, Box 10, PI-163, E-1011

30. RG75, BIA Records, DC, Wheeler Howard Act 1933-1937, Box 4, PI-163, E-1011

31. RG75, BIA Records, DC, Wheeler Howard Act 1933-1937, Box 10, PI-163, E-1011

32. RG75, BIA Records, DC, Wheeler Howard Act, Box 6, PI-163, E-1011

33. Ibid

34. Ibid

35. RG75, BIA Records, DC, Wheeler Howard Act 1933-1937, Box 10, PL-163, E-1011

36. Ibid

## Chapter 6: John Collier Explains

1. RG75, BIA Records, DC, Wheeler Howard Act 1933-1937, Box 10, PI-163, E-1011

2. Ibid

## Chapter 7: Implementation and Sidetracks

1. RG75, BIA Records, DC, Records of Office of Commissioner of Indian Affairs John Collier 1933-45, Box 1, PI-163, Entry 178

2. RG75, BIA Records, DC, Wheeler Howard Act 1933-1937, Box 11, PI-163, E-1011

3. RG75, BIA Records, DC, Records of Office of Commissioner of Indian Affairs John Collier 1933-45, Box 1, PI-163, Entry 178

4. Ibid

5. Ibid

6. Ibid

7. RG75, BIA Records, DC, Records of Commissioner John Collier 1933-1945, Box 2, PI-163, Entry 178

8. RG75, BIA Records, DC, Records of Office of Commissioner of Indian Affairs John Collier 1933-45, Box 1, PI-163, Entry 178

9. RG75, BIA Records, DC, Wheeler Howard Act 1933-1937, Box 11, PI-163, E-1011

10. RG75, BIA Records, DC, Howard Wheeler Act 1933-1937, Box 4, PI-163, E-1011

11. RG75, BIA Records, DC, Howard Wheeler Act 1933-1937, Box 10, PI-163, E-1011

12. Ibid

13. RG75, BIA Records, DC, Records of Office of Indian Affairs Commissioner John Collier file 1919-1945, File of letters sent, Box 1, PI-163, Entry 180

14. RG75, BIA Records, DC, Wheeler Howard Act 1933-1937, Box 1, PI-163, E-1011

15. Ibid

16. RG75. BIA Records, DC, Records of Office of Commissioner of Indian Affairs John Collier 1933-45, Box 1, PI-163, Entry 178

17. RG75, BIA Records, DC, Wheeler Howard Act 1933-1937, Box 8 & Box 9, PI-163, E-1011 and RG75, BIA Records, DC, Records of Office of Commissioner of Indian Affairs John Collier — 1933-45, Box 1, PI-163, Entry 178

18. RG75, BIA Records, KC, Cons. Chip. Agency — Cass Lake, Correspondence of W.F. Meyers, Correspondence of Peter F. Walz, Box 500, Hm:1990, Stack area — US, Row 3, Comp 27, Shelf 7

19. RG75, BIA Records, KC, Cons. Chip. Agency — Cass Lake, Correspondence of W.F. Meyers, Correspondence of Peter F. Walz, Box 500, Hm:1990, Stack area-US, Row 3, Comp 27, Shelf 7

20. Ibid

21. Rg75, BIA Records, KC, Cons. Chip Tribe — Cass Lake, Annual Reports 1942 — 1946, Box 345, Hm:1989, Box 1-5, Row 3, Comp 25, Shelf 4

22. RG75, BIA Records, DC, Office file of Comm Collier 1933-45, Box 14, PI-163, Entry 178

23. Unknown Valor by Martha MacCallum — pg. 37

24. RG75, BIA Records, DC, Records of Commissioner Collier 1933-45, Box 21, PI-163, Entry 178

25. Ibid

26. Ibid

27. Ibid

28. Ibid

## Chapter 8: The U.S. Government Buys Mille Lacs

1.  RG75, BIA Records, KC, Cons. Chip. Agency-Cass Lake, Land transaction case file, Mille Lacs Expendable Land Acquisition Program, Box 542, HM:1990, Row 3, Comp 29, Shelf 2

2.  RG75, BIA Records, KC, Cons. Chip. Agency — Cass Lake, Mille Lacs Expendable Land Acquisition Program, Box 544, Hm:1990, Row 3, Comp 29, Shelf 2

3.  RG75, BIA Records, KC, Cons. Chip. Agency-Cass Lake, Ballots of Constitution Referendum — 1937, Wild Rice Corporate Enterprise, Box 151, HM:1989, Stack area-US, Row 3, Comp 21, Shelf 4

4.  RG75, BIA Records, KC, Cons. Chip. Tribe-Cass Lake, Land transaction case files, Mille Lacs Expendable Land Acquisition Program, Box 542, Hm:1990, Row 3, Comp 29, Shelf 2

5.  Ibid

6.  RG75, BIA Records, KC, Cons. Chip. Agency — Cass Lake, correspondence of W.F. Meyers, correspondence of Peter F. Walz, Box 500, Hm:1990, Stack area-US, Row 3, Comp 27, Shelf 7

7.  RG75, BIA Records, KC, Cons. Chip. Agency — Cass Lake, Box 543, Hm:1990, Row 3, Comp 29, Shelf 2

8.  RG75, BIA Records, KC, Cons. Chip. Agency — Cass Lake, Annual Reports 1937-1941, Box 344, Hm:1989, Stack area — US, Row 3, Comp 25, Shelf 4

9.  RG75, BIA Records, KC, Cons. Chip. Tribe — Cass Lake, Annual Reports 1942 — 1946, Monthly Narrative Reports, Box 345, Hm:1989, Stack Area — US, Row 3, Comp. 25, Shelf 4

10. RG75, BIA Records, KC, Cons. Chip. Agency — Cass Lake, Land Transaction Case Files, Mille Lacs Expendable Land Acquisition Program, Box 542, Hm:1990, Row 3, Comp. 29, Shelf 2

11. RG75, BIA Records, KC, Cons. Chip. Agency — Cass Lake, Annual Reports 1942-1946, Monthly Narrative Reports, Box 345, Hm:1989, Stack area-US, Row 3, Comp 25, Shelf 4

12. RG75, BIA Records, KC, Cons. Chip. Agency — Cass Lake, Land Transaction Case files, Mille Lacs Expendable Land Acquisition Program, Box 542, Hm:1990, Row 3, Comp 29, Shelf 2

13. RG75, BIA Records, KC, Cons. Chip. Agency — Cass Lake, Mille Lacs Expendable Land Acquisition Program, Box 544, Hm:1990, Row 3, Comp 29, Shelf 2

14. RG75, BIA Records, KC, Cons. Chip. Agency — Cass Lake, Mille Lacs Expendable Land Acquisition Program, Box 543, Hm:1990, Row 3, Comp 29, Shelf 2

15. RG75, BIA Records, KC, Cons. Chip. Tribe — Cass Lake, Mille Lacs Expendable Land Acquisition Program, Box 544, Hm:1990, Row 3, Comp 29, Shelf 2

16. RG75, BIA Records, KC, Cons. Chip. Agency — Cass Lake, Annual Reports 1942-1946, Box 345, Hm:1989, Row 3, Comp. 25, Shelf 4, Box 1-5

## Chapter 9: Wild Rice Camp Sites

1. RG75, BIA Records, KC, Cons. Chip. Agency — Cass Lake, Annual Reports 1931-1936, Box 343, Hm:1989, Row 3, Comp 25, Shelf 4

2. RG75, BIA Records, KC, Cons. Chip. Agency — Cass Lake, Land Transaction Case Files, Mille Lacs Expendable Land Acquisition Program, Box 542, Hm:1990, Row 3, Comp 29, Shelf 2

3. RG75, BIA Records, KC, Cons. Chip. Agency — Cass Lake, Land Transaction Case File, Mille Lacs Expendable Land Acquisition Program, Box 542 & Box 543, Hm: 1990, Row 3, Comp. 29, Shelf 2

4. RG75, BIA Records, KC, Cons. Chip. Agency — Cass Lake, Mille Lacs Expendable Land Acquisition Program, Box 544, Hm:1990, Row 3, Comp 29, Shelf 2

5. Ibid

6. RG75, BIA Records, KC, Cons. Chip. Agency — Cass Lake, Land Transaction Case File, Mille Lacs Expendable Land Acquisition Program, Box 542, Hm:1990, Row 3, Comp. 29, Shelf 2

7. RG75, BIA Records, KC, Cons. Chip. Agency — Cass Lake, Mille Lacs Expendable Land Acquisition Program, Box 543, Hm:1990, Row 3, Comp 29, Shelf 2

8. RG75, BIA Records, KC, Cons. Chip. Agency — Cass Lake, Mille Lacs Expendable Land Acquisition Program, Box 544, Hm:1990, Row 3, Comp 29, Shelf 2

9. Ibid

10. Ibid

11. RG75, BIA Records, KC, Cons. Chip. Agency — Cass Lake, Mille Lacs Expendable Land Acquisition Program, Box 544, Hm:1990, Row 3, Comp 29, Shelf 2

12. RG75, BIA Records, KC, Cons. Chip. Agency — Cass Lake, Ballots of Constitution Referendum — 1937, Wild Rice Corporate Enterprise, Box 151, Hm:1989, Stack area -US, Row 3, Comp 21, Shelf 4

## Chapter 10: The Minnesota Chippewa Tribe

1. RG75, BIA Records, DC, Wheeler Howard Act 1933-1937, Box 12, PI-163, E-1011

2. RG75, BIA Records, DC, Commissioner of Indian Affairs Collier 1933-1945, Box 5, PI-163, Entry 178

3. RG75, BIA Records, DC, General records concerning Indian organization 1934-1956, Constitution and Bylaws, Coeur d' Alene tribe to Eastern Shawnee, Box 2, Entry 1012

4. TG75, BIA Records, KC, Cons. Chip. Tribe-Cass Lake, Arrival Reports 1942–1946. Box 345, Hm: 1989, Box 1–5, Row 3, Comp 25, Shelf 4

## Chapter 11: Ten, Fifteen, Seventy-Five, Eighty-Five Years into the Future

1. *Ten Years of Tribal Government Under the I.R.A* by Theodore Has, Chief Counsel, United States Indian Service

2. J. Howard McGrath Papers, Box 28, Truman Library, Independence, MO

3. Hearing before the Committee on Indian Affairs, U.S. Senate, 112th Congress, 1st session, June 23, 2011

4. The Non-Removable Mille Lacs Band of Ojibwe, A thriving tribal culture in East Central Minnesota, Mille Lacs Band of Ojibwe brochure

# The Indian Removal Act

To provide for an exchange of lands with the Indians residing in any of the States or Territories, and for their removal West of the river Mississippi.

*Be in enacted by the Senate and House of Representatives of the United States of America assembled,* That it shall and may be lawful for the President of the United States to cause so much of any territory belonging to the United States, West of the river Mississippi, not included in any State or organized territory, and to which the Indian title has been extinguished, as he may judge necessary, to be divided into a suitable number of districts, for the reception of such tribes or nations of Indians as may choose to exchange the lands where they now reside, and remove there; and to cause each of said districts to be so described by natural or artificial marks, as to be easily distinguished from each other.

Sec. 2. *And be it further enacted,* That it shall and may be lawful for the President to exchange any or all of such districts, so to be laid off and described, with any tribe or nation of Indians now residing within the limits of any of the States or territories, and with which the United States have existing treaties, for the whole or any part or portion of the territory claimed and occupied by such tribe or nation, within the bounds of any one or more of the states or territories where the land claimed and occupied by the Indians, is owned by the United States, or the United States are bound to the state within which it lies to extinguish the Indian claim thereto.

Sec. 3. *And be it further enacted,* That in the making of any such exchange or exchanges, it shall and may be lawful for the President, solemnly to assure the tribe or nation with which the exchange is made, that the United States will forever secure and guaranty to them, and their heirs or successors, the country so exchanged with them; and if they prefer it, that the United States will cause a patent or grant to be made and executed to them for the same: *Provided always,* That such lands shall revert to the United States, if the Indians become extinct, or abandon the same.

Sec. 4. *And be it further enacted*, That if, upon any of the lands now occupied by the Indians, and to be exchanged for, there should be such improvements as add value to the land claimed by any individual or individuals of such tribes or nations, it shall and may be lawful for the President to cause such value to be ascertained by appraisement or otherwise, and to cause such ascertained value to be paid to the person or persons rightfully claiming such improvements. And upon payment of such valuation, the improvements so valued and paid for, shall pass to the United States, and possession shall not afterwards be permitted to any of the same tribe.

Sec. 5. *And be it further enacted*, That, upon the making of any such exchange as is contemplated by this act, it shall and may be lawful for the President to cause such aid and assistance to be furnished to the emigrants as may be necessary and proper to enable them to remove to, and settle in, the country for which they may have exchanged; and, also, to give them such aid and assistance as may be necessary for their support and subsistence for the first year after their removal.

Sec. 6. *And be it further enacted*, That it shall and may be lawful for the President to cause such tribe or nation to be protected, at their new residence, against all interruption or disturbance from any other tribe or nation of Indians, or from any other person or persons whatever.

Sec. 7. *And be it further enacted*, That it shall and may be lawful for the President to have the same superintendence and care over any tribe or nation in the country to which they may remove, as contemplated by this act, that he is now authorized to have over them at their present places of residence: *Provided*, That nothing in this act contained shall be construed as authorizing or directing the violation of any existing treaty between the United States and any of the Indian tribes.

Sec. 8. *And be it further enacted*, That, for the purpose of giving effect to the provisions of this act, the sum of five hundred thousand dollars is hereby appropriated, to be paid out of any money in the Treasury, not otherwise appropriated.

APPROVED, May 28, 1830.

# Indian Citizenship Act

BE IT ENACTED by the Senate and house of Representatives of the United States of America in Congress assembled, That all non-citizen Indians born within the territorial limits of the United States be, and they are hereby, declared to be citizens of the United States: Provided That the granting of such citizenship shall not in any manner impair or otherwise affect the right of any Indian to tribal or other property. (Approved June 2, 1924)

# The Original Collier Proposal

A BILL to grant to Indians living under Federal tutelage the freedom to organize for purposes of local self-government and economic enterprise; to provide for the necessary training of Indians in administrative and economic affairs; to conserve and develop Indian lands; and to promote the more effective administration of justice to matters affecting Indian tribes and communities by establishing a Federal Court of Indian Affairs.

*Be it enacted by the Senate and House of Representatives of the United States of America in Congress assembled.*

## TITLE I — INDIAN SELF-GOVERNMENT

SECTION 1. That it is hereby declared to be the policy of Congress to grant to those Indians living under Federal tutelage and control the freedom to organize for the purposes of local self-government and economic enterprise, to the end that civil liberty, political responsibility, and economic independence shall be achieved among the Indian peoples of the United States and to provide for cooperation between the Federal Government, the States, and organized Indian communities for Indian welfare. It is further declared to be the policy of Congress that those functions of government now exercised over Indian reservations by the Federal Government through the Department of the Interior and the Office of Indian Affairs shall be gradually relinquished and transferred to the Indians of such reservations, duly organized for municipal and other purposes, as the ability of such Indians to administer the institutions and functions of representative government shall be demonstrated, and that those powers of control over Indian funds and assets now vested in officials of the Federal Government shall be terminated or transferred to the duly constituted governments of local Indian communities as the capacity of the Indians concerned to manage their own economic affairs prudently and effectively, shall be demonstrated. It is further declared to be the policy of Congress to assist in the development of Indian capacities for self-government and economic competence by providing for the necessary training of Indians, and by rendering financial assistance and cooperation in establishing Indian communities.

SECTION 2. In accordance with the foregoing purposes, the Secretary of the Interior is hereby authorized to issue to the Indians residing upon any Indian reservation or reservations or subdivision thereof a charter granting to the said community group any or all of such powers of government and such privileges of corporate organization and economic activity, hereinafter enumerated, as may seem fitting in light of the experience, capacities, and desires of the Indians concerned; but no such charter shall take effect until ratified by the three-fifths vote at a popular election open to all adult Indians resident within the territory covered by the charter.

Upon receipt of petition for the issuance of a charter signed by one-fourth of the adult Indians residing on any existing reservation, it shall be the duty of the Secretary of the Interior to make the necessary investigations and issue a proper charter, subject to ratification, or shall proclaim the conditions upon which such charter will be issued; and such petition, with a record of findings and of the action of the Secretary, shall be transmitted by the Secretary of the Interior to Congress: *Provided*, That whenever the Secretary of the Interior shall acquire land not comprised within any existing reservation for the purpose of establishing a new Indian community, pursuant to the authority granted by Title III of this Act, he shall issue a charter to take effect at some future time and shall therein prescribe the conditions under which persons of at least one-fourth degree of Indian blood shall be entitled to become members of such community, and the acceptance of such membership by the qualified persons shall constitute an acceptance and ratification of such charter.

SECTION 3. Each charter issued to an Indian community shall define the territorial limits of the community and the criteria of membership within the community; shall, wherever such community is sufficiently populous and endowed with sufficient territory to make the establishment of local government possible, prescribe a form of government adopted to the needs, traditions, and experience of such community; and shall guarantee the civil liberties of minorities and individuals within the community, including the liberty of conscience, worship, speech, press, assembly, and association, and the right of any member to abandon the community and to receive some compensation for any interest in community assets thereby relinquished, the extent of which compensation and manner of payment thereof to be fixed by chartered provision. Each charter shall further specify the powers of self-government to be exercised by the chartered community, and shall provide for the planned extension of these powers as the community offers evidence of capacity to administer them. Each charter shall likewise prescribe the powers of management or supervision to be exercised by the chartered community over presently restricted real and personal property of individual Indians or tribes, and shall provide for the bonding of any community officials or Federal employees entrusted with the custody of community funds and for such forms of publicity and accounting, and for such continuing supervision by the Office of Indian Affairs over financial transactions and economic policies as may be found by the Secretary of the Interior to be necessary to prevent dissipation of the capital resources of the community or unjust discrimination in the apportionment of income; and each charter shall further provide for the gradual elimination of administrative supervision as the Indian community shows progress in the effective utilization of its resources and the prudent disposal of its assets.

SECTION 4. The Secretary of the Interior is authorized to grant to any community which may be chartered under this Act, either by original charter or by supplement to such charter initiated or ratified by a three-fourths vote, any or all of the powers hereinafter enumerated, subject to the provisions of law fixed by section 8 of this title, or any rule or regulations promulgated pursuant thereto, respecting the terms upon which certain functions of the Federal Government shall be transferred to the chartered community, and to provide, in such original charter or supplement, for the definition, qualification, or limitation of any powers which may be granted, in any manner deemed necessary or desirable for the effectuation of the purposes and policies above set forth.

a.  To organize and act as a Federal municipal corporation, to establish a form of government, to adopt and thereafter to amend a constitution, and to promulgate and enforce ordinances and regulations for the effectuation of the functions hereafter specified, and any other functions customarily exercised by local governments.

b.  To elect or appoint officers, agents, and employees, to define the qualifications for office, to fix the salaries of officials to be paid by the community, to prescribe the qualifications of voters, to define the conditions of membership within the community, and to provide for the adoption of new members.

c. To regulate the use and disposition of property by members of the community, to protect and conserve the property, wildlife, and natural resources of the community, to cultivate and encourage arts, crafts, and culture, to administer charity, and to protect the health, morals, and general welfare of the members of the community.

d. To establish courts for the enforcement and administration of ordinances of the community, which courts shall have exclusive jurisdiction over all offenses of, and controversies between, members of the chartered community, under the ordinances of such community, and jurisdiction exclusive or nonexclusive over all other cases arising under the ordinances of the community, and shall have power to render and enforce judgments, criminal and civil, legal and equitable, and to punish violations of local ordinances by fine not exceeding $500, or, in the alternative, by imprisonment for a period not exceeding six months: *Provided,* That no person shall be punished for any offense for which prosecution has been begun in any other court of competent jurisdiction.

e. To accept the surrender of the tribal, corporate, or community interests of individual members who desire to abandon the community and to pay a fair compensation therefor, to act as guardian or to provide for the appointment of guardians for minor and other incompetent members of the community, and to administer tribal and individual funds and properties which may be transferred or entrusted to the community by the Federal Government.

f. To operate, maintain, and equip any public improvement and, as a Federal agency, to condemn and take title to any lands or properties, in its own name, when necessary for any of the purposes authorized by charter, and to levy assessments for community purposes, or to require the performance of labor on community projects, in lieu of assessments.

g. To acquire, manage, and dispose of property, subject to applicable laws restricting the alienation of Indian lands and the dissipation of Indian resources, to make contracts, to issue nontransferable certificates of membership, to declare and pay out dividends, to adopt and use a corporate seal which shall be judicially noticed in all Federal courts, to sue and be sued in its own name, to employ counsel and to pay counsel fees not in excess of limits to be fixed by charter provision, to have succession until its membership may become extinct, and to exercise any other privileges which may be granted to membership or business corporations.

h.  To compel the transfer from the community for inefficiency in office or other cause, of any employee of the Federal Indian Service locally assigned; to regulate trade and intercourse between members of the community and nonmembers; to exclude from the territory of the community, with the approval of the Secretary of the Interior, nonmembers whose presence endangers the health, security, or welfare of the community; *Provided, however,* That nothing in this section or in this Act shall be construed to forbid the service in the territory of an Indian community of any civil or criminal process of any court having jurisdiction over any person found therein.

i.  To exercise any other powers now or hereafter delegated to the Office of Indian Affairs, or any officials thereof, to contract with government bodies of State or Nation for the reception or performance of public services, and to act in general as a Federal agency in the administration of Indian Affairs, upon the condition, however, that the United States shall not be liable for any act done, suffered to be done, or omitted to be done by a chartered Indian community.

j.  To exercise any other powers, not inconsistent with the Constitution and the laws of the United States, which may be necessary or incidental to the execution of the powers above enumerated.

An Indian community chartered under this Act shall be recognized as successor to any existing political powers heretofore exercised over the members of such community by any tribal, or other native political organization comprised within the said community, not withheld by such tribal or other native political organization, and shall, subject to the terms of said charter, further be recognized as successor to all right, interest, and title to all funds, property, choses in action, and claims against the United States heretofore held by the tribes or other native political organizations comprised within the community, or to a proportionate share thereof, except as such succession may be limited by the charter, subject to existing provisions of law with respect to the maintenance of suits against the United States, and subject further to such provision for apportionment of such assets among nonmembers of the community having vested rights therein, as may be prescribed by the charter.

SECTION 5. When any Indian community shall have been chartered, it shall be the duty of the Commissioner of Indian Affairs to cause reports concerning their respective functions to be made to the constituted authorities of the community, to advise and consult with such authorities on problems of local administration and Federal policy, and to allow such authorities free access to the records and files of the local agency.

Any Indian community shall have the power to compel the transfer from the community of any persons employed in the administration of Indian affairs within the territorial limits of the community other than persons appointed by the community: *Provided, however,* That the Commissioner of Indian Affairs may prescribe such conditions for the exercise of this power as will assure to employees of the Indian Service a reasonable security of tenure, an opportunity to demonstrate their capacities over a stated period of time, and an opportunity to hear and answer complaints and charges.

SECTION 6. The Secretary shall prepare annual estimates of expenditures for the administration of Indian affairs, including expenditures for functions and services administered by an Indian community, pursuant to the authority conferred by section 8 of this title. It shall be the duty of the Secretary to transmit to the authorized representative of an Indian community any estimates and justifications thereof for expenditures to be made in whole or in part within the territorial limits of the community. Any recommendations of the authorized representatives of the community, including the approval or rejection of any item in whole or in part, or the recommendation of any other expenditure, shall be transmitted by the Secretary to the Bureau of the Budget and to the Congress concurrently with the submission of the estimates of the Secretary.

The Secretary shall also transmit to the authorized representatives of an Indian community a copy of any bill, or amendment of a bill, for the benefit of Indians, authorizing, in whole or in part, the appropriation or expenditure, within the territorial limits of such community, of any funds from the Federal Treasury for which the Secretary of the Interior has submitted no estimates, and the Secretary shall transmit their written recommendations to the Congress.

The Secretary shall also transmit to the authorized representatives of an Indian community a description of any project involving the expenditure, in whole or in part, of any funds appropriated for the general welfare within the territorial limits of the community.

No expenditure hereafter authorized or appropriated for by Congress shall be charged against any such Indian community as a reimbursable debt, unless such appropriation and expenditure have been recommended or approved by such Indian community through its duly constituted authorities; and any funds of the community deposited in the United States Treasury shall be expended only by the bonded disbursing agent of such community.

SECTION 7. The Secretary of the Interior may from time to time delegate to any Indian community, within the limits of its competence as defined by charter, the authority to perform any act, service, or function which the United States administers for the benefit of Indians within the territorial limits of the community and may enter into annual agreements with the constituted authorities of the community with respect to the terms and conditions of such delegation.

SECTION 8. The Commissioner is authorized and directed to proceed immediately after the passage of this Act, to arrange and classify the various functions and services administered for Indians by the United States into divisions and subdivisions which may be separately transferred. The Commissioner is further authorized and directed to proceed, immediately after the passage of this Act, to make a study and investigation of the conditions upon which separable functions and services may be transferred to the Indian communities and thereupon to promulgate, direct, and express rules and regulations to such given transfer.

The said rules and regulations shall set forth all conditions reasonably necessary to assure the satisfactory and continued administration of the function or service transferred. The said rules and regulations shall include standards of fitness for Indians with respect to health, age, character, knowledge, and ability, for any position maintained, now or hereafter, before or after transfer to an Indian community, for the administration of functions or services within the territorial limits of any community, and a classification of all positions for which the requisite knowledge and training may be acquired by Indians through experience or apprenticeship in the position, The said rules and regulations shall also set forth for each separable function or services, a condition of its transfer, the positions for which Indians shall qualify and the required number of qualified Indians for each such position, provisions assuring a reasonable security of tenure, and any other conditions reasonably necessary to assure the continued and the satisfactory administration of transferred functions or services.

Any Indian community may, through procedure set up in its charter, appoint a member to any vacant position under the Indian Service maintained for the administration of functions or services for Indians within the territorial limits of the community. The appointee shall not take office until he shall have previously received the certificate of approval of his fitness for the position in question from the Commissioner. The Commissioner shall issue such certificate of approval to any member of an Indian community recommended by the duly authorized representatives of the community and who is qualified for the position under the rules and regulations prescribed pursuant to the section.

Any Indian community may, upon a three-fourths vote at a popular election open to all adult members, request the transfer of any separable function or service, and the Secretary of the Interior shall transfer such function or service and, if necessary, confer by supplement to the community charter, the legal capacity to exercise such function or service, subject only to the following terms and conditions:

(a) The community must comply with all conditions prescribed by the rules and regulations of the Secretary of the Interior pursuant to the authority of this section. The community may transmit to the Congress any objection it may have to the condition imposed, together with its budget recommendations for the next fiscal year.

(b) The Secretary of the Interior shall certify to the Secretary of the Treasury the amount of any sums or any unexpended balance of such sums theretofore or thereafter expressly appropriated, or the proportionate share of any general appropriation, for the administration of such function or service within territorial limits of the community. The Secretary of the Treasury shall place such sums to the credit of the community, to be paid out on the requisition of the bonded disbursing agent of the community. The expenditure of such funds shall be subject to all Federal laws and regulations governing the expenditures of Federal appropriations.

(c) The Commissioner shall aid and advise the community, and the local federal employees shall cooperate in any feasible manner at the request of the community, in the administration of the function or service transferred. The Commissioner shall also make available to the Indian community any facilities, including any lands, buildings, and equipment previously used but no longer needed by the United States in the administration of Indian affairs within the community.

(d) Whenever the Secretary of the Interior shall determine that the community has failed to comply with the conditions imposed for the continued administration of the function or service transferred, the Secretary or the Commissioner of Indian Affairs shall reassume the administration of such function or service and the Secretary shall report to the next regular session of the Congress with appropriate recommendations.

(e) The community, or its duly authorized representatives, shall make on or before September 1 of each year, an annual report of the fiscal year ended June 30, previously, to the Secretary, concerning the administration of the function or service transferred to the community including an account by the disbursing agent of the community of receipts and expenditures of moneys placed to the credit of the community under this section.

(f) The Secretary of the Interior shall make an annual report to Congress on the administration of the functions and services transferred to the community, and shall include in such reports the reports of the Indian communities required by paragraph (e) of this section.

SECTION 9. The Secretary and the Commissioner shall continue to exercise all existing powers of supervision and control over Indian affairs now entrusted to them or either of them which are not transferred by charter or supplement thereto or by Act of Congress to organized Indian communities and shall have power to enforce by administrative order or veto, if so provided within the charter, or, in any event, by legal process in any court of competent jurisdiction, all provisions contained in a charter for the protection of the rights of minorities within the community, all provisions that limit, qualify, or restrict the powers granted to the community.

SECTION 10. The Secretary of the Interior may, upon granting a charter to an Indian community, convey or confirm to such community, as an agency of the Federal Government, any right, interest, or title in property which may be held by the United States in trust for members of the community, and in any lands, buildings, or equipment previously used by the United States in the administration of Indian affairs within the community, and in any liens or credits of the United States held by virtue of loans to or expenditures on behalf of Indian members of the said community.

SECTION 11. Nothing in this Act shall be construed as rendering the property of any Indian community or of any member of such community subject to taxation by any State or subdivision thereof, or subject to the attachment or sale under legal process, or as an expression of intent on the part of the United States to abandon the duties and responsibilities of guardianship of any Indians becoming members of chartered communities.

SECTION 12. There is hereby authorized to be appropriated, out of the funds in the Treasury not otherwise appropriated, such sums as may be necessary, not to exceed $500,000 in any one fiscal year, to be expended at the order of the Secretary of the Interior, and with the consent of the Indian communities concerned, in defraying the expenses of the organization and development of communities chartered under this Act, including the construction and furnishing of community buildings, the purchase of clerical supplies, and the improvement of community lands.

SECTION 13. The following definition of terms used in this title shall be binding in the interpretation of this statute:

(a) The term "Commissioner" whenever used in this Act shall be taken to refer to the Commissioner of Indian Affairs, and the term "Secretary" to the Secretary of the Interior, and the terms "Commissioner" and "Secretary" whenever used in this Act in reference to the exercise of any power shall be construed as authorizing the delegation of such power to subordinate officials.

(b) The term "Indian" as used in this title to specify the persons to whom charters may be issued, shall include all persons of Indian descent who are members of any recognized Indian tribe, band, or nation, or are descendants of such members and were, on or about February 1, 1934, actually residing within the present boundaries of any Indian reservation, and shall further include all other persons of one-fourth or more Indian blood, but nothing in this definition or in the Act shall prevent the Secretary of the Interior or the constituted authorities of a chartered community from prescribing, by provision of charter or pursuant thereto, additional qualifications or conditions for membership in any chartered community, or from offering the privileges of membership therein to nonresidents of a community who are members of any tribe, wholly or partly comprised within the chartered community.

(c) The term "residing upon an Indian reservation" as used in this title to specify the persons to whom charters may be issued shall signify the maintaining of a permanent abode at the time of the issuance of a charter and for a continuous period of at least one year prior to February 1,

1934, and subsequent to September 1, 1932, but this definition may be modified by the Secretary of the Interior with respect to Indians who may reside on lands required subsequently to February 1, 1934.

(d) The term "charter" as used in this Act shall denote any grant of power by the United States, whether or not such power includes the privilege of corporate existence.

(e) The "three-fifths vote" required for ratification of a charter and the "three-fourths vote" required for proposal or ratification of any supplement thereto or transfer of any Federal function or service shall be measured with reference to the total number of votes cast; the chartered community, or, if the community has not yet been chartered, the Secretary of the Interior shall designate the time, place and manner of voting, shall declare the qualifications of voters, and shall be the final judge of the eligibility of voters and the validity of ballots.

(f) The term "disposition of property" as used in this title shall denote any transfer of property by devise or intestate succession, as well as transfer intervivos.

(g) The term "punish" as used in this title shall not be construed to affect the amount or extent of civil judgments.

(h) The term "public" as used in this title shall include all matters affecting either the property owner or controlled by a chartered community, or the health, morals, or welfare of a considerable part of the membership of such community.

(i) The term "dividend" as used in this title shall be construed to include any distribution of funds by a chartered community out of current or accrued income and any other distribution of funds which may be approved by the Secretary of the Interior.

(j) The power "to sue and be sued" as used in this title shall not be construed to grant to the courts of any State any jurisdiction over a chartered community or the members thereof not now possessed over an Indian tribe or its members, nor to sanction execution upon the assets of the community, nor shall this power be construed to deny the right of the United States to intervene in any suit or proceeding in which it now has the right to intervene.

(k) The term "tribe" wherever used in this Act shall be construed to refer to any Indian tribe, band, nation, pueblo, or other native political group or organization.

(l) The term "reservation" wherever used in this Act shall be construed to comprise all the territory within the outer boundaries of any Indian reservation, whether or not such property is subject to restrictions on alienation and whether or not such land is under Indian ownership.

(m) The term "territory of a chartered community" wherever used in this Act shall be construed to comprise all lands, waters, highways, roads, and bridges within the boundaries of an Indian community as fixed by charter, regardless of whether the title to such property is in the United States, an Indian tribe or community, a restricted Indian or the heirs of a restricted Indian, or whether it is in a fee-patent Indian, or any other person, agency, or government.

(n) The term "transfer" as used in this title to apply to any function or service shall designate the relinquishment by the Secretary of the Interior or the Commissioner of Indian Affairs of any rights and duties incident to the performance of such function or service and the assumption of such rights and duties by the Indian community as an agency of the Federal Government.

## TITLE II — SPECIAL EDUCATION FOR INDIANS

SECTION 1. The Commissioner is authorized and directed to make suitable provision for the training of Indian members of chartered communities and other Indians of at least one-fourth degree of Indian blood, in the various services now intrusted to the Office of Indian Affairs and in any additional services which may be undertaken by a chartered Indian community, including education, public-health work, and other social services, the administration of law and order, the management of forests and grazing lands, the keeping of financial accounts, statistical records and other public reports, and the construction and maintenance of buildings, roads, and other public works. The Commissioner may use the staffs and facilities of existing Indian boarding or day schools for such special instruction, and he may provide for the training and education of Indian students in universities, colleges, schools of medicine, law, engineering, or agriculture, or other institutions of recognized standing and may subsidize such training and education under the following conditions:

(a) The Commissioner shall extend financial aid and assistance on the basis of financial need to qualified Indians for the payment of tuition and other costs of education, including necessary costs of support. One-half of the amount so expended shall be a non-interest-bearing, reimbursable loan to be repaid in installments whenever the beneficiary shall have received employment anywhere, but the obligation shall be temporarily suspended during any period of unemployment.

There is hereby authorized to be appropriated, out of any funds in the United States Treasury not otherwise appropriated, a sum not to exceed $50,000 annually to defray subsidies made under the foregoing paragraph.

(b) Notwithstanding the provisions of paragraph (a) of this section, the Commissioner may grant scholarships to any qualified Indian of special promise, no part of which shall be reimbursable.

There is hereby authorized to be appropriated, out of any funds in the United States Treasury not otherwise appropriated, a sum not to exceed $15,000 annually to defray the cost of scholarships awarded under the foregoing paragraph.

Formal contracts shall not be required for compliance with section 3744 of the Revised Statutes (U.S.C. title 41, sec. 16), with respect to the grants of subsidies or scholarships to Indian students under the foregoing provisions.

SECTION 2. It is hereby declared to be the purpose and policy of Congress to promote the study of Indian civilization and preserve and develop the special cultural contributions and achievements of such civilization, including Indian arts, crafts, skills, and traditions. The Commissioner is directed to prepare curricula for Indian schools adapted to the needs and capacities of Indian students, including courses in Indian history, Indian arts and crafts, the social and economic problems of the Indians, and the history and problems of the Indian Administration. The Commissioner is authorized to employ individuals familiar with Indian culture and with the contemporary social and economic problems of the Indians to instruct in schools maintained for Indians. The Commissioner is further directed to make available the facilities of the Indian schools to competent individuals appointed or employed by an Indian community to instruct the elementary and secondary grades in the Indian arts, crafts, skills, and traditions. The Commissioner may contribute to the compensation of such individuals in such proportion and upon such terms and conditions as he may deem advisable. For this purpose the Commissioner may use moneys appropriated for the maintenance of such schools.

## TITLE III — INDIAN LANDS

SECTION 1. It is hereby declared to be the policy of Congress to undertake a constructive program of Indian land use and economic development, in order to establish a permanent basis of self-support for Indians living under Federal tutelage; to reassert the obligations of guardianship where such obligations have been improvidently relaxed; to encourage the effective utilization of Indian lands and resources by Indian tribes, cooperative associations, and chartered communities; to safeguard Indian lands against alienation from Indian ownership and against physical deterioration; and to provide land needed for landless Indians and for the consolidation of Indian landholdings in suitable economic units.

SECTION 2. Hereafter no tribal or other land of any Indian reservation or community created or set apart by treaty or agreement with the Indians, act of Congress, Executive order, purchase, or otherwise, shall be allotted in severalty to any Indian.

SECTION 3. The Secretary of the Interior is authorized to withdraw from disposal the remaining surplus lands of any Indian reservation heretofore opened or authorized to be opened, to sale, settlement, entry, or other form of disposal by Presidential proclamation, or under any of the public land laws of the United States. Any land so withdrawn shall have the status of tribal or community lands of the tribe, reservation, or community within whose territorial limits they are located: Provided, however, That valid rights or claims of any persons to any lands so withdrawn existing on the date of the withdrawal shall not be affected by this Act.

The Secretary of the Interior shall determine what lands, lying outside of the areas classified for consolidation under Indian ownership pursuant to section 6 of this title, are not needed by the Indians, and such lands shall be reopened to sale, settlement, entry, or other lawful form of disposal in accordance with existing law.

SECTION 4. The existing period of trust placed upon Indian allotment and unallotted tribal lands and any restriction of alienation thereof, are hereby extended and continued until otherwise directed by Congress. The authority of the Secretary of the Interior to issue to Indians patents in fee or certificates of competency or otherwise to remove the restrictions on lands allotted to individual Indians under any law or treaty is hereby revoked.

No lands or other capital assets owned by an Indian community, or any interest therein, shall be voluntarily or involuntarily alienated: *Provided, however,* That the community may grant the use of the surface of, or any mining privileges in, any land to a nonmember, by lease or revocable permit for a period of not to exceed one year, or, with the approval of the Secretary, for a longer period, and may, with the approval of the Secretary, sell or contract to sell to a nonmember any standing timber, or dispose of any capital improvements, owned by the community.

SECTION 5. No sale, devise, gift, or other transfer of Indian lands held under any trust patent or otherwise restricted, whether in the name of the allottee or his heirs, shall be made or approved: *Provided, however,* That such lands may, with the approval of the Secretary, be sold, devised, or otherwise transferred to the Indian tribe from whose lands the allotment was made or the chartered community within whose territorial limits they are located: *And provided further,* That the Secretary of the Interior may authorize exchanges of lands of equal value whenever such exchange is in his judgment necessary for or compatible with the proper consolidation of Indian lands classified for the purpose pursuant to the authority of section 6 of this title.

SECTION 6. The Secretary of the Interior is authorized and directed to classify areas of land allotted in whole or in part now under restricted Indian ownership which are reasonably capable of consolidation into suitable units for grazing, forest management, or other economic purposes, and to proclaim the exclusion from such areas of any lands not to be included therein. In order to bring about an orderly and sound acquisition and consolidation of lands and to promote the effective use of Indian resources and the development of Indian economic capacities, the Secretary is hereby authorized and directed to make economic and physical investigation and classification of the existing Indian lands, of intermingled and adjacent non-Indian lands and of the other lands that may be required for landless Indian groups or individuals; to make necessary maps and surveys; to investigate Indian aptitudes and needs in the agricultural and industrial arts, in political and social affairs and in education, and to make such other investigations as may be needed to secure the most effective utilization of existing Indian resources and the most economic acquisition of additional lands. In carrying out the investigations prescribed in this section the Secretary is authorized to utilize the services of any Federal officers or employees that the President may assign to him for the purpose, and is further authorized, with the consent of the States concerned, to enter into cooperative agreements with State agencies for similar services.

SECTION 7. The Secretary of the Interior is hereby authorized, in his discretion, and under such rules and regulations as he may prescribe, to acquire, through purchase, relinquishment, gift, exchange, or assignment, lands or surface rights to lands, within or outside of existing reservations, including trust or otherwise restricted allotments, whether the allottee be living or deceased, for the purpose of providing land for Indians for whom reservation or other land is now available and who can make beneficial use thereof, and for the purpose of blocking out and consolidating areas classified for the purpose pursuant to the authority of section 6 of this title. The Secretary is authorized, in the case of trust or other restricted lands or lands to which fee patents have hitherto been issued to Indians and which are unencumbered, to accept voluntary relinquishments of, and to cancel the patent or patents or any other instrument removing restrictions from the land.

There is hereby authorized to be appropriated, for the acquisition of such lands and for expenses incident thereto, including appraisals and the investigations provided for in section 6 of this title, a sum not to exceed $2,000,000 for any one fiscal year. The unexpected balance of appropriation made for any one year pursuant to this Act shall remain available until expended.

The Secretary of the Interior is hereby authorized to accept voluntary relinquishments from any Indian allottee or Indian homestead entryman, or from his heirs, of all rights in and to any land included in any Indian public domain allotment, homestead, or application therefor, which has heretofore or may hereafter be made, where such land lies within the exterior boundaries of any Indian reservation or area heretofore or hereafter set apart and reserved for the use and benefit of any Indian tribe or band; and the Secretary of the Interior is hereby authorized and empowered to cancel any patent which may have been issued conveying such land, or any interest therein, to any Indian allottee or Indian homestead entryman.

Title to any land acquired pursuant to the provisions of this section shall be taken in the name of the United States in trust for the Indian tribe or community for whom the land is acquired, but title may be transferred by the Secretary to such community under the conditions set forth in this Act.

SECTION 8. Any Indian tribe or chartered Indian community is authorized to purchase or otherwise acquire any interest of any member or nonmember in land within its territorial limits, and may expend any tribal or community funds, whether or not held in the Treasury of the United States, for this purpose, whenever, in the opinion of the Secretary of the Interior the acquisition is necessary for the proper consolidation of Indian lands.

The Secretary of the Interior is authorized to transfer to an Indian tribe or community, and to accept on behalf of the tribe or community, any member's interest in restricted farming, grazing, or timberlands, and shall issue a nontransferable certificate in exchange, evidencing a proportionate interest in tribal or community lands of similar quality, if in his opinion such transfer is necessary for the proper consolidation of Indian lands: *Provided, however,* That any Indian making beneficial use of such transferred lands shall be entitled to continue the occupancy and use of such lands, and to any improvements thereon, or to receive adequate compensation for such improvements, subject to the provisions of section 14 of this title. For the purpose of this section "proportionate interest" shall be construed to mean a right to use or to receive the income from an equivalent amount of tribal or community land of similar quality or to receive the money value of any lawful disposition of the interest transferred if such right of use is not exercised. A member's proportionate interest may descend to the heirs of such member but not to any nonmember, and his right of use of transferred land, if exercised, may similarly descend to the heirs of such member.

The Secretary of the Interior may sell and convey to an Indian, to an Indian tribe, or community, any restricted lands inherited by any member, whenever, in his opinion, the sale is necessary for the proper consolidation of Indian lands.

The time and mode of payment of the purchase price of any lands authorized to be sold or purchased under this section shall be governed by the agreement between parties, but insofar as practicable the purchase price shall be paid in annual installments equal to the estimated annual proceeds realizable from any lawful disposition of the land, and the vendor, if a member, may accept any right of use in tribal or community lands as satisfaction of the purchase price in whole or in part.

SECTION 9. The Secretary of the Interior shall assign the use of tribal or community lands to any member according to the right of interest of such member for a period not to exceed the life of the assignee and shall make rules and regulations governing such assignments. The Secretary of the Interior may in addition assign to any such member the right of exclusive occupancy of any community lands for farming or domestic purposes in proper economic units: *Provided,* That any Indian making beneficial use of land shall be entitled to preference in the assignment of the use of such land and to any improvements thereon or to adequate compensation for such improvements.

All rights of exclusive occupancy of, and all physical improvements lawfully created on, tribal or community lands, shall descend according to rules of descent and distribution to be prescribed by the Secretary of the Interior.

SECTION 10. Wherever the Secretary shall find that existing State laws governing the determination of heirs, so far as made applicable to any restricted Indian lands by congressional enactment, are not adapted to Indian needs and circumstances, he may promulgate independent rules governing such determination, including such rules as may be necessary to prevent any subdivision of rights to lands or improvements thereon which is likely to impair their beneficial use.

The Secretary may delegate to a chartered Indian community the authority conferred by this section.

SECTION 11. On and after the effective date of the passage of this Act, and beginning with the death of the person presently entitled, all right, interest, and title in restricted allotted lands, but not including any proportionate interest acquired pursuant to section 8 of this title or any improvements lawfully erected, shall pass to the chartered community within whose territorial limits such lands are located or, if no community has been chartered, to the tribe from whose lands the allotment was made: *Provided, however,* That the individual who would be otherwise entitled, save for the provisions of this section, shall acquire a contingent interest in such lands, and title to any such lands shall vest in such individuals when and only when the Secretary shall determine that such lands lie outside any area classified for consolidation pursuant to section 6; *And provided further,* That prior to such determination the individual otherwise entitled shall enjoy the use and income realized from any lawful disposition of such lands.

The Secretary shall issue to the individuals otherwise entitled a nontransferable certificate evidencing a descendible interest in tribal or community lands of similar quality in the proportion which the acreage of the farming, grazing, or timber lands, whichever, passing to the tribe or community at any time bears to the total tribal or community acreage of farming, grazing, or timber lands:

*Provided, however,* That such persons shall enjoy a preference in the assignment of lands passing to the tribe or community in accordance with the provisions of this action.

No will purporting to make any other disposition of such lands shall be approved.

SECTION 12. The Secretary of the Interior is authorized and directed to issue to each member of an Indian tribe or community which owns or controls lands allotted in whole or in part a nontransferable certificate evidencing the member's right to an equal interest in all tribal community assets, including the right to make beneficial use of a proportionate share thereof: *Provided, however,* That in the administration of sections 8, 9, 10, and 11 of this title, members so entitled may be given the right to actual beneficial use of more than their proportionate shares of such tribal or community lands and resources: *And provided further,* That in the administration of sections 8, 9, 10, and 11 of this title, appropriate deductions may be made from the undivided interest of any member proportionate in value to any special interest acquired or inherited by such member, in exchange for property passing, transferred, or sold, to a tribe or community, or any restricted lands retained in severalty by such member.

SECTION 13. Each certificate issued pursuant to the authority of any section of this title shall be issued in triplicate, one copy of which the Secretary of the Interior shall retain in a register to be kept for the purpose and the others of which he shall forward to the tribe or chartered community. The said tribe or community shall deliver to the Indian in whose favor it is issuing one of such certificates so forwarded and shall cause the other to be copied into a register of the tribe or community to be provided for the purpose and shall file the same.

The Secretary may delegate to a chartered community the authority conferred by this section and may countersign certificates of interest by such community to its members.

SECTION 14. The Secretary of the Interior is authorized and directed to classify and divide the lands owned or controlled by an Indian tribe or community into economic units suitable for farming, grazing, forestry, and other purposes, and may lease or permit the use of, and may regulate the use and management of, such lands whenever in his opinion necessary to promote and preserve their economic use. The Secretary may delegate to a chartered Indian community the authority conferred by this section.

SECTION 15. The Secretary of the Interior is authorized and directed to make rules and regulations for the operation and management of Indian forestry units on the principle of sustained yield management, to restrict the number of livestock grazed on Indian range units to the estimated carrying capacity of such ranges, and to promulgate such other rules and regulations as may be necessary to protect the range from deterioration, to prevent soil erosion, and like purposes. The Secretary may delegate to a chartered Indian community the authority conferred by this section.

SECTION 16. The Secretary of the Interior is authorized to proclaim new Indian reservations on lands purchased for the purposes enumerated in this Act, or to add such lands to the jurisdiction of existing reservation. Such lands, so long as title to them is held by the United States or by an Indian tribe or community, shall not be subject to taxation, but the United States shall assume all governmental obligations of the State or county in which such lands are situated with respect to the maintenance of roads across such lands, the furnishing of educational and other public facilities to persons residing thereon, and the execution of proper measures for the control of fires, floods, and erosion, and the protection of the public health and order in such lands, and the Secretary of the Interior may enter into agreements with authorities of any State or subdivision thereof in which such lands are situated for the performance of any or all of the foregoing functions by such State or subdivision or any agencies or employees thereof authorized by the law of the State to enter into such agreements, and for the payment of the expenses of such functions where appropriations therefor shall be made by Congress.

SECTION 17. Nothing contained in this title shall be construed to relate to Indian holdings of allotments or homesteads upon the public domain outside of the geographical boundaries of any Indian reservation now existing or to be established hereafter.

SECTION 18. Whenever used in this title the phrase "a member of an Indian tribe" shall include any descendant of a member permanently residing within an existing Indian reservation.

SECTION 19. Whenever used in this title the phrase "lands owned or controlled by an Indian tribe or community" shall include all interest in land of any of its members.

SECTION 20. The provisions of this Act shall not be construed to prevent the removal of restrictions on taxable lands of members of the Five Civilized Tribes nor operate to effect any change in the present laws and procedure relating to the guardianship of minor and incompetent members of the Osage and Five Civilized Tribes, but in all other respects shall apply to such Indians.

SECTION 21. None of the provisions of this Act, except the provisions of title II, relating to Indian educations, shall apply to the Indians of New York State.

## TITLE IV — COURT OF INDIAN AFFAIRS

SECTION 1. There shall be a United States Court of Indian Affairs, which shall consist of a chief judge and six associate judges, each of whom shall be appointed by the President, by and with the advice and consent of the Senate, and shall receive an annual salary of $7,500 payable monthly from the Treasury.

SECTION 2. The said Court of Indian Affairs shall always be open for the transaction of business, and sessions thereof may, in the discretion of the court, be held in several judicial circuits and at such places said court may from time to time designate. The authority of the court may be exercised either by the full court or by one or more judges duly assigned by the court to sit in a particular locality or to hold a special term for a designated class of cases.

SECTION 3. The Court of Indian Affairs shall have original jurisdiction as follows:

(1) Of all prosecutions for crimes against the United States committed within the territory of any Indian reservation or chartered Indian community, whether or not committed by an Indian;

(2) Of all cases to which an Indian tribe or chartered Indian community is a party;

(3) Of all cases at law or in equity arising out of commerce with an Indian tribe or community or members thereof, wherein a real party in interest is not a member of such tribe or community;

(4) Of all cases, civil or criminal, arising under the laws or ordinances of a chartered Indian community, wherein a real party interest is not a member of such community;

(5) Of all actions at law or suits in equity wherein the pleadings raise a substantial question concerning the validity or application of any Federal law, or any regulation or charter authorized by such law, relating to the affairs or jurisdiction of any Indian tribe or chartered community;

(6) Of all actions, suits, or proceedings involving the right of any person, in whole or in part of Indian blood or descent, to any allotment of land under any law or treaty;

(7) Of all cases involving the determination of heirs of deceased Indians and the settlement of the estates of such Indians; of all cases and proceedings involving the partition of Indian lands, or the guardianship of minor and incompetent Indians; and of all cases and proceedings to determine the competency of individual Indians where the issuance of cancellation of a fee patent or the removal of restrictions from inherited or allotted lands, funds, or other property held by the United States in trust for such Indians may be involved: *Provided,* That the Court of Indian Affairs shall exercise no jurisdiction in cases over which exclusive jurisdiction has been granted by Congress to the Court of Claims, or to any other Federal court other than the United States district courts, or in cases over which exclusive jurisdiction may be granted by charter provision to the local courts of an Indian community.

SECTION 4. All jurisdiction heretofore exercised by the United States district courts by reason of the fact that a case involved facts constituting any of the grounds of jurisdiction enumerated in the preceding section, is hereby terminated, reserving, however, to such district courts complete jurisdiction over all pending suits and over all proceedings ancillary or supplementary thereto.

SECTION 5. The Court of Indian Affairs may order the removal of any cause falling within its jurisdiction as above set forth, from any court of any State or any Indian community in which such cause may have been instituted.

SECTION 6. The Court of Indian Affairs shall have jurisdiction to hear and determine appeals from the judgment of any court of any chartered Indian community in all cases in which said Court of Indian Affairs might have exercised original jurisdiction.

SECTION 7. The procedure of the Court of Indian Affairs shall be determined by rules of court to be promulgated by it, existing statutes regulating procedure in courts of the United States notwithstanding. Such rules shall regulate the form and manner of executing, returning, or filing writs, processes, and pleadings; the removal of causes specified in section 5; the taking of appeals specified in section 6; the joinder of parties and of causes of action, legal and equitable; the raising of questions of law before trial; the taking of testimony by examination before trial and other proceedings for discovery and inspection; the issuance of subpoenas to summon witnesses and compel the production of documents at trial; the summoning of jurors and the waiver of jury trial; the form and manner of entry of judgments; the manner of executing judgments; the conduct of supplementary proceedings; the survival of actions and the substitution of parties; the amounts and manner of payment of fees to the clerk or the marshal of the court; the practice of attorneys; and such other matters as may require regulation in order to provide a complete system of procedure for the conduct of the court. In general the rules of court shall conform as nearly as possible to the statutes regulating the procedure in the district courts of the United States, the rules of the Supreme Court governing causes in said district courts, and the practice in the courts of the State in which the controversy arises, save that the rules shall, so far as possible, be nontechnical in character and fitted to the needs of prospective litigants.

SECTION 8. The courts may provide, by rules to be promulgated by it, for appeals to the full court from judgment rendered on circuit by less than a majority of the full court.

SECTION 9. All substantial rights accorded to the accused in criminal prosecutions in the district courts of the United States shall be accorded in prosecutions in the Court of Indian Affairs. The trial of offenses punishable by death or by imprisonment for a period exceeding five years shall be had within or in the vicinity of the reservation or Indian community where the offense was committed.

SECTION 10. In both civil and criminal causes, the right to trial by jury and all other procedural rights guaranteed by the Constitution of the United States shall be recognized and observed.

SECTION 11. In criminal cases the rules of evidence shall be these prevailing in criminal cases in the United States district courts. In civil cases the common law rules of evidence, including the rules governing competency of witnesses, shall prevail: *Provided, however,* That the court shall have the power to amend such rules by rule of court or judicial decision to make them conform as nearly as possible to modern changes evidenced by the statutes and decisions of the United States and the several States, and to adapt them, where necessary, to the solution of problems of proof peculiar to the cases before the court.

SECTION 12. The statutes and decisions of the several States, except where the Constitution, treaties, or statutes of the United States, or the charters or ordinances of Indian communities or orders of executive departments thereunder promulgated, otherwise require or provide, shall be regarded as rules of decision in all civil cases in the Court of Indian Affairs.

SECTION 13. The Court of Indian Affairs shall be a court of record possessed of all incidental powers, including the power to summon jurors, to administer oaths, to have and use a judicial seal, to issue writs of habeas corpus, to punish for contempt, and to hold to security of the peace and for good behavior, which may be exercised by the district courts of the United States, and such powers shall be subject to all limitations imposed by law upon said district courts. The orders, writs, and processes of the Court of Indian Affairs may run, be served, and be returnable anywhere in the United States. The said court shall perform such administrative functions as Congress may assign it. The said court shall have the power to render declaratory judgments, and such judgments, in cases of actual controversy, shall have the same force as final judgments in ordinary cases.

SECTION 14. The judges of the Court of Indian Affairs shall hold office for a period of ten years; they may be removed prior to the expiration of their term by the President of the United States, with the consent of the Senate for any cause.

SECTION 15. The final judgement of the Court of Indian Affairs shall be subject to review on questions of law in the circuit court of appeals of the circuit in which such judgement is rendered. The several circuit courts of appeals are authorized to adopt rules for the conduct of such appellate proceedings, and, until the adoption of such rules, the rules of such courts relating to appellate proceedings upon a writ of error, so far as applicable, shall govern. The said circuit courts of appeals shall have power to affirm, or, if the judgement of the Court of Indian Affairs is not in accordance with law, to modify or reverse the judgement of that court, with or without remanding the case for a rehearing, as justice may require; the judgement of the circuit court of appeals shall be final, except that it may be subject to review by the Supreme Court as provided in the United States Code, title 28, sections 346 and 347.

SECTION 16. The fees of jurors and witnesses shall be fixed in accordance with the provision of law governing such fees in United States courts generally as provided in the United States Code, title 28, sections 600 to 605.

SECTION 17. The costs and fees in the Court of Indian Affairs shall be fixed and established by said court in a table of fees: *Provided,* That the costs and fees so fixed shall not exceed, with respect to any item, the costs and fees now charged in the Supreme Court.

SECTION 18. The Court of Indian Affairs shall appoint a chief clerk, a reporter, and such assistant clerk and marshals, not to exceed seven each, as may be necessary for the efficient conduct of its business. The said officials shall be under the direction of the court in the discharge of their duties; and for misconduct or incapacity they may be removed by it from office; but the court shall report such removals, with the cause thereof, to Congress, if in session, or if not, at the next session.

SECTION 19. The Attorney General shall provide the Court of Indian Affairs with suitable rooms in courthouses or other public buildings at such places as the court may select for its sessions.

SECTION 20. The chief clerk of the court shall, under the direction of the chief judge, employ such stenographers, messengers, or attendants and purchase such books, periodicals, and stationary as may be needful for the efficient conduct of the business of the court, and expenditures for such purposes shall be allowed and paid by the Secretary of the Treasury upon claim duly made and approved by the chief judge.

SECTION 21. The judges of the Courts of Indian Affairs and the clerks and marshals thereof shall receive necessary travelling expenses, and expenses not to exceed $5 per day for subsistence while traveling on duty and away from their designated stations.

SECTION 22. With respect to all matters relating to the receipt of fines, costs, fees, bail, and other payments to officials of the court, the custody of funds and the rendering of accounts therefor, the bonding of court officials charged with such custody, the payment of moneys for salaries, traveling expenses, clerical services, the publication of reports of opinions, and office expenses, the laws, departmental regulations, and rules of court applicable to similar matters in the Supreme Court shall apply to the Court of Indian Affairs except as otherwise provided in this chapter.

SECTION 23. The Secretary of the Interior is hereby authorized to appoint not to exceed ten special attorneys whose duty it shall be to advise and represent such Indian tribes or communities as the Secretary of the Interior may designate, and the individual members thereof. Within ten days of the institution of any proceedings on behalf of such tribes or communities or members thereof, the special attorneys provided for herein shall serve upon the appropriate United States district attorney written notice of the pendency of any such proceedings, together with a copy of all the pleadings on file in any such proceeding.

SECTION 24. As used in this title, the term "circuit court of appeals" includes the Court of Appeals of the District of Columbia.

SECTION 25. Appropriations for the Federal Court of Indian Affairs and for incidental expenses shall be made annually based upon estimates submitted by the Attorney General, and appropriations for the special attorneys shall be made annually, based upon estimates submitted by the Secretary of the Interior.

# Wheeler-Howard Act, June 18, 1934

### (*The Indian Reorganization Act*)

## 48 Stat. 984

—An Act to conserve and develop Indian lands and resources; to extend to Indians the right to form business and other organizations; to establish a credit system for Indians; to grant certain rights of home rule to Indians; to provide for vocational education for Indians; and for other purposes.

BE IT ENACTED by the Senate and House of Representatives of the United States of America in Congress assembled, That hereafter no land of any Indian reservation, created or set apart by treaty or agreement with the Indians, Act of Congress, Executive order, purchase, or otherwise, shall be allotted in severalty to any Indian.

SECTION 2. The existing periods of trust placed upon any Indian lands and any restriction on alienation thereof are hereby extended and continued until otherwise directed by Congress.

SECTION 3. The Secretary of the Interior, if he shall find it to be in the public interest, is hereby authorized to restore to tribal ownership the remaining surplus lands of any Indian reservation heretofore opened, or authorized to be opened, to sale, or any other form of disposal by Presidential proclamation, or by any of the public land laws of the United States; *Provided, however,* That valid rights or claims of any persons to any lands so withdrawn existing on the date of the withdrawal shall not be affected by this Act; *Provided further,* That this section shall not apply to lands within any reclamation project heretofore authorized in any Indian reservation; *Provided further,* That the order of the Department of the Interior signed, dated, and approved by Honorable Ray Lyman Wilbur, Secretary of the Interior, on October 28, 1932, temporarily withdrawing lands of the Papago Indian Reservation in Arizona from all forms of mineral entry or claim under the public land mining laws, is hereby revoked and rescinded, and the lands of the said Papago Indian Reservation are hereby restored to exploration and location, under the existing mining entry or claim under the public land mining laws of the United States, in accordance with the express terms and provisions declared and set forth in Executive orders establishing said Papago Indian Reservation. *Provided further,* That damages shall be paid to the Papago Tribe for loss of any improvements on any land located for mining in such a sum as may be determined by the Secretary of the Interior but not to exceed the cost of the improvements; *Provided further,* That a yearly rental not to exceed five cents per acre shall be paid to the Papago Tribe for loss of the use or occupancy of any land withdrawn by the requirements of mining operations, and payment derived from damages or rentals shall be deposited in the Treasury of the United States to the credit of the Papago Tribe; *Provided further,* That in the event any person or persons, partnership, corporation, or association, desires a mineral patent, according to the mining laws of the United States, he or they shall first deposit in the Treasury of the United States to the credit of the Papago Tribe the sum of $1.00 per acre in lieu of annual rental, as heretofore provided, to compensate for the loss or occupancy of the lands withdrawn by the requirements of mining operations; *Provided further,* That the patentee shall also pay into the Treasury of the United States for the credit of the Papago Tribe damages for the loss of improvements not heretofore paid in such sum as may be determined by the Secretary of the Interior, but not to exceed the cost thereof; the payment of $1.00 per acre for surface use to be refunded to patentee in the event that patent is not acquired.

Nothing herein contained shall restrict the granting or use of permits for easements or rights-of-way; or ingress or egress over the lands for all proper and lawful purposes; and nothing contained herein, except as expressly provided, shall be construed as authority for the Secretary of the Interior, or any other person, to issue or promulgate a rule or regulation in conflict with the Executive order of February 1, 1917, creating the Papago Indian Reservation in Arizona or the Act of February 21, 1931 (46 Stat, 1202).

SECTION 4. Except as herein provided, no sale, devise, gift, exchange or other transfer of restricted Indian lands or of shares in the assets of any Indian tribe or corporation organized hereunder, shall be made or approved; *Provided, however,* That such lands or interests may with the approval of the Secretary of the Interior, be sold, devised, or otherwise transferred to the Indian tribe in which the land or shares are located or from which the shares were derived or to a successor corporation; and in all instances such lands or interests shall descend or be devised, in accordance with the then existing laws of the State, or Federal laws where applicable, in which said lands are located or in which the subject matter of the corporation is located, to any member of such tribe or of such corporation or any heirs of such member; *Provided further,* That the Secretary of the Interior may authorize voluntary exchanges of lands of equal value and the voluntary exchange of shares of equal value whenever such exchange, in his judgment, is expedient and beneficial for or compatible with the proper consolidation of Indian lands and for the benefit of cooperative organizations.

SECTION 5. The Secretary of the Interior is hereby authorized, in his discretion, to acquire through purchase, relinquishment, gift, exchange, or assignment, any interest in lands, water rights or surface rights to lands, within or without existing reservations, including trust or otherwise restricted allotments whether the allottee be living or deceased, for the purpose of providing land for Indians.

For the acquisition of such lands, interests in lands, water rights, and surface rights, and for expenses incident to such acquisition, there is hereby authorized to be appropriated, out of any funds in the Treasury not otherwise appropriated, a sum not to exceed $2,000,000 in any fiscal year; *Provided,* That no part of such funds shall be used to acquire additional land outside of the exterior boundaries of the Navajo Indian Reservation for the Navajo Indians in Arizona and New Mexico, in the event that the proposed Navajo boundary extension measures now pending in Congress and embodied in the bills (S. 2531 and H.R. 8927) to define the exterior boundaries of the Navajo Indian Reservation in Arizona, and for other purposes, and the bills (S. 2531 and H.R. 8982) to define the exterior boundaries of the Navajo Indian Reservation in New Mexico and for other purposes, or similar legislation, become law.

The unexpended balance of any appropriations made pursuant to this section shall remain available until expended.

Title to any lands or rights acquired pursuant to this Act shall be taken in the name of the United States in trust for the Indian tribe or individual Indian for which the land is acquired, and such lands or rights shall be exempt from State and local taxation.

SECTION 6. The Secretary of the Interior is directed to make rules and regulations for the operation and management of Indian forestry units on the principle of sustained-yield management, to restrict the number of livestock grazed on Indian range units to the estimated carrying capacity of such ranges, and to promulgate other rules and regulations as may be necessary to protect the range from deterioration, to prevent soil erosion, to assure full utilization of the range, and like purposes.

SECTION 7. The Secretary of the Interior is hereby authorized to proclaim new Indian reservations on lands acquired pursuant to any authority conferred by this Act, or to add such lands to existing reservations; *Provided,* That lands added to existing reservations shall be designated for the exclusive use of Indians entitled by enrollment or by tribal membership to residence at such reservations.

SECTION 8. Nothing contained in this Act shall be construed to relate to Indian holdings of allotments or homesteads upon the public domain outside of the geographical boundaries of any Indian reservation now existing or established hereafter.

SECTION 9. There is hereby authorized to be appropriated, out of any funds in the Treasury not otherwise appropriated, such sums as may be necessary, but not to exceed $250,000 in any fiscal year, to be expended at the order of the Secretary of the Interior, in defraying the expenses of organizing Indian chartered corporations or other organizations created under this Act.

SECTION 10. There is hereby authorized to be appropriated, out of any funds in the Treasury not otherwise appropriated, the sum of $10,000,000 to be established as a revolving fund from which the Secretary of the Interior, under such rules and regulations as he may prescribe, may make loans to Indian chartered corporations for the purpose of promoting the economic development of such tribes and of their members, and may defray the expenses of administering such loans. Repayment of amounts loaned under this authorization shall be credited to the revolving fund and shall be available for the purpose for which the fund is established. A report shall be made annually to Congress of transactions under this authorization.

SECTION 11. There is hereby authorized to be appropriated, out of any funds in the United States Treasury not otherwise appropriated, a sum not to exceed $250,000 annually, together with any unexpended balances of previous appropriations made pursuant to this section, for loans to Indians for the payment of tuition and other expenses in recognized vocational and trade schools; *Provided,* That not more than $50,000 of such sum shall be available for loans to Indian students in high schools and colleges. Such loans shall be reimbursable under rules established by the Commissioner of Indian Affairs.

SECTION 12. The Secretary of the Interior is directed to establish standards of health, age, character, experience, knowledge, and ability for Indians who may be appointed, without regard to civil service laws, to the various positions maintained, now or hereafter, by the Indian Office, in the administration of functions or services affecting any Indian tribe. Such qualified Indians shall hereafter have the preference to appointment to vacancies in any such positions.

SECTION 13. The provisions of this Act shall not apply to any of the Territories, colonies, or insular possessions of the United States, except that sections 9, 10, 11, 12 and 16 shall apply to the Territory of Alaska; *Provided,* That sections 2, 4, 7, 16, 17 and 18 of this Act shall not apply to the following-named Indian tribes, the members of such Indian tribes, together with members of other tribes affiliated with such named tribes located in the State of Oklahoma as follows: Cheyenne, Arapaho, Apache, Comanche, Kiowa, Caddo, Delaware, Wichita, Osage, Kaw, Otoe, Tonkawa, Pawnee, Ponca, Shawnee, Ottawa, Quapaw, Seneca, Wyandotte, Iowa, Sac and Fox, Kickapoo, Pottawatomi, Cherokee, Chickasaw, Choctaw, Creek, and Seminole. Section 4 of this Act shall not apply to the Indians of the Klamath Reservation in Oregon.

SECTION 14. The Secretary of the Interior is hereby directed to continue the allowance of the articles enumerated in section 17 of the Act of March 2, 1889 (23 Stat. L.894), or their commuted cash value under the Act of June 10, 1896 (29 Stat. L. 334), to all Sioux Indians who would be eligible, but for the provisions of this Act, to receive allotments of lands in severalty under section 19 of the Act of May 29, 1908 (25 (35) Stat. L. 451), or under any prior Act, and who have the prescribed status of the head of a family or single person over the age of eighteen years, and his approval shall be final and conclusive, claims thereafter to be paid as formerly from the permanent appropriation made by said section 17 and carried on the books of the Treasury for this purpose. No person shall receive in his own right more than one allowance of the benefits, and application must be made and approved during the lifetime of the allottee or the right shall lapse. Such benefits shall continue to be paid upon such reservation until such time as the lands available therein for allotment at the time of the passage of this Act would have been exhausted by the award to each person receiving such benefits of an allotment of eighty acres of such land.

SECTION 15. Nothing in this Act shall be construed to impair or prejudice any claim or suit of any Indian tribe against the United States. It is hereby declared to be the intent of Congress that no expenditures for the benefit of Indians made out of appropriations authorized by this Act shall be considered as offsets in any suit brought to recover upon any claim of such Indians against the United States.

SECTION 16. Any Indian tribe, or tribes, residing on the same reservation, shall have the right to organize for its common welfare, and may adopt an appropriate constitution and bylaws, which shall become effective when ratified by a majority vote of the adult members of the tribe, or of the adult Indians residing on such reservation, as the case may be, at a special election authorized and called by the Secretary under such rules and regulations as he may prescribe. Such constitution and bylaws when ratified as aforesaid and approved by the Secretary of the Interior shall be revocable by an election open to the same voters and conducted in the same manner as hereinabove provided. Amendments to the constitution and bylaws may be ratified and approved by the Secretary in the same manner as the original constitution and bylaws.

In addition to all powers vested in any Indian tribe or tribal council by existing law, the constitution adopted by said tribe shall also vest in such tribe or its tribal council the following rights and powers: To employ legal counsel, the choice of counsel and fixing of fees to be subject to the approval of the Secretary of the Interior; to prevent the sale, disposition, lease, or encumbrance of tribal lands, interests in lands, or other tribal assets without the consent of the tribe; and to negotiate with the Federal, State and local Governments. The Secretary of the Interior shall advise such tribe or its tribal council of all appropriation estimates or Federal projects for the benefit of the tribe prior to the submission of such estimates to the Bureau of the Budget and the Congress.

SECTION 17. The Secretary of the Interior may, upon petition by at least one-third of the adult Indians, issue a charter of incorporation to such tribe: *Provided,* That such charter shall not become operative until ratified at a special election by a majority of the adult Indians living on the reservation. Such charter may convey to the incorporated tribe the power to purchase, take by gift, or bequest, or otherwise own, hold, manage, operate, and dispose of property of every description, real and personal, including the power to purchase restricted Indian lands and to issue in exchange therefor interests in corporate property, and such further powers as may be incidental to the conduct of corporate business, not inconsistent with law, but no authority shall be granted to sell, mortgage, or lease for a period exceeding ten years any of the land included in the limits of the reservation. Any charter so issued shall not be revoked or surrendered except by Act of Congress.

SECTION 18. This Act shall not apply to any reservation wherein a majority of the adult Indians, voting at a special election duly called by the Secretary of the Interior, shall vote against its application. It shall be the duty of the Secretary of the Interior, within one year after the passage and approval of this Act, to call such an election, which election shall be held by secret ballot upon thirty days' notice.

SECTION 19. The term "Indian" as used in this Act shall include all persons of Indian descent who are members of any recognized Indian tribe now under Federal jurisdiction, and all persons who are descendants of such members who were, on June 1, 1934, residing within the present boundaries of any Indian reservation, and shall further include all other persons of one-half or more Indian blood. For the purposes of this Act, Eskimos and other aboriginal peoples of Alaska shall be considered Indians. The term "tribe" wherever used in this Act shall be construed to refer to any Indian tribe, organized band, pueblo, or the Indians residing on one reservation. The words "adult Indian" wherever used in this Act shall be construed to refer to Indians who have attained the age of twenty-one years.

*Approved, June 18, 1934.*

# Solicitor Nathan Margold Opinion

*Powers of an Indian Tribe under the IRA*

My opinion has been requested on the question of what powers may be secured to an Indian tribe and incorporated in its constitution and bylaws by virtue of the following phrase, contained in section 16 of the Wheeler-Howard Act (Public No. 383, 73d Congress): "In addition to <u>all powers vested in any Indian tribe or tribal council by existing law</u>, the constitution adopted by said tribe shall also vest \*\*\*."

The question of what powers are vested in an Indian tribe or tribal council by existing law cannot be answered in detail for each Indian tribe without reference to hundreds of special treaties and special act of Congress. It is possible, however, on the basis of the reported cases, the written opinions of the various Executive departments, and those statutes of Congress which are of general import, to define the powers which have heretofore been recognized as lawfully within the jurisdiction of an Indian tribe. My answer to the propounded question, then, will be general, and subject to correction for particular tribes in the light of the treaties and statutes affecting such tribe wherever such treaties and statutes contain peculiar provisions restricting or enlarging the general authority of an Indian tribe.

In analyzing the meaning of the phrase in question, I note that the general confirmation of powers already recognized, is found in conjunction with specific grants of the following powers: "To employ legal counsel, the choice of counsel and fixing of fees to be subject to the approval of the Secretary of the Interior; to prevent the sale, disposition, lease, or encumbrance of tribal lands, interests in lands, or other tribal assets without the consent of the tribe; and to negotiate with the Federal, State, and local Governments." Furthermore, when a constitution has been adopted by a majority of the adults of an Indian tribe or tribes residing on the same reservation, the Secretary of the Interior is directed to "advise each tribe or its tribal council of all appropriation estimates or Federal projects for the benefit of the tribe prior to the submission of such estimates to the Bureau of the Budget and the Congress."

I note, also, as relevant to the question of construction, that one of the stated purposes of the Act in question is "to grant certain rights of home rule to Indians."

I assume, finally, that any ambiguity in the phrase which I am asked to interpret ought to be resolved in accordance with: " *** the general rule that statutes passed for the benefit of dependent Indian tribes or communities are to be liberally construed, doubtful expressions being resolved in favor of the Indians." *Alaska Pacific Fisheries* v. *United States* (248 U.S. 78, 89). And see to the same effect, *Seufert Bros. Co.* v. *United States* (249 U.S. 194); *Choate* v. *Trapp* (234 U.S. 665); *Jones* v. *Meehan* (175 U.S. 1).

Bearing these considerations in mind, I have no doubt that the phrase "powers vested in any Indian tribe or tribal council by existing law" does not refer merely to these powers which have been specifically granted by the express language of treaties or statutes, but refers rather to the whole body of tribal powers which courts and Congress alike have recognized as properly wielded by Indian tribes, whether by virtue of specific statutory grants of power, or by virtue of the original sovereignty of the tribe in so far as such sovereignty has not been curtailed by restrictive legislation or surrendered by treaties. Had the intent of Congress been to limit the powers of an Indian tribe to those previously granted by special legislation, it would naturally have referred to "existing laws" rather than "existing law" as the source of such powers. The term "law" is a broader term than the term "laws" and includes, as well as "laws", the materials of judicial decisions, treaties, constitutional provisions and practices, and other sources controlling the decisions of courts. Furthermore, it was clearly not the purpose of Congress to narrow the body of tribal powers which have heretofore been recognized by the courts. It would therefore be contrary to the manifest intent of the Act to interpret this phrase in a narrow sense as referring only to express statutory grants of specific powers.

Perhaps the most basic principle of all Indian law, supported by a host of decisions hereinafter analyzed, is the principle that <u>those powers which are lawfully vested in an Indian tribe are not, in general, delegated powers granted by express acts of Congress, but rather inherent powers of a limited sovereignty which has never been extinguished</u>. Each Indian tribe begins its relationship with the Federal Government as a sovereign power, recognized as such in treaty and legislation. The powers of sovereignty have been limited from time to time by special treaties and laws designed to take from the Indian tribes control of matters which, in the judgment of Congress, these tribes could no longer be safely permitted to handle. The statutes of Congress, then, must be examined to determine the limitations of tribal sovereignty rather than to determine its sources or its positive content. What is not expressly limited remains within the domain of tribal sovereignty, and therefore properly falls within the statutory category, "powers vested in any Indian tribe or tribal council by existing law."

The acts of Congress which appear to limit the powers of an Indian tribe are not to be unduly extended by doubtful inference. What was said in the case of *In re Mayfield* (141 U.S. 107) is still pertinent:

> The policy of Congress has evidently been to vest in the inhabitants of the Indian country such power of self-government as was thought to be consistent with the safety of the white population with which they may have come in contact, and to encourage them as far as possible in raising themselves to our standard of civilization. We are bound to recognize and respect such policy and to construe the acts of the legislative authority in consonance therewith. *** (At pp. 115-116)

## THE DERIVATION AND SCOPE OF INDIAN TRIBAL POWERS

From the earliest years of the Republic the Indian tribes have been recognized as "distinct, independent, political communities" (*Worcester* v. *Georgia*, 6 Pet. 515, 559), and, as such, qualified to exercise powers of self-government, not by virtue of any delegation of powers from the Federal Government, but rather by reason of their original tribal sovereignty. Thus treaties and statutes of Congress have been looked to by the courts as limitations upon original tribal powers, or, at most, evidences of recognition of such powers rather than as the direct source of tribal powers. This is but an application of the general principle that "It is only by positive enactments, even in the case of conquered and subdued nations, that their laws are changed by the conqueror" (*Wall* v. *Williamson*, 8 Ala. 48, 51, upholding tribal law of divorce).

In point of form it is immaterial whether the powers of an Indian tribe are expressed and exercised through customs handed down by word of mouth or through written constitutions and statutes. In either case the laws of the Indian tribe owe their force to the will of the members of the tribe.

The earliest complete expression of these principles is found in the case of *Worcester* v. *Georgia* (6 Pet. 515). In that case the State of Georgia, in its attempts to destroy the tribal government of the Cherokees, had imprisoned a white man living among the Cherokees with the consent of the tribal authorities. The Supreme Court of the United States held that his imprisonment was in violation of the Constitution, that the State had no right to infringe upon the Federal power to regulate intercourse with the Indians, and that the Indian tribes were, in effect, wards of the Federal Government entitled to exercise their own inherent rights of sovereignty so far as might be consistent with Federal law. The court declared, per Marshall, C.J.:

> "The Indian nations had always been considered as distinct, independent, political communities, ***." (at p. 559.)

> "***and the settled doctrine of the law of nations is, that a weaker power does not surrender its independence — its right to self-government — by associating with a stronger, and taking its protection. A weak state, in order to provide for its safety, may place itself under the protection of one more powerful, without stripping itself of the right of government, and ceasing to be a state. Examples of this kind are not wanting in Europe. 'Tributary and feudatory states,' says Vattel, 'do not thereby cease to be sovereign and independent states, so long as self-government, and sovereign and independent authority, are left in the administration of the state.' At the present day, more than one state may be considered as holding its right of self-government under the guarantee and protection of one or more allies.
>
> The Cherokee nation, then, is a distinct community, occupying its own territory, with boundaries accurately described, in which the laws of Georgia can have no force, and which the citizens of Georgia have no right to enter, but with the assent of the Cherokees themselves, or in conformity with treaties, and with the acts of Congress. The whole intercourse between the United States and this nation, is, by our constitution and laws, vested in the government of the United States. The act of the state of Georgia, under which the plaintiff in error was prosecuted, is, consequently void, and the judgment a nullity. *** (at pp. 560-561.)

In the recent case of *Patterson* v. *Council of Seneca Nation* (245 N.Y. 433, 157 N.E. 734) The New York Court of Appeals gave careful consideration to the present status of the Seneca tribe and of its legislative and judicial organs of government. Reviewing the relevant Federal cases, the court reached the conclusion that the powers which the Seneca Council and the Seneca Peacemakers' Court sought to exercise were powers derived from the sovereignty of the Seneca Nation, and that no act of New York State could diminish this sovereignty although proper legislation, enacted at the request of the Indians themselves, might supplement the provisions of the tribal constitution. After reviewing the relevant State legislation, the court declared:

> ***Thus did the Seneca Nation, far from abdicating its sovereign powers, set up a strong central government, distribute all governmental powers among three departments, empower a legislative body to be called the 'Councillors of the Seneca Nation' to make necessary laws, create a president to execute them, and establish a Peacemakers' Court and a Surrogate's Court to interpret the laws of the Nation and decide causes. Thus did the Legislature of the state of New York twice approve of the Constitution adopted and the government set up. It was not accurate to say, therefore, that the state of New York in the year 1849 'assumed governmental control' of the Indians. On the contrary, in that year and subsequently, by its approval of the Indian Constitution in its original and amended form, the state of New York acknowledged the Seneca Indians to be a separate nation, a self-governing people, having a central government with appropriate departments to make laws, to administer and to interpret them. ***

The force of the Seneca Constitution, the court found, derived not from the sovereignty of New York State, but from the original sovereignty of the Seneca Nation.

> Various statutes passed by the New York Legislature in relation to the Indians are now embodied in the 'Indian Law.' Article 4 of that law is entitled 'The Seneca Indians.' It doubtless embodies the statutes passed pursuant to the request of the Seneca Nation contained in its Constitution of 1848. This article

purports to set up a government for the Seneca Nation, consisting of three departments, exactly as provided in the Indian Constitution. It must be held, however, that the Indian Nation itself created these departments and the system of government set up by its Constitution, the force of which had been expressly acknowledged by the New York Legislature. It purported to set up a Peacemakers' Court. The source of jurisdiction of that court, however, was the Indian Constitution, not the Indian Law. Thus, in *Mulkins v. Snow,* supra, this court said:

The Peacemakers' Court is not a mere statutory local court of inferior jurisdiction. It is an Indian court, which has been recognized and given strength and authority by statute. It does not owe its existence to the state statute and is only in a qualified sense a state court."***

• • • • • • • • • • • • • • • • • • • • • • •

The respondent argues that the jurisdiction of the Peacemakers' Court is limited by the Indian Law (section 46) to 'matters, disputes, and controversies between any Indians residing upon such reservation' which may arise upon 'contracts or for wrongs.' We answer that the Peacemakers' Court is the creation not of the state but of the Indian Constitution; that by such Constitution, as amended in 1898, the Peacemakers' Courts are given 'exclusive jurisdiction in all civil causes arising between individual Indians residing on said reservations, except those which the Surrogate's Courts have jurisdiction of,' without reference to 'contracts' or to 'wrongs'. The Indian law does not deny comprehensive jurisdiction; it merely fails to use terms apparently bestowing it. The Indian Constitution does bestow it. ***

Thus the doctrine first laid down by Chief Justice Marshall in the early years of the Republic was reaffirmed but a few years ago with undiminished vigor by the New York Court of Appeals.

The whole course of judicial decision on the nature of Indian tribal powers is marked by adherence to three fundamental principles: An Indian tribe possesses, in the first instance, all the powers of any sovereign state. Conquest renders the tribe subject to the legislative power of the United States and, in substance, terminates the external powers of sovereignty of the tribe,[4] e.g., its power to enter into treaties with foreign nations, but does not by itself affect the internal sovereignty of the tribe, i.e., its powers of local self-government. These powers are subject to be qualified by treaties and by express legislation of Congress, but save as thus expressly qualified, full powers of internal sovereignty are vested in the Indian tribes and in their duly constituted organs of government.

A most striking affirmation of these principles is found in the case of *Talton* v. *Mayes* (163 U.S. 376). The question was presented in that case whether the Fifth Amendment of the Federal Constitution operated as a limitation upon the legislation of the Cherokee Nation. A law of the Cherokee Nation authorized a grand jury of five persons to institute criminal proceedings. A person indicted under this procedure and held for trial in the Cherokee courts sued out a writ of habeas corpus, alleging that the law in question violated the Fifth Amendment to the Constitution of the United States, since a grand jury of five was not a grand jury within the contemplation of the Fifth Amendment. The Supreme Court held that the Fifth Amendment applied only to the acts of the Federal Government; that the sovereign powers of the Cherokee Nation, although <u>recognized</u> by the Federal Government, were not <u>created</u> by the Federal Government; and that the judicial authority of the Cherokees was, therefore, not subject to the limitations imposed by the bill of rights:

> The question, therefore, is, does the Fifth Amendment to the Constitution apply to the local legislation of the Cherokee nation so as to require all prosecutions for offenses committed against the laws of that nation to be initiated by a grand jury organized in accordance with the provisions of that amendment. The solution of this question involves an inquiry as to the nature and origin of the power of local government exercised by the Cherokee nation and recognized to exist in it by the treaties and statutes above referred to. Since the case of *Barron* v. *Baltimore*, 7 Pet. 243, it has been settled that the Fifth Amendment to the

---

4   Certain external powers of sovereignty, such as the power to make treaties with the United States, have been recognized by the Federal Government. And <u>of</u> *Montoya* v. *United States* (180 U.S. 261; *Scott* v. *United States* and *Apache Indians* (33 Ct. Cl. 486); *Dobbs* v. *United States and Apache Indians* (33 Ct. Cl. 308). The treaty-making power of the Indian tribes was terminated by the act of March 3, 1871 (U.S. Code, Title 25, Sec. 71).

Constitution of the United States is a limitation only upon the powers of the General Government, that is, that the amendment operates solely on the Constitution itself by qualifying the powers of the National Government which the Constitution called into being.

\* \* \* \* \* \* \* \* \* \* \* \* \* \*

"The case in this regard therefore depends upon whether the powers of local government exercised by the Cherokee nation are Federal powers created by and springing from the Constitution of the United States, and hence controlled by the Fifth Amendment to that Constitution, or whether they are local powers not created by the Constitution, although subject to its general provisions and the paramount authority of Congress. The repeated adjudications of this court have long since answered the former question in the negative. In *Cherokee Nation v. Georgia*, 5 Pet. 1, which involved the right of the Cherokee nation to maintain an original bill in this court as a foreign State, which was ruled adversely to that right, speaking through Mr. Chief Justice Marshall, this court said (p. 16):

> Is the Cherokee nation a foreign State in the sense in which that term is used in the Constitution?
>
> 'The counsel for the plaintiffs have maintained the affirmative of this proposition with great earnestness and ability. So much of the argument as was intended to prove the character of the Cherokees as a State, as a distinct political society, separated from others, capable of managing its own affairs and governing itself, has, in the opinion of a majority of the judges, been completely successful. They have been uniformly treated as a State from the settlement of our country. The numerous treaties made with them by the United States recognizes them as a people capable of maintaining the relations of peace and war, of being responsible in their political character for any violation of their engagements or for any aggression committed on the citizens of the United States by any individual of their community. Laws have been enacted in the spirit of these treaties. The acts of our government plainly recognize the

Cherokee nation as a State, and the courts are bound by those acts.'

It cannot be doubted, as said in *Worcester* v. *The State of Georgia*, 6 Pet. 515, 559, that prior to the formation of the Constitution treaties were made with the Cherokee tribes by which their autonomous existence was recognized. And in that case Chief Justice Marshall also said (p. 559):

> 'The Indian nations had always been considered as distinct, independent political communities, retaining their original natural rights. ... The very term 'nation' so generally applied to them, means a 'people distinct from others.' The Constitution, by declaring treaties already made, as well as those to be made, to be the supreme law of the land, has adopted and sanctioned the previous treaties with the Indian nations, and consequently admits their rank among those powers who are capable of making treaties.'

In reviewing the whole subject in *Kagama* v. *United States*, 118 U.S. 375, this court said (p. 381):

> 'With the Indians themselves these relations are equally difficult to define. They were, and always have been, regarded as having a semi-independent position when they preserved their tribal relations; not as States, not as nations, not as possessed of the full attributes of sovereignty, but as a separate people with the power of regulating their internal and social relations, and thus far not brought under the laws of the Union, or of the State within whose limits they reside.'

True it is that in many adjudications of this court the fact has been fully recognized, that although possessed of these attributes of local self government, when exercising their tribal functions, all such rights are subject to the supreme legislative authority of the United States. *Cherokee Nation* v. *Kansas Railway Co.*, 135 U.S. 641, where the cases are fully reviewed. But the existence of the right in Congress to regulate the manner in which the local powers of the Cherokee nation shall be exercised does not render such local powers Federal powers arising from and created by the Constitution of the United States. It follows that as the powers of local self government enjoyed by the Cherokee nation existed prior to the Constitution, they are not operated upon by the Fifth Amendment, which, as we have said, had for its sole object to control the powers conferred by the Constitution on the National Government.*** (at pp. 382-384.)

And see, to the same effect, Ex parte Tiger (2 Ind. T. 41, 47 S.W. 304). It is recognized, of course, that these provisions of the Federal Constitution which are completely general in scope, such as the Thirteenth Amendment, apply to the members of Indian tribes as well as to all other inhabitants of the nation. In re Sah Quah (31 Fed. 327).

Added recognition of the sovereign character of an Indian tribe is found in the case of *Turner* v. *United States and Creek Nation* (51 Ct. Cls, 125, aff'd 248 U.S. 354). Rejecting a claim against the Creek Nation based upon the allegedly illegal acts of groups of Indians in destroying the fence of a cattle company, the Court of Claims declared:

> ***we must apply the rule of law applicable to established governments under similar conditions. It is a familiar rule that in the absence of a statute declaring a liability thereof neither the sovereign nor the governmental subdivisions, such as counties or municipalities, are responsible to the party injured in his person or estate by mob violence.*** (at p. 153.)

An extreme application of the doctrine of tribal sovereignty is found in the case of *Ex parte Crow Dog* (109 U.S. 556), in which it was held that the murder of one Sioux Indian by another upon an Indian reservation was not within the criminal jurisdiction of any court of the United States, but that only the Indian tribe itself could punish the offense.

The contention that the United States courts had jurisdiction in a case of this sort was based upon the language of a treaty with the Sioux, rather than upon considerations applicable generally to the various Indian tribes. The most important of the treaty clauses upon which the claim of Federal jurisdiction was based provided:

> And Congress shall, by appropriate legislation, secure to
> them an orderly government; they shall be subject to the laws of

the United States, and each individual shall be protected in his rights of property, person, and life. (at p. 568.)

Commenting upon this clause, the Supreme Court declared:

> It is equally clear, in our opinion, that these words can have no such effect as that claimed for them. The pledge to secure to these people, with whom the United States was contracting as a distinct political body, an orderly government, by appropriate legislation thereafter to be framed and enacted, necessarily implies, having regard to all the circumstances attending the transaction, that among the arts of civilized life, which it was the very purpose of all these arrangements to introduce and naturalize among them, was the highest and best of all, that of self-government, the regulation by themselves of their own domestic affairs, the maintenance of order and peace among their own members by the administration of their own laws and customs. They were nevertheless to be subject to the laws of the United States, with a voice in the selection of representatives and the framing of the laws, but as a dependent community who were in a stage of pupilage, advancing from the condition of a savage tribe to that of a people who, through the discipline of labor and by education, it was hoped might become a self-supporting and self-governed society.\*\*\* (at pp. 568-569.)

In finally rejecting the argument for Federal jurisdiction the Supreme Court declared:

> \*\*\* It is a case where, against an express exception in the law itself, that law, by argument and inference only, is sought to be extended over aliens and strangers; over the members of a community separated by race, by tradition, by the instincts of a free though savage life, from the authority and power which seeks to impose upon them the restraints of an external and unknown code, and to subject them to the responsibilities of civil conduct, according to rules and penalties of which they could have no previous warning; which judges them by a standard made by others and not for them, which takes no account of the condi-

tions which should except them from its exactions, and makes no allowance for their inability to understand it. (at p. 571.)

The force of the decision in *Ex parte Crow Dog* was not weakened, although the scope of the decision was limited, by subsequent legislation which withdrew from the rule of tribal sovereignty a list of seven major crimes, only recently extended to ten.[5] Over these specified crimes jurisdiction has been vested in the Federal courts. Over all other crimes, including such serious crimes as kidnaping, attempted murder, receiving stolen goods, and forgery, jurisdiction resides not in the courts of the Nation or State but only in the Indian tribe itself.

We shall defer the question of the exact scope of tribal jurisdiction for more detailed consideration at a later point. We are concerned for the present only in analyzing the basic doctrine of tribal sovereignty. To this doctrine the case of *Ex parte Crow Dog* contributes not only an intimation of the vast and important content of criminal jurisdiction inherent in tribal sovereignty, but also an example of the consistent manner in which the United States Supreme Court has opposed the efforts of lower courts and administrative officials to infringe upon tribal sovereignty and to assume tribal prerogatives without statutory justification. The legal powers of an Indian tribe, measured by the decisions of the highest courts, are far more extensive than the powers which most Indian tribes have been actually permitted by omnipresent officials to exercise in their own right.

The doctrine of tribal sovereignty is well summarized in the following passage in the case of In Re Sah Quah (31 Fed. 327):

> From the organization of the government to the present time, the various Indian tribes of the United States have been treated as free and independent within their respective territories, governed by their tribal laws and customs, in all matters pertaining to their internal affairs, such as contracts, and the manner of their enforcement, marriage, descents, and the punishment for crimes committed against each other. They have been excused from all allegiance to the municipal laws of the whites as precedents or otherwise in relation to tribal affairs, subject, however, to such restraints as were from time to time deemed necessary

---

5    U.S. Code, Title 18, sec. 548, analyzed infra, under heading, "The Powers of an Indian Tribe in the Administration of Justice."

for their own protection, and for the protection of the whites adjacent to them. *Cherokee Nat,* v. *Georgia,* 5 Pet. 1, 16, 17; *Jackson* v. *Goodell,* 20 Johns, 193. (at p. 329.)

And in the case of *Anderson* v. *Mathews* (174 Cal. 537, 163 Pac. 902), it was said:

> ***The Indian tribes recognized by the federal government are not subject to the laws of the state in which they are situated. They are under the control and protection of the United States, but they retain the right of local self-government, and they regulate and control their own local affairs and rights of persons and property, except as Congress has otherwise specially provided by law.*** (at 163 Pac. 905.)

See, also, to the same effect, Story's Commentaries, Sec. 1099; 3 Kent's Commentaries (14th ed.) 383-386.

The acknowledgement of tribal sovereignty or autonomy by the courts of the United States has not been a matter of lip service to a venerable but outmoded theory. The doctrine has been followed through the most recent cases, and from time to time carried to new implications. Moreover, it has been administered by the courts in a spirit of whole-hearted sympathy and respect. The painstaking analysis by the Supreme Court of tribal laws and constitutional provisions in the *Cherokee Intermarriage Cases* (203 U.S. 706) is typical, and exhibits a degree of respect proper to the laws of a sovereign state. If verbal recognition is needed, there is the glowing tribute which Judge Nott pays to this same Cherokee Constitution in the case of *Journeycake* v. *Cherokee Nation and United States* (28 Ct. Cls. 281, 317-318):

> The constitution of the Cherokees was a wonderful adaptation to the circumstances and conditions of the time, and to a civilization that was yet to come. It was framed and adopted by a people some of whom were still in the savage state, and the better portion of whom had just entered upon that state of civilization which is characterized by industrial pursuits; and it was framed during a period of extraordinary turmoil and civil discord, when the greater part of the Cherokee people had just been driven by military force from their mountains and valleys in Georgia, and been brought by enforced immigration into the

country of the western Cherokees; when a condition of anarchy and civil war reigned in the territory — a condition which was to continue until the two branches of the nation should be united under the treaty of 1846 (27 C. Cls. R., 1); yet for more than half a century it has met the requirements of a race steadily advancing in prosperity and education and enlightenment so well that it has needed, so far as they are concerned, no material alteration or amendment, and deserves to be classed among the few great works of intelligent statesmanship which outlive their own time and continue through succeeding generations to assure the rights and guide the destinies of men. And it is not the least of the successes of the constitution of the Cherokees that the judiciary of another nation are able, with entire confidence in the clearness and wisdom of its provisions, to administer it for the protection of Cherokee citizens and the maintenance of their personal and political rights. (at pp.317-318.)

The sympathy of the courts towards the independent efforts of Indian tribes to administer the institutions of self-government has led to the doctrine that Indian laws and statutes are to be interpreted not in accordance with the technical rules of the common law, but in the light of the traditions and circumstances of the Indian people. An attempt in the case of Ex parte Tiger (47 S.W. 304, 2 Ind. T. 41) to construe the language of the Creek Constitution in a technical sense was met by the appropriate judicial retort:

If the Creek Nation derived its system of jurisprudence through the common law, there would be much plausibility in this reasoning. But they are strangers to the common law.[6] They derive their jurisprudence from an entirely different source, and they are as unfamiliar with common law terms and definitions as they are with Sanskrit or Hebrew. With them, 'to indict' is to file a written accusation charging a person with a crime.

So, too, in the case of *McCurtain* v. *Grady* (1 Ind. T. 107, 38 S.W. 65) the court had occasion to note that:

---

6    See *Waldron* v. *United States*, 143 Fed. 413; *Hanson* v. *Johnson*, 246 Pac. 868 (Okla.).

The Choctaw constitution was not drawn by geologists or for geologists, or in the interest of science, or with scientific accuracy. It was framed by plain people, who have agreed among themselves what meaning should be attached to it, and the courts should give effect to that interpretation which its framers intended it should have.

The realm of tribal autonomy which has been so carefully respected by the courts, has been implicitly confirmed by Congress in a host of statutes providing that various administrative acts of the President or the Interior Department shall be done only with the consent of the Indian tribe or its chiefs or council.

Thus, U.S. Code, title 25, section 63, provides that the President may "consolidate one or more tribes, and abolish such agencies as are thereby rendered unnecessary," but that such action may be undertaken only "with the consent of the tribes to be affected thereby, expressed in the usual manner."

Section 111 of the same title provides that payments of moneys and distribution of goods for the benefit of any Indians or Indian tribes shall be made either to the heads of families and individuals directly entitled to such moneys or goods or else to the chiefs of the tribe, for the benefit of the tribe, or to persons appointed by the tribe for the purpose of receiving such moneys or goods. This section finally provides that such moneys or goods "by consent of the tribe" may be applied directly by the Secretary to purposes conducive to the happiness and prosperity of the tribe.

Section 115 of the same title provides: The President may, at the request of any Indian tribe, to which an annuity is payable in money, cause the same to be paid in goods, purchased as provided in section 91.

Section 140 of the same title provides that specific appropriations for the benefit of Indian tribes may be diverted to other uses "with the consent of said tribes, expressed in the usual manner."

Other statutory provisions of general import, confirming or delegating specific powers to the Indian tribes or their officers, are:

U.S. Code, title 25, section 48, section 130, section 132, section 159, section 162, section 184, section 218, section 225, section 229, section 371, section 397, section 398, section 402.

These latter provisions are discussed later under relevant headings.

The whole course of Congressional legislation with respect to the Indians has been based upon a recognition of tribal autonomy, qualified only where the need for other types of governmental control has become clearly manifest. As was said in a report of the Senate Judiciary Committee (prior to the enactment of U.S. Code, title 18, sec. 548):

> Their right of self-government, and to administer justice among themselves, after their rude fashion, even in inflicting the death penalty, has never been questioned. (Sen. Rep. No. 268, 41$^{st}$ Congress, 3d session.)

It is a fact that State governments and administrative officials have frequently trespassed upon the realm of tribal autonomy, presuming to govern the Indian tribes through State law or departmental regulation or arbitrary administrative fiat, but these trespasses have not impaired the vested legal powers of local self-government which have been recognized again and again when these trespasses have been challenged by an Indian tribe. "Power and authority rightfully conferred do not necessarily cease to exist in consequences of long non-user." (*United States ex rel. Standing Bear* v. *Crook*, 5 Dill. 453, 460.) The Wheeler-Howard Act, by affording statutory recognition of these powers of local self-government and administrative assistance in developing adequate mechanisms for such government, may reasonably be expected to end the conditions that have in the past led the Interior Department and various State agencies to deal with matters that are properly within the legal competence of the Indian tribes themselves.

Neither the allotting of land in severalty nor the granting of citizenship has destroyed the tribal relationship upon which local autonomy rests. Only through the laws or treaties of the United States, or administrative acts authorized thereunder, can tribal existence be terminated. As was said in the case of *United States* v. *Boylan* (265 Fed. 165) with reference to certain New York Indians over whom State courts had attempted to exercise jurisdiction:

> ***Congress alone has the right to say when the guardianship over the Indians may cease. *U.S.* v. *Nice,* 241 U.S. 591, 36 Sup. Ct. 696, 60 L. ED. 1192; *Tiger* v. *Western Inv. Co.,* 221 U.S. 286, 32 Sup. Ct. 578, 55 L. Ed. 738. Accordingly it has been held that it is for Congress to say when the tribal existence shall be deemed to have terminated, and Congress must so express its intent in relation thereto in clear terms. Until such legislation by Congress, even a grant of citizenship does not terminate the tribal status or relieve the Indian from the guardianship of the

government. *U.S. v. Nice,* 241 U.S. 592, 36 Sup. Ct. 696, 60 L.
Ed. 1192." \*\*\* (at p. 171.)

The court concludes:

> \*\*\*The right of self-government has never been taken from
> them. \*\*\*
>
> At all times the rights which belong to self-government have
> been recognized as vested in these Indians.\*\*\* (at p. 173.)

In the case of *Farrell* v. *United States* (110 Fed. 942), the effect of allotment
in severalty and of the grant of citizenship was considered, and the court declared:

> \*\*\*The agreement to maintain the agent and the retention
> and exercise of the power to control the liquor traffic are not
> inconsistent, as we have seen, with the allotment of the lands
> in severalty, or with the grant to the allottees of the immunities
> and privileges of citizenship. Neither the act of 1887 nor any
> other act of congress or treaty with these Indians required those
> who selected allotments and received patents and the privileges
> and immunities of citizenship to sever their tribal relation, or
> to surrender any of their rights as members of their tribes, as a
> condition of the grant, so that after their allotments, as before,
> their tribal relation continued. And finally the legislative and
> executive departments of the government to which the subject-
> matters of the relations of the Indians and their tribes to the
> United States, and the regulation of the commerce with them,
> has been specially intrusted, have uniformly held that congress
> retained, and have constantly exercised, the power to regulate
> intercourse with these Indians, and to prohibit the traffic in
> intoxicating liquors with them, since these patents issued, to the
> same extent as before their lands were allotted in severalty. It is
> the settled rule of the judicial department of the government, in
> ascertaining the relations of Indian tribes and their members to
> the nation, to follow the action of the legislative and executive
> departments, to which the determination of these questions has
> been especially intrusted. *U.S. v. Holliday,* 3 Wall. 407, 419, 18
> L. Ed. 182; *U.S. v. Earl* (C.C.) 17 Fed. 75, 78. (at p. 951.)

And in the case of *United States v. Holliday* (3 Wall. 407), the Supreme Court declared:

> In reference to all matters of this kind, it is the rule of this court to follow the action of the executive and other political departments of the government, whose more special duty is to determine such affairs. If by them those Indians are recognized as a tribe, this court must do the same. (at p. 419.)

And see, to the same effect, *The Kansas Indians* (5 Wall. 737, 756); *Yakima Joe v, To-is-lap* (191 Fed. 516); *United States v. Flournoy Livestock, etc. Co.* (71 Fed. 576).

There are, of course, a number of instances in which tribal autonomy has been terminated by Act of Congress or by treaty. See, for example, *Wiggan v. Conolly* (163 U.S. 56); *United States v. Elm* (2 Cin. Law Bull. 307, 25 Fed. Cas, No. 15,048); and cf. act of April 26, 1906 (34 Stat. 137). But to accomplish this, the provision of treaty or statute must be positive and unambiguous. (*Morrow v. Blevins*, 23 Tenn. 223; *Jones v. Meehan*, 175 U.S. 1.)

Save in such instances, the internal sovereignty of the Indian tribes continues, unimpaired by the changes that have occurred in the manners and customs of Indian life, and, for the future, remains a most powerful vehicle for the movement of the Indian tribes towards a richer social existence.

## THE POWER OF AN INDIAN TRIBE
## TO DEFINE ITS FORM OF GOVERNMENT

Since any group of men, in order to act as a group, must act through forms which give the action the character and authority of group action, an Indian tribe must, if it has any power at all, have the power to prescribe the forms through which its will may be registered. The first element of sovereignty, and the last which may survive successive statutory limitations of Indian tribal power, is the power of the tribe to determine and define its own form of government. Such power includes the right to define the powers and duties of its officials, the manner of their appointment or election, the manner of their removal, the rules they are to observe in their capacity as officials, and the forms and procedures which are to attest the authoritative character of acts done in the name of the tribe. These are matters that may be determined even in a modern civilized nation by unwritten custom as well as by written law. The controlling character of the Indian tribe's basic forms and procedures has been recognized by State and Federal courts, whether evidenced by written statute or by the testimony of tradition.

Thus, in the case of *Pueblo of Santa Rosa* v. *Fall* (273 U.S. 315) the Supreme Court recognized that by the traditional law of the Pueblo the "Captain" of the Pueblo would have no authority to convey to attorneys the claims of the Pueblo or to authorize suit thereon, and that such acts without the approval of a general council would be null and void.

To the same effect, see 7 Op. Atty. Gen. 142 (1855).

In 5 Op. Atty. Gen. 79 (1849) the opinion is expressed that a release to be executed by the "Creek Indians" would be valid "provided, that the chiefs and headmen executing it are such chiefs and headmen and constitute the whole or a majority of the council of the Creek Nation."

In *Rawlins* and *Presbey* v. *United States* (23 Ct. Cls. 106) the court finds that a chief's authority to act in the name of the tribe has been established by the tacit assent of the tribe and by their acceptance of the benefits of his acts.

In the case of *Mount Pleasant* v. *Gansworth* (271 N.Y. Supp. 78) it is held that the Tuscarora tribal council has never been endowed with probate jurisdiction, that no other body has been set up by the tribe to exercise probate powers, and hence that State court may step in to remedy the lack. Whether or not the final conclusion is justified, in the light of such cases as *Patterson* v. *Council of Seneca Nation* (245 N.Y. 443; 157 N.E. 734), the opinion of the court indicates at least that the limitations which a tribe may impose upon the jurisdiction of its own governmental bodies and officers will be respected.

Not only must officers presuming to act in the name of an Indian tribe show that their acts fall within their allotted function and authority, but likewise the procedural formalities which tradition or ordinance require must be followed in executing an act within the acknowledged jurisdiction of the officer or set of officers.

In 19 Op. Atty. Gen. 179 (1888) it is held that a decree of divorce which has not been signed by a judge or clerk of court, as required by the laws of the Choctaw Nation, is invalid.

*In re Darch* (265 N.Y. Supp. 86) involves action of a special tribal council meeting to which only a few of the members of the council were invited. The action was declared invalid on the ground that the council's rules of procedure required due notice of a special meeting to be given to all the members of the council. Based on an analogy taken from corporation law, the rule was laid down that violation of this requirement rendered the acts of the council invalid.

In 25 Op. Atty. Gen. 308 (1904) it appeared that certain sums were to be paid to attorneys "only after the tribal authorities, thereunto duly and specifically authorized by the tribe, shall have signed a writing \*\*." By resolution of the tribe the business committee had been authorized to sign the writing in question. The signature of the business committee, in the opinion of the Attorney General, met the statutory requirement:

"The proceedings of the council were regular, and the motions were carried by a sufficient number of voters, though less than a majority of those present. See *State* v. *Vanodel* (131 Ind. 388): *Attorney General* v. *Shepard* (62 N.H. 383); and *Mount* v. *Parker* (32 N.J. Law, 341)."

The doctrine of *de facto* officers has been applied to an Indian tribe, in accordance with the rule applied to other governmental agencies, so as to safeguard from collateral attack acts and documents signed by officers acting under color of authority, through subject, in proper proceedings, to removal from office. See *Nofire* v. *United States* (164 U.S. 657); *Seneca Nation* v. *John* (16 N.Y. Supp. 40).

Based upon the analogy of the constitutional law of the United States, the doctrine has been applied to Indian statutes and constitutional provisions that statutes deemed by the court to be violative of constitutional limitations are to be regarded as void. See *Whitmire, Trustee* v. *Cherokee Nation* (30 Ct. Cls. 138) *Delaware Indians* v. *Cherokee Nation* (38 Ct. Cls. 234) 19 Op. Atty. Gen. 229 (1889).

Statutes of Congress have recognized that the authority of an Indian tribe is customarily wielded by chiefs and headmen.[7]

Other congressional legislation has specifically recognized the propriety of paying salaries to tribal officers out of tribal funds.[8]

---

7    U.S. Code, Title 25, Sec. 130: "Withholding of moneys or goods on account of intoxicating liquors. No annuities, or moneys, or goods, shall be paid or distributed to Indians \*\*\* until the chiefs and headmen of the tribe shall have pledged themselves to use all their influence and to make all proper exertions to prevent the introduction and sale of such liquor in their country."

8    U.S. Code, Title 25, Sec. 162, after providing generally for the segregation, deposit and investment of tribal funds, contains the following qualification: "And provided further, That any part of tribal funds required for support of schools or pay of tribal officers shall be excepted from segregation or deposit as herein authorized and the same shall be expended for the purposes aforesaid."

## THE POWER OF AN INDIAN TRIBE TO DETERMINE ITS MEMBERSHIP

The courts have consistently recognized that in the absence of express legislation by Congress to the contrary, the Indian tribe has complete authority to determine all questions of its membership.[9] It may thus by usage or written law determine under what conditions persons of mixed blood shall be considered members of the tribe. It may provide for special formalities of recognition, and it may adopt such rules as seem suitable to it, to regulate the abandonment of membership, the adoption of non-Indians or Indians of other tribes, and the types of membership or citizenship which it may choose to recognize. The completeness of this power receives statutory recognition in U.S. Code, Title 25, Sec. 184, which provides that the children of a white man and an Indian woman by blood shall be considered members of the tribe if, and only if, "said Indian women was *** recognized by the tribe,"[10] The power of the Indian tribes in this field is limited only by the various statutes of Congress defining the membership of certain tribes for purposes of allotment or for other purposes, and by the statutory authority given to the Secretary of the Interior to promulgate a final tribal roll for the purpose of dividing and distributing tribal funds.[11]

---

9    It must be noted that property rights attached to membership are largely in the control of the Secretary of the Interior rather than the tribe itself. See heading, infra, "Tribal Powers Over Property."

10    "Rights of children born of marriages between white men and Indian women. All children born of a marriage solemnized prior to June 7, 1897, between a white man and an Indian woman by blood and not by adoption, where said Indian woman was on that date, or was at the time of her death, recognized by the tribe, shall have the same rights and privileges to the property of the tribe to which the mother belongs, or belonged at the time of her death, by blood, as any other member of the tribe, and no prior Act of Congress shall be construed as to debar such child of such right. (June 7, 1897, c.3, sec. 1, 30 Stat. 90.)"

11    *U.S. Code. Title 25, Sec. 163: "Roll of membership of Indian tribes. The Secretary of the Interior is authorized, wherever in his discretion such action would be for the best interest of the Indians, to cause a final roll to be made of the membership of any Indian tribe; such rolls shall contain the ages and quantum of Indian blood, and when approved by the said Secretary are declared to constitute the legal membership of the respective tribes for the purpose of segregating the tribal funds as provided in the preceding section, and shall be conclusive both as to ages and quantum of Indian blood: Provided, That the foregoing shall not apply to the Five Civilized Tribes or to the Osage Tribe of Indians, or to the Chippewa Indians of Minnesota, or the Menominee Indians of Wisconsin. (June 30, 1919, c.4, sec. 1, 41 Stat. 9.)

The power of an Indian tribe to determine questions of its own membership arises necessarily from the character of an Indian tribe as a distinct political entity. In the case of *Patterson* v. *Council of Seneca Nation* (245 N.Y. 433; 157 N.E. 734), the Court of Appeals of New York reviewed the many decisions of that court and of the Supreme Court of the United States recognizing the Indian tribe as a "distinct political society, separated from others, capable of managing its own affairs and governing itself" (per Marshall, C.J., in *Cherokee Nation* v. *Georgia*, 5 Pet. 1), and, in reaching the conclusion that mandamus would not lie to compel the plaintiff's enrollment by the defendant council, declared:

"Unless these expressions, as well as similar expressions many time used by many courts in various jurisdictions, are mere words of flattery designed to soothe Indian sensibilities, unless the last vestige of separate national life has been withdrawn from the Indin tribes by encroaching state legislation, then, surely, it must follow that the Seneca Nation of Indians has retained for itself that prerequisite to their self-preservation and integrity as a nation, the right to determine by whom its membership shall be constituted.

\* \* \* \* \* \* \* \*

"It must be the law, therefore, that, unless the Seneca Nation of Indians and the State of New York enjoy a relation inter se peculiar to themselves, the right to enrollment of the petitioner, with its attending property rights, depends upon the laws and usages of the Seneca Nation and is to be determined by that Nation for itself, without interference or dictation from the Supreme Court of the state."

After examining the constitutional position of the Seneca Nation and finding that tribal autonomy has not been impaired by any legislation of the state, the court concludes:

"The conclusion is inescapable that the Seneca Tribe remains a separate nation; that its powers of self-government are retained with the sanction of the state; that the ancient customs and usages of the nation except in a few particulars, remain, unabolished, the law of the Indian land; that in its capacity of a sovereign nation the Seneca Nation is not subservient to the orders and directions of the courts of New York state; that, above all, the Seneca Nation retains for itself the power of determining who are Senecas, and in that respect is above interference and dictation."

In the case of *Waldron* v. *United States* (143 Fed. 413), it appeared that a woman of five-sixteenth Sioux Indian blood on her mother's side, her father being a white man, had been refused recognition as an Indian by the Interior Department although, by tribal custom, since the woman's mother had been recognized as an Indian, the woman herself was so recognized. The court held that the decision of the Interior Department was contrary to law, declaring"

"In this proceeding the court has been informed as to the usages and customs of the different tribes of the Sioux Nation, and has found as a fact that the common law does not obtain among said tribes, as to determining the race to which the children of a white man, married to an Indian woman, belong; but that, according to the usages and customs of said tribes, the children of a white man married to an Indian woman take the race or nationality of the mother."

The same view is maintained in 19 Op. Atty. Gen. 115 (1888), in which it is said:

> It was the Indians, and not the United States, that were interested in the distribution of what was periodically coming to them from the United States. It was proper then that they should determine for themselves, and finally, who were entitled to membership in the confederated tribe and to participate in the emoluments belonging to that relation.
>
> The certificate of the chiefs and councilors referred to is possibly as high a grade of evidence as can be procured of the fact of the determination by the chiefs of the right of membership under the treaty of February 23, 1867, and seems to be such as is warranted by the usage and custom of the Government in its general dealings with these people and other similar tribes, (At page 116)

See to the same effect:
In re William Banks (26 L.D. 71);
*Black Tomahawk* v. *Waldron* (19 L.D. 311); 20 Op. Atty. Gen. 711 (1894);
*Western Cherokee Indians* v. *United States,* (27 Ct, Cls. 1, 54);
*United States* v. *Heyfron* (two cases) (138 Fed. 964, 968).

In the Cherokee intermarriage cases (203 U.S. 76), the Supreme Court of the United States considered the claims of certain white men, married to Cherokee Indians, to participate in the common property of the Cherokee Nation. After carefully examining the constitutional articles and the statutes of the Cherokee Nation, the court reached the conclusion that the claims in question were invalid, since, although the claimants had been recognized as citizens for certain purposes, the Cherokee Nation had complete authority to qualify the rights of citizenship which is offered to its "naturalized" citizens, and had, in the exercise of this authority, provided for the revocation or qualification of citizenship rights so as to defeat the claims of the plaintiffs. The Supreme Court declared (per Fuller, C.J.):

> The distinction between different classes of citizens was recognized by the Cherokees in the differences in their intermarriage law, as applicable to the whites and to the Indians of other tribes; by the provision in the intermarriage law that a white man intermarried with an Indian by blood acquired certain rights as a citizen, but no provision that if he marries a Cherokee citizen not of Indian blood he shall be regarded as a citizen at all; and by the provision that if, once having married an Indian by blood, he marries the second time a citizen not by blood, he loses all of his rights as a citizen. And the same distinction between citizens as such and citizens with property rights has also been recognized by Congress in enactments relating to other Indians than the Five Civilized Tribes. Act August 9, 1888, 25 Stat. 392, c.818,; act May 2, 1890, 26 Stat. 96, c.182; act June 7, 1897, 30 Stat. 90, c.3. (At page 88)

> *** The laws and usages of the Cherokees, their earliest history, the fundamental principles of their national policy, their constitution and statutes, all show that citizenship rested on blood or marriage; that the man who would assert citizenship must establish marriage; that when marriage ceased (with a special reservation in favor of widows and widowers) citizenship ceased; that when an intermarried white married a person having no rights of Cherokee citizenship by blood it was conclusive evidence that the tie which bound him to the Cherokee people was severed and the very basis of his citizenship obliterated. (At page 95)

See, to the same effect, 19 Op. Atty. Gen. 109 (1888).

> An Indian tribe may classify various types of membership and qualify not only the property rights, but the voting rights of certain members. Thus in 19 Op. Atty. Gen. 389 (1888) the view is expressed that a tribe may by law restrict the rights of

tribal suffrage, excluding white citizens from voting, although by treaty they are guaranteed rights of "membership."

Similarly, an Indian tribe may revoke rights of membership which it has granted. In *Roff* v. *Burney* (168 U.S. 218), the Supreme Court upheld the validity of an act of the Chickasaw legislature depriving a Chickasaw citizen of his citizenship, declaring:

> The citizenship which the Chickasaw legislature could confer it could withdraw. The only restriction on the power of the Chickasaw Nation to legislate in respect to its internal affair is that such legislation shall not conflict with the Constitution or laws of the United States, and we know of no provision of such Constitution or laws which would be set at naught by the action of a political community like this in withdrawing privileges of membership in the community once conferred. (At page 222)

The right of an Indian tribe to make express rules governing the recognition of members, the adoption of new members, the procedure for abandonment of membership, and the procedure for readoption, is recognized in *Smith* v. *Bonifer* (154 Fed. 883, aff'd. 166 Fed. 846). In that case the plaintiffs' right to allotments depended upon their membership in a particular tribe. The court held that such membership was demonstrated by the fact of tribal recognition, declaring:

> Indian members of one tribe can sever their relations as such, and may form affiliations with another or other tribes. And so they may, after their relations with a tribe has been severed, rejoin the tribe and be again recognized and treated as members thereof, and tribal rights and privileges attach according to the habits and customs of the tribe with which affiliation is presently cast. As to the manner of breaking off and recasting tribal affiliations we are meagerly informed. It was and is a thing, of course, dependent upon the peculiar usages and customs of each particular tribe, and therefore we may assume that no general rule obtains for its regulation.

Now, the first condition presented is that the mother of Philomme was a fullblood Walla Walla Indian. She was consequently a member of the tribe of that name. Was her status changed by marriage to Tawakown, an Iroquois Indian?

This must depend upon the tribal usage and customs of the Walla Wallas and the Iroquois. It is said by Hon. William A. Little, Assistant Attorney General, in an opinion rendered the Department of the Interior in a matter involving this very controversy:

> That inheritance among these Indians is through the mother and not through the father, and that the true test in these cases is to ascertain whether parties claiming to be Indians and entitled to allotments have by their conduct expatriated themselves or changed their citizenship.'

But we are told that:

> means membership in a family; and this in turn constitutes citizenship in the tribe, conferring certain social, political, and religious privileges, duties, and rights, which are denied to persons of alien blood.' Handbook of American Indians, edited by Frederick Webb Hodge, Smithsonian Institute, Government Printing Office, 1907.
>
> Marriage, therefore, with Tawakown would not of itself constitute an affiliation on the part of his wife with the Iroquois tribe, of which he was a member, and a renunciation of membership with her own tribe." (At page 836)

Considering a second marriage of the plaintiff to a white person, the court went on to declare:

> But notwithstanding the marriage of Philomme to Smity, and her long residence outside of the limits of the reservation, she was acknowledged by the chiefs of the confederated tribes to be a member of the Walla Walla tribe. From the testimony adduced herein, read in connection with that taken in the case of *Hy-yu-tse-mil-kin* v. *Smith,* supra, it appears that Mrs. Smith was advised by Homily and Show-a-way, chiefs, respectively, of the Walla Walla and Cayuse tribes, to come upon the reservation and make selections for allotment for herself and children, and that thereafter she was recognized by both these chiefs, and by Peo, the chief of the Umatillas, as being a member of the Walla Walla tribe. It is true that she was not so recognized at first, but

she was finally, and by a general council of the Indians held for
the special purpose of determining the matter. (At page 888)

Where tribal laws have not expressly provided for some certificate of membership (see 19 Op. Atty. Gen.115 (1888), the courts, in cases not clearly controlled
by recognized tribal custom, have looked to recognition by the tribal chiefs as a
test of tribal membership. *Hy-yu-tse-mil-kin* v. *Smith* (194 U.S. 401, 411).

The weight given to tribal action in relation to tribal membership is shown
in the case of *Nofire* v. *United States* (164 U.S. 657). In that case the jurisdiction
of the Cherokee courts in a murder case, the defendants being Cherokee Indians,
depended upon whether the deceased, a white man, had been duly adopted by
the Cherokee tribe. Finding evidence of such adoption in the official records of
the tribe, the Supreme Court held that such adoption deprived the State court
of jurisdiction over the murder and vested such jurisdiction in the tribal courts.

A similar decision was reached in the case of *Raymond* v. *Raymond* (83 Fed,
721), in which the jurisdiction of a tribal court over an adopted Cherokee was
challenged. The court declared (per Sanborn, J):

> It is conceded that under the laws of that nation the appel-
> lee became a member of that tribe, by adoption, through her
> intermarriage with the appellant. It is settled by the decisions of
> the supreme court that her adoption into that nation ousted the
> federal court of jurisdiction over any suit between her and any
> member of that tribe, and vested the tribal courts with exclu-
> sive jurisdiction over every such action. *Alberty v. U.S.*, 162 U.S.
> 499, 16 Sup. Ct. 864; Nofire v. U.S., 164 U.S. 657, 656, 17
> Sup. Ct. 212.

It is of course recognized throughout the cases, that tribal membership is a
bilateral relation, depending for its existence not only upon the action of the tribe
but also upon the action of the individual concerned. Any member of any Indian
tribe is at full liberty to terminate his tribal relationship whenever he so chooses.
In the famous case of *United States ex rel. Standing Bear* v. *Crook* (5 Dill. 453,
25 Fed. Cases No. 14891), in which an Indian secured a writ of habeas corpus
directed against a general of the United States Army, to prevent his removal to
Indian territory, the court found that the petitioner, Standing Bear, had severed
his relationship with his tribe and was, therefore, not subject to the provision of

any treaties or legislation concerned with the removal of the tribe to Indian territory. The court declared (per Dundy, J.):

> Standing Bear, the principal witness, states that out of five hundred and eighty-one Indians who went from the reservation in Dakota to the Indian Territory, one hundred and fifty-eight died within a year or so, and a great proportion of the others were sick and disabled, caused, in great measure, no doubt, from change of climate; and to save himself and the survivors of his wasted family, and the feeble remnant of his little band of followers, he determined to leave the Indian Territory and return to his old home, where, to use his own language, 'he might live and die in peace, and be buried with his fathers.' He also states that he informed the agent of their final purpose to leave, never to return, and that he and his followers had finally, fully, and forever severed his and their connection with the Ponca Tribe of Indians, and had resolved to disband as a tribe, or band, of Indians, and to cut loose from the government, go to work, become self-sustaining, and adopt the habits and customs of a higher civilization. To accomplish that would seem to be a desirable and laudable purpose, all who were able so to do went to work to earn a living. The Omaha Indians, who speak the same language, and with whom many of the Poncas have long continued to intermarry, gave them employment and ground to cultivate, so as to make them self-sustaining. And it was when at the Omaha reservation, and when thus employed, that they were arrested by order of the federal government, for the purpose of being taken back to Indian Territory. They claim to be unable to see the justice, or reason, or wisdom, or necessity, of removing them by force from their own native plains and blood relations to a far-off country, in which they can see little but new-made graves opening for their reception. The land from which they fled in fear has no attractions for them. The love of home and native land was strong enough in the minds of these people to induce them to brave every peril to return and live and die where they had been reared. The bones of the dead son of Standing Bear were not to repose in the land they hoped to be leaving forever,

but were carefully preserved and protected, and formed a part of what was to them a melancholy procession homeward.

***What is here stated in this connection is mainly for the purpose of showing that the relators did all they could to separate themselves from their tribe and to sever their tribal relations, for the purpose of becoming self-sustaining and living without support from the government. This being so, it presents the question as to whether or not an Indian can withdraw from his tribe, sever his tribal relation therewith, and terminate his allegiance thereto, for the purpose of making an independent living and adopting our own civilization.

If Indian tribes are to be regarded and treated as separate but dependent nations, there can be no serious difficulty about the question. If they are not to be regarded and treated as separate, dependent nations, then no allegiance is owing from an individual Indian to his tribe, and he could, therefore, withdraw therefrom at any time. The question of expatriation has engaged the attention of our government from the time of its very foundation. Many heated discussion have been carried on between our own and foreign governments on this great question, until diplomacy has triumphantly secured the right to every person found within our jurisdiction. This right has always been claimed and admitted by our government, and it is now no longer an open question. It can make but little difference, then, whether we accord to the Indian tribes a national character or not, as in either case I think the individual Indian possesses the clear and God-given right to withdraw from his tribe and forever live away from it, as though it had no further existence. If the right of expatriation was open to doubt in this country down to the year 1868, certainly since that time no sort of question as to the right can now exist. On the 27th of July of that year Congress passed an act, now appearing as section 1999 of the Revised Statutes, which declares that: 'Whereas, the right of expatriation is a natural and inherent right of all people, indispensable to the enjoyment of the rights of life, liberty, and the pursuit of happiness; and, whereas, in the recognition of this principle the government has freely received immigrants from all nations, and invested them with the rights of citizenship.

***Therefore, any declaration, instruction, opinion, order, or decision of any officer of the United States which denies, restricts, impairs, or questions the right of expatriation, is declared inconsistent with the fundamental principles of the republic.'"

The tribal power recognized in all the foregoing cases is not overthrown by anything in the case of *United States ex rel. West* v. *Hitchcock* (205 U.S. 80). In that case, an adopted member of the Wichita tribe was refused an allotment by the Secretary of the Interior because the Department had never approved his adoption. Since the Secretary, according to the Supreme Court, had unreviewable discretionary authority to grant or deny an allotment even to a member of the tribe by blood, it was unnecessary for the Supreme Court to decide whether refusal of the Interior Department to approve the relator's adoption was within the authority of the Department. The court, however, intimated that the general authority of the Interior Department under Rev. Stat. 463 (U.S. Code, Title 25, Sec.2),[12] was broad enough to justify a regulation requiring Department approval of adoption, but hastened to add that since the relator would have no legal right of appeal even if his adoption without Department approval were valid, "it hardly is necessary to pass upon that point."

The power of an Indian tribe to determine its membership is subject to the qualification however, that in the distribution of tribal funds and other property under the supervision and control of the Federal Government, the action of the tribe is subject to the supervisory authority of the Secretary of the Interior. See *United States ex rel. West* v. *Hitchcock,* 205 U.S. 80; *Mitchell* v. *United States,* 23 Fed, (2d) 771; *United States* v. *Provoe,* 38 Fed. (2d) 799, reversed on other grounds, 283 U.S. 753. See also *Wilbur* v. *United States,* 281 U.S. 206; The original power to determine membership, including the regulation of membership by adoption , nevertheless remains with the tribe, and in view of the broad provisions of the Wheeler-Howard Act, it is my opinion that the Secretary of the Interior may in the future define and confine his power of supervision in accordance with the terms of the constitution adopted by the tribe itself and approved by him.

## THE POWER OF AN INDIAN TRIBE TO REGULATE DOMESTIC RELATIONS

The Indian tribes have been accorded the widest possible latitude in regulating the domestic relations of their members. Indian custom marriage has been specifically recognized by Federal statute, so far as such recognition is necessary for

---

12  "Duties of Commissioner. The Commissioner of Indian Affairs shall, under the direction of the Secretary of the Interior, and agreeably to such regulations as the President may prescribe, have the management of all Indian affairs and of all matters arising out of Indian relations. (R.S. Sec. 463.)"

purposes of inheritance.[13] Indian custom marriage and divorce has been generally recognized by State and Federal courts for all other purposes. Where Federal law or written laws of the tribe do not cover the subject, the customs and traditions of the tribe are accorded the force of law, but these customs and traditions may be changed by the statutes of the Indian tribes. In defining and punishing offenses against the marriage relationship, the Indian tribe has complete and exclusive authority in the absence of legislation by Congress upon the subject. No law of the State controls the domestic relations of Indians living in tribal relationship. The authority of an Indian tribal council to appoint guardians for incompetents and minors is specifically recognized by statute,[14] although this statute at the same time deprives such guardians of the power to administer Federal trust funds.

The completeness and exclusiveness of tribal authority over matters of domestic relationship is clearly set forth by Mr. Justice VanDevanter in the opinion of the Supreme Court in *United States* v. *Quiver* (241 U.S. 602, at 603 — 605):

"At an early period it became the settled policy of Congress to permit the personal and domestic relations of the Indians with each other to be regulated, and offenses by one Indian against the person or property of another Indian to be dealt with, according to their tribal customs and laws. Thus the Indian Intercourse Acts of May 19, 1796, c. 30, 1 Stat. 469, and March, 1802, c. 13, 2 Stat. 139, provided for the punishment of various offenses by white persons against Indians and by Indians against white persons, but left untouched those by Indians

---

13  U.S.C., Title 25, sec. 371, which provides: "Descent of land. For the purpose of determining the descent of land to the heirs of any deceased Indian under the provisions of section 348, whenever any male and female Indian shall have cohabited together as husband and wife according to the custom and manner of Indian life the issue of such cohabitation shall be, for the purpose aforesaid, taken and deemed to be the legitimate issue of the Indians so living together ***"

14  U.S.C., Title 25, sec. 159, which provides: Moneys due incompetents or orphans. The Secretary of the Interior is directed to cause settlements to be made with all persons appointed by the Indian councils to receive moneys due to incompetent or orphan Indians, and to require all moneys found due to such incompetent or orphan Indians to be returned to the Treasury; and all moneys so returned shall bear interest at the rate of 6 per centum per annum, until paid by order of the Secretary of the Interior to those entitled to the same. No money shall be paid to any person appointed by any Indian council to receive moneys due to incompetent or orphan Indians, but the same shall remain in the Treasury of the United States until ordered to be paid by the Secretary to those entitled to receive the same, and shall bear 6 per centum interest until so paid." (R.S. sec. 2108.)

against each other; and the act of June 30, 1834, c. 161, Sec. 25, 4 Stat. 729, 733, while providing that 'so much of the laws of the United States as provides for the punishment of crimes be in force in the Indian country', qualified its action by saying, 'the same shall not extend to crimes committed by one Indian against the person or property of another Indian.' That provision with its qualification was later carried into the Revised Statutes as Secs. 2145 and 2146. This was the situation when the court, in *Ex parte Crow Dog,* 109 U.S. 556, held that the murder of an Indian by another Indian on an Indian reservation was not punishable under the laws of the United States and could be dealt with only according to the laws of the tribe. The first change came when, by the act of March 3, 1885, c. 341, Sec. 9, 23 Stat. 362, 385, now Sec. 328 of the Penal Code, Congress provided for the punishment of murder, manslaughter, rape, assault with intent to kill, assault with a dangerous weapon, arson, burglary and larceny when committed by one Indian against the person or property of another Indian. In other respects the policy remained as before. After South Dakota became a State, Congress, acting upon a partial session of jurisdiction by that State, c. 106, Laws 1901, provided by the act of February 2, 1903, c. 351, 32 Stat. 793, now Sec. 329 of the Penal Code, for the punishment of the particular offenses named in the act of 1885 when committed on the Indian reservations in that State, even though committed by others than Indians, but this is without bearing here, for it left the situation in respect of offenses by one Indian against the person or property of another Indian as it was after the act of 1885.

We have now referred to all the statutes. There is none dealing with bigamy, polygamy, incest, adultery or fornication, which in terms refers to Indians, these matters always having been left to the tribal customs and laws and to such preventative and corrective measures as reasonably could be taken by the administrative officers."

Recognition of the validity of marriages and divorces consummated in accordance with tribal law or custom is found in the following cases:

*Carney* v. *Chapman*, 247 U.S. 108;
*Boyer* v. *Dively*, 58 Mo. 510;
*Johnson* v. *Dunlap*, 58 Okla. 316, 173 Pac. 931;
*Cyr* v. *Walker*, 29 Okla. 281, 116 Pac. 931;
*Hallowell* v. *Commons*, 210 Fed. 793;
*Earl* v. *Godley*, 42 Minn. 361;
*Ortley* v. *Ross*, 78 Neb. 339;
*People ex rel. La Forte* v. *Rubin*, 98 N.Y. Supp. 787;
*Butler* v. *Wilson*, 54 Okla. 229, 153 Pac. 823;

*Proctor* v. *Foster*, 107 Okla. 95, 230 Pac. 753;

*Davis* v. *Reeder*, 102 Okla. 106, 226 Pac. 880;

*Pompey* v. *King*, 101 Okla. 253, 225 Pac. 175;

*Buck* v. *Branson*, 34 Okla. 807, 127 Pac. 436;

*Johnson* v. *Johnson*, 30 Mo. 72;

*Unussee* v. *McKinney*, 270 Pac. 1096 (Okla.);

and *cf.* *Connolly* v. *Woolrich* (1867), 11 Lower Can. Jur. 197.

Legal recognition has not been withheld from marriages by Indian custom, even in those cases where Indian custom sanctioned polygamy. As was said in *Kobogum* v. *Jackson Iron Co.*, (76 Mich. 498, 43 N.W. 602):

> "*** The testimony now in this case shows that, as matter of history, we are probably bound to know judicially, that among these Indians polygamous marriages have always been recognized as valid, and have never been confounded with such promiscuous or informal temporary intercourse as is not reckoned as marriage. While most civilized nations in our day very wisely discard polygamy, and it is not probably lawful anywhere among English-speaking nations, yet it is a recognized and valid institution among many nations, and in no way universally unlawful. We must either hold that there can be no valid Indian marriage, or we must hold that all marriages are valid which by Indian usage are so regarded. There is no middle ground which can be taken, so long as our own laws are not binding on the tribes. They did not occupy their territory by our grace and permission, but by a right beyond our control. They were placed by the Constitution of the United States beyond our jurisdiction, and we have no more right to control their domestic usages than those of Turkey or India. *** We have here marriages had between members of an Indian tribe in tribal relations, and unquestionably good by the Indian rules. The parties were not subject in those relations to the laws of Michigan, and there was no other law interfering with the full jurisdiction of the tribe over personal relations. We cannot interfere with the validity of such marriages without subjecting them to rules of law which never bound them."

See, to the same effect, *State* v. *McKenney* (18 Nev. 182, 200).

The jurisdiction of a tribal court over divorce actions is recognized in *Raymond* v. *Raymond* (83 Fed. 721); 19 Opn. Atty. Gen. 109 (1888).

## THE POWER OF AN INDIAN TRIBE TO GOVERN THE DESCENT AND DISTRIBUTION OF PROPERTY

It is well settled that an Indian tribe has the power to prescribe the manner of descent and distribution of the property of its members, in the absence of contrary legislation by Congress. Such power may be exercised through unwritten custom and usages, or through written laws of the tribe. This power extends to personal property as well as real property. By virtue of this authority an Indian tribe may restrict the descent of property on the basis of Indian blood or tribal membership, and may provide for the escheat of property to the tribe where there are no recognized heirs. An Indian tribe may, if it so chooses, adopt as its own laws of the State in which it is situated and may make such modifications in these laws as it deems suitable to its peculiar conditions.

The only general statutes of Congress which restrict the power of an Indian tribe to govern the descent and distribution of property of its members are section 5 of the General Allotment Act (U.S. Code, Title 25, Sec. 346)[15], which provides that allotments of land shall descend "according to the laws of the State or Territory where such land is located", the act of June 25, 1910, c. 431, Sec. 1, 36 Stat. 855 (U.S. Code, Title 25, Sec. 372),[16] which provides that the Secretary of the

---

15   *Patents to be held in trust; descent and partition. Upon the approval of the allotments provided for in sections 331 to 334, inclusive, and 336 by the Secretary of the Interior, he shall cause patents to issue therefor in the name of the allottees, which patents shall be of the legal effect, and declare that the United States does and will hold the land thus allotted, for the period of twenty-five years, in trust for the sole use and benefit of the Indian to whom such allotment shall have been made, or, in case of his decease, of his heirs according to the laws of the State or Territory where such land is located, and that at the expiration of said period the United States will convey the same by patent to said Indian or his heirs as aforesaid, in fee, discharged of said trust and free of all charge or incumbrance whatsoever: ***

16   "Ascertainment of heirs of deceased allottees.—When any Indian to whom an allotment of land has been made, dies before the expiration of the trust period and before the issuance of a fee simple patent, without having made a will disposing of said allotment as hereinafter provided, the Secretary of the Interior, upon notice and hearing, under such rules as he may prescribe, shall ascertain the legal heirs of such decedent, and his decision thereon shall be final and conclusive. ***

Interior shall have unreviewable discretion to determine the heirs of an Indian in ruling upon the inheritance of individual allotments issued under the authority of the General Allotment Law, and section 2 of the same act (U.S. Code, Title 25, Sec. 373),[17] which gives the Secretary of the Interior final power to approve and disapprove Indian wills devising restricted property.

These statutes abolished the former tribal power over the descent and distribution of property, with respect to allotments of land made under the General Allotment Act, and rendered tribal rules of testamentary disposition subject to the authority of the Secretary of the Interior. They do not, however, affect intestate succession to personal property or interests in land other than allotments (e.g., possessory interests in land to which title is retained by the tribe). With respect to all property other than allotments of land made under the General Allotment Act, the inheritance laws and customs of the Indian tribe are still of supreme authority.[18]

The authority of an Indian tribe in the matter of inheritance is clearly recognized by the United States Supreme Court in the case of *Jones v. Meehan* (175 U.S. 1), in which it was held that the oldest male child of a Chippewa Indian succeeded to his statutory allotment in accordance with tribal law. The Court declared:

> The Department of the Interior appears to have assumed that, upon death of Moose Dung the elder, in 1872, the title in his land descended by law to his heirs general, and not to his eldest son only.

---

17 \*\*<u>Disposal by will of allotments held under trust.</u> — Any persons of the age of twenty-one years having any right, title, or interest in any allotment held under trust or other patent containing restrictions on alienation or individual Indian moneys or other property held in trust by the United States shall have the right prior to the expiration of the trust or restrictive period, and before the issuance of a fee simple patent or the removal of restrictions, to dispose of such property by will, in accordance with regulations to be prescribed by the Secretary of the Interior: <u>Provided, however,</u> That no will so executed shall be valid or have any force or effect unless and until it shall have been approved by the Secretary of the Interior: \*\*\*

18 The foregoing general analysis is inapplicable to the Five Civilized Tribes, Congress having expressly provided that State probate courts shall have jurisdiction over the estates of allotted Indians of the Five Civilized Tribes leaving restricted heirs. (Act of June 14, 1918, c. 101, sec. 1; 40 Stat. L. 606; U.S. Code, Title 25, sec. 375.)

But the elder Chief Moose Dung being a member of an Indian tribe, whose tribal organization was still recognized by the Government of the United States, the right of inheritance in his land, at the time of his death, was controlled by the laws, usages and customs of the tribe, and not by the law of the State of Minnesota, nor by any action of the Secretary of the Interior. (At page 29.)

In reaching this conclusion the Supreme Court relied upon the following cases:

*United States* v. *Shanks* (15 Minn. 369);
*Dole* v. *Irish* (2 Barb. [N.Y.] 639);
*Hastings* v. *Farmer* (4 N.Y. 293, 294);
*The Kansas Indians* (5 Wall. 737);
*Waupemanqua* v. *Aldrich* (28 Fed. 489);
*Brown* v. *Steele* (23 Kansas 672);
*Richardville* v. *Thorp* (28 Fed. 52).

In the case of *Jones* v. *Meehan, supra,* the tribal authority was exercised through immemorial usage. Other tribes, however, have exercised a similar authority through written law.

In the case of *Gray* v. *Coffman* (3 Dill. 393, 10 Fed. Cases No. 5714), the court held that the validity of the will of a member of the Wyandot tribe depended upon its conformity with the written laws of the tribe. The court declared:

The Wyandot Indians, before their removal from Ohio had adopted a written constitution and laws, and among others, laws relating to descent and wills. These are in the record, and are shown to have been copied from the laws of Ohio, and adopted by the Wyandot tribe, with certain modifications, to adapt them to their customs and usages. One of these modifications was that only living children should inherit, excluding the children of deceased children, or grandchildren. The Wyandot council, which is several times referred to in the treaty of 1855, was an executive and judicial body, and had power, under the laws and usages of the nation, to receive proof of wills, etc.: and this body continued to act, at least to some extent, after the treaty of 1855.

\*\*\*under the circumstances, the court must give effect to the well established laws, customs, and usages of the Wyandot tribe of Indians in respect to the disposition of property by descent and will.

In the case of *O'Brien* v. *Bugbee* (46 Kan. 1, 25 Pac. 428), it was held that a plaintiff in ejectment could not recover without positive proof that under tribal custom he was lawful heir to the property in question. In the absence of such proof, it was held that title to the land escheated to the tribe, and that the tribe might dispose of the land as it saw fit.

Tribal autonomy in the regulation of descent and distribution is recognized in the case of *Woodin* v. *Seeley* (141 Misc. 207; 252 N.Y. Supp. 818). In this case, and in the case of *Patterson* v. *Council of Seneca Nation* (245 N.Y. 433; 157 N.E. 734), the supremacy of tribal law in matters of inheritance and membership rights is defended on the ground: "that when Congress does not act no law runs on an Indian reservation save the Indian tribal law and custom."

In the case of *Y-Ta-Tah-Wah* v. *Rebock* (105 Fed. 257), the plaintiff, a medicine-man imprisoned by the federal Indian agent and county sheriff for practicing medicine without a license, brought an action of false imprisonment against these officials, and died during the course of the proceedings. The court held that the action might be continued, not by an administrator of the decedent's estate appointed in accordance with state law, but by the heirs of the decedent by Indian custom. The court declared, per Shiras, J.:

> If it were true that, upon the death of a tribal Indian, his property, real and personal, became subject to the laws of the state directing the mode of distribution of estates of decedents, it is apparent that irremediable confusion would be caused thereby in the affairs of the Indians \*\*\* (At page 262.)

In a case involving the right of an illegitimate child to inherit property, the authority of the tribe to pass upon the status of illegitimates was recognized in the following terms:

> The Creek Council, in the exercise of its lawful function of local self-government, saw fit to limit the legal rights of an illegitimate child to that of sharing in the estate of his putative father, and not to confer upon such child generally the status

of a child born in lawful wedlock. (*Oklahoma land company* v. *Thomas*, 34 Okla. 681, 127 Pac. 8).

See, to the same effect, *Butler* v. *Wilson* (54 Okla. 229, 153 Pac. 823).

In the case of *Dole* v. *Irish* (2 Barb. 639) it was held that a surrogate of the State of New York has no power to grant letters of administration to control the disposition of personal property belonging to a deceased member of the Seneca tribe. The court declared:

"I am of the opinion that the private property of the Seneca Indians is not within the jurisdiction of our laws respecting administration; and that the letters of administration granted by the surrogate to the plaintiff are void. I am also of the opinion that the distribution of Indian property according to their customs passes as good title, which our courts will not disturb; and therefore that the defendant has a good title to the horse in question, and must have judgment on the special verdict." (At pages 642-643.)

In *George* v. *Pierce* (148 N.Y. Supp. 230), the distribution of real and personal property of the decedent through the Onondaga custom of the "dead feast" is recognized as controlling all rights of inheritance.

In the case of *Mackey* v. *Kaelin* (173 Fed. 216), the court recognized the validity of tribal custom in determining the descent of real and personal property and indicated that the tribal custom of the Puyallup band prescribed different rules of descent for real and for personal property.

## THE TAXING POWER OF AN INDIN TRIBE

Chief among the powers of sovereignty recognized as pertaining to an Indian tribe is the power of taxation. Except where Congress has provided otherwise, this power may be exercised over members of the tribe and over nonmembers, so far as such nonmembers may accept privileges of trade, residence, etc., to which taxes may be attached as conditions.

The case of *Buster* v. *Wright* (135 Fed. 947, app. Diam. 203 U.S. 599), contains an excellent analysis of the taxing power of the Creek Nation:

> Repeated decisions of the courts, numerous opinions of
> the Attorneys General, and the practice of years place beyond
> debate the propositions that prior to March 1, 1901, the Creek
> Nation had lawful authority to require the payment of this tax
> as a condition precedent to the exercise of the privilege of trad-

ing within its borders, and that the executive department of the government of the United States had plenary power to enforce its payment through the Secretary of the Interior, and his subordinates, the Indian inspector, Indian agent, and Indian police. *Morris* v. *Hitchcock,* 194 U.S. 384, 392, 24 Sup. Ct. 712, 48 L. Ed. 1030; *Crabtree* v. *Madden,* 4 C. C. A, 408, 410, 413, 54 Fed. 426, 428, 431; *Maxey* v. *Wright,* 3 Ind. T. 243, 54 S.W. 807; *Maxey* v. *Wright,* 44 C.C.A. 683, 105 Fed. 1003; 18 Opinions of Attorneys General, 34,36; 23 Opinions of Attorneys General, 214, 217, 219, 220, 528. ********

*** It may not be unwise, before entering upon the discussing of this proposition, to place clearly before our minds the character of the Creek Nation and the nature of the power which it is attempting to exercise.

The authority of the Creek Nation to prescribe the terms upon which noncitizens may transact business within its borders did not have its origin in act of Congress, treaty, or agreement of the United States. It was one of the inherent and essential attributes of its original sovereignty. It was a natural right of that people, indispensable to its autonomy as a distinct tribe or nation, and it must remain an attribute of its government until by the agreement of the nation itself or by the superior power of the republic it is taken from it. Neither the authority nor the power of the United States to license its citizens to trade in the Creek Nation, with or without the consent of that tribe, is in issue in this case, because the complainants have no such license. The plenary power and lawful authority of the government of the United States by license, by treaty, or by act of Congress to take from the Creek Nation every vestige of its original or acquired governmental authority and power may be admitted, and for the purpose of this decision are here conceded. The fact remains nevertheless that every original attribute of the government of the Creek Nation still exists intact which has not been destroyed or limited by act of Congress or by the contract of the Creek tribe itself.

Originally an independent tribe, the superior power of the republic early reduced this Indian people to a 'domestic, dependent nation' (Cherokee Nation v. State of Georgia, 5 Pet. 1-20, 8 L.Ed. 25), yet left it a distinct political entity, clothed with the ample authority to govern its inhabitants and to manage its domestic affairs through officers of its own selection, who under a Constitution modeled after that of the United States, exercised legislative, executive and judicial functions within its territorial jurisdiction for more than a half century. The governmental jurisdiction of this nation was neither conditioned nor limited by the original title by occupancy to the lands within its territory. \*\*\*\*\*\*\*\*\*\*\*\*\*

\*\*\*Founded in its original national sovereignty, and secured by these treaties, the governmental authority of the Creek Nation, subject always to the superior power of the republic, remained practically unimpaired until the year 1889. Between the years 1888 and 1901 the United States by various act of Congress deprived this tribe of all its judicial power, and curtailed its remaining authority until its powers of government have become the mere shadows of their former selves. Nevertheless its authority to fix the terms upon which noncitizens might conduct business within its territorial boundaries guaranteed by the treaties of 1832, 1856, and 1866, and sustained by repeated decisions of the courts and opinions of the Attorneys General of the United States, remained undisturbed.

\*\*\*\*\*It is said that the sale of these lots and the incorporation of cities and towns upon the sites in which the lots are found authorized by act of Congress to collect taxes for municipal purposes segregated the town sites and the lots sold from the territory of the Creek Nation, and deprived it of governmental jurisdiction over this property and over its occupants. But the jurisdiction to govern the inhabitants of a country is not conditioned or limited by the title of the land which they occupy in it, or by the existence of municipalities therein endowed with power to collect taxes for city purposes, and to enact and enforce municipal ordinances. Neither the United States, nor a state, nor any other sovereignty loses the power to govern the people within its borders by the existence of towns and cities therein endowed with the usual powers of municipalities, nor by the ownership nor occupancy of the land within its territorial jurisdiction by citizens and foreigners. (At pp. 949-952.)

A similar opinion was rendered by the Attorney General (23 Ops. Atty. Gen. 528) with respect to the right of the Cherokee Nation to impose an export tax on hay grown within the limits of the reservation. The opinion of the Attorney General suggested that tribal authority to impose such a tax would remain "even if the shipper was the absolute owner of the land on which the hay was raised." This suggestion was referred to and approved by the United States Supreme Court in *Morris* v. *Hitchcock* (194 U.S. 384, 392).

In the latter case, the Court of Appeals of the District of Columbia, considering the validity of a tax or fee imposed by the Chickasaw Nation upon the owners of all cattle grazed within the Chickasaw territory, analyzed the status and powers of the Chickasaw Nation in these terms:

A government of the kind necessarily has the power to maintain its existence and effectiveness through the exercise of the usual power of taxation upon all property within its limits, save as may be restricted by its organic law. Any restriction in the organic law in respect of this ordinary power of taxation, and the property subject thereto, ought to appear by express provision or necessary implication. *Board Trustees* v. *Indiana,* 14 How. 268, 272; *Talbott* v. *Silver Bow Co.,* 139 U.S. 438, 448. Where the restriction upon this exercise of power by a recognized government, is claimed under the stipulations of a treaty with another, whether the former be dependent upon the latter or not, it would seem that its existence ought to appear beyond a reasonable doubt. We discover no such restriction in the clause of Article 7 of the Treaty of 1855, which excepts white persons from the recognition therein of the unrestricted right of self-government by the Chickasaw Nation, and its full jurisdiction over persons and property within its limits. The condition of that exception may be fully met without going to the extreme of saying that it was also intended to prevent the exercise of the power to consent to the entry of noncitizens, or the taxation of property actually within the limits of that government and enjoying its benefits. (*Morris* v. *Hitchcock,* 21 App. D.C. 565, 593.)

In the case of *Maxey* v. *Wright* (3 Ind. T. 243, 54 S.W. 807, aff'd. 105 Fed. 1003), the right of an Indian tribe to levy a tax upon a nonmember of the tribe residing on its reservation was held to be an essential attribute of tribal sovereignty, which might be curtailed by express language of a treaty or statute, but otherwise remained intact. In that case the court declared:

> ***in the absence of express contradictory provisions by treaty, or by statute of the United States, the Nation (and not a citizen) is to declare who shall come within the boundaries of its occupancy, and under what conditions. (at page 36.)

See, to the same effect, 17 Ops. Atty. Gen. 134; 18 Ops. Atty. Gen. 34.

In view of the fact, however, that Congress has conferred upon the Commissioner of Indian Affairs exclusive jurisdiction to appoint traders in Indian reservations and to prescribe the terms and conditions governing their admission and operations (see Secs. 261 and 262, Title 25, U.S. Code), an Indian tribe is without power to levy a tax upon such licensed traders unless authorized by the Commissioner of Indian Affairs so to do.

## THE POWER OF AN INDIAN TRIBE TO EXCLUDE NONMEMBERS FROM ITS JURISDICTION

The power of an Indian tribe to exclude nonmembers of the tribe from entering upon the reservation was first clearly formulated in an opinion of the Attorney General in 1821 with respect to the lands of the Seneca Indians:

"So long as a tribe exists and remains in possession of its lands, its title and possession are sovereign and exclusive; and there exists no authority to enter upon their lands, for any purpose whatever, without their consent." (1 Op. Atty. Gen. 465, 466).

It was further said in the course of this opinion that even the United States Government could not enter the Seneca lands, for the purpose of building a road or for any other purpose, without the consent of the Indians.

Although the last implication of this doctrine, if originally valid, has been superseded by many statutes authorizing and directing officers and agents of the United States to enter upon Indian lands for various purposes, the basic principle that an Indian tribe may exclude private individuals from the territory within its jurisdiction, or prescribe the conditions upon which such entry will be permitted, has been followed in a long line of cases.

Two grounds for this power of exclusion are established by the decided cases: first, the Indian tribe may exercise, over all tribal property, the rights of a landowner; second, the tribe may, in the exercise of local self-government, regulate the relations between its members and other persons, so far as may be consistent with Congressional statutes governing trade and intercourse.

In *Rainbow* v. *Young* (161 Fed. 835), it was held that the Indian superintendent and Indian police had power to remove an attorney seeking to collect fees on a day when lease money was being paid to the Indians. In addition to the specific authority to remove undesirable persons granted by Revised Statutes, sec. 2149 (recently repealed by act of May 21, 1934, Public No. 242, 73d Congress), the court found that the power to remove nonresidents was incidental to the general power of a landowner, which the United States was qualified to exercise with respect to Indian lands:

"Besides, the reservation from which Mr. Sloan was removed is the property of the United States, is set apart and used as a tribal reservation and in respect of it the United States has the right of an individual proprietor (citing cases) and can maintain its possession and deal with intruders in like manner as can an individual in respect of his property." (at p. 837.)

See, to the same effect, *United States* v. *Mullin* (71 Fed. 682); 20 Op. Atty. Gen. 245, holding that an injunction by a State court might properly be disobeyed; 14 Op/ Atty. Gen. 451. And with respect to the general power of a government as a landowner to remove intruders see *Canfield* v. *United States* (167 U.S. 518, 524).

As was said in the case of *Stephenson* v. *Little* (18 Mich. 433), in which it was held that the United States Government as a landowner might, through officials of the Land Office, seize and direct the sale of timber cut on public lands even though other timber had been mixed with that so cut:

"It seems to me there can be no doubt that the Government has all the common law rights of an individual in respect to depredations committed on its property, and that where there is no statute making it the duty of any particular official to enforce those rights, it is ex necessitate rei made the duty of the Executive Department of the Government to enforce them." (At page 440).

What is here said of the rights of the United States Government may be said with equal force of the rights of an Indian tribe. In an unallotted reservation, an Indian tribe occupies the position of a landowner in equity, if not in strict law. (*United States* v. *Sturgeon,* 6 Sawy. 29, 27 Fed. Cas. No. 16, 413).

The cases cited with respect to the power of an Indian tribe to tax nonmembers, as a condition of entry or residence within the jurisdiction of the tribe, confirm the foregoing conclusions, and indicate further that the power of an Indian tribe to exclude nonmembers is not limited to lands in tribal ownership.

Over tribal lands, the tribe has the rights of a landowner as well as the rights of a local government, dominion as well as sovereignty. But over all the lands of the reservation, whether owned by the tribe, by members thereof, or by outsiders, the tribe has the sovereign power of determining the conditions upon which persons shall be permitted to enter its domain, to reside therein, and to do business, provided only such determination is consistent with applicable Federal laws and does not infringe any vested rights of persons now occupying reservation lands under tribal authority. *Morris* v. *Hitchcock* (194 U.S. 384) and other cases cited under heading "The Taxing Power of an Indian Tribe".

## TRIBAL POWERS OVER PROPERTY

The powers of an Indian tribe with respect to property derive from two sources. In the first place, the tribe has all the rights and powers of a property owner with respect to tribal property. In the second place, the Indian tribe has, among its powers of sovereignty, the power to regulate the use and disposition of individual property among its members.

The powers of an Indian tribe over tribal property are no less absolute than the powers of any landowner, save as restricted by general acts of Congress restricting the alienation or leasing of tribal property,[19] and particular acts of Congress designed to control the disposition of particular funds or lands.

Statutes restricting tribal powers to lease lands are cited at page 65 below.

The foregoing restrictions are partially modified by the Wheeler Howard Act (Public No. 383, 73d Congress), sec. 4,6,17.

It is recognized that property held by the United States in trust for an Indian tribe is, like other trust property, subject to terms of the trust with respect to the use and disposition of corpus and income. Thus it is provided that tribal funds held by the United States in trust for Indian tribes may be expended only in accordance with annual statutory appropriations, except for certain designated purposes as to which annual statutory appropriation is not required. See act of May 18, 1916, c. 125, sec. 27, 39 Stat. L. 159.

The powers of an Indian tribe with respect to tribal land are not limited by any rights of occupancy which the tribe itself may grant to its members. The proposition that occupancy of tribal land does not create any vested rights in the occupant as against the tribe is supported by a long line of court decisions:

*Sizemore* v. *Brady,* 235 U.S. 441;
*Franklin* v. *Lynch,* 233 U.S. 269;
*Gritts* v. *Fisher,* 224 U.S. 640;

---

19  \* U.S. Code, title 25, sec. 177, provides: "Purchases or grants of lands from Indians. No purchase, grant, lease, or other conveyance of lands, or of any title or claim thereto, from any Indian nation or tribe of Indians, shall be of any validity in law or equity, unless the same be made by treaty or convention entered into pursuant to the Constitution. \*\*\*"

U.S. Code, title 25, sec. 85, provides: "Contracts relating to tribal funds or property. No contract made with any Indian, where such contract relates to the tribal funds or property in the hands of the United States, shall be valid, nor shall any payment for services rendered in relation thereto be made unless the consent of the United States has previously been given, (June 30, 1913, c. 4, sec. 18, 38 Stat. 97,)"

*Journeycake* v. *Cherokee Nation and United States* 28 Ct. Cls. 281;

*Sac and Fox Indians of Iowa* v. *Sac and Fox Indians of Oklahoma and the United States,* 45 Ct. Cls. 287, aff'd 220 U.S. 481;

*Hayes* v. *Barringer,* 168 Fed. 221;

*Dukes* v. *Goodall,* 5 Ind. T. 145, 82 S.W. 702;

In re Narragansett Indians, 20 R. I. 715;

*Terrance* v. *Gray,* 156 N.Y. Supp. 916;

*Reservation Gas Co.* v. *Snyder,* 88 Misc. 209, 150 N.Y. Supp. 216;

Application of Parker, 237 N.Y. Supp. 135;

*McCurtain* v. *Grady,* 1 Ind. T. 107, 38 S.W. 65;

*Whitmire, trustee,* v. *Cherokee Nation,* 30 Ct. Cls. 138;

*Myers* v. *Mathis,* 2 Ind. T. 3, 46 S.W. 178.

In the case of *Sizemore* v. *Brady, supra,* the Supreme Court declared:

> lands and funds belonged to the tribe as a community, and not to the members severally or as tenants in common. (at p. 446.)

Similarly, in *Franklin* v. *Lynch, supra,* the Supreme Court declared:

> As the tribe could not sell, neither could the individual members, for they had neither an undivided interest in the tribal land nor vendible interest in any particular tract. (at p. 271.)

In the case of *Journeycake* v. *Cherokee Nation and the United States, supra,* the Court of Claims carefully analyzed the laws and constitutional provisions of the Cherokee Nation and found that property within the jurisdiction of the Nation was of two kinds: communal property in which each individual had exclusive right of occupancy in particular tracts, rights not subject to transfer or disposition except according to prescribed rules; and national property held by the tribe itself. With respect to the former type of property, the court declared:

> The distinctive characteristic of communal property is that every member of the community is an owner of it as such. He does not take as heir, or purchaser, or grantee; if he dies his right of property does not descend; if he removes from the community it expires; if he wishes to dispose of it he has nothing which he can convey; and yet he has a right of property in the land as per-

fect as that of any other person; and his children after him will enjoy all that he enjoyed, not as heirs but as communal owners.

Analyzing the status of tribal lands not subject to individual occupancy, the court declared:

> With this power of regulation and control of the public domain, and the jus disponendi lodged in the government of the Nation, it is plain that the communal element has been reduced to a minimum and exists only in the occupied lands. And it is manifest that with the growth of civilization, with all of its intricacies, and manifold requirements, the communal management of the public domain would have been utterly insufficient, and if it had continued would have been a barrier to the advancement of civilization itself.
>
> With these powers of absolute ownership lodged in the Cherokee government, the power to alienate, the power to lease, the power to grant rights of occupancy, the power to restrict rights of occupancy, and with the exercise of those powers running back to the very year of the adoption of the constitution, and receiving from that time to the present, the unquestioning acquiescence of the former communal owners, the Cherokee people, it is apparent that the 'public domain' of the Cherokee Nation is analogous to the 'public lands' of the United States or the 'demesne lands of the Crown,' and that it is held absolutely by the Cherokee government, as all public property is held, a trust for governmental purposes and to promote the general welfare.

Similarly, in the case of *Hayes* v. *Barringer, supra,* the court declared, in considering the status of Choctaw and Chickasaw tribal lands:

> ***At that time these were the lands of the Choctaw and Chickasaw Nations, held by them, as they held all their lands, in trust for the individual members of their tribes, in the sense in which the public property of representative governments is held in trust for its people. But these were public lands, and, while the enrolled members of these tribes undoubtedly had a vested

equitable right to their just shares of them against strangers and fellow members of their tribes, they had no separate or individual right to or equity in any of these lands which they could maintain against the legislation of the United States or of the Indian Nations. *Stephens* v. *Cherokee Nation,* 174 U.S. 225, 488, 19 Sup. Ct. 722, 43 L. Ed. 1041; *Cherokee Nation* v. *Hitchcock,* 187 U.S. 294, 23 Sup. Ct. 115, 47 L. Ed. 183; *Lone Wolf* v. *Hitchcock,* 187 U.S. 553, 23 Sup. Ct. 216, 47 L. Ed. 299; *Wallace* v. *Adams,* 143 Fed. 716, 74 C.C.A. 540; *Ligon* v. *Johnston* (C.C.A.) 164 Fed. 670.

So, too, *United States* v. *Lucero* (1 N.M. 422), title to lands within a pueblo is recognized to lie in the pueblo itself, rather than in the individual members thereof.

> The extent of any individual's interest in tribal property is subject to such limitations as the tribe may see fit to impose.

Thus in *Reservation Gas Co,* v. *Snyder, supra,* it was held that an Indian tribe might dispose of minerals on tribal lands which had been assigned to individual Indians for private occupancy, since the individual occupants had never been granted any specific mineral rights by the tribe.

In *Terrance* v. *Gray, supra,* it was held that no act of the occupant of assigned tribal land could terminate the control duly exercised by the chiefs of the tribe over the use and disposition of the land.

In Application of Parker, supra, it was held that the Tonawanda Nation of Seneca Indians had the right to dispose of minerals on the tribal allotments of its members and that the individual allottee had no valid claim for damage.

In the case of *McCurtain* v. *Grady, supra,* a provision of the Choctaw constitution conferring upon the discoverer of coal the right to mine all coal within a mile radius of the point of discovery was upheld as a valid exercise of tribal power.

In *Whitmire, trustee,* v. *Cherokee Nation, supra,* the Court of Claims held that the general property of the Cherokee Nation, under the provisions of the Cherokee constitution, might be used for public purposes, but could not be diverted to per capita payments to a favored class.

The chief limitation upon tribal control of membership rights in tribal property is that found in acts of Congress guaranteeing to those who sever tribal relations to take up homesteads on the public domain,[20] and to children of white men and Indian women, under certain circumstances,[21] a continuing share in the tribal property. Except for these general limitations and other specific statutory limitations found in enrollment acts and other special acts of Congress, the proper authorities of an Indian tribe have full authority to regulate the use and disposition of tribal property by the members of the tribe.

The authority of a tribal council to lease tribal lands is specifically confirmed by U.S. Code, title 25, sections 397, 398 and 402.[22] Although the exercise of such

---

20  U.S, Code, title 43, sec. 189, provides that an Indian severing tribal relations to take up a homestead upon the public domain "shall be entitled to his distributive share of all annuities, tribal funds, lands and other property, the same as though he had maintained his tribl relations." For a discussion of this and related statutes, see *Oakes* v. *United States* (172 Fed. 305).

21  U.S. Code, title 25, sec. 184: "Rights of children born of marriages between white men and Indian women. All children born of a marriage solemnized prior to June 7, 1897, between a white man and an Indian woman by blood and not by adoption, where said Indian woman was on that date, or was at the time of her death, recognized by the tribe, shall have the same rights and privileges to the property of the tribe to which the mother belongs, or belonged at the time of her death, by blood, as any other member of the tribe, and no prior Act of Congress shall be construed as to debar such child of such right. (June 7, 1897, c. 3, sec. 1, 30 Stat. 90.)"

22  U.S. Code, Title 25, Sec. 397: Leases of Lands for grazing or mining. Where lands are occupied by Indians who have bought and paid for the same, and which lands are not needed for farming or agricultural purposes, and are not desired for individual allotments, the same may be leased by authority of the council speaking for such Indians, for a period not to exceed five years for grazing, or ten years for mining purposes in such quantities and upon such terms and conditions as the agent in charge of such reservation may recommend, subject to the approval of the Secretary of the Interior. (Feb. 28, 1891, c. 383, Sec. 3, 26 Stat. 795.)

U.S. Code, Title 25, Sec. 398: "Leases of unallotted lands for oil and gas mining purposes. Unallotted land on Indian reservations other than lands of the Five Civilized Tribes and the Osage Reservation subject to lease for mining purposes for a period of ten years under the preceding section may be leased at public auction by the Secretary of the Interior, for oil and gas mining purposes."

U.S. Code, Title 25, Sec. 402: Leases of surplus lands. The surplus lands of any tribe may be leased for farming purposes by the council of such tribe under the same rules and regulations and for the same term of years as is now allowed in the case of leases for grazing purposes. (Aug. 15, 1894, c. 290, Sec. 1, 28 Stat. 305.)

authority is made subject to the approval of the Secretary of the Interior, it has been said that:

> From the language of this statute it appears reasonably certain that it was the legislative purpose to confer primary authority upon the Indians, and that the determination of the council should be conclusive upon the government, at least in the absence of any evidence of fraud or undue influence. (*White Bear* v. *Barth*, 61 Mont. 322, 203 Pac. 517.)

U.S. Code, title 25, section 179, which imposes a penalty upon persons driving stock to range upon the lands of an Indian tribe, has been construed as recognizing the right of the tribe to permit the use of its lands for grazing purposes, for a consideration.

See: *United States* v. *Hunter,* 4 Mackey (D.C.) 531;

*Kirby* v. *United States,* 273 Fed. 391, aff'd 260 U.S. 423.

Similarly, U.S. Code, title 25, section 180, imposing a penalty upon persons settling on Indian land, has been judicially interpreted as implying that an Indian tribe has power to permit such settlement upon such terms as it may prescribe. The cases on this subject have been analyzed under the heading "The Power of an Indian Tribe to Exclude Nonmembers From Its Jurisdiction."

The authority of an Indian tribe in matters of property is not restricted to those lands or funds over which it exercises the rights of ownership. The sovereign powers of the tribe extend over the property as well as the person of its members.

Thus, in *Crabtree* v. *Madden* (54 Fed. 426), it is recognized that questions of the validity of contracts among members of the tribe are to be determined according to the laws of the tribe.

See, to the same effect:

In re Sah Quah, 31 Fed. 327;

*Jones* v. *Laney,* 2 Tex. 342.

In the latter case the question arose whether a deed of manumission freeing a negro slave, executed by a Chickasaw Indian within the territory of the Chickasaw nation, was valid. The lower court had charged the jury "that their (Chickasaw) laws and customs and usages, within the limits defined to them, governed all property belonging to any one domesticated and living with them." Approving this charge, upon the basis of which the jury had found the deed to be valid, the appellate court declared:

> "Their laws and customs, regulating property, contracts, and the relations between husband and wife, have been respected, when drawn into controversy, in the courts of the State and of the United States." (At p. 348.)

In the case of *Delaware Indians* v. *Cherokee Nation* (38 Ct. Cls. 234, decree mod. 193 U.S. 127), it is said:

"The law of real property is to be found in the law of the situs. The law of real property in the Cherokee country, therefore, is to be found in the constitution and laws of the Cherokee Nation."

In the case of *Myers* v. *Mathis, supra,* the validity of a Chickasaw statute of limitations, whereby an individual Indian suffered a loss of his improvements by reason of his absence for a fixed period, was upheld.

In the case of *James H. Hamilton* v. *United States* (42 Ct. Cls. 282), it appeared that land, buildings and personal property owned by the claimant, a licensed trader, within the Chickasaw Reservation, had been confiscated by an act of the Chickasaw legislature. The plaintiff brought suit to recover damages on the theory that such confiscation constituted an "Indian depredation". The Court of Claims dismissed the suit, declaring:

"The claimant by applying for and accepting a license to trade with the Chickasaw Indians, and subsequently acquiring property within the limits of their reservation, subjected the same to the jurisdiction of their laws," (At p. 287)

The authority of an Indian tribe to impose license fees upon persons engaged in trade with its members within the boundaries of the reservation is confirmed in *Zevely* v. *Weimer* (5 Ind. T. 646, 82 S.W. 941), as well as the various cases cited under the heading "The Taxing Power of an Indian Tribe."

The power of an Indian tribe to regulate the inheritance of individual property owned by members of the tribe has been analyzed under a separate heading.

It clearly appears, from the foregoing cases, that the powers of an Indian tribe are not limited to such powers as it may exercise in its capacity as a landowner. In its capacity as a sovereign, and in the exercise of local self-government, it may exercise powers similar to those exercised by any State or Nation in regulating the use and disposition of private property, save in so far as it is restricted by specific statutes of Congress.

The laws and customs of the tribe, in matters of contract and property generally (as well as on questions of membership, domestic relations, inheritance, taxation, and residence), may be lawfully administered in the tribunal of the tribe, and such laws and customs will be recognized by courts of State or Nation in cases coming before these courts.[23]

## THE POWERS OF AN INDIN TRIBE IN THE ADMINISTRATION OF JUSTICE

The powers of an Indian tribe in the administration of justice drive from the substantive powers of self-government which are legally recognized to fall within the domain of tribal sovereignty. If an Indian tribe has power to regulate the marriage relationships of its members, it necessarily has power to adjudicate, through tribunals established by itself, controversies involving such relationships. So, too, with other fields of local government in which our analysis has shown that tribal authority endures. In all these fields the judicial powers of the tribe are co-extensive with its legislative and executive powers.

*Washburn* v. *Parker* (7 Fed. Sup. 120);
*Raymond* v. *Raymond* (83 Fed. 721);
19 Op. Atty. Gen. 109 (1838)
7 Op. Atty. Gen. 174 (1855).

The decisions of Indian tribal courts, rendered within their jurisdiction and according to the forms of law or custom recognized by the tribe, are entitled to full faith and credit in the courts of the several states.

As was said in the case of *Standley* v. *Roberts* (59 Fed. 836, app. Dism. 17 Sup. Ct. 999 men.):

> *** the judgments of the court of these nations, in cases within their jurisdiction, stand on the same footing with those of the courts of the territories of the Union and are entitled to the same faith and credit. (At page 845.)

---

23  See: Cuthbert Pound, "Nationals Without a Nation", 22 Columbia Law Rev. 97, 101-102 (1922); W. G. Rice, Jr., "The Position of the American Indian in the Law of the United States", 16 Jour. Comp. Leg. (3d Series), part 1, p. 78 (1934).

And in the case of *Raymond* v. *Raymond, supra,* the court declared:

> The Cherokee Nation *** is a distinct political society, capable of managing its own affairs and governing itself. It may enact its own laws, though they may not be in conflict with the constitution of the United States. It may maintain its own judicial tribunals, and their judgments and decrees upon the rights of the persons and property of members of the Cherokee Nation as against each other are entitled to all the faith and credit accorded to the judgments and decrees of territorial courts. (At page 722.)

The question of the judicial powers of an Indian tribe is particularly significant in the field of law and order. For in the fields of civil controversy the rule and decisions of the tribe and its officers have a force that state courts and Federal courts will respect. But in accordance with the well settled principle that one sovereign will not enforce the criminal laws of another sovereign, state courts and Federal courts alike must decline to enforce penal provisions of tribal law. Responsibility for the maintenance of law and order is therefore squarely upon the Indian tribe, unless this field of jurisdiction has been taken over by the states or the Federal government.

It is illuminating to deal with the question of tribal criminal jurisdiction as we have dealt with other questions of tribal authority, by asking, first, what the original sovereign powers of the tribes were, and then how far and in what respect these powers have been limited.

So long as the complete and independent sovereignty of an Indian tribe was recognized, its criminal jurisdiction, no less than its civil jurisdiction, was that of any sovereign power. It might punish its subjects for offenses against each other or against aliens and for public offenses against the peace and dignity of the tribe. Similarly, it might punish aliens within its jurisdiction according to its own laws and customs.[24] Such jurisdiction continues to this day, save as it has been expressly limited by the acts of a superior government.

---

24  This power is expressly recognized, for instance, in the Treaty of July 2, 1791, with the Cherokees (7 Stat. 40) providing: "If any citizen of the United States, or other person not being an Indian, shall settle on any of the Cherokee lands, such person shall forfeit the protection of the United States, and the Cherokees may punish him or not, as they please." (Dec. 8)

It is clear that the original criminal jurisdiction of the Indian tribes has never been transferred to the States. Sporadic attempts of the States to exercise jurisdiction over offenses between Indians, or between Indians and whites, committed on an Indian reservation, have been held invalid usurpation of authority.

The principle that a State has no criminal jurisdiction over offenses involving Indians committed on an Indian reservation is too well established to require argument, attested as it is by a line of cases that reaches back to the earliest years of the Republic. See:

*Worcester* v. *Georgia,* 6 Pet. 515;

*United States* v. *Kagama,* 118 U.S. 375;

*United States* v. *Thomas,* 151 U.S. 577;

*Toy* v. *Hopkins,* 212 U.S. 542

*United States* v. *Celestine,* 215 U.S. 278;

*Donnelly* v. *United States,* 228 U.S. 345;

*United States* v. *Pelican,* 232 U.S. 442;

*United States* v. *Ramsey,* 271 U.S. 467;

*United States* v. *King,* 81 Fed. 625;

In re Lincoln, 129 Fed. 297;

*United States* v. *Hamilton,* 223 Fed. 685;

*Yohyowan* v. *Luce,* 291 Fed. 425;

*State* v. *Campbell,* 53 Minn. 354, 55 N.W. 553;

*State* v. *Big Sheep,* 75 Mont. 219, 243 Pac. 1067;

Es parte Cross, 20 Nebr. 417;

*People ex rel. Cusick* v. *Daly,* 212 N.Y. 183, 105 N.E. 1048;

*State* v. *Cloud,* 228 N.W. 611 (Minn.);

*State* v. *Rufus,* 237 N.W. 671 (Wis.)

A state, of course, has justification over the conduct of an Indian off the reservation.[25] A state also has jurisdiction over some, but not all, acts of non-Indians

---

25  See *Pablo* v. *People* (23 Colo. 134) (upholding State jurisdiction over murder of Indian by Indian outside of reservation).

within a reservation.[26] But the relations between whites and Indians in "Indian country" and the conduct of Indians themselves in Indian country are not subject to the laws or the courts of the several States.

The denial of State jurisdiction, then, is dictated by principles of constitutional law.

On the other hand, the constitutional authority of the Federal Government to prescribe laws and to administer justice upon the Indian reservation is plenary. The question remains how far Congress has exercised its constitutional powers.

The basic provisions of Federal law with regard to Indian offenses are found in sections 217 and 218 of U.S. Code Title 25:

> Sec. 217. <u>General laws as to punishment extended to Indian country.</u> Except as to crimes the punishment of which is expressly provided for in this title, the general laws of the United States as to the punishment of crimes committed in any place within the sole and exclusive jurisdiction of the United States, except the District of Columbia, shall extend to the Indian country. (R.S. Sec. 2145.)

> Sec. 218. <u>Exceptions as to extension of general laws.</u> The preceding section shall not be construed to extend to crimes committed by one Indian against the person or property of another Indian, nor to any Indian committing any offense in the Indian country who has been punished by the local law of the tribe, or to any case where, by treaty stipulations, the exclusive jurisdiction over such offenses is or may be secured to the Indian tribes respectively. (R.S. Sec. 2146; Feb 18, 1875, c. 80, Sec. 1, 18 Stat. 318.)

These provisions recognize that, with respect to crimes committed by one Indian against the person or property of another Indian, the jurisdiction of the Indian tribe is plenary. These provisions further recognize that, in addition to this general jurisdiction over offenses between Indians, an Indian may possess, by vir-

---

26  See *United States* v. *McBratney* (104 U.S. 621) (declining Federal jurisdiction over murder of non-Indian by non-Indian on reservation).

tue of treaty stipulations, other fields of exclusive jurisdiction (necessarily including jurisdiction over cases involving non-Indians). "The local law of the tribe" is further recognized to the extent that the punishment of an Indian under such law must be deemed a bar to further prosecution, under any applicable Federal laws, even though the offense be one against a non-Indian.

Such was the law when the case of *Ex parte Crow Dog* (109 U.S. 556), which has been discussed in an earlier connection, arose. The United States Supreme Court there held that Federal courts had no jurisdiction to prosecute an Indian for the murder of another Indian committed on an Indian reservation, such jurisdiction never having been withdrawn from the original sovereignty of the Indian tribe.

Shortly before the decision in this case, an opinion had been rendered by the Attorney General in another Indian murder case holding that where an Indian of one tribe had murdered an Indian of another tribe on the reservation of a third tribe, even though it was not shown that any of the tribes concerned had any machinery for the administration of justice, the Federal courts had no right to try the accused. The opinion concluded:

> If no demand for Foster's surrender shall be made by one or other of the tribes, founded fairly upon a violation of some law of one or other of them having jurisdiction of the offense in question according to general principles, and by forms substantially conformable to natural justice, it seems that nothing remains except to discharge him.
> (17 Ops. Atty. Gen. 566, 570.)

A similar decision had been reached in State courts. See *State* v. *McKenney* (18 Nev. 182).

The right of an Indian tribe to inflict the death penalty had been recognized by Congress, in the report cited above, at page 20.

Following the Crow Dog decision, Congress passed the act of March 3, 1885, Sec. 9 (23 Stats. L. 385), which, with an amendment, became Sec. 328 of the U.S. Criminal Code of 1910 and now Sec. 548 of Title 18 of the U.S. Code. This section provides for the prosecution in the Federal courts of Indians committing, within Indian reservations, any of the ten (formerly seven, then eight) specifically mentioned offenses (whether against Indians or against non-Indians), viz; murder, manslaughter, rape, incest, assault with intent to kill, assault with a dangerous weapon, arson, burglary, robbery, and larceny.[27]

Although this statute does not expressly terminate tribal jurisdiction over the enumerated crimes, and might, if the question were an original one, be interpreted as conferring only a concurrent jurisdiction upon the Federal courts, it has been construed for many years as removing all jurisdiction over the enumerated crimes from the Indian tribal authorities.

Thus, in the case of *United States* v. *Whaley* (37 Fed. 145), which arose soon after the passage of the statute in question, it had appeared fitting to the tribal council of the Tule River Reservation that a medicine man who was believed to have poisoned some twenty-one deceased patients should be executed, and he was so executed. The four tribal executioners were found guilty of manslaughter, in the Federal court, on the theory that the act of March 3, 1885, had terminated tribal jurisdiction over murder cases. Whether tribal authorities may still inflict the death penalty for offenses other than the enumerated ten major crimes is a matter of some doubt.

The lacunae in this brief criminal code of ten commandments are serious, and indicate the importance of tribal jurisdiction in the field of law and order.

"Assault" cases that do not involve a "dangerous weapon" or where "intent to kill" cannot be proven, cannot be prosecuted in the Federal court, no matter how brutal the attack may be, or how near death the victim is placed, if death does not actually ensue; men brutally beating their wives and children are, therefore, exempt from prosecution in the Federal courts, and as above shown, the State

---

27  *"548. (Criminal Code, section 328.) Indians committing certain crime; acts on reservations; rape on Indian women. — All Indians committing against the person or property of another Indian or other person any of the following crimes, namely, murder, manslaughter, rape, incest, assault with intent to kill, assault with dangerous weapon, arson, burglary, robbery, and larceny on and within any Indian reservation under the jurisdiction of the United States Government, including rights of way running through the reservation, shall be subject to the same laws, tried in the same courts, and in the same manner, and be subject to the same penalties as are all other persons committing any of the above crimes within the exclusive jurisdiction of the United States: Provided, That any Indian who commits the crime of rape upon any female Indian within the limits of any Indian reservation shall be imprisoned at the discretion of the court: Provided further, That as herein used the offense rape shall be defined in accordance with the laws of the State in which the offense was committed.

The foregoing shall extend to prosecutions of Indians in South Dakota under section 549 of this title." (As amended June 28, 1932, c. 284, 47 Stat. 337.)

courts do not have jurisdiction. Even assault with intent to commit rape or great bodily injury is not punishable under any Federal statute.[28]

Aside from rape and incest the various offenses involving the relation of the sexes (e.g., adultery, seduction, bigamy, and solicitation), as well as those involving the responsibility of a man for the support of his wife and children are not within the cases that can be prosecuted in Federal courts.[29]

Other offenses which may be mentioned, to which no State or Federal laws now have application, and over which no State or Federal court now has any jurisdiction, are: kidnapping, receiving stolen goods, poisoning (if the victim does not die), obtaining money under false pretenses, embezzlement, blackmail, libel, forgery, fraud, trespass, mayhem, bribery, killing of another's live stock, setting fire to prairie or timber, use of false weights and measures, carrying concealed weapons, gambling, disorderly conduct, malicious mischief, pollution of water supplies, and other offenses against public health.[30]

It is not clear whether the foregoing offenses, which are not punishable in the Federal courts when committed by one Indian against another, are likewise exempt from punishment when committed by a non-Indian against an Indian, or by an Indian against a non-Indian, if the offense occurs within the boundaries of Indian country.

In these circumstances the wrongdoer is clearly not subject to State law. He is, however, subject to the provision of the United States Criminal Code which deal with a meager list of "offenses within admiralty, maritime and territorial jurisdiction of the United States."[31] The offenses specifically dealt with in this Federal criminal code do not include any of the offenses above enumerated except simple assault, various sex offenses, receiving stolen goods, and attempts at murder. There is, however, in the United States Criminal Code a provision (U.S. Code, Title 18, Sec. 468) which makes acts committed upon land within the exclusive jurisdiction of the United States subject to Federal prosecution whenever made criminal

---

28  *United States* v. *King* (81 Fed. 625).

29  See *United States* v. *Quiver* (241 U.S. 602), discussed above under heading, "The Powers of an Indian Tribe to Regulate Domestic Relations."

30  Cf. statements of Assistant Commissioner Meritt, before House Committee on Indian Affairs, 69th Congress, on H.R. 7826 Hearings ("Reservation Court of Indian Offenses"), p. 91.

31  See *Donnelly* v. *United States* (228 U.S. 243) (murder of Indian by non-Indian upon reservation held within exclusive Federal jurisdiction).

by State law. It may be argued that this provision applies to offenses committed by an Indian against a non-Indian or by a non-Indian against an Indian, but no decision so holding has been found.[32]

On the foregoing analysis the limitations of Federal jurisdiction in the Indian country are apparent. The only offense punishable in the Federal courts when committed within an Indian reservation are: The ten major crimes specially designated in U.S. Code, title 18, section 548; the special "reservation offenses" included in U.S. Code, title 25 (chiefly involving the sale of liquor); the ordinary Federal crimes applicable throughout the United States (such as counterfeiting, smuggling,[33] and offenses relative to the mails), and, with respect to offenses committed by an Indian against a non-Indian or by a non-Indian against an Indian, the special "territorial" offenses for which punishment is provided in chapters 11 and 13 of U.S. Code, title 18.

The difficulties of this situation have prompted agitation for the extension of Federal or State laws over the Indian country, which has continued for at least five decades, without success.[34]

---

32  *United States* v. *Barnaby* (51 Fed. 20) held that this section had no application to crimes committed by one Indian against another. The court declared: "This attempt to adopt territorial and state laws may be classed as indolent legislation, not well adapted to producing order upon Indian reservations, or in those places under the exclusive jurisdiction of the general government, and allowing men guilty of crimes, demanding in all civilized governments punishment, as in this case, to escape their just deserts. The motion in arrest of judgment is sustained, and the defendant discharged from custody."

33  See *Bailey* v. *United States* (47 Fed. (2d) 702), confirming conviction of tribal Indian for offense of smuggling.

34  See Harsha, "Law for the Indians," 134 North American Review 272;

James Bradley Thayer, *A People Without Law,* 68 Atlantic Monthly 540, 676 (1891);

Austin Abbott, "Indians and the Law," 2 *Harv. Law Rev.* 167 (1888)

William B. Hornblower, "The Legal Status of the Indians," 14 Rep. Am. Bar Assn. 261 (1891)

Resolution of American Bar Association, August 1891, in 15 Rep. Am. Bar Assn. 422 (1892)

Cuthbert Pound, "Nationals Without a Nation," 22 Columbia Law Rev. 97 (1922);

Meriam and Associates, "The Problem of Indian Administration," (1928), chapter 13;

Ray A. Brown, "The Indian Problem and the Law", 39 Yale L.J. 307 (1930);

Report of Brown, Mark, Cloud and Meriam on "Law and Order on Indian Reservations of the Northwest," Hearings Subcommittee of the Senate Committee on Indian Affairs, part 26, page 14137, et seq. (1932)

The propriety of the object sought is not here in question, but the agitation itself is evidence of the large area of human conduct which must be left in anarchy if it be held that tribal authority to deal with such conduct has disappeared.

Fortunately such tribal authority has been repeatedly recognized by the courts, and although it has not been actually exercised always and in all tribes, it remains a proper legal basis for the tribal administration of justice wherever an Indian tribe desires to make use of its legal powers.

The recognition of tribal jurisdiction over the offenses of tribal Indians accorded by the Supreme Court in *Ex parte Crow Dog, supra,* and *United States* v. *Quiver, supra,* indicates that the criminal jurisdiction of the Indian tribes has not been curtailed by the failure of certain tribes to exercise such jurisdiction, or by the inefficiency of its attempted exercise, or by any historical changes that have come about in the habits and customs of the Indian tribes. Only specific legislation terminating or transferring such jurisdiction can limit the force of tribal law.

A recent writer,[35] after carefully analyzing the relation between Federal and tribal law, concludes:

"This gives to many Indian tribes a large measure of continuing autonomy, for the federal statutes are only a fragment of law, principally providing some educational, hygienic and economic assistance, regulating land ownership, and punishing certain crimes committed by or upon Indians on a reservation. Where these statutes do not reach, Indian custom is the only law. As a matter of convenience, the regular courts (white men's courts) tacitly assume that the general law of the community is the law in civil cases between Indians, but these courts will apply Indian custom where it is proved." (at p. 90.)

A careful analysis of the relation between a local tribal government and the United States is found in 7 Ops. Atty. Gen. 174 (1855), in which it is held that a court of the Choctaw Nation has complete jurisdiction over a civil controversy between a Choctaw Indian and an adopted white man, involving rights to property within the Choctaw Nation:

"On the other hand, it is argued by the United States Agent, that the courts of the Choctaw can have no jurisdiction of any case in which a citizen of the United States is a party ***.

In the first place, it is certain that the Agent errs in assuming the legal impossibility of a citizen of the United States becoming subject, in civil matters, or

---

35  W.G. Rice, Jr., "The position of the American Indian in the Law of the United States," 16 Jour. Comp. Leg. (3d series), part 1. Page 78 (1934).

criminal either, to the jurisdiction of the Choctaw. It is true that no citizen of the United States can, while he remains within the United States, escape their constitutional jurisdiction, either by adoption into a tribe of Indians, or any other way. But the error in all this consists in the idea that any man, citizen or not citizen, becomes divested of his allegiance to the United States, or throws off their jurisdiction or government, in the fact of becoming subject to any local jurisdiction whatever. This idea misconceives entirely the whole theory of the Federal Government, which theory is, that all inhabitants of the country are, in regard to certain limited matters, subject to the federal jurisdiction, and in all others to the local jurisdiction, whether political or municipal. The citizen of Mississippi is also a citizen of the United States; and he owes allegiance to, and is subject to the laws of, both governments. So also an Indian, whether he be Choctaw or Chickasaw, and while subject to the local jurisdiction of the councils and courts of the Nation, yet is not in any possible relation or sense divested of his allegiance and obligations to the Government and laws of the United States."

In effect, then, an Indian tribe bears a relation to the Government of the United States similar again to that relationship which a municipality bears to a State. An Indian tribe may exercise a complete jurisdiction over its members and within the limits of the reservation,[36] subordinate only to the expressed limitations of Federal law.

Recognition of tribal authority in the administration of justice is found in the statutes of Congress, as well as in the decision of the Federal courts.

U.S. Code, Title 25, section 229, provides that redress for a civil injury committed by an Indian shall be sought in the first instance from the "Nation or tribe to which such Indian shall belong." This provision for collective responsibility evidently assumes that the Indian tribe or Nation has its own resources for exercising disciplinary power over individual wrongdoers within the community.

We have already referred to U.S. Code, Title 25, section 218, with its express assurance that persons "punished by the law of the tribe" shall not be tried again before the Federal courts.

What is even more important than these statutory recognitions of tribal criminal authority is the persistent silence of Congress on the general problem of

---

36  The jurisdiction of the Indian tribe ceases at the border of the reservation (see 18 Op. Atty. Gen. 440, holding that the authority of the Indian police is limited to the territory of the reservation), and Congress has never authorized appropriate extradition procedure whereby an Indian tribe may secure jurisdiction over fugitives from its justice. See Ex parte Morgan (20 Fed. 298).

Indian criminal jurisdiction. There is nothing to justify an alternative to the conclusion that the Indian tribes retain sovereignty and jurisdiction over a vast area of ordinary offenses over which the Federal government has never presumed to legislate and over which the State governments have not the authority to legislate.

The attempts of the Interior Department to administer a rough-and-ready sort of justice through Courts of Indian Offenses, or directly through superintendents, cannot be held to have impaired tribal authority in the field of law and order. These agencies have been characterized, in the only reported case squarely upholding their legality, as "mere educational and disciplinary instrumentalities by which the Government of the United States is endeavoring to improve and elevate the condition of these dependent tribes to whom it sustains the relation of guardian." (*United States v. Clapox*, 35 Fed. 575; and cf. Ex parte Bi-a-lil-le, 12 Ariz. 150, 100 Pac. 450; *United States* v. *Van Wert*, 195 Fed. 974). Perhaps a more satisfactory defense of their legality is the doctrine put forward by a recent writer that the Courts of Indian Offenses "derive their authority from the tribe, rather than from Washington."[37]

Whichever of these explanations be offered for the existence of the Courts of Indian Offenses, their establishment cannot be held to have destroyed or limited the powers vested by existing law in the Indian tribe over the province of law and order and the administration of civil and criminal justice.

## THE POWERS OF AN INDIAN TRIBE TO SUPERVISE GOVERNMENT EMPLOYEES

Although the power to supervise regular Government employees is certainly not an inherent power of Indian tribal sovereignty, it is a power which is specifically granted to the Indian tribes by statute, subject to the discretion of the Secretary of the Interior. U.S. Code, Title 25, Section 48, provides:

> Right of tribes to direct employment of persons engaged for them. Where any of the tribes are, in the opinion of the Secretary of the Interior, competent to direct the employment of their blacksmiths, mechanics, teachers, farmers, or other persons engaged for them, the direction of such persons may be given to the proper authority of the tribe, (R.S. sec. 2072.)

---

37  W.G. Rice, Jr., "The Position of the American Indian in the Law of the United States", 16 Jour. Comp. Leg. (3d Ser.), Part 1, p. 78, 93 (1934).

Under the terms of this statute it is clearly within the discretionary authority of the Secretary of the Interior to grant to the proper authorities of an Indian tribe all powers of supervision and control over local employees which may now be exercised by the Secretary, e.g., the power to specify the duties, within a general range set by the nature of the employment, which the employee is to perform, the power to prescribe standards for appointment, promotion and continuance in office, the power to compel reports, from time to time, of work accomplished or begun.

It will be noted that the statute in question is not restricted to the cases in which a Federal employee is paid out of tribal funds. Senators are responsible to their constituents regardless of the source of their salaries, and therefore most Indian Service employees have been responsible only to the Federal Government, though their salaries might be paid from the funds of the tribe.

In directing the employment of Indian Service employees, an Indian tribe may impose upon such employees the duty of enforcing the laws and ordinances of the tribe, and the authority of Federal employees so acting has been repeatedly confirmed by the courts. See *Morris* v. *Hitchcock* (194 U.S. 384); *Buster* v. *Wright* (135 Fed. 947, app. Dism. 203 U.S. 599); *Maxey* v. *Wright* (3 Ind. T. 243, 54 S. W. 807, aff'd 105 Fed. 1003); *Zevely* v. *Weimer* (5 Ind. T. 646, 83 S.W. 941; 23 Ops, Atty. Gen. 528.

The section in question has not, apparently, been extensively used by the Interior Department, and that Department, under a previous administration, has recommended its repeal. Congress has not seen fit, however, to repeal the statute, and the recommendation of a previous Secretary of the Interior has no particular weight in construing the meaning of the statute.

## CONCLUSIONS

I conclude that under Section 16 of the Wheeler-Howard Act (Public No, 383, 73d Congress) the "powers vested in any Indian tribe or tribal council by existing law", are those powers of local self-government which have never been terminated by law or waived by treaty, and that chief among these powers are the following:

1.   The power to adopt a form of government, to create various offices and to prescribe the duties thereof, to provide for the manner of election and removal of tribal officers, to prescribe the procedure of the tribal council and subordinate committees or councils, to provide for the salaries or expenses of tribal officers and other expenses of public business, and, in

general to prescribe the forms through which the will of the tribe is to be executed.

2. To define the conditions of membership within the tribe, to prescribe rules for adoption, to classify the members of the tribe and to grant or withhold the right of suffrage in all matters save those as to which voting qualifications are specifically defined by the Wheeler-Howard Act (that is, the referendum on the act, and votes on acceptance, modification or revocation of Constitution, by-laws or charter), and to make all other necessary rules and regulations governing the membership of the tribe so far as may be consistent with existing acts of Congress governing the enrollment and property rights of members.

3. To regulate the domestic relations of its members by prescribing rules and regulations concerning marriage, divorce, legitimacy, adoption, the care of dependents, and the punishment of offenses against the marriage relationship, to appoint guardians for minors and mental incompetents, and to issue marriage licenses and decrees of divorce, adopting such State laws as seem advisable or establishing separate tribal laws.

4. To prescribe rules of inheritance with respect to all personal property and all interests in real property other than regular allotments of land.

5. To levy dues, fees, or taxes upon the members of the tribe and upon non-members residing or doing business of any sort within the reservation, so far as may be consistent with the power of the Commissioner of Indian Affairs over licensed traders.

6. To remove or to exclude from the limits of the reservation non-members of the tribe, excepting authorized Government officials and other persons now occupying reservation lands under lawful authority, and to prescribe appropriate rules and regulations governing such removal and exclusion, and governing the conditions under which non-members of the tribe may come upon tribal land or have dealings with tribal members, providing such acts are consistent with Federal laws governing trade with the Indian tribes.

7. To regulate the use and disposition of all property within the jurisdiction of the tribe and to make public expenditures for the benefit of the tribe, out of tribal funds, where legal title to such funds lies in the tribe.

8. To administer justice with respect to all disputes and offenses of or among the members of the tribe, other than the ten major crimes reserved to the Federal courts.

9. To prescribe the duties and to regulate the conduct of Federal employees, but only in so far as such powers of supervision may be expressly delegated by the Interior Department.

It must be noted that these conclusions are advanced on the basis of general legislation and judicial decisions of general import, and are subject to modification with respect to particular tribes in the light of particular powers granted, or particular restrictions imposed, by special treaties or by special legislation. With this qualification, the conclusions advanced are intended to apply to all Indian tribes recognized now or hereafter by the legislative or the executive branch of the Federal Government.

Respectfully.

(Sgd.) Nathan R. Margold
Solicitor.
Approved: October 25, 1934
(Sgd.) Oscar L. Chapman,
Assistant Secretary.

# Composite Indian Reorganization Act for Alaska

Alaska amendment of May 1, 1936:

That sections 1, 5, 7, 8, 15, 17, and 19 of the Act entitled "An Act to conserve and develop Indian lands and resources; to extend to Indians the right to form business and other organizations; to establish a credit system for Indians; to grant certain rights of home rule to Indians; to provide for vocational education for Indians; and for other purposes", approved June 18, 1834 (48 Stat.984), shall hereafter apply to the Territory of Alaska: *Provided,* That groups of Indians in Alaska not heretofore recognized as bands or tribes, but having a common bond of occupation, or association, or residence within a well-defined neighborhood, community, or rural district may organize to adopt constitutions and bylaws and to receive charters of incorporation and Federal loans under sections 16, 17, and 10 of the Act of June 18, 1934 (48 Stat. 984).

Sec. 2. That the Secretary of the Interior is hereby authorized to designate as an Indian reservation any area of land which has been reserved for the use and occupancy of Indians or Eskimos by section 8 of the Act of May 17, 1884 (23 Stat. 26), or by section 14 or section 15 of the Act of March 3, 1891 (26 Stat. 1101), or which has been heretofore reserved under any executive order and placed under the jurisdiction of the Department of the Interior or any bureau thereof, together with additional public lands adjacent thereto, within the Territory of Alaska, or any other public lands which are actually occupied by Indians or Eskimos within said Territory: *Provided,* That the designation by the Secretary of the Interior of any such area of land as a reservation shall be effective only upon its approval by the vote, by secret ballot, of a majority of the Indian or Eskimo residents thereof who vote at a special election duly called by the Secretary of the

Interior upon thirty days' notice: *Provided, however*, That in each instance the total vote cast shall not be less than 30 per centum of those entitled to vote: *Provided further*, That nothing herein contained shall affect any valid existing claim, location, or entry under the laws of the United States, whether for homestead, mineral, right-of-way, or other purpose whatsoever, or shall affect the rights of any such owner, claimant, locator, or entryman to the full use and enjoyment of the land so occupied.

The following provisions of the Indian Reorganization Act of June 18, 1934 (48 Stat. 984), are applicable to Alaska:

That hereafter no land of any Indian reservation, created or set apart by treaty or agreement with the Indians, Act of Congress, Executive order, purchase, or otherwise, shall be allotted in severalty to any Indian.

Sec. 5. The Secretary of the Interior is hereby authorized, in his discretion, to acquire through purchase, relinquishment, gift, exchange, or assignment, any interest in lands, water rights or surface rights to lands, within or without existing reservations, including trust or otherwise restricted allotments, whether the allottee be living or deceased, for the purpose of providing land for Indians.

For the acquisition of such lands, interests in lands, water rights, and for expenses incident to such acquisition, there is hereby authorized to be appropriated, out of any funds in the Treasury not otherwise appropriated, a sum not to exceed $2,000,000 in any one fiscal year: *Provided*, That no part of such funds shall be used to acquire additional land outside of the exterior boundaries of Navajo Indian Reservation for the Navajo Indians in Arizona and New Mexico, in the event that the proposed Navajo boundary extension measure now pending in Congress and embodied in the bills (S. 2499 and H.R. 8927) to define the exterior boundaries of the Navajo Indian Reservation in Arizona, and for other purposes, and the bills (S. 2531 and H.R. 8982) to define the exterior boundaries of the Navajo Indian Reservation in New Mexico and for other purposes, or similar legislation, become law.

The unexpended balances of any appropriations made pursuant to this section shall remain available, until expended.

Title to any lands or rights acquired pursuant to this act shall be taken in the name of the United States in trust for the Indian tribe or individual Indian for which the land is acquired, and such lands or rights shall be exempt from State and local taxation.

Sec. 7. The Secretary of the Interior us hereby authorized to proclaim new Indian reservations on lands acquired pursuant to any authority conferred by this Act, or to add such lands to existing reservations: *Provided,* That lands added to existing reservations shall be designated for the exclusive use of Indians entitled by enrollment or by tribal membership to residence at such reservations.

Sec. 8. Nothing contained in this Act shall be construed to relate to Indian holdings of allotments or homesteads upon the public domain outside of the geographic boundaries of any Indian reservation now existing or established hereafter.

Sec. 9. There is hereby authorized to be appropriated, out of any funds in the Treasury not otherwise appropriated, such sums as may be necessary, but not to exceed $250,000 in any fiscal year, to be expended at the order of the Secretary of the Interior, in defraying the expenses of organizing now chartered corporations or other organizations created under this Act.

Sec. 10. There is hereby authorized to be appropriated, out of any funds in the Treasury not otherwise appropriated, the sum of $10,000,000 to be established as a revolving fund from which the Secretary of the Interior, under such rules and regulations as he may prescribe, may make loans to Indian chartered corporations for the purpose of promoting the economic development of such tribes and of their members, and may defray the expenses of administering such loans. Repayment of amounts loaned under this authorization shall be credited to the revolving fund and shall be available for the purposes for which the fund is established. A report shall be made annually to Congress of transactions under this authorization.

Sec. 11. There is hereby authorized to be appropriated, out of any funds in the United States Treasury not otherwise appropriated, a sum not to exceed $250,000 annually, together with any unexpended balances of previous appropriations made pursuant to this section, for loans to Indians for the payment of tuition and other expenses in recognized vocational and trade schools: *Provided,* That not more than $50,000 of such sum shall be available for loans to Indian students in high schools and colleges. Such loans shall be reimbursable under rules established by the Commissioner of Indian Affairs.

Sec. 12. The Secretary of the Interior is directed to establish standards of health, age, character, experience, knowledge, and ability for Indians who may be appointed, without regard to civil-service laws, to the various positions maintained, now or hereafter, by the Indian Office, in the administration of functions or services affecting any Indian tribe. Such qualified Indians shall hereafter have the preference to appointment to vacancies in any such positions.

Sec. 15. Nothing in this Act shall be construed to impair or prejudice any claim or suit of any Indian tribe against the United States. It is hereby declared to be the intent of Congress that no expenditures for the benefit of Indians made out of appropriations authorized by this Act shall be considered as offsets in any suit brought to recover upon any claim of such Indians against the United States.

Sec. 16. Any Indian tribe, or tribes, residing on the same reservation, shall have the right to organize for its common welfare, and may adopt an appropriate constitution and bylaws, which shall become effective when ratified by a majority vote of the adult members of the tribe, or of the adult Indians residing on such reservation, as the case may be, at a special election authorized and called by the Secretary of the Interior under such rules and regulations as he may prescribe. Such constitution and bylaws when ratified as aforesaid and approved by the Secretary of the Interior shall be revocable by an election open to the same voters and conducted in the same manner as hereinabove provided. Amendments to the constitution and bylaws may be ratified and approved by the Secretary in the same manner as the original constitution and bylaws.

In addition to all powers vested in any Indian tribe or tribal council by existing law, the constitution adopted by said tribe shall also vest in such tribe or its tribal council the following rights and powers: To employ legal counsel, the choice of counsel and fixing of fees to be subject to the approval of the Secretary of the Interior; to prevent the sale, disposition, lease, or, encumbrance of tribal lands, interests in lands, or other tribal assets without the consent of the tribe; and to negotiate with the Federal, State, and local Governments. The Secretary of the Interior shall advise such tribe or its tribal council of all appropriation estimates or Federal projects for the benefit of the tribe prior to the submission of such estimates to the Bureau of the Budget and the Congress.

Sec. 17. The Secretary of the Interior may, upon petition by at least one-third of the adult Indians issue a charter of incorporation to such tribe; *Provided*, That such a charter shall not become operative until ratified at a special election by a majority vote of the adult Indians living on the reservation. Such charter may convey to the incorporated tribe the power to purchase, take by gift, or bequest, or otherwise, own, hold, manage, operate, and dispose of property of every description, real and personal, including the power to purchase restricted Indian lands and to issue in exchange therefor interests in corporate property, and such further powers as may be incidental to the conduct of corporate business, not inconsistent with law, but no authority shall be granted to sell, mortgage, or lease for a period exceeding ten years any of the land included in the limits of the reservation. Any charter so issued shall not be revoked or surrendered except by Act of Congress.

Sec. 19. The term "Indian" as used in this Act shall include all persons of Indian descent who are members of any recognized Indian tribe now under Federal jurisdiction, and all persons who are descendants of such members who were, on June 1, 1934, residing within the present boundaries of any Indian reservation, and shall further include all other persons of one-half or more Indian blood. For the purposes of this Act, Eskimos and other aboriginal peoples of Alaska shall be considered Indians. The term "tribe" wherever used in this Act shall be construed to refer to any Indian tribe, organized band, pueblo, or the Indians residing on one reservation. The words "adult Indians" wherever used in this Act shall be construed to refer to Indians who have attained the age of twenty-one years.

Act of May 17, 1884 (23 Stat. 26):

Sec. 14. That none of the provisions of the last two preceding sections of this Act shall be so construed as to warrant the sale of any lands belonging to the United States which shall contain coal or the precious metals, or any town site, or which shall be occupied by the United States for public purposes, or which shall be reserved for such purposes, or to which the natives of Alaska have prior rights by virtue of actual occupation, or which shall be selected by the United States Commissioner of Fish and Fisheries on the island of Kadiak and Afognak for the purpose of stablishing fish-culture stations. And all tracts of land not exceeding six hundred and forty acres in any one tract now occupied as missionary stations in said district of Alaska are hereby excepted from the operation of the last preceding sections of this act. No portion of the islands of the Pribylov Group or the Seal Islands of Alaska shall be subject to sale under this Act: and the United States reserves, and there shall be reserved in all patents issued under the provisions of the last two preceding sections the right of the United States to regulate the taking of salmon and to do all things necessary to protect and prevent the destruction of salmon in all the waters of the lands granted frequented by salmon.

Sec. 15. That until otherwise provided by law the body of lands known as Annette Islands, situated in Alexander Archipelago in Southeastern Alaska, on the north side of Dixon's entrance, be, and the same is hereby, set apart as a reservation for the use of the Metlakahtla Indians, and those people known as Metlakahtlans who have recently emigrated from British Columbia to Alaska, and such other Alaskan natives as may join them, to be held and used by them in common, under such rules and regulations and subject to such restrictions, as may be prescribed from time to time by the Secretary of the Interior.

Act of March 3, 1891 (26 Stat. 1101):

Sec. 8. ***Provided*, That the Indians or other persons in said district shall not be disturbed in the possession of any lands actually in their use or occupation or now claimed by them but the terms under which such persons may acquire title to such lands is reserved for future legislation by Congress: *And provided further*, That parties who have located mines or mineral privileges therein under the law of the United States applicable to the public domain, or who have occupied and improved or exercised acts of ownership over such claims, shall not be disturbed therein, but shall be allowed to perfect their title to such claims by payment as aforesaid: *And provided also*, That the land not exceeding six hundred and forty acres at any station now occupied as missionary stations among the Indian tribes in said section, with the improvements thereon erected by or for such societies shall be continued in the occupancy of the several religious societies to which said missionary stations respectively belong until action by Congress. But nothing contained in this act shall be construed to put in force in said district the general land laws of the United States.

# Oklahoma Indian Welfare Act

AN ACT to promote the general welfare of the Indians of the State of Oklahoma and for other purposes,

*Be it enacted by the Senate and the House of Representatives of the United States of America in Congress assembled,* That the Secretary of the Interior is hereby authorized, in his discretion, to acquire by purchase, relinquishment, gift, exchange, or assignment, any interest in lands, water rights, or surface rights to lands, within or without existing Indian reservations, including trust or otherwise restricted lands now in Indian ownership: *Provided,* That such lands shall be agricultural and grazing lands of good character and quality in proportion to the respective needs of the particular Indian or Indians for whom such purchases are made. Title to all lands so acquired shall be taken in the name of the United States, in trust for the tribe, band, group, or individual Indian for whose benefit such land is so acquired, and while the title thereto is held by the United States said lands shall be free from any and all taxes, save that the State of Oklahoma is authorized to levy and collect a gross-production tax, not in excess of the rate applied to production from lands in private ownership, upon all oil and gas produced from said lands, which said tax the Secretary of the Interior is hereby authorized and directed to cause to be paid.

Sec. 2. Whenever any restricted Indian land or interests in land, other than sales or leases of oil, gas, or other minerals therein, are offered for sale, pursuant to the terms of this or any other Act of Congress, the Secretary of the Interior shall have a preference right, in his discretion, to purchase the same for or in behalf of any other Indian or Indians or Indians of the same or any other tribe, at a fair valuation to be fixed by the appraisement satisfactory to the Indian owner or owners, or if offered for sale at auction said Secretary shall have a preference right, in his discretion, to purchase the same for or in behalf of any other Indian or Indians by meeting the highest bid otherwise offered therefor.

Sec. 3. Any recognized tribe or band of Indians residing in Oklahoma shall have the right to organize for its common welfare and to adopt a constitution and bylaws, under such rules and regulations as the Secretary of the Interior may prescribe. The Secretary of the Interior may issue to any such organized group a charter of incorporation, which shall become operative when ratified by a majority vote of the adult members of the organization voting: *Provided, however*, That such election shall be void unless the total vote cast be at least 30 per centum of those entitled to vote. Such charter may convey to the incorporated group, in addition to any powers which may properly be vested in a body corporate under the laws of the State of Oklahoma, the right to participate in the revolving credit fund and enjoy any other rights or privileges secured to an organized Indian tribe under the Act of June 18, 1934 (48 Stat. 984): *Provided*, That the corporate funds of any such chartered group may be deposited in any national bank within the State of Oklahoma or otherwise invested, utilized, or disbursed in accordance with the terms of the corporate charter.

Sec. 4. Any ten or more Indians, as determined by the official tribal rolls, or Indian descendants of such enrolled members, or Indians as defined in the Act of June 18, 1934 (48 Stat. 984), who reside within the State of Oklahoma in convenient proximity to each other may receive from the Secretary of the Interior a charter as a local cooperative association for any one or more of the following purposes: Credit administration, production, marketing, consumers' protection, or land management. The provisions of this Act, the regulations of the Secretary of the Interior, and the charters of the cooperative associations issued pursuant thereto shall govern such cooperative associations: *Provided*, That in those matters not covered by said Act, regulations, or charters, the laws of the State of Oklahoma, if applicable, shall govern. In any stock or nonstock cooperative association no member shall have more than one vote, and membership therein shall be open to all Indians residing within the prescribed district.

Sec. 5. The charters of any cooperative association organized pursuant to this Act shall not be amended or revoked by the Secretary except after a majority vote of the membership. Such cooperative associations may sue and be sued in any court of the State of Oklahoma or of the United States having jurisdiction of the cause of action, but a certified copy of all papers filed in any action against a cooperative association in a court of Oklahoma shall be served upon the Secretary of the Interior, or upon an employee duly assigned by him to receive such service. Within thirty days after such service or within such extended time as the trial court may permit, the Secretary of the Interior may intervene in such action or may remove such action to the United States district court to be held in the district where such petition is pending by filing in such action in the State court a petition for such removal, together with the certified copy of the papers served upon the Secretary. It shall then be the duty of the State court to accept such petition and to proceed no further in such action. The said copy shall be entered in the said district court within thirty days after the filing of the petition for removal, and the said district court is hereby given jurisdiction to hear and determine said action.

Sec. 6. The Secretary is authorized to make loans to individual Indians and to associations or corporate groups organized pursuant to this Act. For the making of such loans and for expenses of the cooperative associations organized pursuant to this Act, there shall be appropriated, out of the Treasury of the United States, the sum of $2,000,000.

Sec. 7. All funds appropriated under the several grants of authority contained in the Act of June 18, 1934 (49 Stat. 984), are hereby made available for use under the provisions of this Act, and Oklahoma Indians shall be accorded and allocated a fair and just share of any and all funds hereafter appropriated under the authorization herein set forth: *Provided*, That any royalties, bonuses, or other revenues derived from mineral deposits underlying lands purchased in Oklahoma under the authority granted by this Act, or by the Act of June 18, 1934, shall be deposited in the Treasury of the United States, and such revenues are hereby made available for expenditure by the Secretary of the Interior for the acquisition of lands and for loans to Indians in Oklahoma as authorized by this Act and by the Act of June 18, 1934 (48 Stat. 984).

Sec. 8. This Act shall not relate to or affect Osage County, Oklahoma.

Sec. 9. The Secretary of the Interior is hereby authorized to prescribe such rules and regulations as may be necessary to carry out the provisions of this Act. All Acts or parts of Acts inconsistent herewith are hereby repealed.

Approved, June 26, 1936.

# CONSTITUTION AND BYLAWS OF THE MINNESOTA CHIPPEWA TRIBE[38]

## MINNESOTA

### APPROVED JULY 24, 1936

### PREAMBLE

We, the Minnesota Chippewa Tribe, consisting of the Chippewa Indians of Minnesota under the Consolidated Chippewa Agency, in order to form a representative Chippewa tribal organization, maintain and establish justice for our Tribe, and to conserve and develop our tribal resources and common property; to promote the general welfare of ourselves and descendants, do establish and adopt this constitution for the Chippewa Indians of Minnesota under the Consolidated Chippewa Agency in accordance with such privilege granted the Indians by the United States under an existing law.

### ARTICLE I — ORGANIZATION AND PURPOSE

Section 1. The Chippewa Indians of Minnesota under the Consolidated Chippewa Agency are hereby organized as a tribe under Section 16 of the Act of June 18, 1934 (48 Stat. 984)

Sec. 2. The name of this tribal organization shall be "The Minnesota Chippewa Tribe."

---

38   RG75, BIA Records, DC, General Records concerning Indian Organization 1934-1956, Constitution & Bylaws, Coeur d' Alene tribe to Eastern Shawnee, Box 2, Entry 1012

Sec. 3. The purpose and function of this organization shall be to conserve and develop tribal resources and to promote the conservation and development of individual Indian trust property; to promote the general welfare of the members of the tribe; to preserve and maintain justice for its members and otherwise exercise all powers granted and provided the Indians, and take advantage of the privileges afforded by the Act of June 18, 1934 (48 Stat. 984) and acts amendatory thereof or supplemental thereto, and all the purposes expressed in the preamble hereof.

Sec. 4. The Tribe shall cooperate with the United States in its program of economic and social development of the Tribe or in any matters tending to promote the welfare of the Minnesota Chippewa Tribe of Indians.

## ARTICLE II — REPRESENTATION AND MEMBERSHIP

Section 1. This constitution for representation shall apply to the White Earth, Leech Lake, Fond du Lac, Bois Fort (Nett Lake) and Grand Portage Reservations, and the nonremoval Mille Lacs Band of Chippewa Indians.

Sec. 2. All the Chippewa Indians duly registered on the approved rolls of any of the above reservations or bands of Indians as recognized by the United States pursuant to the Treaty with said Indians as enacted by Congress in the Act of January 14, 1889 (25 Stat. 642) and acts amendatory thereof, are members of this Tribal organization: *Provided, however*, that the governing body of the tribe may make necessary corrections in the rolls subject to the approval of the Secretary of the Interior.

Sec. 3. The governing body of the tribe shall have power to make rules governing the qualifications required for enrollment in the tribe of descendants of members of the tribe, which descendants are not on the approved rolls of the tribe at the time of ratification and approval of such rules. These rules shall not be effective until ratified by the Tribal Delegates at the annual or any special meeting of such delegates, and approved by the Secretary of the Interior. No person shall be enrolled as a member of the tribe unless he is a descendant of a member of the tribe.

Sec. 4. The governing body shall have power to decide applications for membership according to the ratified rules, but no decision shall be effective until ratified by the Tribal Delegates at their annual or special meeting.

## ARTICLE III—GOVERNING BODY

Section 1. The government and management of the affairs of the tribe under this constitution shall be vested in a Tribal Executive Committee, said committee to be composed of not more than two members from each reservation and the band mentioned in Article II, Section 1, which shall include tribal officers, who shall be chosen by ballot by the Tribal Delegates as herein provided.

Sec. 2. The Tribal Executive Committee shall supervise and make such rules as it deems advisable governing the conduct of all elections concerning tribal matters not inconsistent with law or regulations of the Secretary of the Interior or Commissioner of Indian Affairs. It shall designate the time and dates such elections shall be held and further designate the districts or communities where elections are to be held for the election of Tribal Delegates.

## ARTICLE IV — ORGANIZATION OF TRIBAL DELEGATES AND TRIBAL EXECUTIVE COMMITTEE

Section 1. Tribal Delegates, numbering not more than two from any designated district or community, shall be chosen by each community at an annual election to be held on the first Monday in May of each year, unless another date shall be designated by the Tribal Executive Committee. Such Tribal Delegates shall meet at the Village of Cass Lake, Cass County, Minn., within 15 days of their election, such date to be fixed within said time by the Tribal Executive Committee. Such Tribal Delegates shall act until their successors have been elected, and shall be subject to call for special meetings by the Tribal Executive Committee. Any vacancy in the Tribal Delegates shall be filled by the community from which the delegate was elected.

Sec. 2. The Tribal Delegates shall select from the tribal membership two persons from each reservation and the band mentioned in Article II, Section 1, hereof, who shall compose the Tribal Executive Committee. Such Tribal Delegates shall also choose from said Tribal Executive Committee the following officers, to wit: a Tribal president, a Tribal vice-president, a Tribal secretary, and a Tribal treasurer. The Tribal Executive Committee shall elect or appoint all other officers and committees, as may be necessary.

Sec. 3. The members of the Tribal Executive Committee selected, shall meet and take office on the first Monday of the month following their election.

# ARTICLE V —
# POWERS OF THE TRIBAL EXECUTIVE COMMITTEE

Section 1. The Tribal Executive Committee shall manage all the business and affairs of the Tribe, including all matters incident to the welfare of said Tribe and shall make all necessary rules and regulations not inconsistent with law for the management of the business and guidance of the officers, employees, and agents of the Tribe.

Sec. 2. The Tribal Executive Committee shall have power to administer the tribal lands of the Minnesota Chippewa Tribe for the benefit of all the tribe, and to assign such land to reservation or community organizations for public uses, or, under rules which shall be subject to review by the Secretary of the Interior, to individual members of the tribe for as long as they shall use the land but for no longer than their natural lives.

Sec. 3. The Tribal Executive Committee shall have the power to negotiate with the Federal, State, and local Governments, on behalf of the tribe and to advise and consult with representatives of the Interior Department on all activities of the Department that may affect the Minnesota Chippewa Indians.

Sec. 4. The Tribal Executive Committee shall have power to employ legal counsel for the protection and advancement of the rights of the Minnesota Chippewa Tribe and its members, the choice of counsel and fixing of fees to be subject to the approval of the Secretary of the Interior.

Sec. 5. The Tribal Executive Committee shall have the power to prevent the sale, disposition, lease, or encumbrance of tribal land interests or other tribal assets without the consent of the tribe.

Sec. 6. The Tribal Executive Committee shall have the power to confer with the Secretary of the Interior upon all appropriation estimates or Federal projects for the benefit of the Tribe prior to the submission of such estimates to the Bureau of the Budget and Congress.

Sec. 7. The Tribal Executive Committee shall have power to organize and to charter associations of tribal members for economic purposes which are not chartered under Federal or State law, and to regulate the activities of such associations.

Sec. 8. The Tribal Executive Committee shall have no power to interfere with the management of the Red Lake Reservation or to exercise any control over the funds and other property exclusively owned by the Red Lake Band of Chippewa Indians.

Sec. 9. The Tribal Executive Committee may exercise such powers as in the future may be delegated to the Tribe by the Secretary of the Interior or by any person or agency.

Sec. 10. Any rights and powers heretofore vested in the Minnesota Chippewa Tribe but not expressly referred to in this Constitution shall not be abridged by this Article but may be exercised by the people of the Minnesota Chippewa Tribe through the adoption of appropriate bylaws and constitutional amendments.

## ARTICLE VI — TRIBAL EXECUTIVE COMMITTEE

Section 1. The following members and officers of the Tribal Executive Committee appointed to lead the Tribe during the preparation of this constitution shall call and hold the first elections for tribal delegates, and shall serve until the first Tribal Executive Committee is formed under this constitution:

### TRIBAL EXECUTIVE COMMITTEE

White Earth — John Broker, William Anywaush

Leech Lake — Ed Wilson, Jacob J. Munnell

Fond du Lac — Henry LaPrairie, Joseph LaPrairie

Bois Fort — Charles Bowness, Peter Smith

Grand Portage — James Scott, Mike Flatt

Mille Lac — Fred Sam, William Nickaboine

THE TRIBAL OFFICERS

John Broker, Tribal President

Henry LaPrairie, Tribal Secretary

Ed. Wilson, Tribal Vice President

Jacob J. Munnell, Tribal Treasurer

## ARTICLE VII —
## MEETINGS OF THE TRIBAL EXECUTIVE COMMITTEE

Section 1. Regular meetings of the Tribal Executive Committee shall be held once in every 3 months beginning on the first Monday in June of each year and on such other days of any month as may be designated for that purpose.

## ARTICLE VIII — VOTING PRIVILEGE

Section 1. Every member of the tribe, male or female, who has attained the age of 21 years shall be qualified to vote in any election under this constitution.

## ARTICLE IX — DURATION OF TRIBAL CONSTITUTION

Section 1. The period of duration of this Tribal Constitution shall be perpetual or until revoked by lawful means as provided in the Act of June 18, 1934 (45 Stat. 984)

## ARTICLE X — EQUAL REPRESENTATION

Section 1. All districts or communities shall have equal representation of not more than two delegates.

Sec. 2. All reservations shall have equal representation of not more than two members in the Tribal Executive Committee, including officers.

## ARTICLE XI — LOCAL ORGANIZATION

Section 1. Each reservation and district or community may govern itself in local matters in accordance with its customs and may obtain, if it so desires, from the Tribal Executive Committee a charter setting forth its organization and powers.

## ARTICLE XII — MAJORITY VOTE

Section 1. At all elections held under this constitution, the majority of eligible votes cast shall rule, unless otherwise provided by an Act of Congress.

## ARTICLE XIII — QUALIFICATIONS

Section 1. Each reservation and district shall be the sole judge of the qualifications of its own members and delegates.

Sec. 2. The Tribal Delegates shall be the sole judge of the qualifications of the members of the Tribal Executive Committee.

## ARTICLE XIV — EXPENDITURE OF TRIBAL FUNDS

Section 1. No compensation shall be paid to any member of the Tribal Executive Committee, including Tribal Officers, or any other person, from tribal funds under the control of the United States, except upon a resolution stating the amount of compensation and the nature of services rendered, or to be rendered

, and said resolution shall be of no effect until approved by the Secretary of the Interior.

Sec. 2. The Tribal Executive Committee shall have the right to expend funds of the Tribe within its control or any funds entrusted to its care and make proper accounting therefor.

Sec. 3. The Tribal Executive Committee shall require of any person, charged by the Tribe with responsibility for the custody of any of its funds or property, to give bond for the faithful performance of his official duties. Such bond shall be furnished by a responsible bonding company and shall be acceptable to the Tribal Executive Committee and to the Commissioner of Indian Affairs and the cost thereof shall be paid by the tribe.

## ARTICLE XV —
## VACANCIES IN TRIBAL EXECUTIVE COMMITTEE

Section 1. Any vacancy in the Tribal Executive Committee shall be filled by the Indians from the reservation on which the vacancy occurs by election under such rules as the Tribal Executive Committee shall prescribe.

Sec. 2. Any Tribal Executive Committeeman may be removed, after notice and an opportunity to be heard, by a two-thirds vote of the Tribal Executive Committee for repeated unjustified absence from the meetings of the Tribal Executive Committee or for a conviction of a crime.

## ARTICLE XVI — QUORUM

Section 1. Seven members of the Tribal Executive Committee shall constitute a quorum, and Roberts' Rules shall govern its meetings.

## ARTICLE XVII — RATIFICATION

Section 1. This constitution and the bylaws shall not become operative until ratified at a special election by a majority vote of the adult members of the Minnesota Chippewa Tribe, voting at a special election called by the Secretary of the Interior, provided that at least 30 percent of those entitled to vote shall vote, and until it has been approved by the Secretary of the Interior.

## ARTICLE XVIII — AMENDMENT

Section 1. This constitution may be revoked by a majority vote of the qualified voters of the Tribe voting at an election called for that purpose by the Secretary of the Interior if at least 30 percent of those entitled to vote shall vote. No amendment shall be effective until approved by the Secretary of the Interior. It shall be the duty of the Secretary to call an election when requested by two-thirds of the Tribal Executive Committee.

# BYLAWS

## ARTICLE I — DETERMINATION OF MEMBERSHIP

In the determination of membership under Article II, Section 2, of the constitution, the Government annuity rolls, as such rolls may be corrected under this Constitution, shall be used to determine the enrollment status in the Tribe and the same shall be conclusive, the said rolls being the Government official register of the recognized members of the Tribe.

## ARTICLE II — MEETINGS

Section 1. Notice shall be given by the Tribal secretary of the date of all meetings or elections of the Tribe, Tribal Executive Committee and Tribal Delegates, by mailing a notice thereof to the Indians in each designated district or community, to Tribal Executive Committeemen and Tribal Delegates, as the case may be, not less than 15 days preceding the date of the proposed meeting.

In the case of special meetings designated for emergency matters pertaining to the Tribe, or those of special importance, warranting immediate action of said Tribe, the Tribal president may waive the 15 days clause herein provided.

Sec. 2. The Tribal president shall call a special meeting of the Tribe, Tribal Delegates, or Tribal Executive Committee upon a written request of at least one-third of the Tribal Executive Committee or by resolution adopted by the Tribal Executive Committee at any meeting of said Committee.

Sec. 3. The Tribal president shall also call a special meeting of the Tribal Executive Committee when matters of special importance pertaining to the Tribe arise for which he deems advisable the said Committee should meet.

Sec. 4. The notices of the time, place, and purpose of all such special meetings, pursuant to request and call, shall be issued in the manner provided in Article II, section 1, hereof.

Sec. 5. The Tribal president who shall act as chairman of the Tribal Executive Committee shall preside at all meetings of the Tribal Delegates and Tribal Executive Committee and shall cast the deciding vote in all cases of a tie.

Sec. 6. A quorum for the Tribal Delegates shall be, for the election of Tribal officers and Tribal Executive Committeemen, at least two-thirds of the total number of the delegates; the same portion shall be required of such delegates to transact any other business coming properly before them.

Sec. 7. No business shall receive final action at any meeting, annual, regular, or special, unless a quorum of Tribal Delegates or the Tribal Executive Committee be present, but at any meeting where a quorum is present, the majority vote of the members present shall decide all questions.

Sec. 8. The order of business at any meeting so far as possible shall be:

    (1) Calling of roll.

    (2) Proof of notice of meeting.

    (3) Reading and disposal of all unapproved minutes.

    (5) Election of Executive Committeemen.

    (6) Unfinished business.

    (7) New business.

    (8) Adjournment.

## ARTICLE III — TERM OF OFFICE AND COMPENSATION

Sec. 1. Tribal Executive Committeemen who shall be elected by the Tribal Delegates in annual meetings assembled shall have been elected and qualified.

Sec. 2. Compensation, other than as provided in Article XIV of the Constitution, if any, to the Tribal Executive Committee and officers, shall be determined by the members of the Tribal Executive Committee at any meeting of the said committee.

## ARTICLE IV — DUTIES AND POWERS OF OFFICERS

Section 1. The president shall:

    (1) Preside over all meetings of the Tribe, Tribal Delegates, and the Tribal Executive Committee.

    (2) Sign as Tribal president, with the Tribal secretary, all notes, leases, deeds, and conveyances of real estate and contracts.

Sec. 2. In the absence or disability of the Tribal president, the vice president shall preside and perform the duties of the president.

Sec. 3. The Tribal secretary shall:

(1) Keep a complete record of the meetings of the Tribal Delegates and the Tribal Executive Committee.

(2) Sign as secretary, with the president, all notes, deeds, and other instruments.

(3) Be the custodian of all property of the Tribe.

(4) Keep a complete record of all business of the Tribal Executive Committee. Make and submit at the annual meeting of the members, a complete and detailed report of the current year's business and shall submit such other reports as shall be required.

(5) Serve all notices required for meetings or elections.

(6) Perform such other duties as may be required of him by the Tribe or Tribal ExecutiveCommittee.

Sec. 4. The treasurer shall receive all funds of the Tribe entrusted to it, deposit same in a depository selected by the Tribal Executive Committee, and disburse same only on vouchers signed by the Tribal president and the Tribal secretary.

## ARTICLE V — RECORDS AND AUDITS

Section 1. Ample records and an accounting system shall be maintained and such reports as may be required by the Tribal Executive Committee shall be made showing the condition of every enterprise promoted and maintained by the Minnesota Chippewa Tribe.

Sec. 2. The Tribal Executive Committee may examine all accounts at any time or at any meeting, and shall have the books of the Tribe audited at least once a year, such audit to take place during the 30 days preceding the first Monday in June of each year and the report of the audit shall be made to the Tribe.

## ARTICLE VI — MISCELLANEOUS

Section 1. The fiscal year of the Tribe shall begin on the first Monday in June of each year.

Sec. 2. The names of the Tribal Delegates elected under Article IV of the Constitution shall be submitted to the Tribal secretary prior to the meeting of the Tribal Delegates.

Sec. 3. These bylaws may be amended in the same manner as the Constitution.

## CERTIFICATION OF ADOPTION

Pursuant to an order, approved May 22, 1936, by the Secretary of the Interior, the attached Constitution and Bylaws were submitted for ratification to the Minnesota Chippewa Tribe and were on the 20th day of June, duly ratified, by a vote of 1,528 for and 544 against, in an election in which over 30 percent of those entitled to vote cast their ballots, in accordance with section 16 of the Indian Reorganization Act of June 18, 1934 (48 Stat. 984), as amended by the Act of June 15, 1935 (48 Stat. 378).

Edward M. Wilson
*Chairman of Election Board*

Selam Fairbanks
*Secretary of the Election Board*

M.L. Burns,
*Superintendent* in charge of the Agency.

I, Harold L. Ickes, the Secretary of the Interior of the United States of America, by virtue of the authority granted me by the act of June 18, 1934 (48 Stat. 984), as amended, do hereby approve the attached Constitution and Bylaws of the Minnesota Chippewa Tribe.

All rules and regulations heretofore promulgated by the Interior Department or by the Office of Indian Affairs, so far as they may be incompatible with any of the provisions of the said Constitution and Bylaws are hereby declared inapplicable to the Minnesota Chippewa Tribe.

All officers and employees of the Interior Department are ordered to abide by the provisions of the said Constitution and Bylaws.

Approval recommended July 20, 1936.

William Zimmerman, Jr.,
*Acting Commissioner of Indian Affairs.*

Harold L. Ickes
*Secretary of the Interior.*

[SEAL]

Washington, D.C., *July 24, 1936.*

# CORPORATE CHARTER
# OF THE
# MINNESOTA CHIPPEWA TRIBE OF THE
# CONSOLIDATED CHIPPEWA AGENCY[39]
# MINNESOTA

## RATIFIED NOVEMBER 13, 1937

### A FEDERAL CORPORATION CHARTERED UNDER THE ACT OF
### JUNE 18, 1934

Whereas, the Minnesota Chippewa Tribe is a recognized Indian tribe organized under a constitution and by-laws ratified by the Tribe on June 20, 1936, and approved by the Secretary of the Interior on July 24, 1936, pursuant to section 16 of the Act of June 18, 1934 (48 Stat. 984), as amended by the Act of June 15, 1935 (49 Stat., 378); and

Whereas, more than one-third of the adult members of the Tribe have petitioned that a charter of incorporation be granted to such tribe, subject to ratification by a vote of the adult Indians living on the reservations of the Minnesota Chippewa Tribe, namely: the White Earth, Leech Lake, Fond du Lac, Bois Fort, Grand Portage and Mille Lac Reservations.

Now, therefore, I, Oscar L. Chapman, Assistant Secretary of the Interior, by virtue of the authority conferred upon me by the said Act of June 18, 1934 (48 Stat. 984), do hereby issue and submit this Charter of incorporation to the Minnesota Chippewa Tribe to be effective from and after such time as it may be

---

39   RG75, BIA Records, DC, General Records Concerning Indian Organization 1934-1956, Constitution and Bylaws, Coeur d' Alene tribe to Eastern Shawnee, Box 2, Entry 1012

ratified by a majority vote at an election in which at least thirty per cent of the adult Indians living on the above-named reservations shall vote.

*Corporate Existence and Purposes.* 1. In order to further the economic development of the Minnesota Chippewa Tribe by conferring upon the said tribe certain corporate rights, powers, privileges and immunities; to secure for the members of the Tribe an assured economic independence; and to provide for the proper exercise by the Tribe of various functions heretofore performed by the Department of the Interior, the aforesaid tribe is hereby chartered as a body politic and corporate of the United States of America, under the corporate name "The Minnesota Chippewa Tribe."

*Perpetual Succession.* 2. The Minnesota Chippewa Tribe shall, as a Federal Corporation, have perpetual succession.

*Membership.* 3. The Minnesota Chippewa Tribe shall be a membership corporation. Its members shall consist of all persons now or hereafter enrolled as members of the Tribe, as provided by its duly ratified and approved Constitution and By-laws.

*Management.* 4. The Tribal Executive Committee of the Minnesota Chippewa Tribe established in accordance with the said constitution and by-laws of the Tribe, shall exercise all the corporate powers hereinafter enumerated.

*Corporate Powers.* 5. The Tribe, subject to any restrictions contained in the Constitution and laws of the United States, or in the Constitution and By-laws of the said tribe, shall have the following corporate powers already conferred or guaranteed by the Tribal Constitution and By-laws:

(a) To adopt, use, and alter at its pleasure a corporate seal.

(b) To purchase, take by gift, bequest, or otherwise, own, hold, manage, operate and dispose of property of every description, real and personal, subject to the following limitations:

(1) No sale or mortgage may be made by the Tribe of any land, or interests in land, including water power sites, water rights, oil, gas, and other mineral rights, now or hereafter held by the Tribe within the boundaries of the Minnesota Chippewa Tribe.

(2) No mortgage may be made by the Tribe of any standing timber on any land now or hereafter held by the Tribe within the boundaries of any reservation of the Minnesota Chippewa Tribe.

(3) No leases, permits (which terms shall not include land assignments to members of the Tribe) or timber sale contracts covering any land or interests in land now or hereafter held by the Tribe within the boundaries of any reservation of the Minnesota Chippewa Tribe shall be made by the Tribe for a longer term than ten years, and all such leases and permits, except to members of the Tribe, and all such contracts must be approved by the Secretary of the Interior or by his duly authorized representative; but oil and gas leases, water power leases, or any leases requiring substantial improvements of the land may be made for longer periods when authorized by law.

(4) No action shall be taken by or in behalf of the Tribe which in any way operates to destroy or injure the tribal grazing lands, timber, or other natural resources of any reservation of the Minnesota Chippewa Tribe.

All leases, permits, and timber sale contracts relating to the use of tribal grazing or timber lands shall conform to regulations of the Secretary of the Interior authorized by section 6 of the Act of June 18, 1934, with respect to range carrying capacity, sustained yield forestry management, and other matters therein specified. Conformity to such regulations shall be made a condition of any such lease, permit, or timber sale contract, whether or not such agreement requires the approval of the Secretary of the Interior, and violation of such condition shall render the agreement revocable, in the discretion of the Secretary of the Interior.

(c) To issue interests in corporate property in exchange for restricted Indian lands, the forms for such interests to be approved by the Secretary of the Interior.

(d) To borrow money from the Indian Credit Fund in accordance with the terms of section 10 of the Act of June 18, 1934 (48 Stat. 984), or from any other governmental agency, or from any member or association of members of the Tribe, or from any other source, and to use such funds directly for productive tribal enterprises, or to loan money thus borrowed to individual members or associations of members of the Tribe: *Provided*, That the amount of indebtedness to which the Tribe may subject itself, other than indebtedness to the Indian Credit Fund, shall not exceed $150,000, except with the express approval of the Secretary of the Interior.

(e) To engage in any business that will further the economic well-being of the members of the Tribe or to undertake any activity of any nature whatever, not inconsistent with law or with any provisions of this Charter.

(f) To make and perform contracts and agreements of every description, not inconsistent with law, or with any provisions of this Charter, with any person, association, or corporation, with any municipality or any county, or with the United States or the State of Minnesota for the rendition of public services: *Provided,* That any contract involving payment of money by the corporation in excess of $5,000 in any one fiscal year shall be subject to the approval of the Secretary of the Interior or his duly authorized representative.

(g) To pledge or assign chattels or future tribal income due or to become due the Tribe: *Provided,* That such agreements or pledge or assignment, other than an agreement with the United States, shall not extend more than five years from the date of execution and shall not cover more than forty per cent of the net tribal income from any one source: *And provided further,* That any such agreement shall be subject to the approval of the Secretary of the Interior or his duly authorized representative.

(h) To deposit corporate funds, from whatever source derived, in any national or state bank to the extent that such funds are insured by the Federal Deposit Insurance Corporation, or secured by a surety bond, or other security, approved by the Secretary of the Interior; or to deposit such funds in the Postal Savings Bank or with a bonded disbursing officer of the United States to the credit of the corporation.

(i) To sue and to be sued in courts of competent jurisdiction within the United States; but the grant or exercise of such power to sue and to be sued shall not be deemed a consent by the said tribe or by the United States to the levy of any judgment, lien or attachment upon the property of the Tribe other than income or chattels specially pledged or assigned.

(j) To exercise such further incidental powers, not inconsistent with law, as may be necessary to the conduct of corporate business.

*Termination of Supervisory Powers.* 6. Upon the request of the Tribal Executive Committee for the termination of any supervisory power reserved to the Secretary of the Interior under sections 5 *(b)* 3,5 *(c)*, 5 *(d)*, 5 *(f)*, 5 *(g)*, 5 *(h)*, and section 8 of this Charter, the Secretary of the Interior, if he shall approve such request, shall thereupon submit the question of such termination to the tribe for referendum. The termination shall be effective upon ratification by a majority vote at an election in which at least thirty per cent of the adult members of the Tribe residing on the reservations of the Minnesota Chippewa Tribe shall vote. If at any time after ten years from the effective date of this Charter, such request shall be made and the Secretary shall disapprove it or fail to approve or disapprove it within ninety days after its receipt, the question of the termination of any such power may then be submitted by the Secretary of the Interior or by the Tribal Executive Committee to popular referendum of the adult members of the Tribe actually living within the reservations of the Minnesota Chippewa Tribe and if the termination is approved by two-thirds of the eligible voters, shall be effective.

*Corporate Property.* 7. No property rights of the Minnesota Chippewa Tribe, as heretofore constituted, shall be in any way impaired by anything contained in this Charter, and the tribal ownership of unallotted lands, whether or not assigned to the use of any particular individuals, is hereby expressly recognized. The individually owned property of members of the Tribe shall not be subject to any corporate debts or liabilities, without such owners' consent. Any existing lawful debts of the Tribe shall continue in force, except as such debts may be satisfied or cancelled pursuant to law.

*Corporate Profits.* 8. The Tribal Executive Committee shall set aside annually twenty-five per cent of the profits of corporate enterprises for the establishment and building up of a reserve fund which shall be used for the undertaking, construction, operation and improvement of corporate enterprises. The Tribal Executive Committee may devote the remainder of such profits, and any other tribal income remaining after the payment of indebtedness and expenses, to such purposes for the benefit of the Tribe as it may think best not inconsistent with this Charter and the tribal constitution and by-laws.

*Corporate Accounts.* 9. The officers of the Tribe shall maintain accurate and complete accounts of the financial affairs of the Tribe, which shall clearly show all credits, debts, pledges, and assignments, and shall furnish an annual balance sheet and report of the financial affairs of the Tribe to the Commissioner of Indian Affairs. The Treasurer of the Tribe shall be the custodian of all moneys which come under the jurisdiction or control of the Tribal Executive Committee. He shall keep accounts of all receipts and disbursements and shall make written reports of same to the Tribal Executive Committee at each regular and special meeting. The books of the Treasurer shall be audited at the direction of the Committee or of the Commissioner of Indian Affairs, and shall be open to inspection by members of the Tribe or duly authorized representatives of the Government at all reasonable times.

*Amendments.* 10. This Charter shall not be revoked or surrendered except by Act of Congress, but amendments may be proposed by resolutions of the Tribal Executive Committee which, when approved by the Secretary of the Interior, to be effective shall be ratified by a majority vote of the adult members living on the reservations of the Minnesota Chippewa Tribe at a popular referendum in which at least 30 per cent of the eligible voters vote.

*Ratification.* 11. This Charter shall be effective from and after the date of its ratification by a majority vote of the adult members of the Minnesota Chippewa Tribe living on the following reservations: White Earth, Leech Lake, Fond du Lac, Bois Fort, Grand Portage and Mille Lac, provided at least 30 per cent of the eligible voters shall vote, such ratification to be formally certified by the Superintendent of the Consolidated Chippewa Agency and the Tribal President and Tribal Secretary of the Tribal Executive Committee of the Tribe.

Submitted by the Assistant Secretary of the Interior for ratification by the Minnesota Chippewa Tribe of the above-named reservations in a popular referendum to be held on November 13, 1937.

Oscar L. Chapman
*Assistant Secretary of the Interior*
Washington, D.C., *September 17, 1937.*

# CERTIFICATION

Pursuant to section 17 of the Act of June 18, 1934 (48 Stat. 984), this Charter, issued on September 17, 1937 by the Assistant Secretary of the Interior to the Minnesota Chippewa Tribe of the Consolidated Chippewa Agency in Minnesota, was duly submitted for ratification to the adult members of the Tribe living on the reservations of the Tribe and was on November 13, 1937 duly adopted by a vote of 1,480 for, and 610 against, in an election in which over 30 per cent of those entitled to vote cast their ballots.

John L. Pemberton,
*President, Tribal Executive Committee of The Minnesota Chippewa Tribe*

Arthur C. Beaulieu,
Secretary, Tribal Executive Committee.

Louis Balsam,
*Superintendent, Consolidated Chippewa Agency*

# CHARTER OF ORGANIZATION OF THE MILLE LACS BAND OF CHIPPEWA INDIANS[40]

WHEREAS, it is the purpose of the Minnesota Chippewa Tribe, organized under a constitution and bylaws ratified by the tribe on July 20, 1936, and approved by the Secretary of the Interior on July 24, 1936, pursuant to Section 16 of the Act of June 18, 1934, to foster self-government within each of the local groups composing the Minnesota Chippewa Tribe; and,

WHEREAS, the members of the Minnesota Chippewa Tribe residing on the Mille Lacs Reservation and in nearby settlements, wish to exercise their right to organize and to manage their local affairs; and,

WHEREAS, it is desired to obtain for such organization a charter from the Tribal Executive Committee setting forth its organization and powers, as provided in Article XI of the Constitution of the Minnesota Chippewa Tribe.

NOW, THEREFORE, we, the Executive Committee of the Minnesota Chippewa Tribe by virtue of the authority conferred upon us by Article XI of the Constitution of the Tribe, do hereby issue this charter to the members of the tribe residing on the Mille Lacs Reservation and in nearby settlements to be effective when duly adopted.

PURPOSES 1. In order that the Mille Lacs Organization may be recognized as a part of the Minnesota Chippewa Tribe, may engage in local and tribal affairs in a business-like way, and may exercise more effectively rights of local self-gov-

---

40   RG75, BIA Records, KC, Cons. Chip. Agency — Cass Lake, Land Transaction Case File, Mille Lacs Expendable land acquisition program, Box 542, Hm:1990, Row 3, Comp. 29, Shelf 2

RG75, BIA Records, DC, General records concerning Indian organization 1934-56, Constitution and Bylaws, Box 2, Entry 1012

ernment, the aforesaid organization is hereby chartered under the name, "THE MILLE LACS BAND OF CHIPPEWA INDIANS."

MEMBERSHIP 2. Membership in the Mille Lacs Band shall consist of the following:

(A) All Chippewa Indians permanently residing on the Mille Lacs Reservation and at, or near, the villages of Isle, Danbury, East Lake and Sandy Lake, Minnesota, on the date of the adoption of this charter, and their descendants, whose names appear on the approved roll of the Chippewa Tribe as determined by Sections 2 and 3 of the Constitution of the Minnesota Chippewa Tribe;

(B) All Chippewa Indians registered, or will be registered, on said roll as Mille Lacs Indians who shall maintain residence on the Mille Lacs Reservation or on any lands under the jurisdiction of the band.

The Council shall have power to enact ordinances, subject to the approval of the Tribal Executive Committee, providing for the adoption of new members.

ORGANIZATION- 3.

A) STRUCTURE: The Mille Lacs Band shall have a system of democratic local self-government in which the separate settlements of Chippewa Indians composing the Band shall be recognized as the inhabitants of separate districts and accorded proportional representation on the governing body. The electorate shall consist of all members of the Band who are 21 years of age or over.

B) GOVERNING BODY: A council consisting of nine members shall be the governing body of the Band and shall be known as the Mille Lacs Council; such council to be elected on the first Monday in May of each year, for a term of one year, by a popular referendum in each district. Representation on the council by districts shall be the following: Sandy Lake District one councilman, East Lake District one councilman, Danbury District two councilmen, Isle District two councilmen, Vineland District three councilmen. The council may create or change districts and the representation of any district as the needs of democratic organization may require, Provided, any such change shall not cause the representations to be disproportionate to the size of the district populations. A temporary council shall serve for the period between the ratification of this charter and the first annual election of councilmen in May, 1939, this temporary council to be composed of the present tribal delegates and the officers of existing local councils of the above designated districts.

C) <u>REMOVAL FROM OFFICE</u>: Upon petition of at least two-thirds of the eligible voters of a district for the removal of a council member representing said district, the council shall call a public hearing on the case and act as the judicial body. The decision of the council by a two-thirds majority vote shall be final.

D) <u>VACANCIES</u>: Should a vacancy in the council occur for any reason, the council shall appoint a successor from the district so lacking the representative for the remainder of the term.

**[No. 4 missing in original document]**

<u>MEETINGS</u> OF THE <u>COUNCIL</u> 5.

A) Regular meetings of the Council shall be held semi-annually, in May and November.

B) Special meetings may be called at any time by the chairman of the council.

C) The chairman of the council shall call a special meeting of the council upon a written request of at least one-half of the membership of the council, or upon resolution adopted by the council, or upon receipt of a petition signed by at least one-half of the eligible voters of the Band.

D) At any meeting of the council duly called three members shall constitute a quorum, Provided, However, that at least one of the three shall be from the Vermillion Lake Reservation.

<u>DUTIES OF</u> OFFICERS

6. The officers of the council shall recognize and perform the following duties:

A) The Chairman, as Chief Executive Officer of the Band, shall preside over all meetings of the council, affix his signature to official documents, countersign warrants duly drawn by the treasurer against funds of the Band, and shall vote only in case of a tie.

B) The Vice-Chairman shall preside at meetings and otherwise act in full capacity of the chairman in the absence of the chairman.

C) The secretary shall conduct all correspondence, issue public notices, take minutes, record official actions, etc., of the Council, and affix his signature to official documents.

D) The treasurer shall accept, receipt for and safeguard all funds of the Band as directed by the council, and keep complete record of receipts and expenditures. He shall be a bonded officer and shall not disburse any funds of the Band except as duly authorized by the council and he shall report on his accounts and all financial transactions at meetings upon request of the council.

## DUTIES OF THE COUNCIL

7.  The Band council shall exercise the following powers:

    A) To represent the Band and to negotiate with agencies of Federal, State and local government on all matters affecting the Band that, in the discretion of the council, may not more appropriately be handled by the Tribal Executive Committee.

    B) To negotiate with the Tribal Executive Committee on all matters affecting the Band and to advise with said committee on allocations of tribal or government funds and on federal projects, over which the committee may exercise any control.

    C) To manage the enterprises and affairs of the Band.

    D) To manage and use any property exclusively owned by the Band or assigned to it by the Tribal Executive Committee, or from any other source.

    E) To raise, reserve or expend funds of the Band for the purposes of the Band.

    F) To borrow revolving credit funds from the Minnesota Chippewa Tribe in accordance with the regulations of the Secretary of the Interior.

    G) To assign income or pledge chattels of the Band to the Tribe to secure loans from the Tribe.

    H) To distribute earnings and profits from activities of the Band to members of the Band.

    I) To exercise any existing powers of the Band or other powers not inconsistent with law that may be delegated to the Band by the Tribe, or by any authorized official or agency of federal, state or local government.

J) To provide for boards, officers and agents and prescribe their powers, duties and compensation, and to delegate to them powers whose exercise may be subject to review of the council.

K) To prescribe rules and regulations for its own business and for the manner of carrying on the business of the Band.

L) To levy taxes upon members of the Band or to require the performance of labor in lieu thereof; Provided, that any such assessment shall be subject to the approval of a majority of the eligible voters of the Band and who shall vote at special referendum on a given measure.

M) To regulate hunting, fishing and trade, and impose license fees within the territorial jurisdiction of the Band, by ordinance which shall be subject to review by the Secretary of the Interior.

N) To protect the peace and welfare of the Band through appropriate ordinances, subject to review by the Secretary of the Interior, and through the establishment of a court and the definitions of its powers and duties.

O) To manage, assign, lease or otherwise administer all unallotted Indian lands within or near the Mille Lacs Reservation that have been, or will be, acquired by the Band, or assigned to the Band, in accordance with ordinances subject to the approval of the Tribal Executive Committee.

## RIGHTS OF MEMBERS

8. All members of the Band enjoy full rights as citizens of the United States, and in addition the rights.

A) To equal opportunities to share in economic resources and activities of the Band.

B) To bring before the council grievances that are within the authority of the council to adjudicate and satisfy.

## AMENDMENTS 9.

A) This charter shall not be revoked except by action of the Tribal Executive Committee, subject to ratification by a two-third majority of the eligible voters of the Band who shall vote in a popular referendum.

B) This charter shall not be surrendered except upon petition of at least thirty percent of the eligible voters of the Band, requesting the Executive Committee to withdraw the charter, and upon ratification of said committee's action to withdraw the charter by a two-thirds majority of the eligible voters of the Band who shall vote in a popular referendum.

C) Amendments to this charter may be adopted subject to the approval of the Executive Committee, by a majority vote of the Executive Committee, by a majority vote of the eligible voters of the Band who shall vote in a popular referendum on the amendment.

## RATIFICATION

10. This charter shall be effective upon ratification by a majority vote of the eligible members of the Minnesota Chippewa Tribe residing on the Mille Lacs Reservation and in the hereinbefore designated settlements who shall vote such ratification to be formally certified by the Superintendent of the Consolidated Chippewa Agency and by the President and Secretary of the Tribal Executive Committee.

Submitted by the Executive Committee of the Minnesota Chippewa Tribe for ratification by the Mille Lacs Band on a popular referendum to be held on February 16, 1939.

Frank Broker
President, Executive Committee
Minnesota Chippewa Tribe
Cass Lake, Minnesota
October 8, 1938

T.J. Fairbanks
Secretary, Executive Committee
Minnesota Chippewa Tribe

# CERTIFICATION

Pursuant to Article XI of the Constitution and By-laws of the Minnesota Chippewa Tribe this charter, issued on October 8, 1938, by the Executive Committee of the Minnesota Chippewa Tribe to the Chippewa Indians of the Mille Lacs Reservation and was on February 16, 1939, duly ratified and accepted by a vote of 82 for and 16 against.

Frank Broker
President, Executive Committee
Minnesota Chippewa Tribe

T.J. Fairbanks
Secretary, Executive Committee,
Minnesota Chippewa Tribe.

February 22, 1939
Mark L. Burns
Supt. Consolidated Chippewa Agency

# Tribal Jurisdiction Over Non-Members

## A Legal Overview

Jane M. Smith — Legislative Attorney
Congressional Research Service

November 26, 2013

## Summary

Indian tribes are quasi-sovereign entities that enjoy all the sovereign powers that are not divested by Congress or inconsistent with the tribes' dependence on the United States. As a general rule, this means that Indian tribes cannot exercise criminal or civil jurisdiction over nonmembers. There are two exceptions to this rule for criminal jurisdiction. First, tribes may exercise criminal jurisdiction over nonmember Indians. Second, tribes may try non-Indians who commit dating and domestic violence crimes against Indians within the tribes' jurisdiction provided the non-Indians have sufficient ties to the tribes. There are three exceptions to this rule for civil jurisdiction. First, tribes may exercise jurisdiction over nonmembers who enter consensual relationships with the tribe or its members. Second, tribes may exercise jurisdiction over nonmembers within a reservation when the nonmembers' conduct threatens or has some direct effect on the political integrity, the economic security, or the health or welfare of the tribe. These first two exceptions, enunciated in the case of *Montana* v. *United States*, are based on the tribes' inherent sovereignty, and exercises of jurisdiction under them must relate to a tribes' right to self-government. Third, Indian tribes may exercise jurisdiction over nonmembers when Congress authorizes them to do so. Congress may delegate federal authority to the tribes, or re-vest the tribes with inherent sovereign authority that they had lost previously. Indian tribes may also exercise jurisdiction over nonmembers under their power to exclude persons from tribal property. However, it is not clear whether the power to exclude is independent of the *Montana* exceptions.

The question of a tribes' jurisdiction over nonmembers can be very complex. It is fair to say, however, that tribal jurisdiction over non-Indians is quite limited. Tribal jurisdiction over nonmember Indians is more extensive. Federal courts, however, consistently require nonmember defendants to challenge tribal court jurisdiction in tribal court before pursuing relief in federal court.

## Introduction

Originally, Indian tribes exercised sovereign authority over their territory and all the people within it, including non-Indians. However, Indian tribes lost some of that authority by "ceding their lands to the United States and announcing their dependence on the Federal Government." "Indian tribes are prohibited from exercising both those powers of autonomous states that are expressly terminated by Congress *and* those powers *inconsistent with their status.*" Express termination of a tribes' sovereign authority may be found in treaties and statutes. As a sovereign authority lost by virtue of the tribes' status, the Supreme Court has explained, "[t]he areas in which such implicit divestiture of sovereignty has been held to have occurred are those involving the relations between an Indian tribe and non-members of the tribe." By virtue of their "dependent status," therefore, tribes have lost the sovereign authority to determine their relations with nonmembers. Accordingly, in *Oliphant v. Suquamish*, the Supreme Court held that Indian tribes do not have inherent sovereign authority to try non-Indian criminal defendants, and in *Montana v. United States*, the Supreme Court announced the general rule for civil jurisdiction that "the inherent sovereign powers of an Indian tribe do not extend to the activities of non-members of the tribe."

Immediately after announcing this rule for civil jurisdiction in *Montana,* however, the Court identified two exceptions, known as the *Montana* exceptions:

> To be sure, Indian tribes retain inherent sovereign power to exercise some forms of civil jurisdiction over non-Indians on their reservations, even on non-Indian fee lands. A tribe may regulate, through taxation, licensing, or other means, the activities of non-members who enter consensual relationships with the tribe or its members, through commercial dealing, contracts,

leases, or other arrangements. A tribe may also retain inherent power to exercise civil authority over the conduct of non-Indians on fee land within its reservation when that conduct threatens or has some direct effect on the political integrity, the economic security, or the health or welfare of the tribe.

In order to fit within one of these exceptions, nonmember conduct must somehow impinge on a tribe's inherent authority to govern itself and its members.

The Supreme Court has identified the tribes' right as landowners to exclude nonmembers from tribal land as one of the bases for upholding tribal taxes against nonmembers' activities on tribal land. It is unclear, however whether the power to exclude is independent of the *Montana* exceptions.

Tribes may also exercise jurisdiction over nonmembers when Congress authorizes them to do so. Congress has provided for tribal authority over nonmembers related to the sale of alcohol on reservations, enforcement of tribal hunting and fishing ordinances on reservations, and enforcement of certain environmental statutes.

Although tribal jurisdiction over nonmembers is fairly limited, if a nonmember defendant in tribal court believes the court lacks jurisdiction, he or she must first challenge the jurisdiction in tribal court. Only after exhausting the tribal court remedies may the nonmember get relief in federal court.

## Criminal Jurisdiction

In most cases, tribal criminal jurisdiction over non-Indian offenders is clear — as a general rule, Indian tribes do not have it. However, there is an exception for tribes to exercise criminal jurisdiction over non-Indians who commit dating and domestic violence against Indians within a tribe's jurisdiction, provided the non-Indian has sufficient ties to the tribe and the tribe provides certain rights.

Tribal criminal jurisdiction over nonmember Indians is more difficult to discern. Such jurisdiction depends on whether the nonmember Indian is recognized as an Indian by the federal government or the tribal community. This determination turns on factors such as enrollment in a tribe, the degree to which the nonmember Indian has received federal services and benefits for Indians; benefited from tribal rights or services; and participated in tribal ceremonies and social life.

## Over Non-Indians

In *Oliphant v. Suquamish Indian Tribe*, the Court held that tribes lack inherent sovereign authority over non-Indian offenders. The Court first analyzed the history of criminal jurisdiction over non-Indians within Indian country through treaty provisions, executive branch activities and opinions, and lower court opinions, and concluded that historically the legislative and executive branches and lower courts presumed that Indian tribes did not have authority over non-Indians who committed offenses within Indian country. Although the Court wrote that this history was not "conclusive," it determined that it "carries considerable weight." Accordingly, the Court read the Suquamish Tribe's (Tribe's) treaty with the United States in light of the historical presumption against tribal jurisdiction over non-Indian offenders. The Court acknowledged that on its own, the treaty probably would not divest the Tribe of criminal jurisdiction over non-Indian offenders if it otherwise retained that authority. However, the Court determined that Tribe did not retain the authority to try non-Indian offenders.

The Court cited two reasons to support its determination that Indian tribes did not possess the inherent authority to try non-Indian offenders. First, the Court wrote, "Indian tribes are prohibited from exercising those powers *inconsistent with their status.*" The Court identified some of the restrictions imposed on the tribes' sovereignty by virtue of their incorporation into the United States as loss of "the tribes' power to transfer [and] exercise external political sovereignty." In addition, quoting Justice Johnson's opinion from the first Indian case to reach the Supreme Court, the Court wrote, "[T]he restrictions upon the soil in the Indians, amount ... to an exclusion of all competitors [to the United States] from their markets; and the limitation upon their sovereignty amounts *to the right of governing every person within their limits except themselves.*" Noting that protection of its territory within its boundaries is "central" to the sovereign interests of the United States, the Court wrote that "the United States has manifested an equally great solicitude that its citizens be protected by the United States from unwarranted intrusions on their personal liberty. The Court concluded, "By submitting to the overriding sovereignty of the United States, Indian tribes therefore necessarily give up their power to try non-Indian citizens of the United States except in a manner acceptable to Congress."

The second reason the Court gave for determining that Indian tribes did not retain inherent authority to try non-Indian offenders was related to the Court's precedent. In *Ex Parte Crow Dog*, the Supreme Court held that federal courts lacked jurisdiction to try an Indian who had committed an offense against another Indian on reservation land. In that case, the Court looked to the "nature and circumstances of the case" and concluded that the United States was seeking to extend law, by argument and inference only ... over aliens and strangers; over the members of a community separated by race [and] tradition, ... from the authority and power which seeks to impose upon them the restraints of an external and unknown code …; which judges them by a standard made by others and not for them … It tries them, not by their peers, nor by the customs of their people, nor the law of their land ; and, by … a different race, according to the law of a social state of which they have an imperfect conception ….

The Court wrote that the same considerations applied to subjecting non-Indian offenders to the laws of Indian tribes and contradicted the notion that, although the tribes are "fully subordinated to the sovereignty of the United States, [they] retain the power to try non-Indians according to their own customs and procedures."

Although the Court recognized that some Indian judicial systems had become "increasingly sophisticated" and in many respects resemble state court systems; that the Indian Civil Rights Act had extended certain basic procedural rights to anyone tried in tribal court so that many of the dangers for non-Indians that existed a few decades ago have disappeared; and that there is a prevalence of non-Indian crime on Indian reservations, the Court wrote that those factors should be addressed to Congress for it to "weigh in deciding whether Indian tribes should finally be authorized to try non-Indians."

Congress authorized tribes to try non-Indians who commit dating and domestic violence in the Violence Against Women Act Reauthorization (VAWA Reauthorization). In short, the VAWA Reauthorization re-vests Indian tribes with the inherent authority to prosecute non-Indians who commit dating and domestic violence crimes against Indians within the tribes' jurisdictions provided the non-Indians have certain enumerated ties to the tribes and the tribes provide protections for the rights of the domestic abuse criminal defendants.

## Over Nonmember Indians

In *Duro v. Reina*, the Supreme Court applied *Oliphant* to hold that a tribe does not possess authority to exercise criminal jurisdiction over Indian offenders who are not members of the tribe. In response, Congress amended the Indian Civil Rights Act so that the terms "powers of self-government" include "the inherent power of Indian tribes, hereby recognized and affirmed, to exercise criminal jurisdiction over all Indians," and "Indian" means any person who would be subject to the jurisdiction of the United States as an Indian under section 1153 of Title 18 if that person were to commit an offense listed in that section in Indian country to which that section applies." Thus Congress re-vested the tribes with the inherent authority to try nonmember Indians.

The authority to try nonmember Indians, however, does not extend to all persons who are racially Indians. "The term 'Indian' is not statutorily defined, but courts have judicially explicated its meaning. The generally accepted test for Indian status considers '(1) the degree of Indian blood; and (2) tribal or government recognition as an Indian.'"

For the first requirement, there is no set degree of Indian blood that is required. However, the Indian blood must trace back to a federally recognized tribe. The second requirement "requires membership or affiliation with a federally recognized tribe."

"When analyzing this prong, courts have considered, in declining order of importance, evidence of the following: (1) tribal enrollment; (2) government recognition formally and informally through receipt of assistance reserved only for Indians; (3) enjoyment of the benefits of tribal affiliation; and (4) social recognition through residence on a reservation and participation in Indian social life."

Therefore, a person with Indian blood who is not a member of the tribe may be subject to prosecution by the tribe if he or she is enrolled in another Indian tribe; received federal benefits or services for Indians; partook of any of the privileges of tribal affiliation, such as participating in tribal hunting or fishing rights or being arrested by tribal police and tried in tribal courts; resided on the Indian reservation; or participated in tribal ceremonies and social events. It appears that courts look to the cumulative effect of these considerations, with no single factor being determinative.

## Civil Jurisdiction

The general rule that tribes lack civil jurisdiction over nonmembers is deceptively simple. Tribal civil jurisdiction over nonmembers is complicated for several reasons.

First, the two *Montana* exceptions to the general rule for consensual relationships and threats to the tribe do not provide bright line rules. Courts must decide cases involving tribal civil jurisdiction over nonmembers based on the unique facts of each case.

Second, there are two types of civil jurisdiction: legislative and adjudicatory. The court has held that tribal adjudicatory jurisdiction is no broader than tribal legislative jurisdiction. It has not determined whether tribal adjudicatory jurisdiction is as broad as tribal legislative jurisdiction. To answer the question whether a tribal court may adjudicate a case involving nonmember conduct, therefore, the

Court inquires whether the tribe would be able to regulate that conduct. Again, there are no bright line rules.

Third, the court has refused to draw a bright line based on the ownership of the land on which the nonmember conduct takes place. In *Nevada v. Hicks*, the Court held that the *Montana* rule applied to Indian and non-Indian land. The status of the land is one factor — perhaps in some cases even a determinative factor — to consider in determining whether a tribe has jurisdiction over non-Indian conduct.

Finally, it is unclear whether tribes generally have civil jurisdiction over Indians who are not members of the tribe. Although Congress re-vested tribes with jurisdiction to try nonmember Indians for criminal conduct, it did not take any action regarding civil jurisdiction over nonmember Indians. The leading commentator on Indian law, however, believes that because *Oliphant's* analysis focused on the understanding of Congress and the executive branch, in addition to that of the courts, Congress's decision to re-vest tribes with criminal jurisdiction over nonmember Indians alters the Court's analysis of Congress's understanding of tribal jurisdiction over nonmember Indians such that the Court might find that tribes have civil jurisdiction over nonmember Indians even though Congress has not provided for it.

## The Montana Exceptions

Most of the litigation concerning the *Montana* exceptions has concerned the exception for nonmembers who enter consensual relationships with tribes or tribal members. The Supreme Court has significantly limited the exception for threats to the tribe.

## Consensual Relationships

Tribes may exercise jurisdiction over non-Indians when the non-Indians enter consensual relationships, such as "commercial dealing[s], contracts, leases, or other arrangements," with the tribe or tribal members. The Court has interpreted this exception narrowly. Federal courts have rarely found tribal jurisdiction based on a nonmember's consensual relationship. In *First Specialty Insurance v. Confederated Tribes of the Grand Ronde Community of Oregon*, the district court upheld the tribal court's jurisdiction over a claim based on a contract between the Tribes and the insured nonmember investment company. In this case, the Tribes' causes of action were based directly on a formal agreement between the Tribes and the nonmember. The Supreme Court has stated, however, that the consensual relationship need not be formal.

## The Consensual Relationship Must be Related to the Non-Indian Conduct at Issue

In *Atkinson Trading Co. v. Shirley*, in considering a tribal tax, the Court wrote, "*Montana's* consensual relationship exception requires that the tax or regulation imposed by the Indian tribe have a nexus to the consensual relationship itself." " A non-member's consensual relationship in one area thus does not trigger tribal civil authority in another — it is not in for a penny, in for a pound." Similarly, a court's adjudicative jurisdiction must have some nexus to the consensual relationship.

In *Strate* v. *A-1 Contractors,* the defendant in tribal court had a contract with the Three Affiliated Tribes of the Ft. Berthold Indian Reservation to perform landscaping. The contractor found itself a defendant in tribal court in conjunction with a traffic accident that occurred on a state highway within the reservation. The Court held that the tribal court did not have jurisdiction over a claim arising out of the accident. Thus, it is not enough that the nonmember have a consensual relationship with a tribe or a tribal member. The conduct over which the tribe is exercising jurisdiction must be related to that consensual relationship. As the Court put it, even though the contractor had a consensual relationship with the Tribes, they "were strangers to the accident."

## The Consensual Relationship Must Be Private

Not every consensual relationship with tribal members or a tribe is subject to tribal jurisdiction, even if it has a nexus to the nonmember conduct at issue. In *Hicks*, the Court wrote that the relationship must be private. In this case, a tribal member who resided on tribal land sued state game wardens in tribal court for damages to property caused by the wardens violating the terms of their search warrant. The wardens had a consensual relationship with the tribe in that they executed the warrant through the tribal court. However, the Court found that the relationship did not fit within the first *Montana* exception and denied that the tribal court had jurisdiction.

In *MacArthur v. San Juan County,* the U.S. Court of Appeals for the Tenth Circuit extended the *Hicks* requirement to apply to state agencies generally. In *MacArthur*, tribal members sued a county, a county agency, and various agency employees in tribal court for allegedly wrongful conduct in connection with the tribal members' employment by the agency, which was located on non-Indian land within the reservation. The court drew a distinction between "private individuals or entities who voluntarily submit themselves to tribal jurisdiction and 'States or state officers acting in their governmental capacity.'" and held "in the absence of congressional delegation, the tribes may not regulate a State qua State on non-Indian land (even within the exterior boundaries of the reservation) based on a consensual relationship between members of the tribe and the State." The court specifically reserved for another case whether a tribe may exercise jurisdiction over a state that has entered a consensual relationship with a tribe or its members in a non-governmental or proprietary capacity.

## The Consensual Relationship May Consist of Invoking Tribal Court Jurisdiction

A nonmember party who brings suit against a tribal member or the tribe in tribal court has entered into a consensual relationship with the tribe for the purpose of adjudicating claims in which the nonmember is a plaintiff or a defendant in a subsequent related action.

In *Smith v. Salish Kootenai College,* the U.S. Court of Appeals for the Ninth Circuit (Ninth Circuit) upheld the tribal courts' jurisdiction to adjudicate a nonmember's claim against a tribal college. Smith, the nonmember, was driving a tribal college truck with two tribal members in it when the truck overturned, killing one member and seriously injuring Smith and the other tribal member. The estate of the member who died filed suit against Smith and the tribal college. The tribal college filed a cross-claim against Smith. The injured tribal member then filed suit in tribal court against Smith and the tribal college. Smith filed a cross-claim against the tribal college. All the claims except Smith's claim against the tribal college settled. Rather than filing his claim against the tribal college in state court, Smith went to trial in tribal court and lost. He then asserted that the tribal court lacked jurisdiction over his claim. The Ninth Circuit held that even though Smith was originally a defendant, by filing a cross-claim against the tribal college he "knowingly enter[ed] tribal court for the purposes of filing suit against the tribal college [and], by the act of filing his claims, entered into a 'consensual relationship' with the tribe within the meaning of *Montana.*"

In *Ford Motor Co. v. Poitra,* the court extended the holding in *Salish Kootenai College* to uphold tribal court jurisdiction over a member's claim against a nonmember because the nonmember, in a related but separate claim, had invoked the tribal court's jurisdiction as a plaintiff. Ford Credit, as plaintiff, obtained a default judgment in tribal court against the tribal member for failing to make payments on a vehicle that Ford Credit financed. Three years later, in a separate lawsuit, the tribal member sued Ford Credit in tribal court seeking damages as a result of Ford Credit's failure to execute the default judgment. Ford Credit lost in tribal court and sought an injunction against enforcement of the tribal court judgment in federal district court, claiming that the tribal court lacked jurisdiction over it. The district court, citing *Salish Kootenai College,* upheld the tribal court's jurisdiction. Quoting the tribal court of appeals, the court wrote, "A non-Indian cannot utilize a tribal forum to gain relief against a tribal member and then attempt to avoid that jurisdiction when it acts negligently in that same action resulting in potential harm to the tribal member."

## Threat to the Tribe's Integrity

The second *Montana* exception provides that tribes may exercise jurisdiction over nonmembers when the nonmember's conduct "threatens or has some direct effect on the political integrity, the economic security, or the health or welfare of the tribe.' Subsequent cases have limited this exception significantly.

In *Atkinson Trading Co. v. Shirley,* the Court struck down a tribal tax on guests of a nonmember's hotel located on non-Indian fee land within the reservation. The Navajo Nation (Nation) argued that the trading post of which the hotel was a part had "direct effects" on its welfare: the Nation provided services to the trading post; the owner of the trading post was an "Indian trader"; the trading post employed almost 100 tribal members; the trading post derived business from the tourists visiting the reservation; and the trading post was surrounded entirely by tribal land. The Court rejected the Nation's argument.

The [second] exception is only triggered by *non-member conduct* that threatens the Indian tribe, it does not broadly permit the exercise of civil authority wherever it might be considered "necessary" to self-government. Thus, unless the drain of the non-member's conduct upon tribal services and resources is so severe that it actually "imperils" the political integrity of the Indian tribe, there can be no assertion of civil authority beyond tribal lands.

In *Plains Commerce Bank v. Long Family Land and Cattle Co.,* the Court reiterated the limited nature of this exception: "[t]he conduct must do more than injure the tribe, it must imperil the subsistence of the tribal community." One commentator has noted that "the elevated threshold for application of the second *Montana* exception suggests that tribal power must be necessary to avert catastrophic consequences."

There is one recent court of appeals case that upheld a tribal court's jurisdiction over a nonmember based on this second exception. In *Attorney's Process and Investigation Services v. Sac & Fox Tribe of the Mississippi in Iowa,* the U.S. Court of Appeals for the Eighth Circuit upheld the tribal court's jurisdiction over trespass and trade secrets claims against a nonmember for taking over the Tribe's facilities and seizing tribal financial documents. In this case, there had been an ongoing tribal leadership dispute: the elected leaders refused to honor the recall petitions submitted by tribal members, and the opposition leaders took control of the Tribe's government building and casino. The opposition leaders held an election in which a majority voted against the elected leaders. The elected leaders hired the nonmember to remove the opposition from the Tribe's facilities. The nonmember raided the facilities with 30 agents armed with batons. At least one agent had a firearm. Later, the Tribe sued the nonmember in tribal court. After the tribal court found for the tribe, the nonmember challenged the tribal court's jurisdiction in federal court. The court of appeals upheld the tribal court's jurisdiction, finding that the nonmember's raid "threatened the tribal community and its institutions" as well as the "political integrity and economic security of the Tribe."

The dawn attack was directed at the Tribe's community center — the seat of tribal government — and the casino, which the tribal appellate court characterized as "the Tribe's economic engine." As it appears from the allegations, the raid sought to return the [elected leaders] to power despite the majority's rejection of the leadership in the May election. This was a direct attack on the heart of tribal sovereignty, the right of Indians to protect tribal self-government.

The court reinforced its conclusion that the tribal court had jurisdiction over the Tribe's claims against the nonmember with the fact that the raid occurred on tribal land: as the landowner, the Tribe had the power to exclude the nonmember altogether. That power includes the authority to regulate conduct on the tribal land.

Based on the language from *Atkinson* and *Plains Commerce Bank,* the second *Montana* exception appears to be very limited and will be applied only in cases in which the tribe's survival is threatened by nonmember conduct.

## The Power to Exclude

In *Merrion v. Jicarilla Apache Tribe,* decided one year after *Montana,* the Supreme Court upheld the Tribe's authority to impose a severance tax on a nonmember company extracting oil and gas from tribal property, in addition to the negotiated royalty payments under the lease. The Court found the jurisdiction to tax nonmembers on tribally owned land derived from the Tribe's power, as a land-owner, to exclude nonmembers and its "general authority, as sovereign, to control economic activity within its jurisdiction and to defray the cost of providing government services by requiring contributions from persons or enterprises engaged in economic activities within that jurisdiction."

It is not clear, however, if the power to exclude is independent of the *Montana* exceptions. Although the Court has written that "[r]egulatory authority goes hand in hand with the power to exclude," it has also written that "the existence of tribal ownership is not alone enough to support regulatory jurisdiction over non-members." If the power to exclude were independent of the *Montana* exceptions, it seems that the existence of tribal ownership alone would suffice to support regulatory jurisdiction.

Moreover, language in the *Atkinson* opinion, decided in 2001 raises further questions about whether the power to exclude is independent of the *Montana* exceptions. Rejecting the Tribe's argument that *Merrion's* recognition of inherent authority to tax supported an occupancy tax on guests staying at a nonmember hotel on non-Indian land, the Court wrote,

*Merrion* was careful to note that an Indian tribe's inherent power to tax only extended to "transactions occurring on *trust lands* and significantly involving a tribe or its members." There are undoubtably parts of the *Merrion* opinion that suggest a broader scope for tribal taxing authority than the quoted language above. But *Merrion* involved a tax that only applied to activity occurring on the reservation, and its holding is therefore easily reconcilable with the *Montana-Strate* line of authority, which we deem to be controlling. An Indian tribe's sovereign power to tax — whatever its derivation — reaches no further than tribal land.

Thus, because the Court wrote that the *Montana-Strate* line of precedent controlled, it is not clear whether the power to exclude provided authority over nonmembers on tribal land independent of the *Montana* exceptions. Despite this uncertainty, in *Water Wheel Camp Recreational Area, Ind. V. LaRance,* the U.S. Court of Appeals for the Ninth Circuit found that the tribal court had jurisdiction over a non-Indian who had leased land from the Colorado River Indian Tribes but stayed after the lease had expired based on the Tribes' power to exclude, independent of the Tribes' inherent authority under the *Montana* exceptions.

## Statutory Exceptions

In addition to exercising authority over nonmembers pursuant to their inherent sovereign authority, Indian tribes may exercise jurisdiction over nonmembers within reservations when Congress authorizes them to do so. Congress may relax restrictions on tribes' inherent sovereign authority, as it did with tribal criminal jurisdiction over nonmember Indians and non-Indian dating and domestic violence defendants, or delegate federal authority to tribes. Congress may delegate federal authority to tribes through laws authorizing federal enforcement of tribal legal standards or laws authorizing enforcement of federal statutes.

There are two "prominent" examples of Congress providing for federal enforcement of tribal standards. First, Section 1161 provides that the federal criminal statutes prohibiting the introduction of alcohol in Indian country "shall not apply" … to any act or transaction within any area of Indian country provided such act or transaction is in conformity both with the laws of the State in which such act or transaction occurs and with an ordinance duly adopted by the [governing] tribe." In *United States v. Mazurie,* the Supreme Court upheld Section 1161 as a delegation to Indian tribes of Congress's authority to regulate the sale of alcohol by non-Indians within Indian reservations. In *City of Timber Lake v. Cheyenne River Sioux Tribe,* the Eighth Circuit upheld the authority of the Tribe to require nonmembers to obtain tribal liquor and business licenses and to enforce those requirements in tribal court. Second, Section 1165 establishes criminal penalties for anyone who, "without lawful authority or permission, willfully and knowingly goes upon" individual Indian or tribal trust land or any lands reserved for Indian use "for the purpose of hunting, trapping, or fishing thereon." Section 1165, therefore, imposes federal criminal penalties for knowing violations of tribal hunting and fishing licensing requirements.

The Clean Air Act provides an example of Congress delegating federal authority to tribes to regulate nonmember conduct on non-Indian fee land by enforcing their own standards. Under Section 7601(d)(1)(A), Indian tribes may petition the Environmental Protection Agency (EPA) for authority to regulate reservation air quality in accordance with minimum federal standards. If EPA grants a petition, the tribe establishes standards, issues permits, and enforces the standards for all land, including non-Indian land, within the reservation.

## Nonmembers Must First Challenge Tribal Court Jurisdiction in Tribal Court

Although tribal civil jurisdiction over nonmembers is quite limited, a nonmember defendant in tribal court who believes the court lacks jurisdiction must first challenge the tribal court's jurisdiction in tribal court. Federal courts will dismiss an action challenging the jurisdiction of a tribal court if the tribal court defendant has not challenged tribal court jurisdiction through the tribal court appellate process subject to four exceptions:

(1) when an assertion of tribal court jurisdiction is "motivated by a desire to harass or is conducted in bad faith"; (2) when the tribal court action is "patently violative of express jurisdictional prohibitions"; (3) when "exhaustion would be futile because of the lack of an adequate opportunity to challenge the tribal court jurisdiction"; and (4) when it is "plain" that tribal court jurisdiction is lacking, so that the exhaustion requirement "would serve no purpose other than delay."

Once a defendant has appealed his or her challenge of tribal court jurisdiction to the highest tribal court, he or she may then challenge the tribal court's jurisdiction in federal court.

## Conclusion

As a general rule, Indian tribes lack criminal and civil jurisdiction over non-members. However, there are exceptions. First, Congress re-vested Indian tribes with inherent authority to exercise criminal jurisdiction over nonmember Indians, as well as non-Indians who commit dating and domestic violence against Indians within the tribes' jurisdiction, provided the non-Indian has certain enumerated ties to the tribes. Second, under the first *Montana* exception, tribes may exercise civil jurisdiction over nonmembers when the nonmembers have entered private consensual relationships with the tribe or its members, provided the conduct at issue relates to the consensual relationship. Third, under the second *Montana* exception, Indian tribes may exercise civil jurisdiction over nonmembers when the nonmembers' conduct threatens the integrity of the tribe. Fourth, tribes may exercise jurisdiction over nonmembers when Congress authorizes them to do so. Although the Supreme Court has recognized the tribal right to exclude nonmembers from tribal land as a basis for regulatory authority, it is not clear whether the right to exclude is independent of the *Montana* exceptions. While the Supreme Court has drawn tribal jurisdiction over nonmembers narrowly, it has also held that defendants in tribal court who challenge the tribal court's jurisdiction must exhaust their tribal court remedies before seeking relief in federal court.

# Index